The illusion of the Burgundian state

Manchester University Press

Manchester Medieval Studies

SERIES EDITOR Professor S. H. Rigby

The study of medieval Europe is being transformed as old orthodoxies are challenged, new methods embraced and fresh fields of enquiry opened up. The adoption of interdisciplinary perspectives and the challenge of economic, social and cultural theory are forcing medievalists to ask new questions and to see familiar topics in a fresh light.

The aim of this series is to combine the scholarship traditionally associated with medieval studies with an awareness of more recent issues and approaches in a form accessible to the non-specialist reader.

ALREADY PUBLISHED IN THE SERIES

Peacemaking in the middle ages: principles and practice
Jenny Benham

Money in the medieval English economy: 973–1489
James Bolton

The commercialisation of English Society, 1000–1500 (second edition)
Richard H. Britnell

Reform and the papacy in the eleventh century
Kathleen G. Cushing

Picturing women in late medieval and Renaissance art
Christa Grössinger

The Vikings in England
D. M. Hadley

A sacred city: consecrating churches and reforming society in eleventh-century Italy
Louis I. Hamilton

The politics of carnival
Christopher Humphrey

Holy motherhood
Elizabeth L'Estrange

Music, scholasticism and reform: Salian Germany 1024–1125
T. J. H. McCarthy

Medieval law in context
Anthony Musson

Constructing kingship: the Capetian monarchs of France and the early Crusades
James Naus

The expansion of Europe, 1250–1500
Michael North

John of Salisbury and the medieval Roman renaissance
Irene O'Daly

Immigrant England, 1300–1550
W. Mark Ormrod, Bart Lambert and Jonathan Mackman

Medieval maidens
Kim M. Phillips

Approaching the Bible in medieval England
Eyal Poleg

Gentry culture in late medieval England
Raluca Radulescu and Alison Truelove (eds)

Chaucer in context
S. H. Rigby

Peasants and historians: debating the medieval English peasantry
Phillipp R. Schofield

Lordship in four realms: The Lacy family, 1166–1241
Colin Veach

The life cycle in Western Europe, c.1300–c.1500
Deborah Youngs

Neighbours and strangers: Local societies in early medieval Europe
Bernhard Zeller, Charles West, Francesca Tinti, Marco Stoffella, Nicolas Schroeder, Carine van Rhijn, Steffen Patzold, Thomas Kohl, Wendy Davies and Miriam Czock

The illusion of the Burgundian state

Élodie Lecuppre-Desjardin

translated by Christopher Fletcher

MANCHESTER UNIVERSITY PRESS

Copyright © Élodie Lecuppre-Desjardin 2022

The right of Élodie Lecuppre-Desjardin to be identified as the author of this work has been asserted by them in accordance with the Copyright, Designs and Patents Act 1988.

Originally published in France as: *Le royaume inachevé des ducs de Bourgogne (XIVe-XVe siècles)* by Élodie Lecuppre-Desjardin

© Editions Belin / Humensis, 2016

This edition published by Manchester University Press
Oxford Road, Manchester M13 9PL
www.manchesteruniversitypress.co.uk

British Library Cataloguing-in-Publication Data
A catalogue record for this book is available from the British Library

ISBN 978 1 5261 4433 1 hardback
ISBN 978 1 5261 7455 0 paperback

First published 2022
Paperback published 2023

The publisher has no responsibility for the persistence or accuracy of URLs for any external or third-party internet websites referred to in this book, and does not guarantee that any content on such websites is, or will remain, accurate or appropriate.

Typeset
by New Best-set Typesetters Ltd

Contents

List of illustrations	*page* vi
Preface	vii
List of abbreviations	ix
Map	x
Introduction	1
1 The splendours of the Burgundian court, or the limits of symbolic communication	12
2 Nobles in need of love and recognition	43
3 Opportunism and ethics in politics	84
4 The jewels in the crown	122
5 Awake, Picards and Burgundians!	178
6 Measuring and imagining: reflections on territorial consciousness	247
7 'Burgundianisation', or the fantasy of a Burgundian nation	300
Conclusion	332
Bibliography	343
Index	344

Illustrations

1. Image of power in the Montpellier manuscript, fifteenth century. Médiathèque Centrale Emile Zola – Montpellier Méditerranée Métropole. — 145
2. Military ordinance, 1473. London, British Library, Add. MS 36619, fol. 5. — 220
3. Roll of the river Aa, from Saint-Bertin Abbey to Blendecques, c. 1470. Saint-Omer, Bibliothèque d'Agglomération du Pays de Saint-Omer, ms. 1489. — 257
4. Map of Flanders from an Italian version of the *Kroniek van Vlaanderen* (*Cronarche de signiori di Fiandra e de loro advenimenti*), 1452. Bruges, Municipal Library, ms. 685, fols 208v–209r. — 258
5. Map of Brabant by Gilles van der Hecken, c. 1535. Brussels, Bibliothèque royale de Belgique, no. 2088–2098, fol. 87v. — 259
6. Philip the Good surrounded by his coats of arms. Martin Le Franc, *Champion des dames*, 1440. Paris, Bibliothèque nationale de France, ms. fr. 12476, fol. 1 v. Source: gallica.bnf.fr © BnF. — 272
7. 'Treatise establishing the rights of Louis XI over the duchy of Burgundy', late fifteenth century. Paris, Bibliothèque nationale de France, ms. fr. 5079, fol. 1. © BnF. — 274
8. Copperplate with the symbols of power of Charles the Bold, after 1472. Brussels, Bibliothèque royale de Belgique, Prints and Drawings Department, f° Rés. S. 111053. — 276

Preface

This book has a rather long history. It is the result of a decade of questions about the nature and the genesis of the medieval state. From this point of view, I am deeply indebted to the students who never failed to ask me questions which might have seemed obvious, but which were always stimulating, forcing me to re-examine my own research in light of their doubts and their need for clarity. 'What is clearly thought out is clearly expressed', said the French author Boileau … and the necessity to be well understood and to explain again and again what at first seemed obvious led to new questions and to new lines of research. Since the nature of what historians usually call the 'Burgundian state' is the central concern this book, I am also indebted to generations of colleagues past and present whose work has helped me to reinterrogate the notions of state, nation, political communication and belonging at the end of the Middle Ages. This book can be seen as a testimony to the pleasure I have had in reading them and debating with them. Wim Blockmans, Marc Boone, Patrick Boucheron, Philippe Contamine, Estelle Doudet and Pierre Monnet are some of them. Bertrand Schnerb, who accepted to play the game of *pro et contra* for many years in our common seminars, must be particularly thanked.

We are used to saying that 'translation is treason', and I must admit that making my language and concepts relevant for English readers was a major challenge. Fortunately, Christopher Fletcher, as a friend, presumably unaware of the scale of the task, did not hesitate to take up the gauntlet. With patience, subtlety and a remarkable feeling for two languages, he did his best to give a translation as close to the original as possible. I would like to thank him very warmly. My book in this version is now also his. Other good fairies were present at the birth of this book. I would like to thank Graeme Small for his enthusiasm. As a go-between for me and Manchester University Press, he actively argued for an English version of this study and confirmed his true support for my work. At my side two other men helped me to finalise the text. One of them, Alun Richards, exercised critical analysis of the last version. The second, Stephen Rigby, as a sort of reincarnation of Boileau, spared no effort or time to read again and again, chapter after chapter, sentence after sentence, word after word, forcing us to amend and polish the text in the aim to offer to a large audience a study as learned as it was accessible. His role of rigorous series editor has proved indispensable and has been much appreciated.

I was born in the 1970s, and my first civic involvement was an enthusiastic 'yes' in 1993 to the Maastricht treaty. Through the hazards of history, the English version of this book, first published in French in 2016, is now published in the aftermath of Brexit. In the fifteenth century, as in the twenty-first, I am more and more convinced that a political union cannot only be based on administrative institutions and economic treatises. It needs common ambitions, ideas and dreams. That is the story written in this book.

Lille, April 2021

Abbreviations

ADCO	Archives Départementales de la Côte d'Or
ADN	Archives Départementales du Nord
Annales ESC	*Annales. Économies, sociétés, civilisations*
BnF	Bibliothèque nationale de France, Paris
CESM	Centre d'Études Supérieures de Civilisation Médiévale
CNRS	Centre Nationale de la Recherche Scientifique
CTHS	Comité des Travaux Historiques et Scientifiques
PCEEB	*Publications du Centre européen d'Études Bourguignonnes*
PUF	Presses Universitaires de France
PUPS	Presses de l'Université Paris-Sorbonne
PUR	Presses Universitaires de Rennes
SEUH	Studies in European Urban History

Map

Map of the Great Principality of Burgundy before the death of Charles the Bold

Introduction

I, Mongin Contault, councillor to my lord the duke of Burgundy and master of the accounts at Dijon, with Laurens Blanchart, clerk and auditor of the said accounts, summoned and present with me, left Dijon on 25 December 1472 and travelled to the county of Ferrates, that is to say to the place and town of Tanne, where I arrived on 3 January of the aforesaid year [1473]. And the better to work and to enquire concerning the matters declared in the said letters of commission, to the good and profit of my said lord the duke, on 4 January of the said month, I communicated the effect of my commission to Monsieur de Haccambacq, knight lord of Belmont, councillor and master of the household of my said lord, and his high bailiff of Ferrates.[1]

In the winter of 1473 Mongin Contault, master of the Chamber of Accounts of Dijon, took his mule and departed for Alsace in the company of a secretary and a squire of the duke charged with 'leading him by the ways'.[2] The mission turned out to be more than testing. On his arrival, Mongin was shivering with cold and fear. He did not speak the local language, he was afraid of robbers, and he soon gave up hope of visiting the seigneurial castles which overlooked the valleys where he preferred to stay, limiting his enquiries to such information as his informants cared to provide.

This man was one of the officers of the Great Principality of Burgundy. His task was highly important, since he was charged with preparing the complete annexation of Alsace and with this its fiscal assessment. On this date and in this place, he was the ill and shivering representative of Burgundian authority. He was an important cog in the machine of a principality whose achievements included exporting the wines of Beaune across Europe, turning the port of

Bruges into a hub for the world's most exotic products, supporting the artistry of the Van Eyck brothers, sending the first strains of Flemish polyphony as far as Naples and refining a form of curial ceremony that would go on to seduce Versailles and its kings. This was a principality whose masters wielded their influence over much of the European diplomacy of their day. We might be a little surprised by the disjuncture between the majesty and power of the 'Burgundian state' as it appears in the writings of many historians and the rough and ready practice of government as it is described in this rather sordid travel narrative. Yet these few lines help us to remember that behind institutions there were men who, by making contacts with others, through their official authority and through informal practices, constructed little by little an edifice which historical writing has tended to consider in its finished form, without worrying about technical subtleties.

Mongin Contault's narrative makes it possible to put a name and a face on the mass of anonymous individuals who, in the central Chamber of Accounts and courts of justice, but also in local government, transmitted, spoke for and imposed authority. It also and more importantly suggests a new approach to analysing these power mechanisms, how they were perceived and how they were exercised in a real, human setting. There is much to learn from this episode in the life of an officer. The duke's orders sent from Ghent and Valenciennes on 12 and 15 May 1472 were clear: this was a military, political and financial mission, and the course of events accelerated when, in mid-December, Pierre von Hagenbach, the bailiff of Ferrette and Alsace, ordered the president of the Chamber of Accounts, Jean Jouard, to send the said Mongin to Thann by 3 January 1473 at the latest. It was with difficulty that Mongin Contault did as he was told, taking to the road and dealing, as a mere recently ennobled officer, with a rough-mannered local aristocracy who kept him at a distance with a lofty attitude which was as foreign to him as the language they spoke. In the course of his enquiries he listened, asking the pre-set questions which he had had translated. He had no choice but to take the word of the local officials, who were the only ones able to do this job, but who threatened to leave unless they were given an increased salary. He organised his movements following the advice of the Hagenbach brothers, who, just as he was about to leave for the forest towns, frightened him by telling him that a certain pro-French count of Arbrestein was active around Basel, devastating the region.³ Mongin did not dare to move. Despite all this, the ducal officer worked hard to gather the information necessary to strengthen the castles' defences, redeem mortgaged lands and collect taxes which custom reserved to the local lord. Indeed, thirty-seven days later, when he returned to Dijon, still in poor health and worried by the injuries suffered by his beloved mule, his work was praised by the president, Jouard, who took the exceptional step of asking the duke to pay for Mongin's services, so that he might continue to serve at his best.

It is worth asking why a man in poor health should agree to go on a dangerous journey on the order of a prince who, concerned as he was with appearances, had nevertheless made no provision either for the costs of the voyage or for the pay which might motivate his man. Mongin acted, not to work for the territorial reinforcement of a state, nor to guarantee the progress and consolidation of the public weal but, as he wrote himself, for 'the good and the profit of his lord'. Like Hue de Lannoy, like Jean de la Driesche, like Simon van Formelis and many of the individuals we will encounter in the following pages, Mongin, whilst not forgetting his own interests, was committed to serving the man who embodied the superior authority in the territory where he lived. When we look more closely at the career of this financial specialist, clerk of the council in 1453, ennobled in 1466, who finally became president of the Dijon Chamber of Accounts in 1481, we start to see how personal ambitions might overcome the fear of sickness and danger. It becomes understandable how he might decide to make all these willing sacrifices in the hope of the promotion which, in this case, he did indeed receive. Just as Pierre von Hagenbach, Charles the Bold's bailiff, knew how to limit the duke's intrusions into local affairs in order to protect his networks, whilst never losing sight of the prince's interests, so Mongin was part of a system of power which transformed the sum of personal interests into a collective dynamic conflating public interest and service to the prince. How could it have been any other way?

Before we start to examine in detail the precise mechanisms which gave life to Burgundian political society, we cannot avoid considering terminology. The present book emerged from a set of questions, a certain perplexity or hesitation in the face of an imposing territorial complex between France and the Empire, brought together through annexation, marriage, inheritance and wars in a little less than a century (1369–1477), which accumulated duchies, counties and lordships from Frisia to the Mâconnais, without ever imposing a single name on the whole. Placed in a difficult situation, historians, after many and recurring terminological disputes, have more or less adopted the practical and convenient term 'the Burgundian state' to refer to the object of their study. If some reject this term in favour of the plural ('the Burgundian states'), the better to describe the reality of a mosaic of lands and powers, the majority have rallied to a denomination which serves as a convenient shorthand, but which is burdened with a set of connotations which tend to overdetermine analyses of the ideology of power in this space. Officers of the court who served a man or a great dynasty or 'house', urban merchants who worked for the common profit of their crafts, soldiers who waged war and expected their share of the spoils, princes who defended their honour and their inheritance, men and women who lived and worked in the sight of God, all are squeezed into a model of a Burgundian state whose riches, developed institutions, international diplomacy and mastery of the art of war seem to make it obvious that it must have existed.

Yet since words, their use and their meaning condition not only speech, but also the construction of thought, after more than fifty years of the use of a term which is habitually employed but never explicitly defined it seems high time to reconsider in detail the political and cultural elements which are held to have made up 'the Burgundian state' and to subject this concept to a renewed critique. By this means we can hope to find a more appropriate vocabulary and to propose a new reading of the political powers and the political structures at the end of the Middle Ages.

As early as 1987, Richard Vaughan, the biographer of the four Valois dukes of Burgundy, reconsidered in a little-known article the pertinence of the concept of the 'state' in this context, and admitted using it only for want of a better term. In contrast to England and France, Vaughan now admitted, 'Burgundy' lacked what he identified as critical attributes for the construction of a state: specifically a capital, a single language, a king and, above all, a name.[4] Even in governing circles, he continued, there was 'no serious consideration of the nature of the Burgundian polity, indeed no concept of Burgundy as a whole, apart from the person of the duke'.[5] The charge was a serious one. Even if his criteria might be questioned, Vaughan's about-face shows how complex this question is. It raises numerous Burgundian paradoxes which this book will consider, paradoxes which seek to explicate a political entity which seems to suffer from a chronic incompleteness.

In order to assess the pertinence of the notion of 'state' in the context of the Burgundian political laboratory, a more neutral term is needed. From this point of view, because the *princeps* (prince) is etymologically 'the one who holds the first place' and, as Bernard Demotz recalls, 'the principalities emerged from the hereditability of public functions from the end of the ninth century when a count, a duke or a marquis exercised for himself regalian rights, whilst nonetheless accepting to swear an oath of fidelity to the sovereign', the term 'principality' does not seem out of place, as long as it is understood as a form of rule rather than a discrete territory.[6] The dukes of Burgundy and of Brabant, counts of Flanders and of Hainault, lords of Zutphen and so on, the Valois dukes of Burgundy, from one title to the next, were princes who presided over a principate (and not a realm as one often reads) whose common denominator was a 'principality' or supremacy over this assemblage of political territories. This 'principality' took the form of a personal union, or set of personal unions, with the prince. To satisfy historians who are troubled by the ambiguity of the term 'principality', which could refer to one of the components of the territories of the Valois dukes of Burgundy rather than the whole, we shall use here the term 'Great Principality' so as to avoid ambiguity, this also being close to the title of 'Grand Duke of the West' sometimes given to Philip the Good.

If it is difficult to establish a consensus concerning the concept of a 'state', the term 'principality' does not seem to be as controversial. In addition, it makes it possible to consider the political construction we are dealing with in its entirety, in a way that 'states' in the plural does not.[7] To talk of the 'Burgundian states' implies a fragmentation which obstructs consideration of a number of questions which need to be taken as a whole: whether some common dynamic or feeling of community can be found in these territories, for example; what the relationship was between the centre and the periphery; how political legitimacy was established; how important the search for sovereigntywas; and whether the notion of a 'capital' is relevant here, to name but a few. When, as early as 1930, the Dutch historian Johan

Huizinga questioned the idea of a Burgundian state, he objected that the phenomenon so described lacked 'temporal government' and political and national cohesion, and so could be described by the idea of 'reign' (*règne*), but not by the word 'state', which according to Huizinga was unknown in the Middle Ages in its modern sense.[8] We can see that these Burgundian princes suffered from no lack 'temporal government', and for the moment it is enough to cite the establishment of the Chambers of Accounts and of Justice at Dijon and Lille in 1386 and the political significance of these initiatives. We will return to the question of national feeling, too, but it is clear that here also this and related terms are often used by historians without a solid theoretical basis, in an often exaggerated and distorted fashion.[9] That said, as we shall see, the problem of cohesion does indeed appear to be a real fault-line in the political entity we are considering.

The dukes of Burgundy did on occasion attempt to propagate general legislation throughout all their lands, even if for the most part the strength of local privileges and of a powerful customary law forced them to legislate in a strictly bilateral manner.[10] It can also rightly be argued that the professionalisation and regulation introduced into the institutions of Brabant, Holland, Zeeland and so on as they fell, one after another, under Burgundian control also contributed to a certain unification. In the same way, the armies of Charles the Bold, as we shall see, had no reason to blush in comparison with the 'ordinance companies' of Charles VII. But it is not enough simply to add a few more criteria to define a 'state' to make it viable: the concept runs the risk of becoming far too elastic.

In his work on 'the medieval origins of the modern state', Joseph Strayer asserted that the state could be defined as a political unit enduring in time and space, featuring impersonal and relatively permanent institutions and possessing a consensus around the recognition of a supreme authority, accompanied by feelings of loyalty towards that authority.[11] In other words, 'A state exists chiefly in the hearts and minds of its people; if they do not believe it is there, no logical exercise will bring it to life.'[12] This subjective sense of the state is certainly its most essential quality, since although it functions through a certain number of objective phenomena, it must also be desired, understood and experienced by the community over which it claims to rule.

At a time when European unity appears fragile, it seems appropriate that loyalty to an abstract entity should also be at the centre of our enquiry into the great political adventure of the late-medieval dukes of Burgundy. The men we shall meet below were certainly more or less loyal to their family, their clientage networks, the local communities in which they lived, the members of their craft guild and the parishes which looked after their salvation, but did they also feel that they were part of an elect group at the service of a country, which was in turn at the service of God? It is difficult to know the innermost feelings of someone like Nicolas Rolin, high chancellor from 1422 to 1462; of Simon van Formelis, head of the government of the city of Ghent, who came into the service of John the Fearless as president of the Council of Flanders in 1409; of a fighting man like Jean, lord of Lisle-Adam; of Mongin Contault; or of Duke Philip the Good himself. Nonetheless, by fixing our attention on the acts, the commitments, the moments of acquiescence, the rebuffs experienced by these individuals and the culture of this people, we can begin to discern the nature of power in this region, the nature of that capacity to command which leads sometimes to the organisation of a historical community regulated by laws and institutions, but which always expresses the profoundly human need both to find a master and to oppose him. It is beside the point to ask if these people were aware of all the parameters by which we as historians might choose to define a state. Rather, it is better to try to discover whether they were conscious of working towards the formation of a unified state. By seeking to bring together all the assumptions of this period, it may yet be possible to identify the underlying forces which drove this composite society. It is hoped that this will enable us to write the history, not of ever-growing perfection, but of the conditions of possibility and impossibility which lead to the particular directions taken by a government.[13]

Many studies of power and authority begin by establishing a set of questions and criteria in order to study developments over time and provide a solid footing for a narrative which privileges facts, semantic evolutions, innovations and types of government.[14] Indeed, this approach has already been adopted for the Great Principality of Burgundy, with historians reaching the conclusion that it is possible to possess all the attributes necessary for a state (chancery, chamber of accounts, courts of justice, armies, regular if not permanent taxation

...) without contemporaries having been conscious of forming a state or of having any kind of political allegiance apart from a personal one. Here as elsewhere, when one observes the behaviour of the men who took part in the 'Burgundian adventure', it is too easy to take solace in rhetorical paradoxes which solve nothing. It thus seems better to listen to those fifteenth-century voices which, in the *scriptorium* of the Chamber of Accounts, in a court of justice, in the midst of a revolt, in the prince's entourage or on the field of battle, tell us their motivations and the convictions which underlay them. It is better, of course, to examine the speeches, the manifestos and the actions of princes to understand their aspirations. Finally, it is better to analyse the constraints imposed by a territory which lay behind a political culture characterised by multiplicity, by variety and consequently by seeming contradictions which vanish under close observation.

To begin to address these paradoxes, the better to dispel them, Chapter 1 proposes a critical study of political communication, which shows how the historian can be taken in by contemporary propaganda, overlooking the fault-lines in this political dialogue, or more precisely the misunderstandings which it could produce. The extraordinary mastery evident in Burgundian political discourse was considered for a long time to provide irrefutable proof of the existence of a 'modern' political ideology. By exploring some of the characteristics of the Burgundian prince's formidable 'multimedia' propaganda, which nonetheless had difficulty in uniting people around a political abstraction, we will seek to identify the origins of this erroneous historiographical interpretation and look for the causes of this incoherence. In preferring to examine a number of different examples rather than presenting a linear narrative, a movement back from the specific to the general will sometimes be adopted, not because this functions as a guarantee of veracity, but because it enables us to approach things from a new angle. Turning to the question of political loyalty in Chapter 2, we will begin by examining it in the inner circle of the prince's servants, showing that at the top of the pyramid, loyalties were fragile. They were regularly shaken by favours offered and then rescinded, and were frequently undermined by betrayals, which grew in number as the demands of government became more intense. Was this a tactical error on the part of the princes? Was it a problem related to the many different environments

Introduction 9

in which Burgundian rule was exercised, which made it necessary for the dukes to be, at the same time, both the greatest lords of France and the master of their own *pays*, which was itself divided between the different interests of their northern and southern lands? This is the question which Chapter 3 will consider before we pass on, in Chapter 4, to the impact of the principality's excessive dependence on the French Crown, and the late and fragile development of a political consciousness which it implied. In the shadow of a distinctively French political ideology, could the principality succeed in creating an autonomous conception of itself, in a context where the absence of a theory of the public weal (or its late and imperfect development) left a space for the expression of individual interests? This leads us to the question of sovereignty, one essential for the affirmation of a state, but also to those of the dreams of kingdom or of empire which we find in these developments. Chapter 5 will examine more closely the military structures which historians have taken to be a pillar of the construction of the state, and which could provide an excellent means to bring together diverse individuals and groups. The difficulties encountered in this regard invite us to reconsider, in Chapter 6, the problem of unification from the point of view of geography and its perception by contemporaries. Here, we will introduce the question of the importance of belonging to a land or country, which is at the core of the process of identity formation. This will allow us to tackle the problem of the modern myth of 'Burgundianisation' in Chapter 7 and to ask the final question of the place of the nation in the construction of the state.

Taken together, these reflections on the ideology of power in this late-medieval Great Principality help us to identify the moment when the artfulness and cunning of these princes, which had initially enabled them to succeed (since each of their possessions had been annexed peacefully in return for the promise to respect customs and privileges), starts to seem more like a symptom of their weakness, of their difficulty in imposing unity and their inability to develop their many lordships towards a form of rule capable of facing up to the vicissitudes of fortune. A royal or imperial crown might have enabled them to unite their people on the firm foundations of the sacred, but in the end it was no more than an illusion, the improbable attribute of an imaginary kingdom that would feed the myth of the 'Burgundian state'.

Notes

1 Little more is known about Mongin Contault's inquiry than what we find in L. Stouff, *La description de plusieurs forteresses et seigneuries de Charles le Téméraire en Alsace et dans la haute vallée du Rhin par Maître Mongin Contault, maître des comptes à Dijon (1473)* (Paris: L. Lahose, 1902), fol. 5r, p. 22.
2 *Ibid.*
3 *Ibid.*: 'Et pour ce que le chemin d'aller ausdits lieux de Rinfel et de Loffemberg est dangereux à présent, comme il m'a este dit et asseuré par ledit messire Pierre de Haccambacq et autres, et que le conte de Arbrestain, qui tient party François, estoit à Basle ... je ne suis osé ... aller, ne ledit Laurens aussi, en celle marche, ains y ay envoyé Richard de Constantinople, l'un des souldoyers de Anguescey, escripvant et parlant les deux langaiges d'Alemaigne et de Bourgoingne, et est feable à mondit seigneur' (fol. 48r, pp. 62–63).
4 R. Vaughan, 'Hue de Lannoy and the question of the Burgundian State', in R. Schneider (ed.), *Das spätmittelalterliche Königtum im europäischen Vergleich* (Stuttgart: Thorbecke, 1987), pp. 335–346. Vaughan wrote: 'In my books on the Valois dukes of Burgundy I used the phrase "the Burgundian State" for want of a better one' (p. 344) and: 'Both England and France possessed, and had for some time possessed, attributes wholly lacking in Burgundy. Namely a single substantial urban nucleus or capital city, a single language, a king, and perhaps most importantly, a name' (p. 335).
5 *Ibid.*, p. 344: 'Here, I have endeavoured to show that even in the best-informed circles of Burgundian councillors, there is no serious consideration of the nature of the Burgundian polity, indeed no concept of Burgundy as a whole, apart from the person of the duke.'
6 B. Demotz (ed.), *Les principautés dans l'Occident médiéval* (Turnhout: Brepols, 2007), pp. 21–22.
7 J.-M. Cauchies disagreed with the expression ('principality of Burgundy'). J.-M. Cauchies, 'État bourguignon ou états bourguignons? De la singularité d'un pluriel', in P. Hoppenbrouwers, A. Janse and R. Stein (eds), *Power and Persuasion. Essays on the Art of State Building in Honour of W.P. Blockmans* (Turnhout: Brepols, 2010), pp. 49–58, at p. 57.
8 J. Huizinga, 'L'État bourguignon, ses rapports avec la France, et les origines d'une nationalité néerlandaise', *Le Moyen Âge* 40 (1930), 171–193, at p. 173. We need to be precise that the term *status* was used by scholastics and medieval jurists to refer to the condition of a ruler (*status principis*) or to the general state of the kingdom as a whole

(*status regni*). It makes no reference to a power in its immanent aspect. See Q. Skinner, *The Foundations of Modern Political Thought*, vol. 1: *The Renaissance* (Cambridge: Cambridge University Press, 1978).
9 In D'A. J. D. Boulton and J. R. Veenstra (eds), *The Ideology of Burgundy: The Promotion of National Consciousness (1364–1565)* (Leiden and Boston: Brill, 2006), 'nation' is considered to be the expression of political ideas attributed to higher social groups.
10 Ordinances were more general under Charles the Bold. See J.-M. Cauchies, 'La législation dans les Pays-Bas bourguignons: état de la question et perspectives de recherche', *Revue d'histoire du droit* 61 (1993), 375–386.
11 J. R. Strayer, *On the Medieval Origins of the Modern State* (Princeton: Princeton University Press, 1970), p. 5. A similar position was adopted by Albert Rigaudière in 'Loi et État dans la France du bas Moyen Âge', in *Penser et construire l'État dans la France du Moyen Âge* (Paris: Cheff, 2003), pp. 181–208. Burdeau, *L'État* (Paris: Seuil, 1970), pp. 13ff.
12 Strayer, *On the Medieval Origins of the Modern State*, p. 15.
13 By the assumptions of a period, I mean something similar to the idea of *épistémè* as defined by Foucault or the 'preconditions for the possibility of knowledge' as defined by Kant before him.
14 See, for example, S. Clark, *State and Status: The Rise of the State and Aristocratic Power in Western Europe* (Quebec: McGill-Queen's University Press, 1995).

1

The splendours of the Burgundian court, or the limits of symbolic communication

When John the Fearless defined the procedures for the renewal of the magistrature and the control of accounts in the town of Ypres in 1414, his avowed intention was to bring to an end the corrupt mechanisms which had perverted them, and thus to re-establish 'good union and concord' between the inhabitants of the towns and the castellanies. With this aim in mind, great care was taken to back up the election of officials with a public oath:

> And those who will be elected to be eschevins and swear to give justice will be held to make a solemn and public oath, along with the accustomed oath, before our said deputies.[1]

The same duke, when he was enthroned as the count of Flanders at Douai in 1405, had heard, delivered to him through a window of the hall, the oath of the *échevins* and of all the people to be his good and loyal subjects. He then took an oath in his turn, swearing with his hand raised to the saints to respect the town's privileges. Some years later, on 15 May 1472, again at Douai, Charles the Bold took part in the ceremony of the Joyous Entry of the town and modified the content of the oaths, forcing his subjects to speak first as usual and then requiring them to swear to serve him 'towards and against all' ('envers et contre tous').[2] The development of oaths publicly sworn by the civic officials of the towns of Flanders and Brabant sheds comparable light on the evolution of power in this region, as new clauses against corruption were included as a result of the intervention of the central power. From the difficult years of the regency of Maximilian of Austria (1482–88), their rulers put to the test the towns' desire to maintain some form of local autonomy whilst preserving their allegiance to a lord, to the exclusion of any form of republicanism.³ For the moment, however, without going further into the nature of political discourse, it is important to note simply the need of both the prince and the towns to articulate, to proclaim and to publicise the nature of the power relations between the king and his subjects by means of more or less elaborate ceremonies.

This mastery of political communication in the many public places which the towns provided, founded on a repertoire of ideas shared by princes and by civic officials – the love of the common good, the preservation of peace, the desire to do justice and so forth – can create the illusion of mutual understanding and of coherence and cohesion between ruler and ruled.⁴ Yet, in fact, such communication was often a dialogue of the deaf, with each side having its own idea of the common good, of peace and of justice. The symbolic communication of the powers which existed in the Burgundian space we are examining certainly attained heights of subtlety, but the historian who observes them must keep a critical eye. Despite a vocabulary shared by all, and a common underlying culture, the discourses, gestures and even the emotions which structured symbolic manifestations of power could be understood in many different ways.

Reality and *trompe-l'oeils*

In an important article published in 1992, Philippe Contamine pointed out the dangers of *trompe-l'oeils*, optical illusions which cause the viewer to take the representation for the real, for any historian engaged in deciphering the projects of the Valois dukes of Burgundy.⁵ Carried away by the whirl of princely celebrations, by the chapter meetings of the Golden Fleece, by the treasures of the manuscript collections recently displayed by the Bibliothèque royale of Belgium or the Bibliothèque nationale de France, by courtly ceremonial and magnificent banquets, the modern observer risks being seduced by the sirens of Burgundian propaganda, concluding too quickly that there must have been an extraordinary political power to match the level of expense associated with this policy of display.

In one of my earlier works, I analysed in detail this practice of government founded on an art of display, in accordance with good Aristotelian and later Machiavellian principles, as an alternative to crudely applying theories of the 'society of the spectacle' which ascribe to all ceremonies the ability to lay the foundations of a political construction. Rather, as ceremonies seemed to me to be tests which revealed the nature and the quality of relations between protagonists in the political society in question, I concluded that 'the Burgundian state was a developing modern state which used its public space with greater or lesser skill to broadcast the progress of its development'.[6] Now that I have put this assertion to the test of sceptical reappraisal and of comparative history, ceremonies still seem to me to be instruments of communication rather than of the creation of power. Nevertheless, the nature of the Burgundian political entity now seems to be in need of reconsideration. As with the critique of universals undertaken by Michel Foucault, the aim of this fresh research project is not to start with a key concept, such as the modern state, and then to demonstrate its existence or non-existence. Instead, by examining a certain number of different themes, I aim to invert this process, to bring to the fore the unsystematic diversity of practices and of ideas which can lead to the establishment of a specific form of government in its own cultural context.

That said, I do not intend to reduce the present enquiry to a list of cases which would serve to undermine to a greater or lesser extent the applicability of the concept of the modern state to the phenomena which concern us here. After all, few would deny that a historical study should not simply involve an attack on past positions, likely to end up in further value judgements and arid system building, but should rather constitute a search for truth. Thus, before turning to the features which distinguish the principality from a unitary and coherent state, let us quickly consider its primary characteristics.

The distinguishing features of a principality

When Henri Pirenne replied to Johan Huizinga's critique of the concept of Burgundian state construction, he explained, quite diplomatically, that it was all a matter of perspective. If one privileged ideas over facts then Burgundian state construction appeared fragile, whereas if one reversed the point of view, then the Burgundian state incontestably existed.[7] It is worth considering this question of perspective for a moment. Pirenne's reasoning has the attraction of suggesting that all parties to that argument were in fact in agreement, leaving historians to admit, with a certain sigh of relief, that, constrained by the combined force of limited sources and their own subjectivity, they can only describe 'their own truth'. Although there is something of that in any historical enquiry, it can still be suggested that, by taking into account the numerous studies on this subject, and associating them with fresh research and a new approach, we might broaden our field of vision, rather than simply putting the problem into a new light.

Paul Bonenfant drew up in turn a practical description of what he called, as a matter of convenience, the 'Burgundian state'.[8] After listing its territorial acquisitions, he suggested describing Burgundian rule as 'monocratic', since power was exercised by a prince who had personal links with each of the counties and duchies which were nonetheless autonomous entities attached to privileges and customs which limited this monocratic power. This was a form of power without sacred connotations, since no religious ceremony comparable to royal coronations accompanied the taking of oaths, and the dukes' use of the formula 'by the grace of God' in their title was just a result of the adoption of this practice of the dukes of Brabant when Philip the Good was enthroned in that duchy in 1430.[9] Legitimacy was feudal in nature; the dukes were subject to the overlordship of the king of France and the emperor, although they were also careful to secure their subjects' consent, notably by means of reciprocal oaths. The extent of the ruler's power was also limited by the existence of representative bodies: the Four Members in Flanders and the Estates General elsewhere. The prince for his part relied on his chancellor and on a series of councils, which were regularly reformed, a mobile Great Council, which took on a permanent character under Philip the Good, with a more restricted subdivision in the 'secret and privy council', and the Chambers of Accounts and of Justice in Lille and in Dijon. Provincial councils were retained in newly acquired territories to deal with day-to-day administration. Finally, Burgundian officials assisted local officials so as to ensure the transmission of orders and to coordinate the different elements of the administration.

On the basis of the descriptive synthesis presented by Jan van Rompaey in his *Nouvelle histoire générale des Pays-Bas*, Marc Boone assessed the real and fictive innovations of the Burgundian administration, focusing on areas where the princes were resident and in which institutions developed, namely the northern part of the ducal territories.[10] The reorganisation of the Chambers of Accounts followed the rhythm of the dukes' acquisitions, applying models which had already been tested elsewhere to new territorial contexts. Following this pattern, the Chamber of Accounts of Dijon was reformed according to the Parisian model. Philip the Bold worked on the basis of what already existed (the Audience and the Chamber of the *Renenghe* in Flanders) to create a juridical and financial chamber which was finally divided between a judicial council for Flanders, which was located in Ghent from 1409 onwards, and a Chamber of Accounts in Lille. The progress of the 'Burgundian state' is thus often assessed in the Flemish historiography on the basis of a strong opposition between the independent jurisprudence of the towns and the development of overarching institutional structures in the hands of the prince. This is despite that fact that the prince in question, for example Philip the Bold, often had other priorities. This was pointed out in a comment added to a petition of the Members of Flanders on the question of residence: 'since my lord has other lands to govern and the business of the kingdom [to attend to]; my lady is not able etc.; [and since] my lord of Nevers often has to go away, etc.'[11] Under Philip the Good, territorial gains required a new and greater administrative oversight, which was undertaken by the Great Council for juridical affairs (which became the Parlement of Malines under Charles the Bold between 1473 and 1477). But, despite occasional revolts and opposition movements, at the other end of the period in question, the functions of Burgundian juridical institutions were found to be useful and were accepted locally. The same can be said of the Chamber of Accounts. The idea of a general centralisation and unification of all the duke's lands can be found in the project elaborated by Charles the Bold at Malines in 1473, but this was rejected by the Estates. The techniques put in place in all these institutions were adopted only insofar as they could still be divided up in such a way as to respect the autonomy of each individual territory. To paraphrase Marc Boone, institutions which pre-existed the new dynasty were incorporated relatively easily into new ones, without this posing any real problem.

Although the existence of this administrative system cannot be denied, it still has to be admitted that when one leaves the level of each separate territory to consider the whole, the question of the feeling of belonging to this whole comes to the fore. In fact, this feeling seems to have been weak, or even non-existent. This was despite the duke's symbolic communication, which was working at full pelt in this period in order to promote such a sentiment around the figure of the prince, the central pillar of the dynastic state.

The prince and his theatre

Political and symbolic communication was an important instrument of power which the dukes of Burgundy mastered perfectly. It served to magnify the prince, the only real common denominator in this mosaic of territories. It was thus logically around the prince and his family that Burgundian propaganda was first organised. In the context of the Joyous Entries, of judicial audiences, in church and in the tournament stalls, in the hall of festivities and in the ceremonial procession, the prince was the focus of everyone's attention.

The splendours of the court projected by the many festivities which the dukes of Burgundy organised could not have been easy to forget. Luxury is of course a means of displaying power, but the celebrations and family events open to all, such as baptisms, marriages and funerals, also possessed strong unifying possibilities as 'affective analogies where each one is tempted to come out of themselves in order to commune with the other in rituals where the collective, figures of identification and the power of the imagination predominate'.[12] Burgundian ceremonies show that the fifteenth-century population was susceptible to being wooed by these joyful celebrations, which sought to play on the common humanity of all despite social barriers and physical distance, much as a modern audience might be moved by a royal wedding at a time when the rest of the news is far from joyous. Naturally it would be wrong to move too easily from one period to another, or to argue that medieval and modern communities have the same capacity to mobilize, to celebrate and to believe. Though 'these enthusiasms are of all places' and of all times, the present enquiry is a historical one. Nevertheless, this modern comparison does help to open up the question of images and their capacity to create a 'collective being', to 'transform a "they" into an "us"', with greater or lesser durability.[13] The political advantages of such manifestations of collective joy are obvious. The happy and festive moment helps the observer to forget dissension, criticism and rancour, and invites them to join a hymn of solidarity to the union of the people brought together around its princes. What can we say, for example, of the wedding of Charles the Bold and Margaret of York at Bruges in 1468? The corteges of guests, overflowing with gold, with brocade, with silk and with precious stones, inundated the streets of the town, whilst ceremonial combats enlivened the festival, in a joyous atmosphere in which the spirit of revolt so familiar in the towns of Flanders evaporated, at least for a time. The dramatisation of the prince and of the princely family in the heart of this event was the essential element, since in a medieval society in which power could be conceived of only when it was incarnated, the first act of political communication lay in being seen and in how one appeared.

Even in the heart of a county of Flanders which was regularly disturbed by revolts that were mainly directed against the economic and fiscal policies of the Valois princes, the presence of the duke of Burgundy was strongly desired.[14] His presence was wanted for political and commercial reasons, but also to establish an almost physical contact with the prince. Condemned to be regularly itinerant, the duke had to manifest himself to show that he was attentive to his subjects and concerned to listen to their requests, but also sometimes simply to prove that he was still alive. This was the case at All Saints (1 November) 1455, when, after ten years of absence, Philip the Good was forced to go to Holland to put the lie to rumours that he was dead.[15] In the wake of the analysis of the grand tour of France organised by Catherine de Medici for the young Charles IX in 1564–66, we know that 'the mobility of kings was consubstantial with their power' and that their movements helped to strengthen bonds of fidelity and provided the opportunity to deploy the symbolism of power which solemn entries into welcoming towns permitted.[16] Social and political relations were woven around the visible body of the prince, guaranteeing a hierarchical pyramid dominated by the majesty of the prince. The performance of street spectacles, interludes (*entremets*) and sketches (*saynètes*) helped to open up a dialogue in which townspeople could make themselves heard, and sometimes their grievances too, but in which the prince retained his iconic position, manifesting the majesty of his rank and affirming his authority.

Of course, the Middle Ages had inherited from classical antiquity the view that tyranny involved the ruler's own enrichment, whereas good government was associated with disinterestedness. Yet in the fourteenth and fifteenth centuries this conception evolved, in the kingdom of France for example, towards the veritable exultation of magnificence, even amongst theologians. A prince richly clothed was a powerful prince, a living prince. An anecdote concerning Louis XI illustrates how this art of self-presentation was raised to an art of government. The king, who had been very modest in dress and in accoutrements throughout his life, began to acquire luxurious items as the end grew near with the express purpose, according to Commynes, of showing that he was not dead and that he was still powerful.[17] The prince's power and authority were expressed and affirmed above all through his superior splendour, through the well-publicised expenditure which fed the political imagination. The Aristotelian principle according to which magnificence was part and parcel of the qualities of the wise man had been read and understood not only by Christine de Pizan, who vaunted the qualities of Charles V as he did honour to the sumptuousness of the House of France, but also by Guillaume Fillastre, counsellor to Philip the Good, who did not fail to recall that magnificence was a princely virtue.[18]

But the question this raised was how such a display of luxury could be accepted, even appreciated, by a public which was certainly varied but which, for the most part, was crushed by numerous taxes. For Lydwine Scordia, royal magnificence was the best way to make apparent the uses of taxes in a time of peace.[19] Since administrative development had never met with much enthusiasm on the part of the king's subjects, royal splendour and majesty were the acceptable face of expenditure funded by taxation. It seems to me doubtful, however, that the townspeople of Tours or of Poitiers felt reassured that their taxes were being well spent as princely magnificence was paraded before them. This explanation seems rather too easy, though it does provide the opportunity to reconsider another set of ideas concerning princely ceremonial. The popular fervour which surrounded majesty was not, I think, the result of a fiscal imagination which made it possible to develop around the prince and around state expenditure the love of the community he represented. Although war did make it possible for a threatened and consequently united people to swallow the necessary pill of permanent taxation to defend their country, the prince's magnificence in no way stimulated blind allegiance to a spendthrift king. We know, for example, in another country, how much the opponents of Richard II stigmatised the exponential growth of the expenses of the royal household in the 1390s to underline the hubris, the inconstancy and finally the irresponsibility of a king who multiplied his magnificent public appearances in these years.[20] Other parameters need to be considered if we are to understand why royal and princely majesty was so effective in winning over the public it was addressed to. Aesthetic sublimation and religious analogies are the key to understanding the effectiveness of this form of symbolic communication, based as it was on the ephemeral.

Admiration and devotion

The beautiful sparks a process of attraction to, admiration of and often attachment to the person who displays such a quality, a process often accompanied by consent to whatever they represent. In this regard, late-medieval imposters provide useful clues, as it were in negative, to understand the attributes of majesty, as many of them were distinguished by their elegance, their beauty and their natural charisma. Hans Stock, the false Conradin, was noticed by German soldiers and also in certain towns in Italy and Switzerland on account of his handsomeness, which corresponded to the reputation of the Staufen family. Lambert Simnel, the false Edward of Warwick, was also vaunted for his attractiveness, his courtly allure and his sprightly conversation. And what can we say of the famous Perkin Warbeck, the false Richard of York, who, before winning over the courts of Europe, including that of Burgundy-Habsburg, used to work as a model for Pregent Meno, a Breton merchant trading in rich textiles?[21] There ought to be nothing surprising in this, if we reflect that 'mirrors for princes' never ceased to repeat that the sovereign's physical appearance ought to represent his moral qualities. In his portrait of Charles VI, the chronicler of the abbey of Saint-Denis adopted, word for word, the characteristics used by William of Tyre two centuries before to describe the kings of Jerusalem. A monarch ought to be a big man, with strong limbs, a full beard and a good head of hair. If this was not the case, rhetoric could be deployed to minimise these deficiencies. Charles VI, of medium height, just like Godfrey of Bouillon, was thus described as follows: 'whilst being smaller than the biggest, he was bigger than those of medium stature'.[22] In short, it was appearance that first made the prince. His body was given majesty through clothes, jewels and sumptuous horses. Such distinctive apparel expressed his power. In the late-medieval Low Countries, sumptuary laws were relatively rare, which made easier, because it was legal, a form of communication through luxury and clothing backed up by allegorical reference to the heavenly and the next life. Indeed, appreciation of nobles' habits of dress and furniture was almost immediately followed by a form of imitation which aimed to redefine social and political status. This, however, posed the problem of the maintenance of boundaries, since the wealth of the prominent burgesses allowed them to gain speedy access to the spheres of luxury and magnificence.[23] Fashions circulated, and the urban authorities distributed robes of very high quality to their representatives, even if this meant burdening the municipal budget. This was an open form of competition, which permitted the circulation of cultural signals, essentially from the top downwards, as Walter Prevenier sees it, without neglecting a process of adaptation to local customs, as when Philip the Good decided to have robes cut in the manner of Holland or Brabant in the years which followed the Burgundian acquisition of these territories.[24]

The second cultural matrix which enabled this form of symbolic communication to flourish was that of religious imitation, because religion provided a spontaneous language, one universally spoken in the Middle Ages. By analysing, for example, the use of light in princely processions, it can be shown that the movement between liturgical and political light confirms Johan Huizinga's suggestion that any common feeling in the Middle Ages needed some kind of visible sign or appeal to support it. Light and the sacred value which accompanied it fulfilled an emblematic and federative function which redounded to the greater glory of the prince whom it illuminated.[25] This conflation of meanings can be seen working to the benefit of princely self-publicity in the ceremonies which accompanied the organisation of the chapter meetings of the Golden Fleece. This chivalric order, founded by Philip the Good at Bruges on 10 January 1430, on the occasion of his marriage to Isabella of Portugal, has too often been considered to be an exclusively noble phenomenon. In reality, the procession of knights took place in towns, displaying chivalric cohesion and fraternity to the urban world in a highly religious atmosphere. This conferred a kind of ecclesiastical dignity on the prince, at least according to the chronicler Matthieu d'Escouchy, who, in the context of the meeting at Mons in 1451, asserts of Philip the Good that he 'went … alone, as the dean goes on procession behind the canons of a church'.[26] Sometimes the prince took the place not of a simple officiant but of the reliquary which was at the heart of any procession, stimulating a veritable *affectus devotionis* on the part of his subjects and reinforcing his superiority in the process.

This same principle was at work in the general processions ordered by Philip the Good and Charles the Bold. These processions, besides putting the prince once more at the centre of attention, demonstrate the increasingly powerful need at the end of this period to bring people together in a single devotional experience. Indeed, whilst Philip the Good issued orders in a relatively traditional fashion for prayers to be said for himself, for his health or for his victories across his lands in the context of great general processions, Charles the Bold, whose different political trajectory will soon become apparent, insisted that these events took place in different places but on the same day, perhaps hoping in this way to abolish the disparity of his territories through his mastery of time. In the same way, when events drove him to the field of battle, Charles took the time to send letters to the mendicants specifying the content of the sermons they were to preach at the various popular and religious meetings they were called upon to organise, for example between 1472 and 1475. In these ways, the possibility of stimulating a common religious experience organised around the prince and in the company of the saints offered an exceptional opportunity to promote ideas of unity and consensus. Devotion and the religious element of medieval life, which will not be considered separately in what follows, must nonetheless be considered essential motivations – not just vital but determining the essence of those who experienced them – of all the choices and attitudes which we will have cause to consider.

These examples, which could of course be elaborated by considering any number of other *magnificences*, as the chronicler George

Chastelain calls them, remind us that the body of the prince in performance, in the street, at court, in the real space of his appearance or in the imaginary space which it evokes, is the first element in a form of symbolic communication which seeks to impose authority through the tools of seduction and emotional conquest. This is also the reason why the prince, who could not be everywhere at once, made use of his family, of his heralds of arms, of his courtiers, his ambassadors, his coats of arms, his seal and so forth, deploying them as so many avatars of his power, wearing his colours and embodying his honour.[27] These ceremonies of majesty could even draw on the memory of the glorious prince, who was transformed into a matchless and missed sovereign by the dangers of the present day coupled with an appropriate dose of nostalgia. Charles the Bold showed that he had well understood this when, knee-deep in wars of conquest and suffering from the bad reputation particular to those princes who never stop increasing taxes, he decided to transfer the remains of his father, Philip the Good, and his mother, Isabella of Portugal, from Bruges to Dijon during the winter of 1473–74. This was not an appropriate season for travel, and yet Charles organised with great care this 'itinerary of the dead', whose route recalled the territorial bases of a duke who sought a royal crown and who felt the need to revive his subjects' allegiance.[28]

Political communication over the long term

The introduction of the question of memory makes it possible to address another time scale essential to Burgundian propaganda. For if appearances were an effective part of the political communication of the dukes of Burgundy, what remained when the party was over? Surely it was this: a reputation for being powerful dukes, an upsurge of admiration of the kind which led Diego de Valera in his *Cirimonial de principes* (c. 1462) to exalt the duke of Burgundy as a model to follow, and the recognition of a highly perfected chivalric culture, although one which was no doubt more international than simply Burgundian. The ceremonies of the dukes definitely promoted their fame outside their lands, but they were limited by their immediacy, which restricted their contribution to the long-term development of princely power within their own domains. Making memory was another kind of challenge.

The tree of ancestors

In making memory, the dukes of Burgundy lacked neither initiative nor means. If their civic investments were in general relatively limited – in comparison with other kinds of expenditure – the conquest of time over the long term was supported by literary patronage designed to confirm legitimacy through ancestry. They sought to maintain the memory of a glorious past, one which omitted more controversial events the better to unite the population around its lords. This was probably the most dangerous part of the political communication between governors and governed and the one which required the most patience. For, if this way of proceeding was traditional amongst noblemen, it took time to pass from one paradigm to another and so to permit an individual to be recognized not only within a local community but also as a full member of a larger and less tangible political entity. It is worth repeating that since authority was based on legitimacy and thus on ancestry, reviving a mythic past was an obligation for Burgundian political communication. The latter went significantly beyond the closed circle of the *scriptoria* of court writers. For while it is legitimate to ask Graeme Small's question – 'who read the chronicle of George Chastelain?' – the wide diffusion of this princely work is not in doubt.[29] To measure the extent of the public consumption of the dukes' political communication, it is necessary to turn to sources other than great chronicle works: short works, poems, roundels, songs and images which circulated far more widely and whose echoes could be heard in every street of this vast territory.

This familiarity, which we can detect in the use and comprehension of ancestral lines, was nourished by the wide diffusion of genealogical images in a great variety of formats. The genealogical culture which lay behind this attempt to harness the passage of time was not only deployed in manuscripts, in the form of chronicles or the heraldic works available only for perusal by an expert few. It was also found in many public places and took on sometimes surprising forms. Genealogical works based on mythical foundations and inserted into regional histories, celebrating the great families of Hainault,

Flanders and Artois, did not remain confined to the restricted society of the court, destined for private reading, after having circulated from the workshop of one scribe to another. Other means of diffusion existed. The Joyous Entries of towns and other official ceremonies provided history in the form of theatre. Thus Edmond de Dynter's *Chronicle of Brabant*, to which we shall return, certainly circulated in the milieu of the chancery, but the genealogical enquiries which it stimulated and which it contained would also inspire, a few years later, a play performed on the arrival of the count of Charolais, the future Charles the Bold, at Brussels in January 1466. This work of entertainment, called *Van menych sympel*, dramatised, on the public square of Brussels, the *menych sympel* (simple folk), the *outgedachte* (the patricians) and Cronyke (Lady Chronicle), who together retraced Charles's origins, insisting in particular on his relationship to his namesake Charlemagne.[30] Following this text, Duke Charles was even called on to the stage at the moment when Lady Chronicle found his place in the lineage these characters presented. Whilst it is impossible to measure the impact of this kind of stimulation of the historical consciousness, the fact of bringing together on the public stage the past and present lords of the land, through the use of allegorical figures designed to persuade a large number of spectators, bears witness to a simultaneously didactic and mobilizing method. A theatrical performance could thus be put to the service of a multi-nodal political grouping designed to integrate, case by case, each of the duke's territories.

The genealogical image outlived ephemeral festivities to be displayed in a more lasting form over the doors of municipal buildings. Consider, for example, the statuettes retracing the genealogy of the counts of Flanders installed on the facade of Bruges town hall and painted in polychrome by Jan van Eyck – a procedure which we find again in Brussels.[31] The dukes placed their most distant ancestors on these buildings visible to all, and also on certain tombs. Thus, when Philip the Good decided to erect a fitting tomb for his great grandfather Louis de Male in the collegial church of Saint-Pierre de Lille, he once more entrusted the task to Jan van Eyck. In the niches in the lower structure of the tomb, twenty-four statuettes were to depict Louis's descendants and thus Philip the Good's family line. This new procession of illustrious individuals displayed a form of legitimacy, irreproachable in the eyes of a public which was often exposed and ever attendant to this kind of demonstration, in the heart of one of the sanctuaries of the counts of Flanders.

This variety of genealogical celebration would change in form at the end of the century, but it was still being called upon to render service when Maximilian of Austria put together his plans for the tomb of his dead wife, Mary of Burgundy, in the church of Notre-Dame de Bruges, showing that political intentions continued to be expressed and thus to be conceived of in terms of lineage. On the two sides of the tomb, constructed between 1488 and 1494, was a genealogical tree, bearing on the tip of its branches the coats of arms of Mary's ancestors surrounded by angels, representing, on the one hand, the Burgundian paternal family and, on the other, the maternal line of Isabelle of Bourbon. The five generations displayed there served to recall that Mary was the heiress of a patrimony which was at that time threatened by the ambitions of the king of France.[32] However, images were not the only medium which could be used to represent the illustrious ancestors of princes. In the principality of Burgundy, the ducal family tree was narrated, mimed, painted and sung. The existence of songs which placed the House of Burgundy in a line of kinship descending vertically, for the most part in the lineage of the House of France, but also moving horizontally, recalling the numerous marriage alliances across Europe, obviously served to promote ducal power, as we shall see. Towns also offered a medium of choice for writing the long-term narrative of politics, a long view expressed through the accumulation, the seemingly endless lists, which were essential tools of medieval intellectual representation. Memory, 'the present of the past', was an essential parameter of political communication which addressed all with the essential aim of legitimizing power and providing a base for an authority which also had to project itself towards the future in order to affirm itself.

The rich foliage of political information

In fifteenth-century Europe it was increasingly becoming a necessity for governments to control the flow of political information. Crises – civil wars in France and England for example – undoubtedly intensified the attention paid to propaganda in all its forms. Political action was no longer conceived without paying attention to the (filtered) information which accompanied it. The public space given to announcement, rather than dialogue, grew larger and certainly led to the formation of a political society which, even if it did not understand all the subtleties of the alliances and the quarrels of the great, were nonetheless aware of their deeds. An instructive study by Claire Billen serves to show how interested the inhabitants of the countryside were in recent political and military events.[33] She analyses an investigation carried out by the *bailli* of the area around Tournai in the name of Louis XI at a time when the town of Mortagne, earlier bought by the king, had just been retaken by the Burgundians on the eve of the War of the Public Weal. At Hollain, where travellers coming from Lille or Tournai could take the boat to Mortagne, peasants often came across messengers, as well as men-at-arms. The inhabitants obtained their information in taverns, by following messengers, sometimes by opening their correspondence or by listening to local gossips. All of this was not so much for the purpose of taking sides or serving a particular party but rather to be ready and to evaluate the risk of the arrival of a large number of men-at-arms of whatever stripe. What counted for them was 'to be well prepared', leaving aside any allegiance to the king or to the duke. This conclusion should obviously inspire the greatest prudence in us if we are to avoid being fooled by the distorting mirror of propaganda. The duke's political communication was technically very accomplished, but the nature of its messages was not always understood, and indeed sometimes it could not be.

It was not enough for Philip the Good to embark on an epistolary campaign worthy of his father in the days of the 'accursed war' to ensure that his failure before Calais in 1436 would stimulate a desire for revenge amongst his subjects.[34] The letters sent to the nobles of his lands and to the princes of Europe were written more to preserve his honour than they were to galvanize a people grappling with an insulting enemy. Nonetheless, the dukes of Burgundy certainly did try to involve their different subjects in one way or another in their various European intrigues.

Here we need to distinguish several levels of propaganda which, spreading out from the court, reached the different layers of Burgundian society. Historians have long been enthralled by the writings of court rhetoricians, to the point of constructing a history of the principality almost exclusively from them, treating them as the repositories of a kind of universal truth. But on the subject of truth, we are aware today of the degree of play in writing, or of the 'writing games' which authors are capable of. Of course, these rhetoricians were orators, but although their poetic battles involved a stylistic subtlety which would only be appreciated by the masters of the genre, their public discourse and their literary conflicts involved them in a field larger than that delimitated by the *scriptorium*. This was not always the case. Thus, when Chastelain evoked a veritable scandal, related to the composition of his *Dit de vérité* and the explication which followed it, the *Exposition sur vérité mal prise*, the modern historian has enough information to see in this polemical work, supposedly diffused to the world for the greater glory of the duke of Burgundy but also according to Chastelain to bring peace between Charles VII and Philip the Good, nothing but a mystification, a probably fictional and carefully amplified debate, with Philip the Good as its sole audience.[35] On the other hand, when the same Chastelain praised the dead duke Philip the Good in 1467 in the ballad of the *Lion rampant*, he did not know that his text would be imitated by Jean Molinet the following year with the aim, going beyond a simple tribute, of allowing the young writer to denounce the bitter attacks of the king of France in the midst of the War of Liège. In this new ballad, which linked Louis XI to the image of the 'universal spider', Chastelain's verse 'Lïon rempant en croppe de montagne' ('Lion rampant on the summit of the mountain') becomes a refrain which court poets, those of France this time, also used, in the reply of the shepherd to the shepherdess, to attack the reputation of the House of Burgundy in a mocking tone:

> Do not think that we will believe you any more
> Lion rampant on the summit of the mountain.[36]

One might reply that these wars of words were accessible only to an erudite public and that this political communication was once again limited to the princely courts where it was developed. But this would be to ignore the role played by the figure of the rhetoricians amongst the *rederijkers*.

In the Low Countries, the court poets (rhetoricians) developed along similar lines to the town poets (*rederijkers*).[37] The first were paid by the prince, the second by the rich cities of Flanders and Brabant, but this did not prevent their voices from coinciding, sometimes to the advantage of the prince. Thus, Anthonis de Roovere (c. 1430–82), master mason and *rederijker* of Bruges, was very quickly noticed by Charles the Bold and employed to vaunt his merits to the population of the town. It was he, for example, who spoke next after Chancellor Hugonet in front of the Estates General, haranguing the people, reminding them that whilst they were amusing themselves in the tavern or enjoying the heat of the hearth, the prince was venturing out on the field of battle to defend their prosperity:

> We stay comfortably at home
> And he, whether he likes it or not,
> Puts up with snow and hail.[38]

George Chastelain himself, on the occasion of the solemn entry of Charles the Bold into Mons in 1468, was solicited by the townsfolk of Valenciennes to write a play and so attract the attention and the favours of the new duke. *La mort du duc Philippe, mystere par maniere de lamentacion* thus dramatised the allegories of Earth, Heaven and Men in search of the dead duke's body. The play rapidly turned to the question of the meaning of this death and the future of the principality. It was then the job of the court poet, addressing an urban public, to reassure the people of dynastic continuity. For 'if the body of Philip is lost with no hope of return, if his soul waits for the prayers of his subjects to reach salvation, it is in his son that stability here below will be maintained'.[39] The memory of the prince was revived in the urban dramatic space by means of a form of communication accessible to all. The use of this medium also reminds us of the multiform nature of a kind of political propaganda which I have described elsewhere as 'multimedia communication'.[40] This is seen clearly if we take the time to compare different sources, and so find again and again, in the sermons of preachers, in the fragments of speech of ducal harangues, from the pens of poets, chroniclers and dramatists, under the artist's brush or the sculptor's chisel, the same recurring themes of the long ancestral line, the sacrifice of the prince for his people, the desire for peace and the love of justice.

The rustling of rumour

Alongside this strident form of princely communication, we must also consider the rather different, softer or deeper notes which nonetheless attest to the skill and to the breadth of the field of action of these fifteenth-century rulers. A study of the use of rumour by French, English and Burgundian princes at the end of the Middle Ages has shown how far Charles the Bold used this popular 'instrument of communication' to win over his subjects, uniting them around his person and against the evils that threatened him.[41] When he learnt of the death of the duke of Guyenne, brother of Louis XI, for example, Charles waxed indignant, appropriating the rumour of that the duke had been poisoned to rise against the king of France once again in 1472. In the letters which the duke sent out into his territory, he declared that the duke of Guyenne had been assassinated on the order of the king 'by poison, curses, sorcery and diabolical conjurations' and that for this reason he was ready, as a vigorous knight, to avenge this murder, so help him God. At the same time, he sought the sympathy of his subjects by taking advantage of rumours of assassination attempts directed against his own person. Rumour, this 'news which spreads amongst a given public and whose origin, as much as its veracity, is uncertain', was not the monopoly of the street, and was not restricted to those stories which circulated amongst the people and which the authorities opposed by ritualised, publicised and official speech, to follow Claude Gauvard's taxonomy.[42] Rumour of course could upset those in power, through its anonymity and its subversive potential. In the English context, Charles Ross, for example, said much the same: rumour was essentially corrosive and biting, and so propaganda was often constructed in response to such seditious news.[43] Yet a number of cases make it possible to show that it is no longer necessary simply to diametrically oppose rumour to official discourse. They also suggest a number of reflections on the evolution of political discourse at the end of the Middle Ages.

The range of possible options was broad, making it possible to redefine the link between authority and rumour. The prince could, for example, let a rumour run and allow it to grow, before then contradicting it publicly. This was the case, for example, in the affair of the Bastard of Rubempré. In the autumn of 1465, rumours accused Louis XI of having wanted to seize and even to assassinate the heir of Burgundy, the future Charles the Bold, following the revelations of an agent of the king intercepted in Holland. At first discreet, the royal counter-attack won the day after the publication of this 'calumny' in a public square of Bruges. Commynes, reporting what Joël Blanchard calls a 'dressing down at the court of Burgundy', explains that royal ambassadors sent to Lille complained first of all of the publication of this affair at Bruges, a centre of international circulation, by Olivier de la Marche – whose arrest Louis XI demanded.[44] De la Marche does not mention this trip through Bruges when he describes his voyage from Holland to Hesdin to report the arrest of the Bastard of Rubempré to Philip the Good.[45] But according to Louis XI, it was he who had spread this rumour during his voyage, even ordering a Bruges preacher to include it in his sermons. We can see how several different discourses set themselves into these events. First there was the measured discourse of the duke of Burgundy and his diplomats, who took refuge in the law: a man who was the subject of numerous suspicions had been arrested to facilitate an inquiry into his intentions. Then came the voice of the count of Charolais, the future Charles the Bold, who argued that he had acted properly in arresting a man who was suspected by those who knew him on a number of charges, which were subsequently confirmed by confessions which Charles could not reveal in detail, out of respect for the royal person, but which had sincerely grieved him. Finally, there was the royal discourse which denounced the defamatory rumour spreading in the Burgundian lands to the effect that the king was the potential assassin of his own cousin.

Rumour was thus at the heart of a form of propaganda extensively used both by Louis XI and by Charles the Bold. In rumour the different time scales invoked at the beginning of this chapter came together. Every rumour said something about the recent past (Louis XI wanted to assassinate the count of Charolais), about the present (he was dismantling the Burgundian lands), or about the near future (he was a danger to the prosperity of the duke's territories). It was a kind of three-pronged weapon, making use of past information carefully chosen to call to mind earlier difficult situations, weakening the present and the confidence which one had in it and raising concerns for the future, all of which must have moved subjects who were alert for any situation of potential war. But if this kind of argument worked well in the middle of the Hundred

Years War, in the propaganda of Charles VII, a French monarch who also knew how to play on the sensibilities of a people in its struggle against an ancestral enemy, this invocation of threats close by was not enough to unite the population of Flanders, Hainault, Brabant, Artois, Dijon and so forth under the leadership of Charles the Bold.

It can be seen that, despite the efforts of the duke's political communication to point the finger at England for its insults to Philip the Good, at France and the threats of Louis XI, or even at the Empire and the effrontery of Frederick III, these all still seemed improbable enemies to the collective consciousness, since they ultimately threatened only the honour of the prince, which was not enough to inspire the whole people. Although this propaganda was impeccably organised, it often chose the wrong object. To build links between rulers and ruled more was needed than the dramatisation of the figure of the prince, the antiquity of his lineage and the ambitions of his house (for example, the quest for a royal crown for Charles the Bold). For this was a territory composed of an unavoidable plurality of cultural identities.

Union in sacred duty?

The quest for universal order may have helped to overcome this internal lack of natural unity. Once again, Burgundian political communication made considerable use of this field of meaning to found part of its discourse of legitimacy. From this point of view, the creation of the Order of the Golden Fleece in 1430, considered a 'divine pledge' (*divine emprise*) based on the Order of the Garter, whilst enabling Philip the Good to avoid joining it, was certainly a key moment in this political project. Similarly, the crusading drive was not just a posture, but a means for the dukes to present themselves as new champions of Christendom. Since Burgundian history writing was especially active in this area, a number of studies have considered this subject in depth.[46] It is thus not necessary to consider them once again in detail. Rather, these matters are discussed here in order to emphasise the power of the chivalric ideal throughout Europe at the end of the Middle Ages, and to sketch out the full extent of this policy of self-presentation.

'A noble state and order of chivalry'

In the year following the celebration of the first chapter of the Order of the Golden Fleece at Bruges in January 1430, the complete statutes of the order were decreed on 27 November 1431, linking the defence of the Catholic faith and the protection of the public weal:

> by which the true Catholic faith ... and the tranquillity and the prosperity of the public weal [*chose publicque*] should be ... kept and maintained[47]

This citation could easily lead to the conclusion that Philip the Good's initiative, which was also inspired by his predecessors' attempt to establish an Order of the Golden Tree, served a desire to make elite chivalric conceptions coincide with public duties in a way which would unite all his territories. After all, the constitution of a confraternity united by its 'true love' for its prince, granted distinction by the latter's care and drawn from the four corners of the Great Principality, could have provided the basis for the perfection of a network of influence capable of unifying such diverse territories around ancient but living ideals. The designation of Dijon as the seat of the order and the desire to move the festival of the Golden Fleece to different towns mostly situated in the north also suggest a plan to master the dukes' territory which recognised its multi-polar nature. The commandments and the organisation of this fraternity sought to ensure that its knights would devote themselves to the worship of God and the glory of chivalric society, on the basis of shared fidelity between the prince and his men.

Yet in fact it now appears, following the initial reflections of Jean Richard, which were later developed by Françoise de Gruben, that the distribution of livery collars concerned the Burgundians of the two Burgundies (i.e. the county and the duchy) only a little, and that a confraternity which could have been opened up widely to the nobility was in fact quite restricted.[48] From very early on, it was not the links that could have united the person of the prince to these different lands through the intermediary of its nobility which were privileged by the order but rather the chivalric qualities of noble men drawn from across Europe, according to diplomatic priorities and to favours attributed to certain families such as the Luxembourg, the Croÿ, the Lannoy, the Lalaing and so on. As a result, whilst the Golden Fleece was progressively opened up to foreign personalities, to the barons of France or the Empire or, as in 1445, to the king of Aragon in the person of Alfonso V, out of twenty-nine members of the ducal council in 1438, only ten, albeit the most important ones, were members of the order. This selective orientation which privileged a chosen few, singled out for their deeds in arms, did not help to spread a network of influence over the Burgundian territories, as one might have expected. The chapter meetings, which allowed each member of the confraternity to be judged collegially and so allowed the prince to watch over his men in a context of mutual sociability, could have served, on a larger scale, as an effective instrument of power. Limited to thirty or so men, it remained simply a context for an examination of members' consciences. Whilst the order enjoyed an undeniable international prestige whose dignity still impressed the Emperor Charles V, it turned out to have a relatively limited usefulness either for the constitution of a group of faithful followers devoted to the king and his interests, or for the elaboration of a Burgundian national identity. D'Arcy Boulton, who initially stressed the limited influence of the order amongst those with power, has recently changed his opinion, seeing this foundation and especially the association of the livery collar with the arms of the prince as a foundational element of the 'Burgundian nation', without however explaining this change of heart.[49] It has to be said, with Gert Melville, that to a significant extent the order functioned as a society of mutual emulation in which this elite nobility 'found new foundations for its legitimation', whereas the dispersed nature of this fraternity, which was spread across Europe, was overcome from time to time in the symbolic performance of community at its various festivals.[50] It is certainly true that during these festivities, the court, oscillating between public representation and the confidentiality of the chapter, displayed to all present the coherence of the select group, whilst at the same time suggesting models of excellence whose memory was guaranteed by the fraternity's coats of arms, which hung in every church where the chapter meetings took place. But this symbolic importance was of only limited duration. Although the model of the worthy knight, admired by all Europe, might seduce a Burgundian nobility hungry for noble deeds, it could not provide a unifying motif for a whole people. The dream of the crusade, on the other hand, was more widely influential.

Unity in defence of the cross

Whilst it behoved the knights of the Golden Fleece gathered around Philip the Good to meet and to work together to defend 'the true Catholic faith', the ideal of the crusade, a *Leitmotif* in the policies of the four dukes of Burgundy, appealed to a broader public, one which was very much aware of their purpose and of their position in an area whose interest was beginning to wane in the eyes of most European monarchs. By bringing up to date the system of values which ordered and ranked the chivalric world, the ideal of the crusade put forward models of respect, of unity, of togetherness and of just war which echoed the principles of the Order of the Golden Fleece, but it also allowed the dukes to ascribe to themselves a form of honour usually reserved for royalty. In alliance with the papal court, Philip the Good emerged very early on as a knight of Christ, and this position did not fail to increase his prestige in all the courts of Europe. The image of the crusader prince thus became an attribute of ducal power. And so, although he was ruined by the cost of the Nicopolis expedition, Philip the Bold organised festivities in all the towns on the route of John the Fearless from Dijon to Lille to celebrate the return of the young prince. When Philip the Good left for Regensburg in 1454 to submit his project to the emperor, he announced his ambitions in public ceremonies in Arras and elsewhere. Before that, the famous Feast of the Pheasant had made Lille the focus of attention, whilst the town listened to the rhythm of the echoes of the banquet taking place in the Palais de la Salle. General processions, referred to above, were also part of this ducal project, and the question of how it was to be financed was resolved by the organisation of lotteries with the participation of the duke's subjects in Hainault and elsewhere.

Yet it was perhaps in 1463–64 that Philip the Good, feeling that he was on the point of finally being able to accomplish his crusading vow, made the greatest effort to project his stature as the champion of Christendom. Whilst a 'Letter to the House of Burgundy on the Crusade' was being composed during a meeting of the Estates General at Lille on 8–12 March 1464, and Philip had to delay his departure once more, he nonetheless publicly announced his imminent voyage to the Levant.[51] Supported by pontifical propaganda, Burgundian political communication was deployed in numerous processions, as at Douai, starting on 3 July 1457, and then at Ghent and at similar events scattered through Flanders. As Jacques du Clercq reports:

> And at this time also a large number of people took the cross, and for the most part all young men, and left by the road, here ten, here twenty, here forty together without captains, and some with little money or equipment for war, and on foot, and they all made their way to Rome; and it was said that from the lands of the duke many of them went in large numbers, and even up to the number of twenty thousand or more.[52]

Although the towns were apparently answering a papal appeal, it would be wrong to neglect such details as the coat of arms marked with the cross of Saint Andrew worn by the inhabitants of the little town of Axel, proving their awareness of the link between this sacred duty and the duke of Burgundy.[53] In the injunction which the bishop of Tournai made to the president of Burgundy on 6 June, ordering him to organise the preaching of the crusade, to place collection boxes in the churches and to detain future crusaders until the arrival of the duke, Guillaume Fillastre explained how he had orchestrated this publicity campaign in the north, noting that he had had the papal bull for the crusade translated into Flemish and French in order to have it read every Sunday.

Popular emotion was great, and it was perhaps because enthusiasm for this sacred duty was ultimately disappointed that popular songs attacked the attitude of the duke of Burgundy when, after the death of Pious II on 15 August 1464, he definitively renounced his project. In the streets of his northern lands, one could hear a poem-dialogue dripping with deeply felt mockery (and word play impossible to render into English):

> Hello, Watier! Where have you been? – In Picardy.
> What have you brought? – Some very good news.
> But does it matter to you? – What? What the Picard says [*Que Picard die*]?
> Are you giving some of them? We're giving some good ones.
> Where is the duke of Burgundy? – At Brussels.

> And what is he doing? – He bathes all day long.
> And what does he say? – Who about? – About the infidels.
> He fights them by his fireplace.[54]

The call of the East, the sacred journey, could perhaps have united the people behind their prince, such was the power of the faith. But for this to happen the princes actually had to go on crusade. Religion, the sublime and its trappings were, as the Milanese ambassador Prospero da Camogli underlined, powerful tools which allowed the dukes to transmit a lesson of order, of rigour and of strength addressed at once to the great of the House of Burgundy, to the watching towns and to the courts of Europe, who listened eagerly to news of the dukes' magnificent entertainments. Yet the desire to form a kind of moral family at the summit of noble society, the will to project an ideal and eternal history and to give oneself the illusion of participating in it, through the thousand ruses of symbolic communication, all this was not enough to galvanise a people when the world demanded that words should be matched by deeds.

The creation of the Order of the Golden Fleece and the dream of crusade were international prestige operations which had little influence on internal politics. In these initiatives, which a recent historiography has attempted to graft on to the themes of state formation and nation building, we should notice above all the search for a form of glory which was all the more coveted since it was displayed to the eyes of the world, or more exactly to a world of insiders. For in these two projects, one of which was concrete, the other ideal, these princes showed above all that they were noble and lived according to their estate, with its values, its obsessions, its emulations. Symbolic communication served to obtain access to the goods of subjects, who were involved only in order to satisfy the impulsions of a chivalric elite.

We can clearly see that the rulers of Burgundy used every means at their disposal to influence 'public opinion'. Images, poems, letters, rumours, processions, solemn entries – all these made it possible to address a wide and fragmented media space. The mastery of the present and the introduction of the past into this exchange between rulers and ruled were deployed as best they could be. Nevertheless, the limits of this often illusory dialogue must be recognised. The mastery of the means available was not enough to guarantee the effectiveness of a discourse which had to go beyond the level of propaganda to achieve that of shared certitudes. For, over the long term, the policy of projecting a prestigious heritage, a magnified present and a common future had necessarily to go further if it was to be capable of constructing a collective identity which went beyond customs, the rules of each trade and the ties of neighbourhood, without however denying them. If the mirage of a princely ceremony charged with affective resonances might achieve this symbiosis for the length of time it took the cortege to pass, the project became harder to maintain once the spectacle was over, and conflict and the hardness of life made their inevitable return. Unsurprisingly, as we shall see in the next chapter, the court was no exception in the way that it too revealed these dissonances.

Notes

1 'Et ceulx qui seront esleuz a estre eschevins et miz en loys seront tenuz de faire serement solennel et publique, avec le serement accoustumé, devant nosdiz commissaires.' Document no. 225 (Ghent, 1 October 1414), in J. M. Cauchies (ed.), *Ordonnances de Jean sans Peur (1405–1419)*, Recueil des ordonnances des Pays-Bas, first series (1381–1506), part 1, vol. III (Brussels: Service public fédéral Justice, 2001), pp. 372–375.
2 An analysis of all these oaths can be found in É. Lecuppre-Desjardin, *La ville des cérémonies. Essai sur la communication politique dans les anciens Pays-Bas bourguignons*, SEUH 4 (Turnhout: Brepols, 2004), pp. 141–148.
3 See J. Van Leeuwen, 'Municipal Oaths, Political Virtues and the Centralised State: The Adaptation of Oaths of Office in Fifteenth-Century Flanders', *Journal of Medieval History* 31 (2005), 185–210.
4 See the distinction between 'public places' and 'public space' in P. Boucheron, 'Espace public et lieux publics: approches en histoire urbaine', in P. Boucheron and N. Offenstadt (eds), *L'espace public au Moyen Âge. Débats autour de Jürgen Habermas* (Paris: PUF, 2011), pp. 99–117.
5 P. Contamine, 'La Bourgogne du XVe siècle', in *Des pouvoirs en France, 1300–1500* (Paris: Presses de l'École Normale Supérieure, 1992), pp. 61–74.
6 Lecuppre-Desjardin, *La ville des cérémonies*, p. 329.
7 See M. Boone, 'L'automne du Moyen Âge: Johan Huizinga et Henri Pirenne ou "plusieurs vérités pour la même chose"', in P. Moreno and

G. Palumbo (eds), *Autour du XVe siècle. Journées d'étude en l'honneur d'Alberto* Vàrvaro (Liège: Presses Universitaires de Liège, 2008), pp. 27–51.
8 P. Bonenfant, 'L'État bourguignon dans le cadre de la monocratie', in *Philippe le Bon, sa politique, son action*, ed. A.-M. Bonenfant-Feytmans (Brussels: De Boeck Université, 1996), pp. 365–376.
9 The formula 'by the grace of God' could be used only by sovereigns who were at the head of the 'feudal pyramid'. In this case, Philip the Good was a vassal of the king of France for most of his territories, except for those which were dependent on the Empire, such as the duchy of Brabant.
10 See M. Boone, 'L'État bourguignon, un État inventeur ou les limites de l'invention', in W. Paravicini (ed.), *La cour de Bourgogne et l'Europe* (Ostfildern: Thorbecke, 2012), pp. 133–156.
11 W. Prevenier, 'Briefwisseling tussen de Vier Leden van Vlaanderen en Filips de Stoute, hertog van Bourgondië en diens echtgenote Margareta van Male, over de inbreuken op de Vlaamse privilegies door vorstelijke ambtenaren en instellingen (1398–1402)', *Bulletin de la Commission royale* 150 (1984), 506–522, at p. 511.
12 M. Maffesoli, 'Communion et communication. Penser le mystère de la socialité contemporaine', *Sociétés* 91:1 (2006), 7–10.
13 Terms inspired by R. Debray, *Les communions humaines. Pour en finir avec "la religion"* (Paris: Fayard, 2005).
14 The literature concerning Flemish revolts is abundant. See, for example, J. Dumolyn and J. Haemers, 'Patterns of Urban Rebellion in Medieval Flanders', *Journal of Medieval History* 31 (2005), 369–393.
15 George Chastelain, *Œuvres*, ed. J. Kervyn de Lettenhove, 8 vols (Brussels: F. Heussner, 1863–66), vol. III, book IV, ch. XIII, p. 69.
16 J. Boutier, A. Dewerpe and D. Nordman, *Un tour de France royale. Le voyage de Charles IX (1564–1566)* (Paris: Aubier, 1984).
17 Philippe de Commynes, *Mémoires*, ed. J. Blanchard (Geneva: Droz, 2007), book VI, ch. 7, p. 472.
18 Guillaume Fillastre, *Premier volume de la Toison d'Or, suivi du second* (1530 edition), Bibliothèque municipale de Lille, no. 43533, fols XVv–XVI.
19 L. Scordia, *Le roi doit vivre du sien. La théorie de l'impôt en France (XIIIe–XVe siècle)* (Turnhout: Brepols, 2005), pp. 333–362.
20 C. Fletcher, *Richard II: Manhood, Youth and Politics, 1377–1399* (Oxford: Oxford University Press, 2008), pp. 192–220.
21 For the nature of princely charisma, see G. Lecuppre, *L'imposture politique au Moyen Âge. La seconde vie des rois* (Paris: Presses Universitaires de France, 2005), pp. 138–146.

22 B. Guenée, 'Le portrait de Charles VI dans la Chronique du Religieux de Saint-Denis', *Journal des Savants* (1997), no. 1, pp. 125–165.
23 For the ideal of 'vivre noblement', see F. Buylaert, W. Declercq and J. Dumolyn, 'Sumptuary Legislation, Material Culture and the Semiotics of "vivre noblement" in the County of Flanders (14th–16th c.)', *Social History* 36:4 (2011), 393–417.
24 W. Prevenier, 'Imitation et comportements spécifiques', in W. Prevenier (ed.), *Le prince et le peuple. La société du temps des ducs de Bourgogne* (Anvers: Fonds Mercator, 1998), p. 157.
25 É. Lecuppre-Desjardin, 'Les lumières de la ville: recherche sur l'utilisation de la lumière dans les cérémonies bourguignonnes (XIVe–XVe siècles)', *Revue historique* 301:2 (609) (1999), 23–43.
26 Matthieu d'Escouchy, *Chronique*, ed. G. du Fresne de Beaucourt, 3 vols (Paris: Jules Renouart, 1843–53), vol. I, ch. LV.
27 L. Hablot, 'Revêtir le prince. Le héraut en tabard, une image idéale du prince. Pour une tentative d'interprétation du partage emblématique entre prince et héraut à la fin du Moyen Âge à travers le cas bourguignon', *Revue du Nord* 88, 366–367 (2006), 755–803.
28 É. Lecuppre-Desjardin, 'La balade des trépassés. L'évocation d'un âge d'or bourguignon au service des ambitions royales de Charles le Téméraire', in *Desir n'a repos. Hommage à Danielle Bohler, Eidôlon* 115 (2015), 269–283.
29 G. Small, 'Qui a lu la chronique de George Chastelain?', *PCEEB* 31 (1991), 101–111. The author demonstrates that recognition of this work came late.
30 R. Stein, 'Cultuur in context. Het spel van *Menych sympel* (1466) als spiegel van de brusselse politieke verhoudingen', *Bijdragen en Mededelingen betreffende de geschiedenis de Nederlanden* 113 (1998), 289–321.
31 For the use of genealogy in ducal propaganda, see É. Lecuppre-Desjardin, 'Un prince, des fiefs, des ancêtres. Des généalogies en partage dans la principauté de Bourgogne au XVe siècle', in O. Rouchon (ed.), *L'opération généalogique. Cultures et pratiques européennes, XVe–XVIIIe siècle* (Rennes: PUR, 2014), pp. 51–71.
32 A. M. Roberts, 'The Chronology and Political Significance of the Tomb of Mary of Burgundy', *The Art Bulletin* 71–73 (1989), 376–400. Thanks to the genealogy, Maximilien could prove that the maternal grandmother of Mary was the sister of Philip the Good, Agnes of Burgundy, which strengthened the Burgundian origin of his wife.
33 C. Billen, 'Mouvances, dépendances et pouvoirs dans un village tournaisien au XVe siècle', *Mémoires de la Société royale d'histoire et d'archéologie de Tournai* 2 (1981), 81–90.

34 During the 'accursed war' (*maudite guerre*), the French civil war between Armagnacs and Burgundians, John the Fearless sent dozens of manifestos and letters all over the kingdom of France to explain and legitimate his war.
35 On this point, see E. Doudet, *Poétique de George Chastelain (1415–1475). Un cristal mucié en un coffre* (Paris: Champion, 2005), *passim*.
36 'Ne pense pas que nous te croyons encore / Un lion grimpant au flanc de la montagne.' E. Doudet, 'Contraintes, concurrences et stratégies d'autonomisation chez les Rhétoriqueurs francophones', in D. Coigneau and S. Mareel (eds), *Met eigen ogen: de rederijker als dichtend individu (1450–1600)*, De Fonteine 58 (2009), 69–86.
37 For the success of Chambers of Rhetoric, see A.-L. Van Bruaene, *Om beters wille. Rederijkerskamers en de stedelijke cultuur in de Zuidelijke Nederlanden (1400–1650)* (Amsterdam: Amsterdam University Press, 2008).
38 'Wy ligghen thuys wel ende saechte gheleydt / Ende, hy wedert hem mishaecht of greyt / Moet ligghen daer sneeuw ende hagel smelt.' Poem by Anthonis de Roovere, quoted by J. B. Oosterman, '"Oh Flanders, weep!" Anthonis de Roovere and Charles the Bold', in M. Gosman *et al*. (eds), *The Growth of Authority in the Medieval West* (Groningen: Forsten, 1999), pp. 257–267.
39 E. Doudet, 'Présence du corps absent. Théâtre et disparition du prince au XVe siècle', *Cahiers de recherches médiévales et humanistes / Journal of Medieval and Humanistic Studies* 32 (2016), 19–36.
40 Lecuppre-Desjardin, *La ville des cérémonies*, *passim*.
41 For numerous examples of this kind, see G. Lecuppre and É. Lecuppre-Desjardin, 'La rumeur: un instrument de la compétition politique au service des princes de la fin du Moyen Âge', in M. Billoré and M. Soria (eds), *La rumeur au Moyen Âge. Du mépris à la manipulation (V[e]–XVe siècles)* (Rennes: PUR, 2011), pp. 149–175.
42 C. Gauvard, 'Rumeurs et stéréotypes à la fin du Moyen Âge', in *La circulation des nouvelles à la fin du Moyen Âge. XIVe congrès de la S.H.M.E.S.P. (Avignon 1993)* (Paris: Presses de la Sorbonne, 1994), pp. 157–177.
43 C. Ross, 'Rumour, Propaganda and Popular Opinion during the Wars of the Roses', in R. A. Griffiths (ed.), *Patronage, the Crown and the Provinces in Later Medieval England* (Gloucester: Humanities Press, 1981), pp. 15–32.
44 Commynes, *Mémoires*, ed. Blanchard, vol. I, pp. 5–6.
45 Olivier de la Marche, *Mémoires*, ed. H. Beaune and J. D'Arbaumont, 4 vols (Paris: Renouard, 1883–88), vol. III, book I, ch. XXXV, p. 3.

46 For the Order of the Golden Fleece, see amongst others C. Van den Bergen-Pantens and P. Cockshaw (eds), *L'ordre de la Toison d'or, de Philippe le Bon à Philippe le Beau (1430–1505). Idéal ou reflet d'une société?* (Turnhout: Brepols, 1996).
47 Jean Lefèvre de Saint Remy, *Chronique*, ed. F. Morand, 2 vols (Paris: Renouard, 1876–81), vol. II, p. 211.
48 Even if the headquarters of the order was settled in Dijon, only eight of the twenty-four knights came from the duchy and the county of Burgundy in 1430. See J. Richard, 'La Toison d'Or dans les deux Bourgogne', *PCEEB* 5 (1963), 47–52. During the total period under consideration, the total number was sixty-three out of 246 knights. See F. de Gruben, *Les chapitres de la Toison d'Or à l'époque bourguignonne (1430–1477)* (Leuven: Leuven University Press, 1997).
49 J. D. A Boulton, 'The Order of the Golden Fleece and the Creation of Burgundian National Identity', in Boulton and Veenstra (eds), *The Ideology of Burgundy*, pp. 21–97.
50 G. Melville, "Le "mystère" de l'ordre de la Toison d'Or. Symbole de l'élite aristocratique et instrument du pouvoir du prince au bas Moyen Âge', in Paravicini (ed.), *La cour de Bourgogne et l'Europe*, pp. 217–228.
51 Letter ed. G. Doutrepont in *Analectes pour servir à l'histoire ecclésiastique de la Belgique* 32 (1906), 144–195.
52 Jacques du Clercq, *Mémoires*, ed. Baron de Reiffenberg (Brussels: Arnold Lacrosse, 1835–36), vol. IV, pp. 52–53.
53 For more details on this example and the others, see J. Paviot, *Les ducs de Bourgogne, la croisade et l'Orient (fin XIVe–XVe siècle)* (Paris: PUPS, 2003), pp. 171–176.
54 M. Löpelmann (ed.), *Die Liederhandschrift des Cardinals de Rohan (XV. Jahrh.)*, Gesellschaft für Romanische Literatur 44 (Göttingen, 1923), pp. 32–33, quoted in *ibid.*, pp. 175–176.

2

Nobles in need of love and recognition

> As much as it hurts and displeases me greatly ... I must, not without great displeasure, declare and cite the causes which moved me to do this [i.e. leave the court]. The first was ... that the said Charles so-called of Burgundy has very vile, detestable and disreputable [habits] against God our Creator, against our law and against all order of nature which it is preferable to keep silent out of respectability rather than to speak of, and with regard to which I will not, cannot and must not comment openly without greatly offending God, our law, and endangering my conscience and my honour. The other cause was for the great hatred which the said Charles so-called of Burgundy has against me because of what I did not want to finish with him in the great and unnatural cruelty which he did to my said most redoubtable lord, my lord the late duke, Philip of Burgundy, whose obedience and authority he usurped over these lands and this lordship ...[1]

Honour insulted, hatred, jealousy, humiliation, a toxic atmosphere, corrupt morals: the arguments advanced by Baudouin de Lille, in his letter of defence of December 1470, bear witness to a profound malaise at the court of Charles the Bold. In this document, the Bastard of Burgundy replies word for word to the accusations made by Duke Charles in a manifesto intended to be read publicly across the whole territory and by preachers in church.[2] In this document, Charles the Bold, in his familiar paternal tone, calls his subjects to witness: Baudouin had conspired with Jean d'Arson and Jean de Chassa to kill him 'by the sword or by poison'. There was nothing new in this conspiracy, and after the plots of the Bastard of Rubempré and Jean Coustain, it appeared that Charles's life was threatened once more. Damaging rumours circulated, and heads had to roll to preserve the prince's. If we believe Thomas Basin, it was obvious that the duke of Burgundy had reasons to be on his guard, and once again it was Louis XI's perfidy which had inspired the treachery of Baudouin, whose ingratitude, according to the duke, was equalled only by his rapacity.[3] The personality of the Bastard of Burgundy, as Jean-Marie Cauchies has reconstructed it, could support the idea of an unscrupulous adventurer motivated by a taste for intrigue, a desire for vengeance and the possibility of material gain.[4] But it is not our purpose here to establish the guilt or otherwise of Charles's half-brother. The more or less discreet but certainly multiple allusions, the cryptic denunciations, the scandals which brought the king's anger out into the open, all attest to a more profound unease in the highest circles of power.

Baudouin was neither the first nor the last noble to leave Charles's court. For a long time, historians of the Burgundian dukes were particularly bashful on this subject, concentrating solely on Philippe de Commynes, who, almost alone, was held to embody the figure of the traitor at court.[5] Historians who had no fear of precise figures or dates nonetheless preferred a certain vagueness when it came to those who swam in the troubled waters of Burgundian rule. The quantity of fugitives was never dealt with except through formulas such as: 'he fled the court ... like ... many others of Charles the Bold's men', 'evidence of hostility punctuated his rule and accumulated in its epilogue', and so on.[6] More recently, however, 'the dark side of Burgundian splendour' has been exposed, along with a 'behind the scenes' world marked by plots, betrayal, murder and scandal, although the introduction to one essay collection is careful to note that 'devouring ambitions, betrayals, partisan struggles ... are naturally not Burgundian specificities'.[7] Charles the Bold's court was, of course, not the only one to exhibit such disorders, and the comparative examples cited in the coming pages will bring the necessary nuance to this picture. But the accumulation of these troubles, the particular way they were expressed and the variety of their motivations take us away from the ordinary clashes which are inherent in any manifestation of princely favour and disgrace. This phenomenon helps to reveal a progression in political ideas at the Burgundian court which cannot be revealed by focusing only on the ordinances and regulations of the household and the hall council, however subtly they are analysed. A significant place must be reserved for human relations and for the differences of culture which can exist within the same historical world. The questions which come to the fore when we read through letters of defence and official narratives, where the reference to sudden departures did not go without a certain embarrassment, are simple enough. Why did men who had received everything from the prince desert him? What do these desertions reveal about the functioning and the malfunctions of the court? Finally, to what were these men, who never cease to invoke their sense of honour, loyal?

Desertions and betrayals

As Badouin took care to point out in his letter of 1470, he had left Charles's court with great reluctance. The suddenness of his departure was due to his fear of the ferocity of his half-brother, and it was only because duty obliged him to defend his honour that he had been forced to reveal family secrets which seriously damaged the reputation of the duke of Burgundy. Even if they were reconciled five years later, by making honourable amends, the spoilt child of Philip the Good felt ill-treated by Charles the Bold, a prince of 'new hard habits', as Chastelain put it.[8] The reasons behind this move are not clearly identified, but incompatibility of temperament, dislike and even hatred, probably explain why a number of noblemen preferred to leave the court, whether temporarily or for good.

Betraying the prince: A tediously familiar phenomenon

In 1463 Jean de Nevers departed from court, not without a certain rancour, exclaiming to his servants on the steps of the castle, 'Well, there you go! Ha! The son wanted to dishonour me, and the father kicks me out of his house. What's to be done? At least I'll be allowed to live until I die.'[9] In 1465 Antoine, Jean and Philippe de Croÿ put themselves under the protection of Louis XI, whilst Duke Charles, in a manifesto published on 12 March, accused the clan of fraud and treason. For Chastelain, it was despair which pushed Antoine de Croÿ to go and 'take strength from the king'.[10] It was in a state of 'bereavement' that Guillaume Rolin, the son of the great chancellor Nicholas, also quit the kingdom, ruined by the duke by 1470. Charles the Bold's death accelerated the movement, and even the most faithful, including, with Antoine, the Great Bastard of Burgundy, Jacques de Luxembourg, Philippe de Crèvecoeur, Jean Damas and Philippe Pot, could not resist the siren calls of the French. To get away from a vague vocabulary and to form a clearer idea of this population of defectors, we need to turn from Burgundian to French chroniclers, as well as ploughing through an extensive monographic literature. The figures cannot be definitive, but the work undertaken by Pierre Roger Gaussin on the counsellors of Louis XI already provides a solid basis, identifying as many as twenty-seven individuals of Burgundian origin, amongst whom we find Jean de Baudricourt, Guillaume Gouffier, Guiot Pot, Jean de la Driesche and of course Philippe de Commynes.[11] Admittedly, the defectors present in the council of the king of France were not all of Burgundian origin, but although the men of Aquitaine or Anjou also found their way into the king's embraces, it is Burgundy which wins the prize. This phenomenon would also be less surprising if, in earlier years and given the coolness of relations between France and the principality of Philip the Good, the royal council had not been almost forbidden to Burgundians. After all, under Philip the Bold and John the Fearless, the overt goal of the Valois princes had been to colonise the royal council. We should not forget that after the letter of defiance of July 1411, John the Fearless, who held Paris and had no reason to try to win over the Armagnac party, engaged in a veritable purge of the personnel of the royal government, installing his men and his allies.[12] But under Charles the Bold and after years of absence, the Burgundians returned to France, not with the agreement of their lord, but regretfully, or so they said, either because they were trying to escape from him or because he had expelled them.

We should not go too far. Although Louis XI did indeed work to siphon away the noble members of the Burgundian court, we need to reject a reading which would make Charles the only object of royal resentment, the victim of a veritable obsession.[13] In reality, this movement grew out of disturbed circumstances which the king of France exploited in the Burgundian territory and elsewhere: it was the opportunity that made the thief. It is the sheer number of these events that attracts our attention rather than simply the phenomenon itself.

We need to keep in mind that these movements between one master and another were not exceptional. Charles the Bold was not the only one to provoke desertion, abandonment or betrayal. In the House of Burgundy itself, Philip the Good had faced a pro-French party which led several court nobles to sign separate alliances to protect their domains in the 1430s. Louis de Chalon, prince of Orange, joined the French court in 1432; Jean de la Trémoille, lord of Jonvelle and knight of the Order of the Golden Fleece, was accused of spying for France on the occasion of the order's third chapter in 1433. In the same year, Guillaume de Chateauvillain rallied to Charles VII and promptly attacked Burgundian lands.[14] Further from the court, what should we make of the case of Jean de Granson, who betrayed Philip, spread agitation in the county of Burgundy in 1455 and was suffocated between two mattresses on the order of the prince?[15] Nor does the shadow of suspicion fail to fall on John the Fearless. Philippe Munier, a.k.a. Jossequin, for example, rallied to the faction of his master's assassins after the duke's murder at Montereau. He was subsequently described as a 'false traitor' by the Burgundian camp, and this parvenu who had enjoyed excessive favour from the dead duke saw his goods confiscated.[16] Others did not wait for the duke's death to cross the Rubicon. The career of Lourdin de Saligny, described by Bertrand Schnerb, shows how the wheel of fortune could gather up its victims through their love of riches and glory, but also through the jealousy which the latter provoked. Lourdin, 'most privy and familiar of the duke', was accused of plotting against his prince in the autumn of 1412, was imprisoned and banished from the court in 1413 only to return in 1418, and became the counsellor and chamberlain of Philip the Good in 1423.[17]

Noble rebellion in the Franche-Comté did not spare Philip the Bold either. One of his sergeants was assassinated by the party of Jean de Chalon, prince of Orange and baron of Arlay, because his privileges had been reduced by the ordinance of 1386.[18] The world of *practiques*, those negotiations through which fidelity is bought whilst fear is at work as much as money, evidently did not spare the court of France any more than that of England. There is no point multiplying examples, but even without invoking the series of trials launched by Louis XI to chastise the 'malcontents' of his reign who had dared to defy him, the case of Jean II, duke of Alençon, nephew of Charles VII, accused of the crime of *lèse-majesté* in 1458 for having become too close to the English, is one of the example of the wolves who were present in the sheepfold of the king's court.[19] The princes of France were just as untrustworthy as the English nobility, about whom Henry VI lamented that he was faced with attacks on both sides of the Channel. It has to be said that in the context of the Wars of the Roses, the monarch's fragile position encouraged the development of an art of intrigue of which the earl of Warwick was by no means the only exponent. Aristocratic opposition had a fine future ahead of it. Abandoning the prince and his house had nothing extraordinary about it. On the other hand, the causes of these betrayals, or simply of these changes of camp, reveal the varied profiles of these defectors, allowing us to go further in our analysis of the shaky nature of Burgundian state-building.

Over-fed parvenus

Amongst these men who found themselves accused, chastised, on the run, sometimes pardoned or definitively banished, we find the figure of the parvenu, the ambitious and successful man of humble origins, against whom contemporary chroniclers expended a considerable amount of vitriol. Chastelain deploys his rhetoric to pick them out: when they do not give themselves away, they are there, hidden in the shadows, giving their evil counsels, spreading discord and leading honest souls into disloyalty and inconstancy. This is how he explains the fall of Jean de Nevers, who kept very bad company after the death of his two mentors, the lord of Rochefort and Messire Hue de Longueval. His malevolent servant, a certain Boutillard, led him to his ruin by inciting him to claim the duchy of Brabant.[20] Chastelain also puts into the mouth of Philip the Good himself an accusation concerning the bad influence which Guillaume de Bische had over Charles the Bold. According to the chronicler, Duke Philip, in his great wisdom, had been careful to distance this evil subject from his son's entourage in 1457. Louis XI's partner in debauchery, Guillaume de Bische, was, according to the old duke of Burgundy, 'the worst crafty boy under heaven' ('le pire subtil garcon qui fust sous la nue'). Raised up by Charles, he became an essential actor in ducal diplomacy, becoming very rich in the process, notably at the expense of the towns of Holland, much like Guillaume de Clugny, archdeacon of Avallon, and Jean Gros, first secretary and *audiencier*. Yet at Charles's death, Bische surrendered Péronne to Louis XI and joined his service. Clugny did much the same and died in 1481 as bishop of Poitiers. Jean Gros, after having first accepted the honorific post of treasurer of the Order of the Golden Fleece from Mary of Burgundy, finally joined the camp of the king of France.[21] But the most famous of these ungrateful men, who did not wait for Charles's death to betray him, or who even helped him to his demise, was Jean Coustain. Coustain was:

> the most privy that [the duke] had, and so privy that there was no office in the lands of the said duke which the said duke granted, which did not pass through the hands of the said Coustain and from which he did not get something.[22]

When he arrived at court, 'wearing a poor canvas smock', he was welcomed by Philip the Good. The duke went on to make Coustain's fortune, much to the chagrin of the nobles whose place he stole. Was he really a traitor? Had he really procured poison to dispose of a prince who, as he admits in his confession, would no doubt have dismissed him once he was enthroned? Was he the right-hand man of the de Croÿ, as Charles the Bold wanted his father to believe? In any event it is clear that Chastelain decided to make Coustain's arrest and speedy execution an example to warn princes against such unscrupulous folk of humble origins, petty-spirited and motivated by covetousness. Although it takes more than ten pages for the chronicler to demolish the reputation of a man whose physical aspect was said to have shown the blackness of his soul, it is all summed up in Philip the Good's exclamation: 'Jean! Jean! I fed you up too fat!'[23] Social mobility disturbed the court, and the jealousies provoked by liberal grants of favour worsened when the recipient was a man whose origins upset the hierarchy of the aristocratic order.

Stripped and humiliated nobles

Yet it was not only 'men raised from the dust' who changed sides when questions of money encouraged them to do so. The word 'covetousness' was not used by the court historiographer when he described the departure of Louis of Luxembourg, count of Saint-Pol, but he did write: 'since he judged in himself that goods should be taken where they were offered, whereas they were refused in the place where he was'. Jean de Chassa, implicated in the affair of the Bastard of Burgundy, is likewise presented as a handsome knight who nonetheless lived above his means. Having contracted numerous debts, he saw in Louis XI's overtures a means to escape from a tight corner. Guillaume Rolin, one of the sons of the chancellor, incurred the wrath of Charles the Bold when he appealed to the Parlement of Paris in a case in which he was implicated. The duke confiscated all Rolin's goods, 'stripping him of everything' and thus inciting him to stay 'all safe in France, where others followed'.[24] Philippe de Commynes, until Joël Blanchard's efforts to rehabilitate his reputation, used to be presented as motivated by gain alone, in the light of the quantity of royal favour he received after his flight in 1472, bringing a precarious economic situation to an end.[25]

The defence of a noble's patrimony played an important role in motivating loyalty or its transference to another party. Richard Vaughan raises the question of the applicability of the concept of betrayal in the case of the House of Chalon, whose lands both in Burgundy and in France put them in a delicate situation. Is it reasonable to talk of treason in the case of Guillaume de Chalon, who was dispossessed by his younger brothers who were well-placed at the court of Charles the Bold, expelled from the principality of Orange and thus forced to join Louis XI whether he liked it or not?[26] In a comparable fashion, many frontier lords found themselves in a very uncomfortable position on the death of Charles the Bold. As Philippe de Commynes explains, the location of their possessions forced them to opt for the French camp: 'They turned [to the king] out of necessity, because they were situated or lived close to towns or in those which were in obedience to the said lord [the king].'[27] We will consider these defections later in greater detail, but it is worth noting at this point that Philippe de Crèvecœur, lord of Esquerdes, Jacques of Luxembourg, lord of Richebourg, and Antoine of Burgundy, known as the 'Great Bastard', were all very involved in Artois, in Picardy and in the south of Flanders, whereas Philippe Pot, Jean Damas and Jean II of Neufchâtel had lands in the duchy or the county of Burgundy. An instinct for survival, for the protection of their patrimony or the networks associated with these nobles must be taken into account in explaining their defections.

Money and favour cannot explain everything of course. Jean Jouffroy, for example, a protégé of Philip the Good, who granted him the bishopric of Arras in 1453, joined the king's service after meeting him during his exile at Genappes, no doubt with the intention of taking advantage of the favour he enjoyed with Louis to bring an end to the Pragmatic Sanction, which aim was achieved as early as October 1461.[28] His hard work earned him a cardinal's hat, and his allegiance to the king, stronger than his loyalty to the pope, won him the glittering prize of the bishopric of Albi in 1462.[29]

The situation of the Croÿ clan was probably more delicate. The departure of these men could simply be ascribed to the context of the end of a reign in which, almost classically, the favourites of the father were displaced by those of the son. Nevertheless, the change took place at a speed which suggests that something more than competition between clientage networks was at work. The different political positions of father and son were central to this violent relegation. Antoine de Croÿ had succeeded in winning the confidence of Philip the Good to the extent that he was considered by Charles the Bold to be a powerful, threatening, Francophile lord, who had, moreover, played a central role in the loss of the Somme towns. After many confrontations and indirect attacks, Charles finally levelled the accusation of high treason against the de Croÿ, who had by this time sought refuge in France. In this case, it could be suggested that the son's policies displeased the de Croÿ and that, on the basis of the interests of their patrimony, these well-established and powerful lords had no confidence in the heir to the House of Burgundy.[30] The language of defiance, of fear, of despair proves that the nobility was not reassured by a prince whose anger was prompt and whose hatred was great and cruel.[31] When the mediators in this conflict tried to reconcile Antoine with Charles for the umpteenth time, promising amongst other things that the duke would confirm his faithfulness in writing, the clan patriarch replied that he despaired of believing in either the prince's grace or his word. The de Croÿs' lack of mutual interest with the duke, their different political vision and their absence of confidence in him came together with the factors traditionally invoked to explain this rupture. When Chastelain has the lord de la Roche, who was supposed to have kept Antoine informed about the rumours circulating about him, finally reveal the extent of the charges which were being laid against him and the risks that he would end up running, the chronicler cannot resist putting into de la Roche's mouth a moralising excursus on the pride of nobles motivated by blind cupidity and avarice.³²

Personal feelings were certainly mixed with the lure of profit and the taste for power which went with riches. Louis XI succeeded from this point of view in upping the bidding, organising a veritable transfer market in the kingdom of France during his reign. As was argued earlier, Burgundy was not the only princely house to be touched by Louis's policy of active recruitment. It has to be admitted that weakening the principalities by depriving them of many of their important figures was a key element in royal self-assertion. Commynes makes this clear when he points out that the king:

> worked to win a man who could serve him or who could hurt him. And he was not concerned at all if he was refused once by a man whom he sought to win, but persisted, liberally promising him and giving him the money and estate which he knew would please him.³³

Money flowed freely, and the distribution of lands proceeded on a substantial scale. Each defection was adequately compensated, even negotiated to the sound of gold and silver coins, without forgetting lands and offices. Philippe de Commynes received amongst other things the principality of Talmont and a pension of 22,000 *livres*. Antoine of Burgundy was granted the county of Guines. The *bailli* of Vermandois, Guiot Pot, was given as many as seventeen castellanies. Jacques of Luxembourg was pleased to take on the lordships of Lens and La Bassée. Crèvecœur kept his offices as governor of Picardy, Peronne, Roye and Montdidier, as seneschal of Ponthieu, as captain of Boulogne and Hesdin, and so on and so forth. Louis XI certainly knew how to attract men to his side who would be useful to him, as he made clear in a letter of 24 March 1477, addressed to the lord of Craon, where he asks him to be generous to all those who might damage the French out of rancour.³⁴ It was in the same spirit, that of buying loyalty, that he tried to gently incorporate the duchies and counties of Burgundy by exonerating them from taxes which were imposed everywhere else, and by declaring the abolition of all the taxes established by Charles the Bold in all the lands which now escheated to the crown. This approach did much to persuade even the most recalcitrant. It almost succeeded in killing in embryo the Dijon rebellion or *mutemaque* of June 1477.

These men with growing needs were naturally attracted by royal generosity, however obvious its motivation, even though the House of Burgundy had not been especially ungenerous. It is in this light that it becomes possible to understand the true meaning of the gift and perhaps to imagine other reasons behind a superficially venal transfer of loyalties, suggested for example when Antoine de Croÿ, tired of the mediators' solicitations, let slip:

> Sir, let me say by way of conclusion and without wasting any more breath: I do not want to leave the service of a king of France for that of a count of Charolais. Excuse me and good bye.[35]

In this context, it is worth asking what loyalty, fidelity and allegiance meant to these seemingly so fickle noblemen.

Love, glory and money

> Do not forget to increase the fiefs of the needy with good rents and fertile lands, each according to his estate; you will lose nothing by this, but you will win their hearts; your lands will be better defended by courageous men if they possess them through you alone, because you are only one man and your power depends on them.[36]

Literature cultivates the art of succinct summary. The principles of liberality as a means of government are particularly well expressed in this thirteenth-century romance, the *Prose Lancelot*. Some readers might be surprised to see this citation at the opening of a discussion of the role of the gift in the fifteenth century, but this would be to forget that at the Burgundian court romance literature and the realities of power came together in a manner which is certainly disconcerting, but also meaningful. These few words said it all. The generosity of princes, whether it is aligned with Christian virtue as it was by Christine de Pizan, or with cold political calculation as in Machiavelli, was a universal rule of good governance when magnanimity rhymed with equity. If it was still possible to complain in the 1980s that there was a lack of research which took into account the work of Marcel Mauss on the gift, historians have now largely made good this lacuna, and the principality of Burgundy is no exception.[37] The work of Hans Cools, Jan Dumolyn, Mario Damen and Carol Chattaway, to name but a few, has directly or indirectly identified principles which, in the context of networks of reciprocal obligations, linked individuals to power.³⁸ From a simple gift to a reward of pensions and rents, the prince's generosity was the keystone of an edifice based on distribution and redistribution.

Largesse! A principle of government

Court nobles live by the recognition of merits and of men through the expression of favour by the first amongst them. In giving this well-known advice, Ghillebert de Lannoy identified the three things which enabled a noble to enrich himself: war, marriage and service to the prince.

> Through the said virtues which are in you … your prince, who will hear of them and who will perceive them by their effect, will commit you to such an office and so high, from which so many goods and profits shall come to you, that you will be rich and powerful.³⁹

Liberality is one of the recurrent themes of 'mirrors for princes'. It provided an essential cement for court relations. We know that Louis XI did not hesitate to spend more than he probably ought to have done in order to attach men to him. Some decades later Claude de Seyssel would criticise this policy, accusing the king of spreading rewards in an inequitable fashion, impoverishing the poor and enriching the wealthy.⁴⁰ The act of giving certainly did not have the same significance in the case of Charles the Bold, who preferred to give a small amount to everybody, which led nineteenth-century historians to see him as a miserly prince. We can nuance this picture, helped as much by the information provided by the accounts of the prince's treasurer as by new interpretations of the gift, of princely favour and of clientage networks.

Did the nobles who wanted to leave Charles's court suffer from the latter's lack of generosity? According to Chastelain, the count of Nevers had nothing to complain about, since 'there was no prince of the blood better maintained than he, as much in gifts of land as of goods as for his estate better maintained than others'.⁴¹ Is this simply the blindness of a Burgundian encomiast? Charles was not known for his great liberality, but the quantification of his gift-giving does not suggest that he was especially exposed to criticism in this regard. Philippe Pot, for example, according to the account for

1468, received 331 *livres* in January in return for his good services, on top of 170 *livres* he received in the previous month, 300 *livres* for the same reasons in May and a further 108 *livres*, giving a total of 909 *livres* for this account alone, or the equivalent of about 4,000 days' work for a Douai master mason![42] In 1468 Baudouin of Burgundy received a pension of 1,200 *écus* of 32 *gros*, and that of the Great Bastard Antoine came to 4,800 francs of 32 *gros*.[43] John Bartier remarked some time ago that working to promote the prince's fortune also improved one's own, for the commoner as much as the gentleman. Although the grants given to the nobility were far superior (although hard to quantify, since the gift of an office was normally synonymous with the gift of a pension), grants of all kinds were plentiful, from a prince or from a clientage network whose extent could be measured by its cost. An examination of the account of the general receipt of 1440 reveals that noblemen 'appear to have been even more rapacious than the clerics' and that rewards rained down on Robinet de Lucques, Philippe de Ternant, Guiot Pot, Simon de Lalaing and the like. The bastard of Saint-Pol, Jean, lord of Haubourdin, received in that year 1,000 *écus* of 48 *gros*, plus 360 *livres* of 40 *gros* for a satin cloth covered in gilded silver for a tournament at Saint-Omer, and 80 *livres* in return for a *chevauchée* against the English. As is well known, Philip the Good made the fortune of the Rolins but also of the de Croÿs, to such an extent that Antoine could lend the duke 6,000 *livres* in a single instalment for 'his present army against those of Ghent' in 1452.[44]

It was moreover the particularly intense demands for service in arms under Charles the Bold which sapped the resources of part of the nobility, as we shall see. For the moment, the tone was set by Philip the Bold, who started his rule as he meant to go on, spoiling his nobility and making gift-giving into a veritable principle of government. He pursued this spendthrift policy up until his death, to such an extent that Marguerite de Male placed on the body of her husband his belt, his purse and his keys in a sign of renunciation of the toxic inheritance which her husband had left her, so heavy were his debts. It has to be said that with the riches of Flanders and his pensions and gifts from the French king, the duke of Burgundy had what it took to satisfy a very demanding court. Carol Chattaway thus estimated that the new year's gifts reached almost 15 per cent of the demesne revenues for the 1390s. In her study of the Order of the Golden Tree, Chattaway calculated that the badges made and distributed were each worth between 25 and 600 francs. Since the quality and weight of gold of the jewel offered corresponded to the rank of its knightly recipient amongst the nobility, Pierre de la Trémoille considered that a brooch valued at 50 francs was unworthy of him and demanded one worth 250 francs instead.[45] This incident shows how far the nobility understood the meaning of all these gifts. One can thus say that the growth of the Burgundian principality was supported by a system of gifts and pensions which were intended to reinforce the loyalty of the men and women best positioned to serve the prince. This technique of government helped to reinforce the personal power of the prince, but it also served to confuse ever more thoroughly private interests and the interests of the public weal.

Mixing 'public' and 'private' interests

In the Burgundian principality, the prince did not forget his favourite courtiers when it came to his conquests. His nobles were directly involved in their prince's fresh acquisitions through the distribution of his favour. If we consult the ordinances of Hainault, for example, we can see that the arrival of Philip the Good as the ruler of this territory led almost immediately to a redistribution of lands in favour the de Croÿ family. The terminology employed in the grants of Hainault lordships, which can also be found in accounts, is revealing:

> We let it be known that we [Philip the Good], considering that the great, notable and pleasing services which ... our very dear and beloved cousin, Messire Antoine, lord of Croÿ and of Renty, has done for us and ... in order that he should be more held and tied to our said service we, to the same lord of Croÿ ... have ... given ... all the right and action that we have and can have over the town, land, lordship and justice of Ruels in the said country and county of Hainault ...[46]

The formula is quite clear in describing how a favour was designed to reinforce the fidelity of a man to his lord and not to the principality which he represented. The most telling example of this confusion of priorities is of course that of the War of the Public Weal. We shall return soon to consider at length the desire for reform expressed in this insurrection, but this feudal revolt also clearly showed how dangerous it was to offend great lords accustomed to their privileges and their substantial pensions. One of the rebels, Nemours, even frankly admitted in 1466 that the king ought to have been more just, succoured his people and given more substantial pensions to the lords.[47] Jacques Krynen is right in thinking that this rising was based on a genuine governmental project supported notably by the men of the Parlement.[48] But we can also doubt the commitment of great lords who put down their arms the moment the king attended to their particular interests. The fee that won over a supporter could be a dangerous tool, since although it stimulated loyalty at a particular moment, it also reduced fidelity to a simple calculation. At the cry of 'largesse!', men come together; at the cry of 'measure!', they split up. In the higgledy-piggledy political logic so characteristic of this period, it seems that Charles the Bold, one of the rebel princes, saw no problem in upbraiding the king for an attitude which he himself demonstrated in his own principality, namely pursuing a political programme based on favouritism. But whilst Louis XI understood the need to change rhythm and tactics, Charles stubbornly persisted, and so could call on no superior principle to bring men together.

The gifts and favours which were at the heart of all power relations in the Burgundian principality were thus a principle of government. To take up the central question of Valentin Groebner's study of the link between gifts and politics at the end of the Middle Ages, we must now ask whether these gifts encouraged the development of a so-called 'modern' state, or whether they impeded it.[49] Groebner, criticising the principle of the 'total phenomenon' established by Marcel Mauss and refined by Maurice Godelier, is particularly concerned to escape from the dichotomy between an archaic economy based on the gift and a monetary economy accompanied by the rise to power of the state in which the gift no longer has a place. Gift exchange could still occupy a dominant position in the construction of 'modern' administrative apparatus. Wim Blockmans suggested a similar reading as early as 1985 when he reconsidered the practices of venality, patronage and 'brokerage' in the principality of Burgundy.[50] In the fifteenth- and sixteenth-century Low Countries, the state was still fragile and needed to build on informal relations which would eventually establish its power whilst also smoothing over tense relations with local powers. Both Blockmans's article and Groebner's book try to extract pure social, economic and political phenomena from the impure feudal ore, the better to place them in the satisfying setting of a new model of the state. In so doing, they follow the familiar teleological thinking which has marked the last few decades of research in political history – despite energetic protests to the contrary – which seeks above all else to locate the emergence of the modern state. Yet there is something contradictory about labelling these practices as 'feudal' whilst also including them as elements in the process of modernisation of a state which eventually had to turn its back on these feudal contracts. To escape from this paradox, we need to abandon the conscious or unconscious prejudices which make us reason in terms of building models, which can certainly be useful but can also be much too schematic. With this aim in mind, let us turn back to the actual men of the fifteenth century.

Hue de Lannoy: a manager at the service of the prince and his demesne

What did a Burgundian noble think about the way his duke displayed his authority by apportioning grants with a close attention to the recipients' status, befitting a court renowned throughout Europe for its elaborate ceremonial? In his *Avis bailé à monseigneur le duc de Bourgogne* ('Advice submitted to my lord the duke of Burgundy') of 1439, Hue de Lannoy put forward a programme of governmental reform designed both to repair the duke's finances and to ensure support for the prince in the event of a threat to his lands.[51] An oath was required to guarantee the fidelity and equity of a council of eight to twelve councillors, 'notable men, of good renown and conscience', who would swear amongst other things to make no 'petitions to my said lord which touch gifts of finances, benefices of offices, graces, pardons ...' except during sessions of the council. He also anticipated the kind of practices which could lead the councillors astray, by making them promise not to accept any wages from other lords or princes without the duke of Burgundy's agreement.[52] Finally, he wanted to reduce the total cost of all gifts to 12,000 *livres*, both to prevent conflicts of interest and to save money.

On the basis of this proposal and others he wrote, one might think that Hue de Lannoy was working in a spirit of transparency, and that he was committed to protecting a political structure threatened by venal officials and the budgetary problems brought about by unnecessary expenditure. Yet we might also suspect that this 'official conscience' was linked to personal frustration when we reflect that, one year previously, the duke had wanted to abolish his salary as the *stadhouder* of Holland, after having already halved it in 1436 for reasons of economy. In a message sent on 2 March 1438, Hue bitterly complained against any such decision, he who had always served faithfully and who had accepted a post which did not suit him despite his illness. He argued subtly in favour of the group of officers from Holland whom he defended and who would all suffer from a budgetary economy which he considered a disgrace. He then came to his own case, recalling in a few lines the service he had rendered as a knight for thirty-two years and as a counsellor to John the Fearless and Philip the Good for twenty-two years, without forgetting – and the phrase is important – his unshakeable loyalty, even though he had not received the slightest gift, pension or grant of land.[53] Had Hue de Lannoy been less well treated than his brothers Ghillebert and Jean? Had this situation stimulated a less personal interpretation of the public weal? Maybe, but it would certainly be a transposition of present-day values to ascribe to this fifteenth-century noble a desire to strengthen an organic set of institutions in the service of an historical community. We should not forget that in the same proposal, Hue de Lannoy invited Philip the Good to 'live off his own' and that in other texts, such as in his advice on the warfare, he conceives of the Burgundian territories as so many lands to bring together, but also to cede or to transfer to some allies, so important was the alliance with France to his spirit of feudal loyalty. His understanding of the prince's government was not that of a state in the modern sense. His thinking was not motivated by a desire to establish an independent administrative system for the ruler, but simply focused on a political edifice ruled by a *deus ex machina*, who would govern according to that powerful ideal of medieval government, the golden mean. His efforts aimed to organise the management of a private demesne, not of a public administration.

The princes themselves did not respect the ordinances promulgated to limit gifts and pensions, keeping well in mind how the favour they granted or denied reinforced their authority. Indeed, in the ordinance of 1433 as many as eleven articles out of fifty-five dealt with gifts and their limitation, stipulating for example that a favour could not be requested several times in a single year.[54] In 1437 an ordinance suspended gifts for good, such was the threat of war. But none of this latter stopped Charles the Bold rewarding his men several times during the same accounting year, nor did the Duchess Mary hesitate to increase pensions in her ordinance of March 1477 so as to limit the ever-growing number of defections to France.[55] In 1454 Philip the Good issued a new restrictive ordinance. The pensions of the duke of Clèves and Nicolas Rolin were suppressed, that of Antoine de Croÿ was greatly reduced, and the count of Étampes lost all his emoluments except for his pension. Yet this turn of the screw provoked no fresh departure from the court. It was probably the spirit in which such ordinances were promulgated which determined their impact. To remove a pension was as heavily charged with meaning as to grant one. This could be done discreetly, with an explanation to hand, or brutally, with humiliation as an aim, and the two produced very different results.

Cooling hearts and the decay of personal relationships

From the moment of his accession, Charles the Bold changed the tune. His father had been too lenient a ruler. From now on, everyone must follow the new rules he imposed, under threat of 'incurring his indignation'. Gifts were, once more, to be regulated, and the desire to purge the corruption at court was clearly expressed. In this way, all the gifts and corrupting promises to members of the court were condemned 'on pain of deprival of offices and punishment in body and in goods at his will'.[56] In 1469 a financial bonus was indeed granted to the nobles of the court, but it was conditional on proof of uninterrupted service. Moreover, grants now had to be demanded in writing and not by word of mouth, without expectation of an oral reply, but only a written one. The reply was to be deferred until the next day and formulated by a secretary, once more in written form. In a nutshell, Charles the Bold had, through his reforms, succeeded in draining gift-giving of its primary purpose, namely to reinforce the personal links between men.

Documents made for apparently practical purposes, when examined with close attention to their formulation, show a depersonalisation or even a certain contempt, an abruptness, which characterised the new prince's government. The new rigour of Burgundian governance was to be displayed through the multiplication of sanctions. Every failure was to be severely punished by the loss of one day's wages for the guilty party and also for anyone who failed to report the fault. The atmosphere was one of surveillance, of mistrust, of denunciation. In his desire to control everything, Charles also wanted to correct personally the 'delinquents and ... to praise the good and obedient for what they did well'.[57] When we compare the ordinances of Philip the Good with those of Charles, we notice very quickly that the former concern named individuals, whereas the latter treat officers anonymously. When Philip refers to the office of the chamberlain, of the pantry squire, of the quartermaster, he is thinking of particular men to whom he gave his confidence, whereas Charles takes the position of the legislator, and his ordinances focus on functions, not the individuals who carried them out.

The prince's desire for rigour must have helped to isolate him and to break the links which, in a climate of confidence and shared honour, bound the great lords to their prince. Chastelain clearly felt and transmitted this change of approach and of atmosphere. But whereas we might suspect that the chronicler was over-dramatising a situation which was not very significant, seeking to explain through his rhetoric forms of behaviour which were promoted by a policy which was simply pragmatic, the examples cited above demonstrate that this was no exaggeration. The chronicler simply coloured with emotions what can be observed through figures and injunctions. Yet political intelligence cannot do without an awareness of feelings, of love and of confidence. Chastelain, when he describes the departure of Guillaume Rolin, states the matter directly:

> All the kingdom in that time was full of murmurs against this House of Burgundy; and it could be seen how the king, in length and in breadth, and from a distance imagined his ruin, with that the duke himself was cause enough of it, by being too firm and too hard to his men in many different unaccustomed ways, especially to noble men, whom he maintained in and wanted to subject to close servitude ... and for that many good men were worn down and became all cold.[58]

The chronicler explains how a nobility used to the joyous extravagance of the father bridled at the austerity of the son. With Charles, boredom soon took over during audiences where it was essential to sit silently, as if at a sermon. In another chapter, Chastelain describes in detail these audiences which were definitely 'in external appearance, a magnificent thing', but which tortured the nobility for three hours, three times a week. Everyone had to sit on a bench, ordered by rank, without fail, on pain of losing his wages for the day.[59] Threats were another weapon which Charles used effectively, ceding to the worst cruelty under cover of implacable justice.

One particular anecdote captured by Chastelain's restrained but captivating pen expresses all the brutality, or even inhumanity, of a prince who certainly knew how to hurt his nobility. On the pretext of demonstrating the new ducal justice, the court chronicler forcefully relates the details of the execution at Bruges of the bastard son of the lord de la Hameyde, in Hainault, several days before Charles's marriage to Margaret of York.[60] Hernoul de la Hameyde, described as a magnificent young man of twenty-four years, had been thrown into prison by the duke's sergeants, on the appeal of the family of another young man whom he had killed. As was common practice, the prisoner's family came to plead in favour of Hernoul, who had served Charles at the battle of Montlhéry. But the duke simply replied that he had to meet the demands of the plaintiffs and avenge the death by strict justice. Strangely, however, Chastelain cannot stop himself from making the following aside: 'some of those present said privately that they had heard him [the duke] swear under his breath by Saint George, that he [Hernoul] would die for it one way or another'. What was more, Hernoul's kin then succeeded in reaching a financial arrangement with the family of the victim, who asked for mercy for the young man held in the gatehouse gaol. But Charles stubbornly refused to listen, becoming angry, and his words seemed far removed from the faultless and reasoned rigour which he pretended to embody: 'But the duke replied little, and what he did say was quite difficult to understand.'[61] The writer then establishes a subtle play of contrast between the lack of seriousness of the duke, who thinks only about going bathing and who replies to the intercession of his mother with words of delay, and the dryness of the orders to the gaoler of Bruges to put the young man to death immediately. As the knights of Hainault quit the court scandalised, and the women of Bruges swooned before such a handsome man, promising to marry him in the hope of saving him, Hernoul was beheaded. At this point, the duke's cruelty, far from the model of divine mercy, becomes clear as Charles in his last order comes across as a new Pontius Pilate:

> But what I complained of of most of all was that the body was fixed in two pieces on the wheel between the worst murderers in the world; and the duke had ordered that it should be done thus.[62]

Buried in holy ground, three days later, as if to develop the metaphor, Hernoul was to serve as an example to the nobles present *en masse* for the ducal wedding at Bruges, but also to the whole world, which ought to fear the rigour and determination of this new prince. This, at least, was the final interpretation which Chastelain delivered to praise the new, just order of his lord and master, before nevertheless reporting rumours that it was for other reasons than a mere manslaughter that a young man was condemned to death who but a few days before had walked abroad and chatted at court.

One could contrast this with the attitude of John the Fearless, who, in the context of the arrest of Lourdin de Saligny, who was even suspected of treason, had listened to the pleas of Lourdin's family and set him free.[63] Charles, for his part, did not take care of his men in general and his nobility was no exception. To give another example, whereas John the Fearless took great care to ensure that Elyon de Jacqueville, captain of Paris during the Cabochien revolt, was far away during the anti-Burgundian reaction in the city, appointing him as keeper of a fortress in the Franche-Comté, that is to say in the Empire, Charles the Bold did not hesitate to send Philippe de Commynes into the English hornets' nest in October 1470. Charles simply told his servant that if Commynes was captured, the duke would bail him out, causing the memorialist to remark that the duke was not worried about sacrificing a loyal servant in order to advance his cause.

This affective rupture in the unity of the body which the prince was supposed to form with the nobility, who also increasingly took positions at court, was seen even more clearly on the field of battle. Thomas Basin provides us with a passage which deserves to be cited in full, so clearly does it reveal the contempt suffered by a group which ducal ordinances had tried to reduce to a mere ornament of princely majesty:

> Even better, all, of whatever condition they were, murmured against him: the nobles because before Neuss and on many other campaigns

they had fought for him in great peril and at their own cost, because, in the evil season, and especially in the winter, he had forced them to suffer for a long time in his camps for a lack of necessary provisions, and this in the cold, the ice, the rain and the snow, without receiving from him the slightest mark of humanity, following which many died in hunger and privation, and others, in large numbers, from many kinds of disease; because, moreover, without precautions or consideration, he had exposed them to great perils, following which many had succumbed under the blows of the enemy. Those who managed to escape from this sad fate were not rewarded with honours or advantages of any kind; many, rich before, had to sell or mortgage their goods, and so they had been and were condemned to great poverty.[64]

Basin's last remark did not apply to the greater nobility, but the fact that this critic of Louis XI underlined the duke's lack of humanity deserves our attention.

The excesses of a 'too redoubted' lord

From the story of Philippe de Commynes, 'booted' by Charles the Bold on his return from the hunt, to the slap received by the count of Campobasso before the walls of Nancy, or the insults addressed to the members of the Estates, there is no need to look far for examples of Charles's petulance and coldness towards his intimates. The court historiographers, Chastelain and Molinet, paid to sing the praises of Burgundy, could not hide the impetuous, cruel and sometimes shameful behaviour of their master. The anecdotes accumulate if we listen out for them, and we begin to see them subtly attracting comment. Although, in his *Les hauts faits du duc de Bourgogne* ('The great deeds of the duke of Burgundy'), Chastelain does condemn certain excesses, he nonetheless excuses them. 'Some said that he was hard on his men in war and lacked reserve', but it was well known that he did not hesitate to put himself in danger. 'He was tenacious in his will, and sometimes sharp in his words',[65] but this did not prevent him from loving his servants. Anger explained many excesses: it could be a prerogative of the great, but when it was not mastered, not balanced by the art of mercy, it put fear and sometimes hatred into men's hearts. Charles Soillot, addressing Philippe de Croÿ in *La moelle des affections des hommes* ('The substance of men's affections'), explains the importance of the balance between anger and compassion, and warns the lord who did not known how to show solicitude.[66] Laurent Smagghe has analysed in detail all the signs which led even the most faithful subjects to admit their discomfort and even their terror of Charles the Bold.[67] Olivier de la Marche admitted that he participated in the abduction of the duchess of Savoy in June 1476 only for fear of losing his life.[68] It is hard to forget the pitiful confusion of the great lords unable to find the courage to tell Charles of the defeat of his armies. As Molinet puts it, with a pen freed by the events of the battle of Nancy on 5 January 1477, 'He [Philip the Good] was much loved for his easy manner with all, and you [Charles the Bold] are well served because you are feared.'[69]

Once again, it was all a matter of measure, or lack of measure, and of context. Charles was not the only duke to show cruelty. John the Fearless, at Othée, as the battle turned into a massacre, was said to have replied to one of his captains who asked him if the bloodbath should continue, 'They fought together, let them die together', forbidding that the enemy be taken for ransom. Nor was he the only duke to inspire fear. Werner Paravicini, analysing the record of the interrogation of the constable de Saint-Pol, has shown how all the lords implicated in the War of the Public Weal lived in fear that the king would 'run after them' and that this fear made them 'potentially dangerous', since the best form of defence was attack.[70]

It cannot be said that Louis XI was a particularly merciful king or that he was especially respectful of the courtiers who surrounded him. But the kingdom of France which he embodied was sufficiently well established to resist a noble league. Because Charles the Bold endangered the rules of friendship, which were particularly sensitive at the court of Burgundy, the coldness of the prince towards his courtiers was felt intensely. As Klaus Oschema has shown, the men of the fifteenth century did not have to wait for Montaigne to express the sentiments which had been examined by earlier generations of historians in a utilitarian, functionalist paradigm which put the analysis of clientage networks at centre stage. After all, how can we analyse highly personalised decision-making mechanisms if we treat emotions and sentiments as unimportant abstractions? This approach can seem dangerous at first, since it emphasises the irrational part of human nature, one which is all the more difficult to analyse because it was played out in a society which is culturally distant from our own. Yet the chivalric culture in which the protagonists of our story were immersed shows the extent to which individual sentiments penetrated the social order and intimately linked the private and the public sphere. This friendship had nothing to do with the calculated *amicitia* of the Romans.[71] It was at the origin of a harmonious and unified atmosphere which could be found not only at tournaments but also in the heat of battle.[72] There again, the vocabulary of affection infiltrated diplomatic relations as much as the expressions used in everyday human relations. Thus when Jacques de Lalaing died in combat, it was not regret for the loss of a valorous knight that was invoked but a bereavement 'so great for the whole host, that it seemed that they had each lost one of their best friends', and when Chastelain describes the departure of the count of Nevers, he cannot stop regretting an attitude which had made the duke 'lose the love of his fellows ... the heart of noble men'.[73]

These emotions were the warp and weft of a court society which imagined itself along the lines of the chivalric model of the Round Table, and where the Order of the Golden Fleece as conceived by Philip the Good was meant to reinforce bonds which were just as powerful as those of kinship. Accused of high treason, Antoine de Croÿ was first invited to plead before a tribunal of his peers, even though Charles the Bold finally decided to judge him without the counsel of the knights, because his family was accused of *lèse-majesté* and only Charles could judge this crime. Amongst the numerous letters he sent between 1465 and 1468, to obtain an audience, defend himself or attack, Antoine de Croÿ called his brothers of the order to intercede in his favour in the name of their fraternity:

> I am of the Order of the Golden Fleece, and one of the oldest, your brother and your companion. You know how much you in this order are bound to me, and me to you.[74]

In 1468 the count of Nevers, for his part, recalled to mind the foundations of an order which he now held to be despised, forcing him to give up the collar of the order, because there was no more good grace and love in the heart of the prince who had been the first to neglect his duties.[75] The affection which the duke's nobles searched for, invoked and regretted the loss of seems to have been lacking under Charles's rule, or at the very least to have furnished a powerful argument when it came to formulate a political attack or defence against the prince. Was this coldness so much criticised that it inspired a man who had been expelled from court for having chosen the de Croÿ clan over the des Rolins? Perhaps. In any case, Guillaume Fillastre, in a treatise which essentially compiles the theories of ancient philosophers concerning friendship, nonetheless gives his opinion on the question, and especially on the kind of relationship that a prince should have with his nobility:

> But in private [the prince must maintain] familiarity with his barons, with his nobles, with his counsellors, showing them a grave and joyful amiability, which behaviour will lead them to love him, to cherish him, to fear him and to honour him.
>
> For always maintaining the rigour of his gravity to everyone and in all places could not be reputed a virtue in him, but a vice which we call harshness, pride, asperity or bitterness.[76]

His message was clear and not particularly original. It was part of the long tradition of 'mirrors for princes' and homiletic literature in general, going back to the Bible. Nevertheless, Guillaume Fillastre, in his counsels on the cultivation of friendship taken as a whole, did not only want to elaborate on the constitutional love founded on a hierarchical relationship which made it possible to recognise power and its omnipotence through the love and fear inspired by the sovereign image of God. Rather, emotion here provides the spirit of his argument when he affirms, glossing Aristotle, that friendship is like 'one soul in two bodies' and that the security of the kingdom does not lie in its army, nor in its riches, but in the fidelity of true friends.

Once more, theories of the 'genesis of the modern state' have tended to downplay the importance of emotions and sentiments which could be expressed only in this reasoned affirmation of power in a ritualised and controlled manner, the 'myth of passions' upsetting the coherence of a consciously rational system.[77] There is no need for us to try to ascertain the authenticity of the sentiments expressed in these varied sources. Sentiments are considered here solely because they form part of the argument of these noblemen who had reason to complain of the behaviour of their prince towards them. Insofar as they bear witness to a form of frustration which inspired a later decision, such personal feelings have a political meaning which must be taken into account just as much as the receipts of accounts or legislative ordinances.

The chapter meetings of the Golden Fleece provide an interesting perspective on the degradation of relations between the prince and his nobility. Traditionally, the chapters of the order were supposed to supervise the behaviour of its members, including the first amongst them. Under Philip the Good, not much is to be found in the record of the chapters' proceedings, apart from some suspicions of treason, and the prince's behaviour was never questioned. By contrast, starting with the first chapter meeting in 1468, the knights complained bitterly of Charles's words to some of his 'servants', to which the duke replied with a formal answer promising to correct himself.[78] But at the chapter meeting held at Valenciennes in 1473, the criticisms became more precise and revived some of those expressed five years before. The members of the order once more complained of unjust and biting words spoken against his loyal servants:

> That sometimes my said lord speaks a little caustically to his servants. ... whom he calls treacherous servants, which is a word that sounds ill, with all respect, and shameful for his loyal servants.[79]

Charles's reply is even more interesting than the complaints made against him, so clearly does it express a new order, a new way for the prince to express his love for his subjects. According to him, the fear which he inspires in his subjects is necessary to keep them on the right path. It was thus necessary to make the distinction between the correction which pertains to mendicant friars and the punishment which is dispensed by the prince. And moreover, since he is nearly forty years old and has seen many things in his lifetime, he knows that there are many who put their private interest before that of the common weal. It is thus sometimes necessary to correct them 'caustically, using somewhat cutting words in general to be able to bring them back to understanding by this means'. But there was no need to worry: the good had nothing to fear, and only the guilty would be corrected.

Charles did not apologise in the slightest but instead asserted himself in a paternalistic and authoritarian tone. The image of the good father who knew how to punish his children when they deserved it was not restricted to him, but here it served an extreme conception of his own authority, and allowed him to bring an end to any discussion. He might as easily have said: you are only children, you will understand when you are grown up. The Biblical allegory of the 'good shepherd', used notably by Christine de Pizan in her *Corps de policie*, present in two copies in the ducal library, is here perverted, insofar as the shepherd is no longer just he who must protect his sheep from wolves and preserve good order amongst them, but also the one who will drive his people, at the rhythm of a forced march in the service of his dream of a crown. Charles amply developed this idea of the prince who can ask anything of his men, because he is the first to sacrifice himself for them. Thanks to the 'multimedia' propaganda, which we have had cause to consider and which was particularly refined in this area, the chroniclers, the rhetoricians, the mendicant friars in the general processions and the prince himself in numerous speeches to the nobility, whether to the Four Members or to the Estates, all developed the figure of the prince who exposed his body and his possessions, 'sparing nothing' in order to preserve the repose, the tranquillity and the security of his subjects whilst the latter stayed warm at home. Gratitude to individual servants no longer had any place in the relations of power he established. The abnegation of a prince who was entirely devoted to his political programme had taken form by increasing the anonymity and depersonalisation of relations of authority, and the unravelling of what Theodor Mayer called in 1939 *Personenverbandsstaat* or personal ties.[80] In Charles's case, immediate emotions had triumphed over more enduring feelings. The dramatic gestures, the sudden expressions of affection and the rapid and cruel judgements had suffocated the culture of negotiation inherent in the natural *benevolentia* of the prince. The common weal had become central, but without any common and accepted definition, it did not command unanimous loyalty. On the contrary, it nourished division.

An ideological rupture

As we shall see, Charles the Bold made the *chose publique* or common weal into one of the fundamental bases of his political edifice. But can we explain the toxic atmosphere we have been discussing by the fact that the notion of the common weal was not part of the cultural values of the court nobility? On the contrary, Bernhard

Sterchi has noted that this expression occurred more and more commonly in the course of the fifteenth century as it developed in the public sphere of political discussion. Brunetto Latini had set out in the thirteenth century 'How the lord should protect the common weal', and authors such as Martin Le Franc, Hue and Guillebert de Lannoy now regularly used the expression to lead their noble readers to the path of virtue.[81] Nevertheless, it would seem that, in the absence of a clear definition, the common weal was no more than a motif heard by an ideal reader but without effective application in actual political life. In other words, the nobility appropriated this notion without really understanding its meaning or its ideological force. Bernhard Sterchi cites as proof a private exchange of letters between Philippe of Clèves and Charles de Lalaing in 1513 in which the former, in an ironic tone, expressed his wish to take advantage of the latter's position as a favourite of the Emperor Charles V to draw attention to his own interests under cover of the common weal. Just as the 'common good' was one of those expressions which provoke only unanimity because of the ambiguity of its content, so the notion of the common weal allowed a malleable usage which first incited discomfort and, finally, discord.[82] As we have seen, Charles the Bold asserted his political programme at the same time as his mode of government tended towards a kind of 'absolutism' which was incompatible with the political ideas and the culture of most of the nobles who surrounded him. Their desertions were not simply betrayals and were not just acts of pure venality: they were also symptoms of incomprehension and profound disagreement with the new Burgundian policy.[83]

A feudal pyramid shaken to the core

Many obstacles can be identified in the steep path which ought to have led to the construction of a unitary state. The ambitions of Charles the Bold did not suit a nobility which respected the feudal order dominated by the king, where each and every one received a patrimony which he must protect above all else, and which guaranteed the power and honour of his line.

Charles's desire to detach himself from the king of France was profoundly shocking to many of his noble courtiers. We shall see that ideas of Burgundian royalty were understood at the court by only a handful of theoreticians who accompanied the duke in his fall. The first Valois dukes, Philip the Bold and John the Fearless, thought of themselves above all as princes of the *fleur-de-lys*. They nourished a pro-French sentiment which became almost natural at court, and the Francophile interests, despite some changes of allegiance under Philip the Good, continued to make their voices heard. Even when John the Fearless, threatened by Armagnac's armies in 1413, asked for the 'aid and counsel' of the nobles of Artois and Picardy, the latter replied that they would 'gladly serve him against all his enemies, except the king and his children'.[84] When Charles the Bold took the crucial step of renouncing his bonds of vassalage to the French king, his attitude troubled nobles whose place in the feudal pyramid put them in an uncomfortable position when they were faced with question of the relative importance of different fidelities. For Commynes, Charles had committed the crime of *lèse-majesté* by imprisoning the king at Péronne, which served to explain his defection to the camp of Louis XI as a consequence of his legitimism. We find the same discourse in the mouth of Baudouin of Burgundy when he writes that he went to the king's court because he was his natural sovereign. The end of this letter also insists upon the subordination of the duke to his sovereign lord, making Charles the Bold a felon, because the latter did not respect the sovereignty of the king of France and had forgotten that he held his lands from him.[85] Of course Baudouin was probably not expressing himself freely and his text served as propaganda for Louis XI, as is suggested by the carefully directed language of his letter and by additions which reveal a desire to damage the House of Burgundy (the phrase 'so-called of Burgundy' was added to Charles's name between the lines of the manuscript). But the breaking of feudal allegiance and the rise in power of Burgundian sovereignty in a particularly aggressive climate disturbed a nobility uncomfortably attached to older convictions.

When Charles the Bold greeted the French ambassadors at Saint-Omer on 15 July 1470, raised up on five steps on a dais worthy of an emperor, hardly greeting them and replying to their peace proposition that the Portuguese were accustomed to condemn their enemies to 'the hundred thousand devils of hell', the court, present in its full array, was highly offended 'because it was ill done tacitly to command the king of France to all the hundred thousand devils'.[86]

Chastelain, who describes this scene, was of course pro-French, but his opinions were shared by a nobility who felt neither Portuguese nor English but who presented themselves as the subjects of a prince who was himself 'a subject of the king and honoured and adorned by the arms of the *fleurs-de-lys*, the glory and splendour of his visage and the brightest of his titles'. This umpteenth aside by the duke of Burgundy thus provided the opportunity to denounce an attitude which fed ideological division within the court itself, since the duke's servants had little sympathy for the opinions of their master.[87] In this regard, the drama of the battle of Nancy on 5 January 1477 pushed men to choose their side. The weakness of the ideological construction of the House of Burgundy stood revealed. Numerous defections amongst the nobility can be understood as a desire to protect lands which were directly held from the French king.

An allegiance to the land

This dilemma was quickly resolved for the frontier lords whom we considered earlier. The fact that some of them were members of the Order of the Golden Fleece, the supposed cement of the dynasty of the House of Burgundy, carried little weight in the face of the crown of France, whose ancestral authority was the legitimate and ultimate reference in matters of sovereignty. In the months which followed the difficult beginning of the rule of Mary of Burgundy, the number of defections to the king of France was large and catastrophic, including many at the top of the Burgundian government. An ordinance of 26 March 1477 and another issued in November of the same year legislated in the hope of flattering and retaining the support of a nobility which threatened to change sides. Concretely, the stakes were raised once again, as is shown in the case of Philip of Burgundy, the son of the Great Bastard, who had already joined the French cause. When Louis XI created the title of count of Sainte-Menehould for Philip's father in 1478, he made the son's inheritance conditional on joining the French side. In reply to this, Maximilian offered Philip the rule of the county of Namur, to which he added, in 1480, the status of captain of Picardy and Artois, thus clinching the deal.[88]

It is true that other nobles such as Adolph of Cleves and Louis of Bruges closed ranks around the young heiress Mary of Burgundy, which leads Jelle Haemers to describe them as the 'guardian angels of the dynasty'.[89] If the historian of this difficult period of transition recognises that the aim of these noblemen was to secure their own position, the temptation is nonetheless great for those such as Haemers to see these noble alliances at court as proof of a Burgundian identity, the sign of loyalty to a House of Burgundy, despite the upheavals which tormented it. By taking the example of the marriage of Philippe of Cleves (Adolph of Cleves's heir) to Anne of Borssele (the daughter of Wolfert of Borssele), celebrated in 1481 with Maximilian's approval, Haemers argues that the union of these two families, who were extraordinarily powerful in Flanders, Brabant, Holland and Zeeland, attests to the existence of a conscious identity. But what becomes of this conscious identity if we consider the frustrations of Wolfert of Borssele, who was forced out of his functions as governor of Holland, and Adolph of Cleves, who was deprived of the command of the Hainault troops in favour of Philippe de Croÿ, all of which suggests that revenge provided as powerful a motive? What are we to make of the supposed spirit of fidelity when we reflect that Wolfert had married a relative of Louis XI, that Adolph's brother-in-law belonged to the royal council, and that these individual relationships could be used at any moment to provide a means to blackmail a Habsburg prince who had no interest in reducing the privileges and titles of a noble group which was also politically and economically powerful? When we look more closely, we see that the energy of those who remained around Mary, some of whom had a genuine affection for her, derived essentially from their concern for their own interests, their fear of seeing a superior power destroy their privileges, fortune and influence. From the spring of 1477 onwards, the nobles as much as the towns tore apart the edifice constructed by Charles the Bold. The ordinances of Thionville in particular gave back to the court nobility the functions which had been seized by the Parlement of Malines. Those who remained could look out for themselves and their own business, as Commynes underlines.

With Maximilian's arrival in August 1477, autocracy returned and with it renewed noble discontent. It is clear that the solidarity of the nobles who stayed to serve Mary of Burgundy was not founded on the need to preserve an ideology of state but on a culture which privileged lineage, patrimony and familial interests. There was no spirit of rebellion such as can be found in the noble leagues of sixteenth-century France. Like Jacob van Artevelde, head of the Ghent revolt of 1348, who turned his back on the possibility of a city-state by changing allegiance and swearing fidelity to the king of England, the nobles had no plan of governmental reform; they simply wanted to return to a state of privilege in which everyone, by his birth, received what was his due in honours and graces, without having to sacrifice his estate to the common weal.

The dream of a Burgundian identity and of a nobility loyal to a princely house fell apart just as completely in the south of the Burgundian lands. If the Franche-Comté escaped French rule until the reign of Louis XIV this was because, as Lucien Fèbvre puts it, 'it was not embodied, was not at all summed up in its entirety by a dynasty born on its soil or raised on its soil – in a natural lord'.[90] The fact that it remained a Burgundian territory after the death of Charles the Bold was the result of Maximilian's successful policy of favour and above all of the desire to avoid the excessively strong royal rule which the people of Franche-Comté could expect from Louis XI. It is still possible to believe in some fidelity to Mary of Burgundy, so ferocious was the resistance to the king. Dole capitulated only during the second invasion of spring 1479, and a long list of nobles of the two Burgundies gave their support to the young princess. Yet as Marie-Thérèse Caron stresses, how could the nobility of the duchy have felt attached to a princess brought up in Flanders, who had never visited it, or to the memory of a prince who had made only a brief appearance in his lands and, moreover, had not worried at all about the devastation carried out in reprisals for his bellicose enterprises?[91] In fact, Maximilian knew how to keep them on side by offering them numerous offices of chamberlain in his household.

It is true that these noblemen were not in an easy position, and their choices could be no more than bets on the future. Jean II de Neuchâtel, knight of the Golden Fleece, preferred to surrender to Louis XI in 1479, whilst Claude de Toulongeon, one of the leaders of the revolt, was forced to abandon his lands and take refuge in the Low Countries in 1480. There again, we can always imagine that if Louis XI had kept his word and given the government of the 'land of Burgundy' to Jean de Chalon as he had promised, rather than giving it to the sire de Craon, the noble grouping brought together to support the king of France by de Chalon would not have changed sides and joined Mary of Burgundy's service. In any event, as Jean Richard notes, few of those who were faithful to Charles the Bold's heiress were drawn from the higher nobility. It was the middling nobility which joined the ranks of the resistance alongside the towns, even if they were more attached to their own local interests than to the autonomy of a feudal princedom.

It is difficult to assess the true nature of the sentiments which were expressed in each particular context. Attachments were born in a local culture which was based on local particularities and powerful family networks, which extended on both sides of the border created between the duchy and the county of Burgundy after their separation.[92] In this complicated network of alliances, arrangements within lineages could counteract the effects of royal confiscations over the long term. Thus when Louis XI seized the lands of Guillaume de Jaucourt, sire de Villarnoult and the head of Maximilian's household, giving them instead to his brother Aubert, the latter returned them in 1493. It was land that determined allegiance, and the legal position which its possession implied, not adhesion to the political ambitions of a distant and ill-understood prince. Without a state, with an aristocracy who had not detached itself from its local moorings, with the intact memory of a natural allegiance to the Valois dukes of the king of France and despite the political ups and downs of Philip the Good and the new ambitions of Charles the Bold, there was little chance of forging a 'faith of Burgundy' (*foy de Bourgogne*) synonymous with a supra-regional Burgundian identity. That was the whole problem.

I would like to conclude by putting men and their acts at centre stage once again, in this case the personality of Jean de Chalon. The 'thirty pence prince', as Louis XI nicknamed him, shows perfectly the rapid reactions of a nobility faced with fast-changing events. Born in 1443, Jean de Chalon ceaselessly swapped from one side to the other. Although he was initially faithful to the House of Burgundy, Louis XI soon made approaches to him, organising his marriage to a daughter of the duke of Bourbon to help bring the nobility of the Franche-Comté on side in 1467. He left Charles the Bold in 1470 following a judgement which favoured the half-brothers of his father, Guillaume VII, for the inheritance of his grandfather Louis. Banished from the principality by the duke for his 'offences, insults and shameful actions',[93] he allied himself with the French court and the duchy of Brittany. On Charles's death, he worked to win the Franche-Comté for the kingdom of France at the Estates of Dole in February 1477. Yet when Louis XI, forgetting his promises, entrusted the government of the two Burgundies to Georges de la Trémoille, Jean joined the resistance to the French king for two years. Expelled from the kingdom, hanged in effigy in numerous towns, Jean took refuge at Basel and then in the Low Countries, where he tried to ally Brittany with England alongside Maximilian. The peace signed at Arras on 23 December 1482 between Louis and Maximilian put him once more in a difficult position, and he chose to go to Brittany to do what he could against the kingdom which had ended his hour of glory. Jean's tribulations in Brittany take us away from our main subject, but it is enough to note that by giving, taking back, feigning and doubling his loyalties, serving first the interests of Anne de Beaujeu, then Anne of Brittany, plotting in favour of a marriage between the heiress of the duchy and the king of the Romans and finally working for an alliance with Charles VIII, Jean succeeded at last in becoming governor of Brittany in the king's name on 2 November 1492, and governor of the Franche-Comté for the emperor on 5 November 1495. As Michel Harsgor notes, though Jean II de Chalon might superficially appear to spin 'like a weathervane, in fact, he was as constant as the northern star'.[94] This great noble of the Franche-Comté continuously pursued the preservation and the consolidation of his own position of authority. In this, he had much in common with Adolph of Cleves and Louis of Bruges, who, in the north, quickly understood that their support for the House of Burgundy guaranteed their position, their riches and their power, which were then compromised once more by Maximilian's arrival.

This story of defectors and fragile loyalties at the Burgundian court expresses no more or less than the frustrations and the fears of 'an aristocratic community which was acutely aware of its dependence on offices and pensions and would not accept the misdirection [or the disappearance] of what it considered to be its right'.[95] It shows how far this 'society of loyalties', sensitive both to affective bonds and to favour justly distributed, could – with time and the monarch's skill – work in the service of the state and for the construction of the kingdom in France, dominated by the sacrality of its sovereign. Yet it also shows how, in the absence of a prince who knew how to inspire love as much as fear, or of a superior abstract entity which could command loyalty, even within the same culture, with the same reflexes and the same expectations, different forms of particularism developed, for the better or the worse. We have also seen that the sovereign state based on the nation was not the ultimate form of rule for a certain number of men. Some had no other ambition than to guarantee their prosperity by means of the royal fountain of honours; others preferred to distance themselves from it to prolong a world where more contractual relations came to the fore and where power was shared.

Notes

1 Excerpts from an undated letter by Baudouin de Bourgogne regarding the criminal allegations recorded by Charles the Bold in one of his manifestos (December 1470), BnF, ms. fr. 5041, fols 184–185.
2 Letter written by Charles the Bold to the *échevinage* of Mons about a conspiracy against him, 11 [recte 13] December 1470, ed. in L. P. Gachard, *Analectes belgiques* (Brussels: A. Wahlen, 1830), vol. I, pp. 66–70.
3 For more details of this affair, see T. Basin, *Histoire de Louis XI*, ed. C. Samaran (Paris: Belles-Lettres, 1963), book III, ch. IV.
4 J.-M. Cauchies, 'Baudouin de Bourgogne (v. 1446–1508), bâtard, militaire et diplomate. Une carrière exemplaire?', *Revue du Nord* 77 (1995), 257–281.
5 See, for example, H. Dubois, *Charles le Téméraire* (Paris: Fayard, 2004), p. 280. For a rehabilitation of Commynes, see J. Blanchard, 'Commynes n'a pas "trahi": pour en finir avec une obsession critique', *Revue du Nord* 91 (2009), 327–360.
6 See Cauchies, 'Baudouin de Bourgogne'; R. Vaughan, *Charles the Bold* (London and New York: Boydell, 1973; new edn, 2004), p. 399.
7 W. Paravicini and B. Schnerb (eds), *La face noire de la splendeur: crimes, trahisons et scandales à la cour de Bourgogne aux XIVe et XVe siècles, Revue du Nord* 91 (2009); *L'envers du décor. Espionnage, complot, trahison, vengeance et violence en pays bourguignons et liégeois*, PCEEB 48 (2008).
8 Chastelain, *Chronique*, vol. V, book VII:2, ch. XI, p. 473: 'Un prince de nouvelle dure mode'. [AQ]
9 *Ibid.*, vol. V, book VI:2, ch. CI, p. 71.

10 Ibid., vol. V, book VI:2, ch. CXXX, p. 183.
11 P. R. Gaussin, 'Les conseillers de Louis XI (1461–1483)', in B. Chevalier and P. Contamine (eds), *La France de la fin du XVe siècle. Renouveau et apogée* (Paris: CNRS, 1985), pp. 104–134. P. R. Gaussin, *Louis XI, un roi entre deux mondes* (Paris: A. G. Nizet, 1976), p. 137, mentions around forty defectors.
12 A. Demurger, 'Guerre civile et changement de personnel administratif dans le royaume de France de 1400 à 1418. L'exemple des baillis et sénéchaux', *Francia* 6 (1978), 151–298.
13 J.-M. Cauchies, in his book *Louis XI et Charles le Hardi. De Péronne à Nancy (1468–1477): le conflit* (Brussels: De Boeck Université, 1996), recommends avoiding the romantic fixation of an eternal rivalry between Louis XI and Charles the Bold, as if these two historical figures were exclusively obsessed by each other.
14 R. Vaughan, *Philip the Good: The Apogee of Burgundy* (Woodbridge: Boydell, 1970; new edn, 2004), pp. 65–67.
15 Dom Urbain Plancher, *Histoire générale et particulière de Bourgogne*, 4 vols (Dijon: De A. de Fay, 1739–81), vol. IV, p. 286.
16 B. Schnerb, *Jean sans Peur. Le prince meurtrier* (Paris: Payot, 2005), pp. 371–381.
17 B. Schnerb, '"Familiarissimus domini ducis". La succession des favoris à la cour de Bourgogne au début du XVe siècle', in J. Hirschbiegel and W. Paravicini (eds), *Der Fall des Günstlings. Hofparteien im Europa von 13. bis zum 17. Jahrhundert* (Östfildern: Thorbecke, 2004), pp. 177–189.
18 M. Bubenicek, *Entre rébellion et obéissance. L'espace politique comtois face au duc Philippe le Hardi (1384–1404)* (Geneva: Droz, 2013).
19 See P. Contamine, 'Le premier procès de Jean II, duc d'Alençon (1456–1458): quels enjeux? quels enseignements politiques?', in P. Hoppenbrouwers, A. Janse and R. Stein (eds), *Power and Persuasion: Essays on the Art of State Building in Honour of W. P. Blockmans* (Turnhout: Brepols, 2010), pp. 103–122.
20 Chastelain, *Chronique*, vol, V, book VII:1, ch. XIII, pp. 280–282.
21 Ibid., vol. IV, book VI:1, ch. XXIX, pp. 115–116, and book VI:2, ch. LXXIII, 481. See also J.-P. Ward, 'Guillaume de Clugny, Guillaume de Bische and Jean Gros: Mediators between Charles the Bold of Burgundy and the Cities of Holland (1460–1477)', *Francia* 33:1 (2006), 69–99.
22 This quotation and the next ones are taken from Du Clercq, *Mémoires*, vol. IV, book V, ch. XLI, p. 214.
23 Chastelain, *Chronique*, vol. IV, book VI:1, ch. LXXXI, p. 259.
24 For all these quotations see *ibid.*, vol. IV, book VI:1, ch. LXIX, p. 216, and vol. V, book VII:2, ch. X, pp. 470–471. The defection of

Guillaume Rolin was a passing one as he was to be found in ducal armies in 1471 and as captain of Dijon in 1475. Vaughan, *Charles the Bold*, pp. 257–258.

25 We must take into account the opposite opinions of J. Dufournet, *La destruction des mythes dans les mémoires de Philippe de Commynes* (Geneva: Droz, 1966), and J. Blanchard, 'Commynes n'a pas "trahi"'.

26 Vaughan, *Charles the Bold*, pp. 231–232.

27 On this topic and the reasons of defections among lords of the Golden Fleece after the death of Charles the Bold, see H. Cools, 'Noblemen on the Borderline: The Nobility of Picardy, Artois and Walloon-Flanders and the Habsburg-Valois Conflict, 1477–1529', in W. Blockmans, M. Boone and T. De Hemptinne (eds), *Secretum Scriptorum. Liber alumnorum Walter Prevenier* (Louvain-Apeldoorn: Garant, 1999), pp. 371–382.

28 The Pragmatic Sanction was a sovereign solemn decree issued by Charles VII at Bourges in July 1438 which established the 'liberties' of the Gallican Church, whilst also making French clergy subject to the will of the king. It was revoked by Louis XI in 1461 to please Pius II and soften diplomatic relations with the pope.

29 C. Märtl, *Kardinal Jean Jouffroy († 1473). Leben und Werk*, Beiträge zur Geschichte und Quellenkunde des Mittelalters 18 (Sigmaringen: Thorbecke, 1996).

30 V. Soen, 'La cause Croÿ et les limites du mythe bourguignon: la frontière, le lignage et la mémoire (1465–1475), *PCEEB* 52 (2012), 81–97.

31 For more details about forms of behaviour, accusations and arguments in defence, see B. Sterchi, *Über den Umgang mit Lob und Tadel* (Turnhout: Brepols, 2005), pp. 471–526.

32 Chastelain, *Chronique*, vol. V, book VI:2, ch. CXXV, p. 168 and ch. CXXXI, pp. 186–187.

33 Commynes, *Mémoires*, ed. Blanchard, vol. I, book I, ch. 10, pp. 61–62.

34 J.-F. Lassalmonie, *La boîte à l'enchanteur. Politique financière de Louis XI* (Paris: Comité pour l'histoire économique et financière de la France, 2002), p. 442, and pp. 448–458 for what follows.

35 Chastelain, *Chronique*, vol. V, book VI:2, ch. CXXXI, p. 192.

36 *Lancelot*, in A. Micha (ed.), *Textes choisis* (Paris: Union générale d'éditions, 1983), pp. 168–169.

37 For other examples, see A. Guéry, 'Le roi dépensier. Le don, la contrainte et l'origine du système financier de la monarchie française de l'Ancien Régime', *Annales ESC* 39 (1984), 1241–1269.

38 H. Cools, *Mannen met macht. Edellieden en de moderne Staat in de Bourgondisch-Habsburgse landen (1475–1530)* (Zutphen: Walburg Pers, 2001).

39 Ghillebert de Lannoy, *Les enseignements paternels*, in *Œuvres de Ghillebert de Lannoy*, ed. C. Potvin (Louvain: Impr. de P. et J. Lefevre, 1878), p. 470.
40 Claude de Seyssel, *Histoire de Louys XII, roy de France* (Paris, 1615), p. 103.
41 Chastelain, *Chronique*, vol. V, book VI:2, ch. CII, p. 73.
42 A. Greve and E. Lebailly (eds), *Comptes de l'argentier de Charles le Téméraire duc de Bourgogne, année 1468* (Paris: De Boccard, 2001), vol. I, nos 329, 845 and 1009. For Baudouin's pension see no. 375, and for Antoine's see no. 374.
43 Many systems of money of account were used in the Burgundian Great Principality. The type of gold coin mentioned here is the *écu* of 32 *gros* (groats). (The groat is a silver coin. The most common coin in ducal accounts was the *livre* of 40 Flemish groats.)
44 These examples are provided by J. Bartier, *Légistes et gens de finance au XVe siècle. Les conseillers de Philippe le Bon et Charles le Téméraire* (Brussels: Académie Royale de Belgique, 1955), pp. 262–270.
45 C. Chattaway, *The Order of the Golden Tree: The Gift-Giving Objectives of Duke Philip the Bold of Burgundy* (Turnhout: Brepols, 2007).
46 Gift of the land and lordship of Roeulx in favour of Antoine de Croÿ, Brussels, 9 August 1431, in J.-M. Cauchies (ed.), *Ordonnances de Philippe le Bon pour le comté de Hainaut (1425–1467)*, Recueil des ordonnances des Pays-Bas, 1st series, section 2, vol. III (Brussels: Académie Royale de Belgique, 2010), no. 43, pp. 77–78.
47 P.-R. Gaussin, *Louis XI*, p. 227.
48 J. Krynen, 'La rébellion du Bien Public (1465)', in M.-T. Fögen (ed.), *Ordnung und Aufruhr im Mittelalter* (Frankfurt: V. Klostermann, 1995), pp. 81–97.
49 V. Groebner, *Liquid Assets, Dangerous Gifts: Presents and Politics at the End of the Middle Ages*, trans. P. E. Selwyn (Philadelphia: University of Pennsylvania Press, 2002).
50 W. Blockmans, 'Corruptie, patronage, makelaardij en venaliteit als symptomen van een ontluikende staatsvorming in de Bourgondisch-Habsburgse Nederlanden', *Tijdschrift voor sociale geschiedenis* 11 (1985), 231–247.
51 *L'avis de 1439*, in *Œuvres de Ghillebert de Lannoy*, pp. 201–326.
52 *Ibid.*, p. 301: 'Et, d'autre part, que vous ne prendrez gages, ne pencions quelzconques d'autres princes ne seigneurs, sinon de mondit seigneur le duc, se ce n'estoit par son ordonnance et bon plaisir, passé en plain conseil.' For the next quotation see *ibid.*, p. 309.
53 BnF, ms. fr. 1278, fols 124–125b.

54 W. Paravicini, 'Die Hofordnungen Herzog Philipps des Guten von Burgund Edition IV. Die verlorenen Hofordnungen von 1431/1432. Die Hofordnung von 1433', *Francia* 15 (1987), 183–231, at pp. 215–217.
55 J. Haemers, *For the Common Good: State Power and Urban Revolts in the Reign of Mary of Burgundy (1477–1482)*, SEUH 17 (Turnhout: Brepols, 2009), p. 106; ADN B 19945, fols 303r–304v.
56 This and the next quotations from W. Paravicini, 'Ordre et règle. Charles le Téméraire en ses ordonnances de l'hôtel', in *Menschen am Hof der Herzöge von Burgund*, ed. K. Krüger, H. Kruse and A. Ranft (Stuttgart: Thorbecke, 2002), pp. 671–713.
57 *Ibid.*, Ordonnance de l'Hôtel, 1469, paragraph 8.
58 Chastelain, *Chronique*, vol. V, book VII:2, ch. X, pp. 469–470.
59 *Ibid.*, vol. V, book VII:1, ch. XL, pp. 370–371.
60 *Ibid.*, vol. V, book VII:1, ch. XLVIII, pp. 397–405. For more details about the narration of this torment, see E. Doudet, who describes this wedding as a 'bloodwedding'. Doudet, *Poétique de George Chastelain*, pp. 374–376.
61 Chastelain, *Chronique*, vol. V, ch. XLVIII, pp. 397–405.
62 *Ibid.*
63 Schnerb, '"Familiarissimus domini ducis"'.
64 Basin, *Histoire de Louis XI*, book V, ch. X, p. 321.
65 G. Chastelain, *Les hauts faits du duc de Bourgogne*, in *Œuvres*, vol. VII, pp. 229–230.
66 C. Soillot, *La moelle des affections des hommes* (Österreichische Nationalbibliothek, Ms 3391, fols 32–40v), ed. in Sterchi, *Über den Umgang*, pp. 590–597.
67 See L. Smagghe, *Les émotions du prince. Émotion et discours politique dans l'espace bourguignon* (Paris: Classiques Garnier, 2012).
68 See É. Lecuppre-Desjardin, *'Je fiz ce qu'il me commanda, contre mon cœur; et prins Madame de Savoye. Le déshonneur d'une chevalier délibéré au cœur de la débâcle bourguignonne'*, *Cahiers de recherches médiévales et humanistes / Journal of Medieval and Humanistic Studies* 39 (2020), 133–149.
69 Jean Molinet, *Chroniques*, ed. O. Jodogne, 3 vols (Brussels: Palais des Académies, 1935–37), vol. I, p. 93.
70 W. Paravicini, 'Peur, pratiques, intelligences. Formes de l'opposition aristocratique à Louis XI d'après les interrogatoires du connétable de Saint-Pol', in Chevalier and Contamine (eds), *La France de la fin du XVe siècle*, pp. 183–196, at pp. 186–187.
71 B. Sère, 'Essai sur un oxymore normatif: l'amitié politique à la fin du Moyen Âge', *Parlement(s), revue d'histoire politique*, hors-série 11 (2016), 87–100.

72 For this notion of harmony between fellows, see K. Oschema, *Freundschaft und Nähe im spätmittelalterlichen Burgund. Studien zum Spannungsfeld von Emotion und Institution* (Cologne: Böhlau, 2006), p. 289.
73 Chastelain, *Chronique*, vol. II, book III:2, ch. XXVIII, p. 363, and vol. V, book VI:2, ch. CII, p. 73.
74 Letter from Antoine de Croÿ to the knights of the Golden Fleece, 26 March 1465, ed. in S. Dünnebeil, *Die Protokollbücher des Ordens vom Goldenen Vlies*, vol. I: *Herzog Philipp der Gute (1430–1467)* (Stuttgart: Thorbecke, 2002), p. 188, 'Regesten', no. 147.
75 This argument can be found in Dünnebeil, *Die Protokollbücher des Ordens vom Goldenen Vlies*, vol. II: *Das Ordenfest 1468 in Brügge unter Herzog Karl dem Kühnen* (Stuttgart: Thorbecke, 2003), pp. 43–44.
76 K. Oschema, *Le traité de l'amitié. Guillaume Fillastre sur l'idéal de l'amitié*, Cour de France.fr, http://cour-de-France.fr/article1908.html, sections 140 and 141 (accessed 2013).
77 See D. Boquet and P. Nagy, 'L'historien et les émotions en politique: entre science et citoyenneté', in D. Boquet (ed.), *Politiques des émotions au Moyen Âge*, Micrologus Library 34 (Florence: SISMEL Edizioni del Galluzzo, 2010), pp. 5–30.
78 The prince's words are quoted in Dünnebeil (ed.), *Die Protokollbucher*, vol.I, p. 120, and vol. III, p. 98.
79 *Ibid.*
80 This notion helps to qualify the non-formalised relationships between the socio-political actors of the medieval world. See T. Mayer, 'Die Ausbildung der Grundlagen des modernen deutsche Staates im hohen Mittelalter', *Historische Zeitschrift* 159 (1939), 457–487.
81 Numerous examples in Sterchi, *Über den Umgang*, pp. 252–253.
82 See É. Lecuppre-Desjardin and A.-L. Van Bruaene, 'Du Bien Commun à l'idéal de Bien Commun', in É. Lecuppre-Desjardin and A.-L. Van Bruaene (eds), *De Bono Communi. The Discourse and Practice of the Common Good in the European City (13th–16th c.)*, SEUH 22 (Turnhout: Brepols, 2010), pp. 1–9.
83 As A. Maczak points out, nobles were facing a difficult transition period at that time. A. Maczak, 'The Nobility–State Relationship', in W. Reinhard (ed.), *Power Elites and State Building* (Oxford: Oxford University Press, 1996), pp. 189–206.
84 Enguerrand de Monstrelet, *Chronique*, ed. L. Douet d'Arcq (Paris: Renouard, 1857–67), vol. II, p. 467.
85 BnF, ms. fr. 5041, fol. 185. 'D'autre part, nature, loyauté, noblesse et fidélité me donnent courage et bien raisonnablement et par honneur ne de vouloir et désirer servir et honorer le tres-chrestien roy de France

mon souverain seigneur duquel je suis un subgect et pareillement est son subgect ledit Charles de Bourgoigne.'
86 Charles's mother was Isabella of Portugal, daughter of John I of Portugal and Philippa of Lancaster. Charles liked to remind people of his Portuguese and English parentage.
87 For this episode, see Chastelain, *Chronique*, vol. V, book VII:2, chs III and IV, pp. 450–454.
88 For this flood of privileges, see Haemers, *For the Common Good*, pp. 81–83, 121–122.
89 *Ibid.*, p. 106.
90 L. Fèbvre, *Philippe II et la Franche-Comté. Étude d'histoire politique, religieuse et sociale* (Paris: Champion, 1912; new edn, Paris: Flammarion, 1970), pp. 7–8, quoted in H. Cools, 'Quelques considérations sur l'attitude des nobles comtois entre 1477 et 1500', PCEEB 42 (2002), 167–182.
91 M.-T. Caron, 'La fidélité dans la noblesse bourguignonne à la fin du Moyen Âge', in P. Contamine (ed.), *L'État et les aristocraties. XIIe–XVIIe siècles, France, Angleterre, Ecosse* (Paris: Presses de l'École Normale Supérieure, 1989), pp. 103–127.
92 For a reflection on the Burgundian identity in border zone, see K. A. Edwards, *Families and Frontiers: Re-Creating Communities and Boundaries in the Early Modern Burgundies* (Boston: Brill, 2002), especially pp. 354–355.
93 Archives du Doubs, E 1335, ed. in J.-B. Duhem, 'Un Franc-Comtois au service de la Bretagne', *Bulletin de la Société polymathique du Morbihan* (1929), 103–158, at pp. 153–154.
94 M. Harsgor, 'Fidélités et infidélités au sommet du pouvoir', in Y. Durand (ed.), *Clientèles et fidélités en Europe à l'époque moderne. Hommage à R. Mousnier* (Paris: PUF, 1981), pp. 259–277.
95 G. Lecuppre, 'Faveur et trahison à la cour d'Angleterre au début du XIVe siècle', in M. Billoré and M. Soria (eds), *La trahison au Moyen Âge. De la monstruosité au crime politique (V^e–XVe siècle)* (Rennes: PUR, 2009), pp. 197–206.

3

Opportunism and ethics in politics

The dukes of Burgundy, until the accession of Charles the Bold, were by nature French princes. Whether by sympathy or by opposition, their origins never ceased to draw them into the heart of the affairs of France. This filial bond not only had consequences for their diplomatic choices, but also instigated a political logic which, in the process of being adapted to local circumstances, lost coherence and threatened to lapse into opportunism. Although telling the people what they want to hear might be thought to show political skill, at worst incurring the accusation of demagoguery, saying two different things in two different places runs the risk of discredit and of a fundamental loss of sense. These remarks might be universally true, but relating them to the Burgundian context quickly confirms their medieval applicability. Placing a number of manifestos and political postures in a broader context makes the ambiguities of Burgundian political thought apparent once more. For although the declarations of the dukes in the kingdom of France are just as well known as their demands in their own principality, few historians have considered them together, nor have they used them to assess the coherence and the ideological foundations of Burgundian politics.

The manifesto of 1405: words meet deeds

Consider first a text which is often cited but not often considered in detail: the manifesto of the 'Burgundian brothers' addressed to Charles VI on 6 August 1405.[1] The context of its composition is well known, and the historiography devoted to it is as voluminous as the events it considers are important.[2] The crisis between the House of

Orléans and that of Burgundy was worsening. The unexpected return to Paris of John the Fearless surprised Louis of Orléans, who left the capital in the company of Queen Isabeau, giving orders that the dauphin, Louis of Guyenne, should be brought to join them. John the Fearless, however, after a rapturous reception by the Parisian population on his arrival on 19 August, immediately rode out to intercept the infant Louis and to bring him back under guard to the Louvre.[3] Here as elsewhere, politics was a matter of relative strength, and 'the Council's control was only total when it was accompanied by the person of the king or of his sons'. Nonetheless, any such manoeuvre needed to be justified.[4] The civil war, as it simmered and then boiled over, had accelerated the development of contrasting forms of political propaganda in the different camps. John the Fearless took the path of solemnity, publicity, popularity and unanimity. Louis of Orléans, by contrast, although he sent out just as many letters and manifestos to justify his position, unhesitatingly assumed the role of the solitary defender of the kingdom of France and reproved anyone who presumed to involve themselves in the affairs of the princes of the blood. The public declaration of August 1405 thus used terms that were already well established in Burgundian discourse. It was read by the ducal counsellor, Jean de Nielles, to a gathering presided over by the dauphin in the absence of the king, in the name of John the Fearless and his brothers, Antoine de Rethel and Philippe de Nevers, and was widely diffused in towns throughout the kingdom. The declaration sought to expose the malfunctions of the present government and with them all that impugned the 'honour and profit' of the king and his kingdom. In four points, the ducal counsellor denounced the bad treatment of the person of the king; the deficiencies of the system of justice; the excesses of taxation; and the oppression which burdened the three orders of society: the clergy, the nobility and the people. The familiar topics of the king's majesty, justice, tax and the body politic constructed a discourse which has long been considered by historians to be positively archaic when compared with Louis of Orléans desire to modernise the institutions of the monarchy.

Yet these ideas, first deployed by Philip the Bold and later adopted and enriched by his son, were more than just worthy old chestnuts. They were part of an established current of thought backed by numerous texts.⁵ Consider for example Pierre le Fruitier, also known as Pierre Salmon. It is widely known that this humble servant of Charles VI was won over by the Burgundian cause. But if his 'mirror for princes', addressed to the king in 1409, theorised to perfection the remonstrances of 1405, it nonetheless remains a product of its time. So where John the Fearless was indignant about the neglect of the apparel which befitted the royal estate, Pierre Salmon wrote that the king on his throne should be 'clothed and adorned with royal apparel', since his first function is to 'shine amongst everyone and over everyone in his kingdom in virtues and in wisdom, by grace and by all good *mores*'.⁶ Where the 1405 manifesto defended the principle of election of officers as a guarantee of good justice, Pierre Salmon affirmed that any good prince should 'know how to take care to give rewards and offices to good people'. Finally, where John the Fearless expressed a desire to limit taxation and to submit its grant to the consideration of an enlightened council, Pierre Salmon threatened any prince who dared to 'gather the treasure of the goods of his subjects by extortion'.⁷

So what do these remonstrances say when we examine them in detail? As we shall see, whereas for Jean Juvénal des Ursins and others all these arguments were advanced with no other aim but the control of the affairs of the kingdom, they nonetheless bear witness to a political culture and a political vision which goes beyond mere self-promotion. They cannot be understood simply by setting up a facile dichotomy between a conservative and an innovative vision of the *res publica* and how it should be strengthened.⁸

Loyalty to the king

First and foremost, this text affirms an unceasing loyalty to the king's person. Later, loyalty would justify the duke of Burgundy's ultimate act, the assassination of Louis of Orléans, since this was necessary to eliminate the threat posed to the king by his brother. It is of course possible, following Corinne Leveleux's analysis of canon law theory, to find in this act a weakening of the strength of the duke's oath, which had been repeatedly reiterated in sworn alliances between the two princes but was brutally broken on the night of 23 November 1407.⁹ Yet the duke's deed also drew on the power of ultimate loyalty to the person of the king and the absolute duty to protect the royal majesty. As we have seen, kinship obligated the duke of Burgundy with regard to his cousin Charles, but beyond lineage, beyond marriage links, it was legalism, a recurring and powerful characteristic of noble culture, which dictated the behaviour of John the Fearless, along the lines begun by his father. In this context we can invoke the oath which the old duke was supposed to have extracted from his sons on his death bed:

> And, in conclusion, it was said that my late lord of Burgundy, whom God forgive, in his last will, had charged my said lord ... and my lord of Limburg, his brother, and made them swear that, after God, they would love the king, his good and his honour, and that of his kingdom, and after him my lord the dauphin, his son, and that they would take pains and act diligently to serve him well and obey him ...[10]

Whether this oath was really taken or not, what is important for our present purposes is that this was indeed the political argument put forward to explain the arrival of the princes of Burgundy in Paris and the almost sacred nature of their mission. It was in this context that the question of personal fidelity arose, and the relationship with the king's body intensified this issue. John the Fearless complained in particular that the government blocked access to the king, such that his loyal servants could 'have no audience with him'. The idea of personal fidelity to the royal person, in this case that of Charles VI, retained its power throughout this period. For example, on a later occasion, when John the Fearless was back in his own lands in 1413, his council assembled at Lille advised him to take advantage of the presence at the court of Hainault of the second son of Charles VI, Jean de Touraine, to turn him into a king he could control. Yet the duke calmed the enthusiasm of his lords, reminding them that what they suggested would be an act of treason towards the present king, whom it was his duty to protect, notwithstanding his current disgrace. The mission he pursued was the same one that had occupied his own father. It was the same one defended by Christine de Pizan and Jean Gerson, for example when the former affirmed that princes should work towards 'the good and the profit of this land ... and the particular good of the person of the king', or when the latter declared that these same princes formed 'the crown of the king'.[11]

One could moralise at length on the perversion of this mission, once it fell to the son of Philip the Bold and to his nephew, as it was transformed from a collective task (the council of the princes) to an authoritarian and egotistical bid for power. John the Fearless soon became guilty of the very faults of which he had accused his enemy, the duke of Orléans, as he isolated Charles VI and packed different councils with his own creatures. For example, the programme of establishing 'election' within the royal administration and choosing the most competent officers, as in the good old days of Charles V, instead giving offices to the highest bidder, would have been more convincing and would have suggested a political thought detached from all favouritism, were it not for the fact that at each return to grace the duke of Burgundy immediately expelled the men of the duke of Orléans, whether they were competent or not, and replaced them with his own personnel, their allegiance being more important than their objective worth. Indeed, the assistance promised to the king to remedy all the specified abuses suggests that one 'system' would replace another: 'And to do this, we offer you riches, body and friends.'[12] The duke clearly wanted to recover the place his father had occupied at the king's side, and this had nothing scandalous or shocking about it. After all, Jean Gerson, in his *Vivat rex*, reinforced the Burgundian position by repeatedly asserting that the power of the king could not be exercised without the advice of the community represented by the king's council and by the Estates General, the latter being precisely the body that John the Fearless had proposed to summon at the end of his manifesto.

Nonetheless, as Jean Juvénal des Ursins scathingly observed, as pretty as these words may have been, they served only to gild the particular interests of the lords who pronounced them.[13] For what made matters more complicated was that both the new protagonists had decided to work alone. In contrast to Philip the Bold, who dominated the council but was nonetheless part of it, Louis of Orléans and John the Fearless turned their backs on the family tradition which had, it is true, enabled the king's brothers to take advantage of the royal coffers for their own interests, but had at least allowed them to do so together. It could be argued that the young Louis was the first to break this implicit contract. It was the duke of Orléans who took advantage of the absence of his uncle Philip to seize control of the royal finances. It was he who humiliated his extended family by disdaining to attend the ceremony which accompanied the presentation of the arm of Saint Benedict in the abbey of Saint Denis in the company of all the princes of the blood on 21 March 1401. Finally, it was Louis who broke the duke of Burgundy's word, by announcing a new *taille*, allegedly with the latter's agreement.[14] This was too much for Philip, who sent a letter of protestation to the *prévôt* of Paris, ordering it to be read out in public. Those who declared that the duke of Burgundy had accepted the levy of a new tax in return for 200,000 francs had 'said and spread pure lies and slanders'.[15] Yet in this letter, transmitted by the Saint Denis chronicler, Philip had also set out in writing the political programme which the Burgundian clan now published in the capital and throughout the kingdom.

Against 'novelties' in Paris and for the Calfvel in Bruges

The general line of the 1405 manifesto, also to be found in texts like the 'Cabochienne ordinance' of 1413, was already clearly established in the letter which Philip the Bold had ordered to be publicly read on 26 October 1401:

> He [Philip the Bold] addressed his letter to the *prévôt* of Paris, with the order for it to be read to the people; he said therein that he had never consented to the said exaction, and that the edict contained a falsehood. Then showing a great compassion for the inhabitants of the kingdom, who had just been struck down by an epidemic which lasted three years and had been ruined by other exactions, he declared that the new tax was intolerable, and that if the treasury was exhausted, it needed to be refilled, not at the expense of the people, but with the money of those who unjustly enriched themselves with the king's largesse, and who he well knew would get all the money from this new *taille*.[16]

The Burgundians in Paris opposed this special excise duty and loudly condemned growth in royal expenditures, which were funded by continuing increases in taxation. They did not accept that the taxation of the king's subjects without negotiation and without justification was essential for the good of the *res publica*. In the manifesto of 1405, the argument was taken further: the king, according to the formula, 'must live off his own', that is to say on the revenues of a royal domain which was insufficiently or badly managed, leaving in peace an exhausted population which, under fiscal burdens and the oppressions of men of war, might rise in rebellion. This position has nothing obviously demagogic or archaic about it. Instead, it reflected a largely accepted idea, developed for example by the preacher Jacques Legrand. As Lydwine Scordia has shown, for some the union of the king with his subjects was ideally based on a 'form of union in grace', comparable to that of the faithful with Christ. This theory had powerful spiritual connotations, but in the face of financial realities which were just as insistent, it presented the prince with numerous material difficulties.[17] Indeed, from 1402 onwards, with the king ill once more and the royal coffers empty, Philip the Bold had decided to raise a new tax, despite the opinions on the matter which we have just seen him express.

This divide between ideal and reality was not only the result of intellectual confusion. Deprived of his share of royal *aides* after the death of his father, John the Fearless saw his income from pensions collapse from 185,300 to 37,000 *livres*. What could the duke do to raise the money which he needed to gain access to the royal coffers once more, and so obtain funds which would allow him to maintain his position, and so keep on receiving them? Françoise Autrand asks this question, although she does not answer it: 'How can one raise a *taille* on one's own lands when one has said repeatedly that the king can live without the revenues of taxation and live on the revenues of his *domaine*?'[18] We can see that the political ideas which they propagated in the kingdom of France quickly tied the political actions of the Burgundians in uncomfortable knots. It thus makes more sense to consider their position not in terms of an opposition between archaism and modernity, but rather from the point of view of the coherence or the ambiguity of their twofold roles, as both great lords of the kingdom and masters of their principality. Indeed, when they ruled their territories directly, the dukes were not guided by the ideals posted up and publicly declared in the streets of Paris and the most important towns of the kingdom. In their northern lands, in the contrast, their fiscal policy took shape through a series of trials of strength which frequently involved clashes with their subjects.

To answer Françoise Autrand's question, it has to be said that John the Fearless did not much worry about his declarations to the good people of Paris when he sought to put in place regular, if not permanent, taxation in Flanders. This can be seen for example in the episode of the *Calfvel*, which is regarded as a kind of *coup d'état* by Flemish historians, and which had much to surprise those who took the duke at his word as it was pronounced in the streets of Paris in 1405. Just two years later, in 1407, John the Fearless played on the internal divisions of the city of Bruges to dispose of the patrician faction then in power, whom he opportunistically accused of financial corruption, and to replace it with his own men.[19] The new rulers of Bruges manipulated the craft guilds in order to obtain acceptance of an ordinance, known as the *Calfvel* (calf skin) which stipulated that the city would now have to send one seventh of its revenues to the duke. They would later opine that they had not grasped the subtleties of the affair, asserting that they had signed a document which they did not understand. This tax of the seventh penny was of an exceptional nature, and was entirely unprecedented. Whilst the towns of French-speaking Flanders and Artois, with one or two exceptions, automatically sent one quarter of the profits of their assizes, the Flemish-speaking towns had succeeded until then in paying a fixed levy, independent of their real income.[20] The dukes and counts of Flanders had to negotiate with the Members of Flanders to collect *aides*, and the large towns came to arrangements thereafter to divide up the sum due between themselves and the 'subaltern towns' according to their field of influence, the smaller towns of the *plat pays* contributing proportionally much more than the giants of the county. With the *Calfvel*, John the Fearless succeeded in imposing on Bruges a financial policy which his father had already envisaged. Unsurprisingly, the pill proved difficult to swallow, and force had to be used in the form of banishments and fines. The tense political atmosphere which followed the duke's manipulation of factional strife is less tangible for the historian than the sanctions ordered in ducal ordinances, but it is just as important for understanding the consequences of this act. Once again, whilst in Paris John the Fearless's propaganda played on ideas of community, solidarity and his proximity to the 'man in the street', whilst his wine flowed freely and badges in his image were widely distributed to galvanise the united people behind this self-proclaimed loyal servant of the king of France, at home the same duke played divide and rule with his own Flemish people.

In the poem entitled 'De zeven poorten van Brugge' ('The Seven Gates of Bruges'), extant in the famous Gruuthuse manuscript and no doubt composed during these delicate years, the author and orator Jan van Hulst disguises himself as a hermit during a Twelfth Night celebration held by the company of the White Bear, appealing to the king of the company and denouncing the lack of brotherly love ('Broederlike minne') in the city of Bruges. In a recent study of this poem, Jan Dumolyn has closely analysed its lexical field to show how the latter accords perfectly with the narrative of the chronicler Olivier van Dixmude. The word *nide* (envy or hatred) occurs repeatedly, but where the poem evokes matters in general without an *ad hominem* denunciation, Olivier van Dixmude targets the origins of the quarrels amongst patricians:

> At this time a great hatred arose amongst the people of Flanders, and those who ate and drank together would have preferred to eat their own heart.[21]

It would of course be wrong to pretend that John the Fearless was the sole cause of this urban discontent. The factions which characterised the towns of Flanders had not waited for his intervention to fight amongst themselves. On the other hand, the duke did not play the role of peace-maker which we might expect of him. On the contrary, without worrying about the people, he played the card of division and disharmony to fill his coffers and to serve his French interests.

He did not stop there. In the following year, 1408, John the Fearless took a further step towards ever greater fiscal pressure by modifying the so-called *transport de Flandre*. To summarise without going into excessive detail, the *transport de Flandre* was the system used to share out the *aides* between the different towns and regions of the county. It had been defined by the Treaty of Athis-sur-Orge (1305). As one might imagine, economic realities had inevitably changed over the following century. It was to answer a request for greater equity between tax-payers that the duke of Burgundy ordered a modification of the amounts raised, notably after the plague of 1400–01 and the Saint Elizabeth's day flood of 1404. However, when we observe the results of the inquest of Oudenburg, which takes its name from the place where the new *transport* was promulgated, we can see that the duke arranged matters for his own profit and that, to accompany the development of commercial policy between Flanders and England, he raised an *aide* of 108,000 *doubles écus*. But, even if the rhetoric of the ordinance repeatedly announced a just and faithful policy, protecting the weak and working solely for the common good of the land, the duke did not really take into account the frailty of the new economic conditions of the country.[22] Whereas six places, including the towns of Ghent and Ypres, saw their contribution reduced, four remained unchanged, and twenty-eight, including Bruges, actually paid more. If the dukes tried from time to time to impose a more equitable fiscal system which was less biased in favour of the largest towns of Flanders, it has to be admitted that they failed, the real priority being to increase the duke's revenues with the complicity of local elites.[23] The dukes, particularly John the Fearless in the years of civil war, based their Flemish policies on their dynastic ambitions.

John the Fearless only went back on the *Calfvel* when forced to do so, when the Flemish troops deserted his army after the siege of Ham in the Vermandois in 1411. The Bruges militia, keeping their arms for this purpose, returned to their city and revolted against and expelled the Scutelare faction. At the city gates, they sent a seven-point petition to the Magistrat which demanded amongst other things the abolition of the *Calfvel*. When this was sent to the count of Charolais at Ghent, who represented his father in the latter's absence, it was discussed in the ducal council which, fearing the dangers of unrest and the impossibility of dealing with it in current circumstances, conceded all the petitioners' demands. The two letters of 24 May 1407 in which the Magistrat and the craft guilds of Bruges had accepted the seventh penny, by then kept in Lille, were taken to Ghent. They were 'torn up piece by piece', and their seals ripped off, according to the memoranda of Thierry Gherbode.[24] Even if John the Fearless hoped to escape on a technicality, arguing that the abolition of this tax had been extorted from his son by force, the *Calfvel* was finished. Worse still, three years later, the balance of power was further inverted and the Four Members of Flanders took advantage of the fragile position of their count to make their financial aid conditional on the acceptance of a twelve-point petition which included the abolition of all *nouvelletés* (novelties) which had appeared under John the Fearless or his father. The count-duke did not give in entirely, but his ostensible aim was already to play for time.

In Paris, the dukes defended a theory, that of a kingdom without direct levies, which they themselves contradicted in practice when they attempted to impose regular taxation, without total success, in their Flemish lands. This contradiction makes clear the weaknesses of a system in which it was becoming more and more difficult to act at the two levels imposed by the structure of the French state and its principalities. They needed the principality under their lordship to be well managed and powerful in order to strengthen their position within the kingdom. From this point of view, John the Fearless's mission was precisely the same as that of Louis of Orléans.[25] Since they gave priority to their status as princes of France, the two first dukes of Burgundy never wanted to construct their own state within their territory. Indeed, the dynastic policy they pursued in France was the primary obstacle against forging a common identity with their northern subjects. Following the metaphor of the body politic which was so popular in the later Middle Ages, one might go so far as to say that if the stomach was Flanders, Artois and Burgundy, the heart was still in Paris.[26]

A return to war against England

Historians who have studied the construction of national identity in the kingdom of France have all underlined the catalysing effect of war in accordance with the universal principal by which a group constructs itself by opposition to others. Unassisted by modern philosophers and psychologists, medieval actors were well aware of the power of a warlike argumentative stance. Indeed, John the Fearless's political discourse did not question the reopening of the war with England. He simply argued that if taxes were correctly used, they would not weigh any more heavily on the people of France. For the duke of Burgundy, in contrast, full advantage ought to be taken of the tensions which were pulling apart the kingdom of England in 1405, making war on the enemy whilst the time was ripe. In his manifesto, he called on France to remember the enormities which the English enemy had perpetrated, from the captivity of King John II to the poor treatment recently inflicted on Isabelle, daughter of Charles VI and widow of Richard II of England, as a means to attack the supposed passivity of Louis of Orléans. From a strictly military point of view, this declaration might have appeared persuasive. Several months before reaching Paris in spring 1405, the duke had had to face English raids which threatened the whole of the Flemish coastline and specifically the isle of Cadzand. After having assembled his men-at-arms at Male, he defended the port of Sluys on 25 May and succeeded in repulsing the enemy *in extremis*.[27] Nonetheless, we should not forget that the revival of the Anglo-French war was the result of the letters of defiance which Louis of Orléans had been careful to send to 'Henry, king of England' as early as 7 August 1402. By accusing the government of France, and thus indirectly Louis of Orléans, of passivity, John the Fearless was evidently acting in bad faith. The true scandal in his eyes lay in the lack of support for French troops in Picardy and Flanders, since Louis had preferred to focus the military effort on Guyenne, leaving exposed his enemy's lands in the north.

The duke of Burgundy's duplicity is apparent once again when we compare his words to the Parisians with the parallel negotiations he undertook with the English to maintain the provision of commercial treaties in his county. The lie is also apparent when we consider that, before as well as after his visit to Paris, John the Fearless gave in to the requests of his Flemish subjects for the re-establishment of diplomatic relations to protect their trade with England. After the duke's declaration in favour of war, we find Burgundian diplomats at work in Calais on 23 October, with barrels of wine fulfilling their accustomed role as a means of softening the English enemy. It has to be said that the Flemish towns had acquired their own quasi-autonomous tradition of negotiation. Even if the duke of Burgundy limited this privilege, he could not ignore the economic and thus political demands of their northern subjects with regard to England.[28] As Walter Prevenier has noted, if Philip the Bold and John the Fearless feared the resurgence of a pro-English party in Flanders, their economic interests were nonetheless different from those of the king of France. The duality of their position was apparent each time they met with the English at a diplomatic conference.[29] One thing is certain: the prosperity of Flanders was a topic which generally united the merchants, those of Bruges in particular, with their Burgundian princes, the former seeking to protect their own trade, the latter seeing in this flourishing economy an indispensable support for their political and military power. From this point of view, the favour accorded by Duke John to the Scutelare clan on the eve of the *Calfvel* affair can also be read as part of his desire to strengthen relations with England, since this family was particularly well established across the Channel and had received an annuity from the English king's Wardrobe as long ago as 1340.

It is clear that when John the Fearless took up arms in the spring of 1405 it was certainly not as a result of any desire to re-ignite the Anglo-French war, but rather to defend his own lands. The ambivalence which we have already seen in the case of taxation thus recurred in the matter of war. The aim of his double discourse was the same: to acquire the financial resources he needed to maintain his pre-eminent position in the kingdom. The manifesto of 1405 thus had its own logic, arguing in favour of a political line which dominated the thinking of the first dukes of Burgundy, who were above all great princes determined to administer their lands as efficiently as possible in order to win influence with the French king and in his service.

Witches, rebels and brigands: strange contrasts

Let us move forward a few years to focus on another kind of ambiguity. The long reign of Philip the Good provides abundant material for anyone who wishes to understand the difficulty of uniting a territory which, because of the distances it involved, dictated differing courses of action. Decisions made by princes were often contradictory and so weakened the manifestation of their authority. Under John the Fearless, if administrative advances were often followed by spectacular reversals, this might be explained by a civil war which made it difficult to implement ducal decisions. In more settled circumstances after 1435, the governance of Philip the Good was no less chaotic, as the following examples suggest.

The Grande Vaudrie *of Arras: a political witch craze?*

In the streets of Arras in 1461, pamphlets were circulating. The people were 'discontented', and a search for heretics and witches had caused considerable damage. The chronicler Jacques du Clercq reports the contents of one of these pamphlets denouncing the legal attacks on townspeople and nobles whose reputation and goods had been damaged to the great disturbance of the entire city.[30]

The well-known episode of the *Grande Vauderie* of Arras began in 1459, at the instigation of the Dominican friar Pierre le Broussard, who claimed to have identified a mysterious demon-worshipping group: the sect of the Vaudois. Two individuals on the edges of society, a prostitute and a poet-painter, were quickly arrested. They confessed under torture to participating in 'witches' sabbaths' and gave the names of their alleged accomplices, amongst whom were many wealthy people. The case took on such dimensions that it frightened certain judges into trying to avoid scandal by freeing the prisoners. Nonetheless, the zeal of the Dominican and of the suffragan bishop of Arras, the Franciscan Jean Fauconnier, was met favourably by Jean de Bourgogne, count of Étampes and captain general of the Marches of Picardy in the name of Philip the Good, who intervened personally in support of the inquisitors' actions. On 9 May 1460 the poet Jean Tannoye and five prostitutes were burned, whilst a further dozen people were arrested and a number of the most prominent citizens of Arras were incriminated. Six more were burned at the stake on 7 July. A final victim was burned on 22 October 1460. In the meantime, the town had begun to attack the tribunal's actions, arguing that the whole affair was simply a machination to seize the goods of some nobles and burgesses and to secure their condemnation by notoriety. Since the duke of Burgundy had not disowned the inquisitors' actions, the surviving victims approached the king, first demanding the end of hostilities and then asking reparation for the unjust and unfounded punishments they had suffered. The inquisitors having conveniently disappeared in the meantime, the Parlement of Paris judged the case in June 1461, but it was not until 20 May 1491 that a complete and definitive judgement was passed annulling the trials of 1459 to 1460.[31]

The rereading of this episode by Franck Mercier has usefully brought to the fore the political implications of an affair which was long considered by historians to be a simple *fait-divers* or even a judicial error. To quote Mercier, its most recent student, 'the prince's shadow' falls long over a plot whose details have probably not yet been totally elucidated.[32] But to speak of a shadow is all the more appropriate when we note that Philip the Good made no clear or open declaration concerning the affair. This is a surprising omission on the part of a prince who, according to Mercier, saw this moment as an opportunity to affirm his majesty. In this interpretation, the *Vauderie* of Arras should be seen as symptomatic of the duke's quest for sovereignty in opposition to the ambitions of the king of France. It is true that the 1450s had been particularly disturbed and that the war waged successfully against the rebels of Ghent between 1447 and 1453 was marked by not only military but also ideological struggle. The manifesto of 1452, sent in the form of letters to all the duke's Estates, took the traditional form of a declaration to all of the truth as seen by the prince, demonstrating the rightfulness of his action whilst rehearsing all the attacks by 'rebellious and disobedient enemies' against the sovereign power which he embodied. Nonetheless, the crime of *lèse-majesté* is never actually mentioned in a text whose arguments could have been made to point in that direction.[33]

If the opposition between the duke and his rebel subjects is expressed particularly violently, it otherwise takes its place in the tradition of revolts which were one important element of political communication in this region.[34] It is not true, as Mercier implies, that this revolt was built on shadowy crimes or on secret plots which menaced the authority of the prince. For example, the capture of a cutler named Brillekin (the nickname of a Ghentish captain who defended Waasland but whose real name is not known and who does not appear in local sources), to whom the Ghentish were supposed to have promised the county, has nothing to do with the tradition of the pretender or substitute prince.[35] Imitation is the very basis of the usurpation of identity, but this so-called Brillekin had rough manners that were completely at odds with the refinement of the duke of Burgundy. He simply provided fuel for a form of Burgundian propaganda which sought to consolidate the image of an arrogant people who dared to defy their lord unjustly. It played effectively on the memory of Jan Breydel, Peter de Conninck and, of course, the Arteveldes, all great leaders of the urban uprisings which run through the history of the county. Brillekin was not a menacing double of the duke but rather the fictional representation of a very real threat, that of a popular leader capable of inspiring the people to defend the privileges which were put at risk by the prince's centralising efforts.[36]

The accusation of *lèse-majesté* was not yet formulated, since another, darker shadow was cast over this conflict by the king of France. The ambassadors of Charles VII were probably bribed by Philip the Good to make a declaration which would ultimately redound to the benefit of the latter, but they nonetheless also replied to the calls of the people of Ghent for the intercession of the sovereign lord of the counts of Flanders, as they felt the law required. The duke of Burgundy was of course not particularly satisfied with an intervention which was felt as an incursion since, in this judgement, it was the king of France who held the title of 'sovereign lord', whereas the duke of Burgundy remained the 'most redoubtable lord and natural prince'.[37] We will consider the notion of *lèse-majesté* later in more detail. For the moment, it is enough to note that the employment of this notion by the duke quickly ran into a superior authority recognised by all parties, that of the king of France, and that it was only expressed in a hesitant and preliminary fashion. For if the war with Ghent can be seen as the umpteenth manifestation of a tradition of Flemish rebellion, whose political significance lay in the habitual tit-for-tat between lord and subjects around the question of disputed privileges, the *Vauderie* of Arras was a very different kind of affair and a very delicate one at that. Once again, the authority of the king of France can be discerned behind these trials, which has divided historians between those offering theologico-political interpretations and those who favour a more 'secular' view privileging the thesis of vengeance between noble clans.[38] It would be presumptuous to present the analysis that follows as any kind of arbitration between the two. Yet the richness of the arguments which have been developed in this context make it possible to widen the range of observation. The *Grande Vauderie* of Arras can certainly be seen as an inquisitorial trial motivated by the desire to purge the town of elements which threatened the spiritual life of the capital of Artois. Nonetheless, this was not its only function. For the high-ranking individuals implicated in this trial, such as Jean de Bourgogne and Philippe de Saveuse, the defence of personal interests and religious convictions were by no means incompatible. The arrival by way of reinforcements during the second phase of the trial in June 1460 of men devoted to the duke's party resulted in the indictment of individuals such as Pierre du Carieulx, Colard de Beaufort and Martin Cornille who had built their fortune in the service of the duke of Burgundy. Cornille had already had trouble with ducal justice for embezzlement in 1449.[39] It would be wrong to deny that the sire de Saveuse was generally committed to the service of God, but one cannot ignore the 'war of friends' that opposed him to Colard de Beaufort. It is pointless to choose one perspective over the other. When we consider both points of view, it becomes apparent that the context in which they are considered dictates how these events should be understood.

From the point of view of the court, the *Vauderie* of Arras was a war against the enemies of the faith. It was in line with the crusading spirit of a nobility whose chivalric culture, still very much alive if somewhat disconnected from reality, nonetheless guided their behaviour in the smallest detail. From this point of view, the ageing Philip the Good, now primarily resident in Brussels, could only have been stimulated and enthused by a mission which compensated in part the great voyage to the Holy Land which he had wanted to accomplish. Indeed, the idea of the crusade still haunted him, as can be seen, for example, in 1463, when he replied to the rebels of g who had come to meet him at Bruges: 'take care that I do not come to you and that you are not the Turks and Turkey, whom I travel to meet'.[40] On the other hand, in practice, the *Vauderie* was an opportunity not only to show pious fervour, but also to attack a party which was felt by some to be excessively Francophile. A reference to the Croÿ clan in the archives of the Parlement of Paris certainly demonstrates a more partisan link. According to Jean de Popaincourt, Pierre du Carieulx allegedly declared as he went to the stake that he 'had falsely accused many people whom he had been made to name including the lord of Croÿ, governor of Arras, and other lords'.[41] Other details point to the strong influence of the king in this fragile region. Colart de Beaufort, for example, was forcibly freed from prison and placed under the protection of the French superior court, and the author of a pamphlet which condemned the exactions of Jean de Bourgogne and his secretary Jean Forme finally found shelter under French royal authority after an elaborate flight.

Arras was situated geographically in the kind of frontier zone which often escaped authority, which was difficult to control and whose liminal situation might stimulate not only nests of witches but also unshakeable fidelities (if we think of the accusations against Joan of Arc, a native of Lorraine, another border zone with unclear boundaries). The case of the maid of Orléans reminds us that fidelity to the kingdom of France was deeply established in local mentalities. In 1431, on the way to her martyrdom, Joan was held in the prison of Arras, where, thanks to complicity between towns, the citizens of Tournai were able to send her funds they had raised to improve the conditions of her detention. During the hard months of December 1434 and January 1435, her memory was evoked during a winter festival where people expressed their culture and political opinions with the aid of snowmen.[42] Loyalty to the kingdom was also inscribed in the very stones of the town, for example in a long text praising the deeds of Philip Augustus at the battle of Bouvines which had been carved into the St-Nicolas gate as early as 1214, given in Latin facing the countryside and in Picard facing towards the town.[43] Arras, which had resisted the troops of Louis XI in 1477, to the point of being emptied of its inhabitants, was nonetheless a nest of Francophiles.

It is worth reflecting on the fact that a form of attack from the margins was particularly favoured by the French court. The case of the bastard of Rubempré a few years later, in 1465, moved the attacks against the Croÿ clan to Holland. The condemnation of Jean Coustain, which also served to weaken the same clan, drew amongst other things on accusations of necromancy already formulated at Arras.[44] In short, the political implications of this trial are clear, and the role of the king of France, as shown through the use of protections and the judgements of the Parlement, is incontestable.

But what has this to do with Philip the Good? Was he affirming his majesty through the crime that threatened it? Some would argue that the increase in condemnations for sodomy during this period in the northern territories of the duke of Burgundy, especially in Bruges, suggest a link between this new rigour and *lèse-majesté* towards God and, by extension, towards the prince.[45] But although Philip the Good was invited to attend the trials, he did not come. Asked to give his opinion, he deferred to the theologians of the university of Leuven. If he was so concerned with the majesty of his authority, would this same prince have granted the exercise of sovereign justice in Lovendegem and Zomergem to his favourite

Jean Coustain, a far from isolated example of the delegation of the exercise of this highly symbolic power? In short, the *Vauderie* of Arras is certainly not an affair which illustrates the strengthening of princely majesty. Philip the Good remained a servant of the king of France. This was why the ambassadors whom he sent to Charles VII at Montbazon in 1458 ended their presentation of the duke's recriminations by making it clear that the duke prayed the king to have him in his 'good grace'. The duke would always 'to the pleasure of God' be 'good, true, frank, loyal and obedient' to the king of France.[46] Charles VII replied to this by inviting the duke to stop complaining and to behave himself like a 'good relation and servant'. Yet, quite apart from the power relations between the king and the duke, the desire to regard the excesses at Arras as an opportunity to restore moral order amongst his devoted subjects, and thus to affirm, through an implacable exercise of justice, the ultimate power of Burgundian authority, seems above all to be an opportunist reaction. It does not appear to derive from any political ideology which could be applied to the entirety of the duke's territories.

A crime syndicate in Dijon in 1454: corruption and omertà *in the ducal archives*

Indeed, a little later, another episode comes to our attention which has something of the quality of a striking but trivial local news story. This incident has been considered more fully by literary scholars than by historians, with the exception of Valérie Toureille's monograph on brigandage in the north of the kingdom of France.[47] Yet the trial of the *Coquillards* or 'Companions of the Shell' which was initiated by the town prosecutor of Dijon, Jean Rabustel, in the autumn of 1455 has much to recommend comparative study. Indeed, Jean Rabustel's investigation revealed a widespread disorganisation in the social fabric of the town of Dijon, the capital of the duchy of Burgundy and, for certain historians, capital of the Burgundian territorial complex as a whole. Following a number of accusations made by the town's inhabitants, complaining of the trouble caused by a band of all sorts of criminals, the town prosecutor, who also directed the police, launched a raid on the town brothel in which a dozen people were arrested; the witness reports would later yield around sixty names.[48] We can easily imagine that the town aldermen would have wanted to protect their authority by acting quickly, in the duke's name, even without his more or less direct intervention. We also know that Philip the Good was very rarely present in the duchy. Yet the revelations made in the witness statements obtained by the prosecutor reveal the outlines of a mafia-like crime syndicate governed by rules of *omertà*, which was particularly well established in Dijon and its surrounding area. Indeed, if most of the crimes that were complained of occurred outside the town walls, the so-called Companions of the Shell operated their prostitution network within Dijon itself. It was in the town, too, that stolen goods were fenced, with the assistance of prominent individuals, like the marshal of the horses or the landlord of the brothel, Jacquot de la Mer, who was also an important town official and who was probably responsible for passing on information essential for the group's survival. Indeed, the gang was particularly well established, even respectable, within the town, to the point that 'it is notable that, for a long time before the said associates were accused, the said Jacquot would drive them and walk with them arm and arm, at all times of day and night, through the town'. The gang was powerful enough to threaten the civic authorities in the middle of the trial with reprisals if its members were prosecuted.[49] The investigating judge's report probably imposed a formal structure on this shadowy network to understand it better, lending it a king, a hierarchy and a language. But the 'sect and trickery' of the Shell was nonetheless a perfectly integrated organisation in the town, evolving in a kind of unhealthy parallel world and therefore posing an even more menacing danger for the kind of order that the authorities wanted and should have guaranteed. We should add that these disturbances to public order did not come out of nowhere in 1455, nor did they disappear immediately after the trial. The raid just cited occurred after two years of complaints, and later, in 1458, Jean Rabustel demanded a new edict against the mayor, directed this time against 'unknown companions who are sunk in sloth [*qui sont oiseulx*]'.[50] The frustration of the duke's subjects expressed itself in different contexts, for example on stage, where the laxity of the authorities was denounced in verse.

Indeed, another subject had already attracted the attention of Jean Rabustel. This was the mystery play of Saint Eloi, ordered by the Carmelites and performed on Sunday, 29 October 1447 by a group of Dijon artisan-actors. An interlude was introduced into this performance which repeatedly impugned the honour of the king and the dauphin, causing a number of prominent individuals to leave in disgust in order to avoid hearing 'such foolish and outrageous words'.[51] For Louis Petit de Julleville, the trial was provoked by the excessively explicit reference to the *écorcheurs* (the much hated mercenary troops of Charles VII), which was replaced in the text by the term *estradeurs* (a lighter but also more depreciative word).[52] The play also probably alluded to the siege of Montbéliard and the atrocities perpetrated there. Jean Rabustel does not give details of the words which were spoken, quoting only the beginning and the end of the offending dialogue. This, as Marie Bouhaïk has observed, was because the Lex Julia of the Code of Justianian (book 48 of the Digest), the imperial law concerning crimes against the *res publica* which defined the concept of *lèse-majesté*, forbade the copying of the incriminating words in this judicial context. The rest of the report shows the embarrassment of the prosecutor, who admits that he does not know how seriously to punish these troublemakers without knowing exactly what they said and instead asks the members of the town council to give their opinion. He is however sure that the matter is important, for the honour and reputation of the town is in question. The sources do not reveal how the case was concluded, but we can nonetheless make a number of remarks.

First, it seems that the king's honour was held in such high esteem that an assault on it provoked an immediate reaction designed to protect the town's reputation. Second, Jean Rabustel has particular difficulty in deciding how to proceed, in part because the absence of either a bishopric or a university in Dijon meant that he had no learned counsels to fall back on. Finally, although the concept of *lèse-majesté* can be discerned behind these accusations against a few actors, it is not to be found at all in the trial of the Companions of the Shell. This is surprising, since they were not only thieves, hustlers and murderers but also counterfeiters, and to falsify the coinage was a crime of *lèse-majesté*. Bearing in mind what we saw above in the case of the duke's northern territories, how should we interpret the inertia of the duke against a gang which threatened his own authority?[53] It could be argued that the efforts made by the king of France in the ordinance of Louppy-le-Chatel of 26 May 1445 to discipline brigands, false beggars and the misdeeds of men of war

Opportunism and ethics in politics

lacked firmness, even as a permanent army was established. But this was not for want of repeated declarations of intent, as royal ordinances multiplied and the Estates of 1456 proposed to send thieves 'to the galleys'. As Valérie Toureille has pointed out, effective or not, 'the offensive against brigandage appears as one of the most visible markers of the re-appropriation of royal majesty', and robbery in particular was often presented as the work of the Devil.[54] Even if prosecutions for falsifying the coinage did not always lead to the kind of execution these crimes called for, namely being plunged into a cauldron of boiling oil or water before hanging, they nonetheless permitted the sovereign to define limits, to demonstrate his superiority over a judicial terrain which was too often divided into many parcels and to propagate the image of a prince who, alone, could invoke rigour or mercy as he saw fit. Thus, although the forger might threaten the ruler's majesty through his activities, he might just as easily consolidate it through the prince's visible reaction.[55] Similarly, the affair of the Companions of the Shell should have offered a particularly promising opportunity to demonstrate the legitimacy and power of the prince.

As we pull together the threads of this affair, two interpretations come to the fore. First of all, the town authorities, who reacted promptly to punish actors who mocked royal authority in 1447, did not show the same zeal when it came to putting an end to all kinds of crimes perpetrated by a gang which corroded the local economy and threatened public order and with it the authority of Philip the Good. Second, whereas in Arras it was prominent officers of the duke who attacked the witches and sorcerers, the latter were absent in Dijon, even though, as we have observed, falsifying the coinage was a crime of *lèse-majesté* and had indeed been the object of firm legislation by the duke, repeated in every meeting of the Estates.[56] Historians have tended either to focus on the production of legislative ordinances or to consider in isolation particularly scandalous cases scattered through the territories of the duke of Burgundy. As a result, they have neglected the lack of uniformity either in enforcement or in the expression of ducal authority. Taken together, these disparities suggest that, beyond simple opportunistic reflexes, there was no coherent strategy in the duke's policies which would have permitted the formation of a political ideology to impose his indisputable superiority. For a prince to exert power through majesty he had to create a political distance from his subjects which would enable him to overcome the spatial distance imposed by the extent of his territories. This was the path followed by Philip the Good's heir, albeit without avoiding a certain number of contradictions.

A conveniently flexible belief system: Charles the Bold and the League of the Public Weal

Flexibility was one of the essential qualities of these political words unburdened by genuine doctrines. The pretensions of Philip the Good were asserted in one context even as they were neglected in another. The reforming faith of John the Fearless crumbles away in the close examination of a Cabochienne ordinance which was certainly intended to enact an administrative purge, but was much less strict when it came to the fundamental reconfiguration of power relations. This programme contained no clear political provisions, since its purpose was to seize power, not to limit it. The idea of reform thus suffered an undeniable decline after 1420, only to return later in the form of intervention by the French state, for example in the 1454 ordinance of Montil-lès-Tours and in the perceptible concern to control public finances during these years in the kingdom of France.[57] Yet it was understood that, for the Crown, sovereignty was not shared with the masses, however reasonable they might be, and that the summoning of the Estates was only a lesser evil, when it was not equated with the crime of *lèse-majesté*.[58] Nonetheless, in 1465, the princes rebelled, presenting themselves as reformers who wanted to limit the power which they actually coveted, as in 1405 and 1413. Charles, at that time count of Charolais, joined this league of dissatisfied nobles, adopting in the process a vocabulary and an argumentative style which he quickly abandoned when it came to asserting his own sovereignty. Charles the Bold's behaviour, however, should not be interpreted in quite the same way as his father's and grandfather's. Charles's strategy, although seemingly identical, did not aim to achieve the same results. Unlike his grandfather, Charles did not want to occupy a privileged position in relation to the king of France. On the contrary, his policy was to weaken the latter in order to increase his own power.

'Before a year is out, he will regret it'

In a morality play which its editor, Joël Blanchard, has suggested can be dated to 1468, new allegories erupted on to the dramatic stage. The play's leading characters, Bien Public and Outrage, evidently support royal propaganda designed to win back public opinion after the military devastation and the diplomatic contortions which had marked the rebellion of the magnates against the tyranny of Louis XI:

LABOUR

> If Public Weal is not unified and perfect
> And the members are bitter and restive
> Not obeying their head, I declare to you:
> Labour is nought, and will not be done again
> And Outrage, which has done so much evil,
> Will come and cover us with blame ... (lines 193–198)[59]

As Labour puts it, with great wisdom, it is time for reconciliation, time to reunite around the king, the head of a body torn apart by the disobedience of Outrage (a.k.a. the rebellious princes), whose misdeeds still threaten the peace. In this political allegory, the principles of a strong monarchy are hammered home whilst the public weal can only be the result of a harmonious body politic governed by a single individual. Yet it was nonetheless in the name of the harmony of the endangered body politic that Charles, the king's brother, François II, duke of Brittany, Jean II, duke of Bourbon, Charles, count of Charolais, Jean, duke of Calabria, and then the duke of Nemours, the duke of Alençon, the count of Dunois and the rest came together in 1465 to put a stop to a despotic king who abused all his powers. The Burgundian chroniclers almost all present their lords, father and son, as joining a collective enterprise.[60]

> The said duke of Burgundy and the count of Charolais his son, loving with all their heart and desiring the good and the tranquillity of the kingdom and desiring the service and the pleasure of the duke of Berry ... agreed that a very large army be raised throughout the kingdom.[61]

In this short extract, Jean de Haynin does not fail to point out that blood lines obliged the family of Burgundy to protect a French kingdom threatened by a king unworthy of his office. It can be seen that, whilst John the Fearless went to the aid of a king harassed by the tyrannous influence of his intimates, Philip the Good and Count Charles decided to join princes who had suffered from the unchecked authority of Louis XI. Once more the duke and the count of Charolais publicly adopted the position of followers rather than initiators. It was from the obligations imposed on them by a duty of solidarity and fraternity towards their cousins that they were compelled to help a sickening kingdom, or at least that is what official chronicles kept repeating. After the appeal of the duke of Berry, Philip and Charles summoned the Estates General to Brussels for 25 April, when Pierre de Goux, on their instructions, read out the letter of the king's brother written at Nantes on 15 March. It was this which determined the duke's actions and justified the decision to raise an army under the command of Charles of Charolais, who was at the same time recognised as Philip the Good's legitimate heir.[62] A financial contribution was also demanded for the army, on the grounds that the duke intended to 'employ himself for the good and relief of the kingdom'. He took up the duke of Berry's argument, which described a kingdom in a piteous state, 'lacking order, justice, and policy',[63] where the poor people were exhausted and the brother of the king himself felt endangered. The duke's act was thus a simple reaction to multiple aggressions by the king. Philip the Good, through his son, was compelled to respond to such an urgent appeal. His honour was involved, and the security of lands was threatened by a king whose ambitions knew no limits.

Yet, for Philippe de Commynes, Charles of Charolais was no simple soldier acting out of filial obedience and family solidarity. On the contrary, he was in fact the originator of a full-blown plot designed to imperil royal authority. Commynes cites as evidence the half-concealed threats which Charles had made to the royal ambassadors, headed by Pierre de Morvilliers, when they came to complain about the count of Charolais's attitude in the affair of the Bastard of Rubempré. After a humiliating meeting, Charles was supposed to have said *sotto voce* to the archbishop of Narbonne, one of the French diplomats:

> Recommend me most humbly to the good grace of the King, and tell him that he has given me a good seeing to here through this chancellor, but before a year is out, he will regret it.[64]

Philippe de Commynes is careful to substantiate this alleged threat with a remark attributed to Louis XI: after the conflict was over, the king flattered the count of Charolais, saying that he was truly a gentleman of the House of France, since he knew how to express himself correctly even in his threats! Apart from this anecdote, we should remember that Charles had started to align himself with the duke of Brittany as early as the summer of 1463, when he concluded a secret alliance with him. He had also signed a treaty with Jean d'Anjou, duke of Calabria, on 10 December 1464, and had made overtures to the duke of Cleves, the king of Scotland and the duke of Bavaria amongst others.[65] We should not forget that Charles had many personal reasons to join the other princes of France. He had never received the pension of 35,000 francs promised by Louis XI, and he was determined to recover the Somme towns. As a first step, he had freed himself from the Francophile influence of the de Croÿ by denouncing them in his manifesto of 12 March 1465, forcing them to flee. It only remained to face down the king and so recover his possessions, including Péronne, Roye and Montdidier. These towns had been granted by Philip the Good to Jean de Bourgogne, count of Étampes, who had in turn gone over to the enemy in 1463 after having been accused of making wax images with the intention of hurting and threatening the life of Charles of Charolais. Vengeance was certainly amongst the count's motives for taking up arms.

Reformatio: *a political programme?*

It is clear that personal interests were not absent from a war justified by the desire to defend the public weal of the kingdom. It is true that the motivations expressed in different manifestos issued during the rebellion are quite vague, employing formulas which had become veritable commonplaces, so venerable was the desire to promote the *reformatio* of the realm.[66] The duke of Berry's manifesto of 26 March 1465 simply refers to the 'great calamity into which the public weal of the kingdom' had fallen. It asserted that 'justice is extremely wounded and crushed, that the people of the Church are oppressed' and that it is necessary 'to expel and repel these enemies of the public weal for the relief of the poor people'.[67] In the letter which he addressed to the inhabitants of the town of Amiens, the language becomes more precise, although without proposing a genuine programme of reform.

Working for the public weal, restoring justice, relieving the poor people of the many taxes which burden them, bringing order back to the kingdom by returning each and every one to the place which is reserved for him: who could disagree with these worthy goals? Many recent studies have demonstrated that the common good never ceased to provide matter for political arguments at the end of the Middle Ages. In the Great Principality of Burgundy, this concept notably took part in a discursive struggle between the duke and the towns, who each worked to defend 'their' common good. As elsewhere, the use of this commonplace of political language once again proves itself to be 'an excellent measure of the historical relationship between the state and the individual', to quote Pierre Monnet.[68] We know, moreover, that this renewed desire to reform the government would attract many imitators. Again in 1484, when the Estates met to discuss the regency of Anne de Beaujeu, a morality play gives voice to the man-in-the-street, affirming this powerful desire for change through the intervention of Reason, a key word in the political vocabulary of the period:

REASON

For this cause I have commanded
The kings, the princes and the dukes.
All the nobles have come here
To do reformation
And to put it in unity. (lines 320–324)[69]

Jacques Krynen has quite rightly noted that historiography has neglected the place of local notables in this conflict, those for whom the noble uprising was an opportunity for real change, those amongst the prominent burgesses and the judicial class, on the margins of a Parisian population which was loyal to the king, who risked plotting to deliver the capital to the Bretons or the Burgundians. It cannot be denied that 'prominent burgesses, university figures, churchmen, officials of the Châtelet, of the Parlement, of the chambers of account and of the city government took the side of the public weal'.[70] The monarchy, in the aftermath of this crisis, was obliged to move towards a new type of government involving deliberative assemblies with a right of expression which could seriously diminish the king's sovereignty. Even if Louis XI had no intention of keeping his promises, the letters ratifying the Treaty of Conflans dated 27 October 1465 implied a *regalis deminutio* or loss of royal dignity. The commission of the Thirty-Six (twelve ecclesiastics, twelve nobles, twelve notables) was given the responsibility for defending the public weal of the kingdom.[71] The royal office lost something of its sovereign substance.

Charles of Charolais fully adhered to a programme which threatened the full authority of the king of France. Nevertheless, it is necessary to distinguish several phases in the development of his position. In their first public declarations, the princes of Burgundy certainly manifested no desire to establish any kind of 'parliamentary' government in the kingdom of France, and indeed made no ideological argument. The defence of the public weal was simply a popular movement, at once profitable and unifying. Regarding the first alliances with the duke of Brittany and the duke of Bavaria, the terms of these treatises insist on the necessity of defending the ducal lands against the evil intentions of a badly counselled king. The alliance signed by the duke of Brittany built on a not inconsiderable premise when it came to theorise the defence of Breton and, by extension, Burgundian sovereignty. The two princes united their powers because it was their duty

> To maintain themselves and their principalities in obedience to God, and to increase and augment them in estate, virtue, magnificence and tranquillity, to which [end] each and every Prince and Lord must carefully attend and intend.[72]

As we can see, the princes' duty of obedience extended only to God. This declaration rings strangely when we remember the multiple declarations of fidelity made by the dukes of Burgundy to the king of France. It seems more than likely that, whatever the complaints of Charles of Charolais, the initiative for this provocation against Louis XI came from the duke of Brittany, whose political philosophy was far more coherent and complete.[73] Indeed, when the king abandoned many of his prerogatives first in the Treaty of Conflans and then in the Treaty of Saint-Maur, the duke of Brittany was the only rebel baron who did not recognise the authority of the Thirty-Six. François II had probably understood the considerable breadth of their powers and, out of a consistent concern to maintain its independence, did not want to submit his duchy to them.[74] The Breton duke's refusal can be situated in the context of a series of acts from the refusal of liege homage and of oaths under Jean IV to the ducal orders of 1480 which made the prince the natural protector of a common land where he could freely raise taxes and mobilise the army to resist those who threatened it. At the end of the fifteenth century, the duke of Brittany acknowledged 'no sovereign or creator who had made him duke or king except Almighty God'.[75] The position of the lands of the duke of Burgundy was not as clear. Indeed, by his acceptance of the Treaty of Conflans and the creation of the commission of Thirty-Six whilst recovering lands which Louis XI had bought from his father, the count of Charolais agreed that he would not cede from the kingdom of France and did homage for the towns he had recovered.

All that being so, in the War of the Public Weal, Charles had joined with those who criticised the tyranny of a king who was called upon to listen to his counsellors so as to govern his country justly and, of course, to satisfy the individual interests of each and every one of the princes who leagued against him.

From shared authority to 'united obedience'

Yet 1465 might also be regarded as the year in which Charles seized power in his father's principality. Even before Philip the Good's death two years later, contemporaries and historians agree that he had begun to put in place a new and ambitious political programme, marked by a kind of inflexible rigour, a love of regulation and a clear propensity for 'absolutism'.[76] We have already seen in the previous chapter how Charles managed to isolate himself from his nobility by dressing them down at meetings of the chapter of the Golden Fleece. Charles's desire to suppress all criticism was not limited to the armigerous class. In the famous speech which he made to the Estates of Flanders at Bruges in 1475, he made clear that, in his view of the world, everyone, ecclesiastics, knights and townspeople, ought to obey his orders without question.[77]

It has to be said that substantial changes in the art of governing had taken place. Chancellor Hugonet explained to the same Estates, summoned to Bruges in January 1473, that there were three forms of government, one of which took decisions through the community, another which placed its destiny in the hands of a virtuous aristocracy and a third based on the government of a single individual. He then went on to assert that 'amongst the three, the most useful, the most expedient and the most fruitful is that by a single prince'.[78]

The next chapter will consider the progressive development of this doctrine of sovereignty under the last Valois duke of Burgundy. For the moment, it is important simply to note that the desire to make the Estates General into a mere rubber stamp for ducal decisions had not always been dominant. Charles, count of Charolais, had been more diplomatic in his dealings with these same Estates in January 1464, when his rift with his father had seemed insoluble. The members of the Estates well understood that this family argument was very damaging for the government of the region. They spared no efforts to bring about a reconciliation which was absolutely necessary since Philip the Good was about to leave his lands to go on crusade. The representatives were essential go-betweens, and, when all options seemed closed, Charles appealed to them to encourage a meeting and to get the negotiations moving. In this family tiff, the defence of the interests of the state was taken on not by the princes but by the lord of Gruuthuse, the representative for Flanders, the lord of Berg, for Brabant, or the lord of Boussut, for Hainault, to name but three. Charles thanked them warmly for their vital assistance. The future would show how he expressed his gratitude!

When Charles took power, the desire to reinforce Burgundian power and to resist the threat from France was undeniable. The young prince's reading was dominated by an Augustinian world view in which the divine nature of the king's authority on earth was underlined. His relations with the duke of Brittany, who had for decades asserted his full and entire sovereignty, no doubt refined the count of Charolais's ambitions. All the same, the future duke could have sought to apply the mode of government which he pleaded for at the level of the kingdom and which would no doubt have particularly suited a region of towns whose political ideology repeatedly affirmed a natural taste for negotiation and deliberation. As Philippe Contamine reminds us, three political tendencies can be discerned at the end of the Middle Ages: the first, corresponding to government by Estates, was that which John the Fearless invoked in his Parisian propaganda; the second was absolutism; and the third, that favoured by the French monarchy, could be described as a monarchy 'regulated' by the machinery of justice, of accounting, of ordinances promulgated for many years and so forth.[79] The reformist ideology, which was pushed so far by John the Fearless as to make Pierre Cochon assert in his *Chronique normande* that 'Burgundy wanted the kingdom to be governed by the three estates', might have developed over the decades to become more than a simple demagogic formula by which the duke sought to crush his Orléanist enemies.[80] It might have led to a theory of state closer to the English than the French model. After all, the Estates General of the dukes' northern territories continued to pay for their wars. Charles's dream of a crown was perhaps not an immediately comprehensible aspiration for these northern representatives, but it seems very likely that it would have been well received by them if the would-be king had agreed to negotiate how his powers would be exercised and if he had accepted some sharing of decision-making powers. Yet for Charles the Bold, the public weal, in whose name he had fought and which he often invoked in his public declarations, had no Aristotelian basis, and, from this point of view, the prince could not be a mere representative of the community charged with serving the common good.[81] Rather his vision remained an Augustinian one, privileging a hierarchy in which the duke was a *dominus* with uncontested, indivisible and ultimately divine authority. Although, in contrast with his predecessors, the last duke of Burgundy had no desire to act as a mere support for the French monarchy, the model of royalty which that same monarchy had developed continued to inspire him. The adoption of a model of sovereignty so ill-adapted to the lands he ruled and their political culture undoubtedly impeded the construction of any Burgundian state.

Out of cunning, out of ambition, but sometimes simply out of a lack of consistency or coherence, as we saw with the *Vauderie* or with the Companions of the Shell, the dukes of Burgundy were disturbingly ambiguous in their political ideology, insofar as they can be said to have had one. A sense of incompleteness runs through the political ideology of these men and these lands, which successive historians have not succeeded in conjuring away by appealing to a kind of redeeming alternative history. Existing historical interpretations have tended to try to 'fix the frontiers, to recognise after the fact the winners and the losers'.[82] Such approaches might be divided between those for whom political opportunism is an effective weapon as part of a larger strategy and those for whom it can only lead inevitably to failure. But rather than concerning ourselves with such imponderables, it seems better to ask what this lack of coherence reveals. Does it suggest a morality ultimately dictated by the needs of action and the desire for victory, untroubled by principles of fidelity and integrity which are nonetheless put centre stage in discourse? Or does it suggest a defective ideological system or an incomplete political programme? Probably a little of both. Yet on the other hand, close observation of the ideological fluidity displayed by the dukes of Burgundy reveals a notable disjuncture between the words pronounced in one place and the acts committed in another, allowing us to understand a little better how and why they used the range of arguments they mobilised in the way that they did. The Kantian principle by which one must act according to a maxim which can become a universal law is not easy to reconcile with the reality of the political game. This vision of moral action leaves no place for opportunist reasoning, yet politics constantly puts intentions to the test of what can be done in the world and so requires constant creativity. The balance of interests was a constant in any political morality long before the Fronde and before Machiavelli theorised this principle. It would be naïve to upbraid the dukes for their cynicism and their demagoguery. Nevertheless, the distance between words and deeds, and the duplicity which they produced, certainly weakened the position of the dukes of Burgundy in the lands of their principality, making it difficult for their inhabitants to identify with these princes, who thought of themselves as the children of France. For some, if one had to serve the Valois Crown of the Valois, the allegiance to the king ought to have been automatic, and the pretentions of Charles the Bold were vain. For others, in their northern lands in particular, if one had to reject the kingdom so that the duchy could become a genuine state, the principles of government of the French monarchy also had to be put into question and a new model found. The ideas of reform propagated in Paris by the dukes of Burgundy, starting with Philip the Bold, could therefore have formed a powerful unifying basis for a population whose political culture encouraged them to a form of loyalism founded on deliberation and consultation. Commynes, whose analyses no doubt drew on his urban assumptions, himself agreed that there was nothing to fear from a well-constituted assembly of Estates which knew how to give advice without refusing the king what he needed.[83] Indeed, these princes demonstrated a lack of political intelligence when they failed to transform their political opportunism in one place into a welcome opportunity in another.

Notes

1. Monstrelet, *Chronique*, vol. I, pp. 115–119.
2. The literature about the civil war between Armagnacs and Burgundians is considerable. See, for example, B. Schnerb, *Les Armagnacs et les Bourguignons. La maudite guerre* (Paris: Perrin, 1988) and B. Guenée, *Un meurtre, une société. L'assassinat du duc d'Orléans, 23 septembre 1407* (Paris: Gallimard, 1992).
3. L. Mirot, 'L'enlèvement du dauphin et le premier conflit entre Jean sans Peur et Louis d'Orléans (juillet–octobre 1405)', *Revue des questions historiques* 95 (1914), 329–355, and 96 (1914), 47–68 and 369–419.
4. Quotations from C. Beaune, 'Les monarchies médiévales', in Y.-M. Bercé (ed.), *Les monarchies* (Paris: PUF, 1997), p. 195.
5. Examples in F. Autrand, 'La guerre des gens de finance en 1406 d'après le *Songe véritable*', in J. Kerhervé and A. Rigaudière (eds), *Finances, pouvoirs et mémoire. Hommages à Jean Favier* (Paris: Fayard, 1999), pp. 292–300.
6. G. A. Crapelet, *Les demandes faites par le roi Charles VI, touchant son état et le gouvernement de sa personne, avec les réponses de Pierre Salmon, son secrétaire familier* (Paris: Imprimerie de Crapelet, 1822), pp. 23–24.
7. For an analysis of Pierre Salmon's ideas, see A. Rigaudière, 'Le bon prince dans l'œuvre de Pierre Salmon', in *Penser et construire l'État*, pp. 497–516.
8. Jean Juvénal des Ursins, *Histoire de Charles VI*, ed. J. A. C. Buchon (Paris, 1843), p. 437.
9. C. Leveleux, 'Le lien politique de fidélité jurée (XIIIe–XVe siècle)', in A.-H. Allirot *et al.* (eds), *Une histoire pour un royaume (XIIe–XVe siècle). Hommage à Colette Beaune* (Paris: Perrin, 2012), pp. 197–217.
10. Section of the letter of Jean Chousat (receiver of accounts) to the members of the Chamber of Accounts in Dijon, 21 August 1405, ed. in L. P. Gachard, *Rapport à Monsieur le ministre de l'intérieur sur les documents concernant l'histoire de la Belgique dans les Archives de Dijon* (Brussels, 1843), pp. 104–105.

11 Quotations taken from J. Krynen, *Idéal du prince et pouvoir royal en France à la fin du Moyen Âge* (Paris: Picard, 1981), pp. 141–144.
12 Monstrelet, *Chronique*, vol. I, p. 119.
13 Juvénal des Ursins, *Histoire de Charles VI*, p. 437.
14 For an idea of the broad context, see F. Autrand, *Charles VI* (Paris: Fayard, 1986), pp. 384ff.
15 *Chronique du Religieux de Saint-Denis*, ed. L. Bellaguet, 6 vols (Paris: Crapelet, 1839–42), vol. III, ch. II, p. 29.
16 *Ibid.*
17 Scordia, *Le roi doit vivre du sien, passim.*
18 Autrand, *Charles VI*, pp. 386ff.
19 J. Dumolyn, *De Brugse opstand van 1436–1438*, Ancien pays et assemblées d'états 101 (Heule: UGA, 1997), pp. 129–143.
20 For the taxes on consumer goods and the tax policy of Philip the Bold more generally, see A. Van Nieuwenhuysen, *Les finances du duc de Bourgogne Philippe le Hardi (1384–1404)* (Brussels: Éditions de l'Université de Bruxelles, 1984), ch. IX, pp. 273–288.
21 J. Dumolyn, 'Une idéologie urbaine "bricolée" en Flandre médiévale: les *Sept portes de Bruges* dans le manuscrit Gruuthuse (début du XVe siècle)', *Revue belge de philologie et d'histoire* 88:4 (2010), 1039–1084.
22 See the ordinance of John the Fearless, 31 August 1408, ed. in W. Buntinx, 'De enquête van Oudenburg. Hervorming van de repartitie van de beden in het graafschap Vlaanderen (1408)', *Bulletin de la Commission Royale d'Histoire* 134 (1968), 91–94.
23 Wim Blockmans admits that, despite all these efforts, no fair tax system was imposed everywhere for all the orders of the society. W. Blockmans, 'Finances publiques et inégalité sociale dans les Pays-Bas aux XIVe–XVe siècles', in J.-P. Genet and M. Le Mené (eds), *Genèse de l'État moderne. Prélèvement et redistribution* (Paris: CNRS, 1987), pp. 77–90.
24 All these documents are edited in L. Gilliodts van Severen, *Inventaire des archives de la ville de Bruges*, 7 vols (Bruges: Imp. de E. Gailliard, 1871–78), vol. IV, pp. 114ff.
25 I agree with the conclusions of Autrand, *Charles VI*, pp. 408–409.
26 For more information about tax policy in the duchy of Burgundy, see H. Dubois, 'Naissance de la fiscalité dans un État princier au Moyen Âge: l'exemple de la Bourgogne', in Genet and Le Mené (eds), *Genèse de l'État moderne. Prélèvement et redistribution*, pp. 91–100.
27 Schnerb, *Jean sans Peur*, pp. 159–161.
28 É. Lecuppre-Desjardin, 'Par-delà la muraille. La conscience politique urbaine dans les anciens Pays-Bas bourguignons à l'épreuve de la politique extérieure', *Revue historique* 315:2 (666) (2013), 259–288.

29 W. Prevenier, 'Les perturbations dans les relations commerciales anglo-flamandes entre 1379 et 1407. Causes de désaccord et raisons d'une réconciliation', in *Économies et sociétés au Moyen Âge. Mélanges offerts à Édouard Perroy* (Paris: Publications de la Sorbonne, 1973), pp. 477–497.
30 Satirical tract edited in Du Clercq, *Mémoires*, vol. III, book IV, ch. XVI, pp. 81–84.
31 Full details of this affair can be found in *ibid.*
32 See F. Mercier, *La Vauderie d'Arras. Une chasse aux sorcières à l'automne du Moyen Âge* (Rennes: PUR, 2006), especially pp. 145–162. The author bases his argument on his observations of Flemish history.
33 L. P. Gachard (ed.), *Collection de documents inédits concernant l'histoire de la Belgique*, 3 vols (Brussels: L. Hauman, 1833–35), vol. II, pp. 96–111.
34 See Dumolyn and Haemers, 'Patterns of Urban Rebellion'.
35 Mercier, *La Vauderie d'Arras*, p. 187.
36 For more details of this conflict, see J. Haemers, *De Gentse Opstand (1449–1453). De strijd tussen rivaliserende netwerken om het stedelijke kapitaal* (Kortrijk: UGA, 2004), especially pp. 228ff.
37 See the text of the award made by the French royal ambassadors, 4 September 1452, in M. Boone, 'Diplomatie et violence d'État. La sentence rendue par les ambassadeurs et conseillers de Charles VII, concernant le conflit entre Philippe le Bon, duc de Bourgogne et Gand en 1452', *Bulletin de la Commission Royale d'Histoire* 156 (1990), 1–54.
38 For a clear explanation of the controversy, see the review of F. Mercier's book by R. Muchembled, *Revue belge de philologie et d'histoire* 84:4 (2006), 1186–1190 and the author's reply in the same journal, 86:2 (2008), 595–601.
39 H. Kruse, 'Les malversations commises par le receveur général Martin Cornille à la cour de Philippe le Bon d'après l'enquête de 1449', *Revue du Nord* 310 (1995), 283–312.
40 Chastelain, *Chronique*, vol. IV, book VI:1, ch. LXV, p. 470.
41 See F. Mercier, 'L'enfer du décor ou la Vauderie d'Arras (1459–1491): les enjeux politiques d'un procès d'inquisition à la fin du Moyen Âge', *Hérésis* 40 (2004), 95–121, at p. 120.
42 É. Lecuppre-Desjardin, 'Une simple agitation de surface? Evénement et festival de neige à Arras à l'hiver 1434–1435', *Le Moyen Âge*, forthcoming.
43 R. Rodière and A. de Loisne, *Épigraphie du département du Pas-de-Calais* (Fontenay-le-Comte: Commission départementale des monuments historiques, 1927), vol. VIII:2, pp. 856ff.

44 For the case of the bastard of Rubempré, see M. Prietzel, 'Rumeurs, honneur et politique. L'affaire du bâtard de Rubempré (1464)', *PCEEB* 48 (2008), 159–176.
45 See M. Boone, '"Le tres fort, vilain et detestable criesme et pechié de zodomie": homosexualité et répression à Bruges pendant la période bourguignonne (fin XIVe–début XVIe siècle)', in H. Soly and R. Vermeir (eds), *Beleid en bestuur in de oude Nederlanden. Liber amicorum prof. Dr. M. Baelde* (Ghent: Vakgroep Nieuwe Geschiedenis van de Universiteit Gent, 1993), pp. 1–17.
46 For the details of recriminations and the responses provided, see D'Escouchy, *Chronique*, vol. II, ch. CLI, p. 413.
47 V. Toureille, *Vol et brigandage au Moyen Âge* (Paris: PUF, 2006).
48 Details of the inquiry in V. Toureille, 'Une contribution à la mythologie des monarchies du crime: le procès des Coquillards à Dijon en 1455', *Revue du Nord* 89 (2007), 495–506. The author notes the composition and organisation of this band of criminals, but does not take into account the opinion of the urban authorities on those public disorders.
49 *Ibid.*, p. 501.
50 ADCO, BII, 360/6 quoted in V. Toureille, 'Voleurs et brigands au nord du Royaume de France à la fin du Moyen Âge (v. 1450–1550)', unpublished PhD thesis, Université Paris I, 2000, p. 392.
51 See M. Bouhaïk-Gironès, 'Le procès des farceurs de Dijon (1447)', *European Medieval Drama* 7 (2003), 117–134.
52 L. Petit de Julleville, *Répertoire du théâtre comique en France au Moyen Âge* (Paris: L. Cerf, 1886), pp. 330–335.
53 It should, however, be pointed out that in Dijon, the mayor administered low and high justice. Nonetheless, the duke could intervene in exceptional circumstances.
54 Toureille, *Vol et brigandage*, p. 253.
55 For details of the punishment of the boiling cauldron in the Great Principality, see J.-M. Cauchies, 'Faux monnayeur et justice du chaudron à Valenciennes (1438)', *Cercle archéologique et historique de Valenciennes. 1926–1976, Mélanges du cinquantenaire* (Valenciennes, 1977), pp. 81–93.
56 See P. Spufford, *Monetary Problems and Politics in the Burgundian Netherlands 1433–1496* (Leiden: Brill, 1970).
57 P. Contamine, 'Réformation: un mot, une idée', in *Des pouvoirs en France*, pp. 37–47.
58 Commynes, *Mémoires*, ed. Blanchard, vol. V, p. 19.
59 J. Blanchard, 'La *Moralité du Bien Public* (1468). Musée Condé ms. 685', *Bibliothèque d'humanisme et Renaissance* 70:3 (2008), 615–661.

60 A selection of Burgundian chronicles on this topic appears in J. Devaux, 'Les chroniqueurs bourguignons et la Guerre du Bien Public', in T. Van Hemelryck and M. Colombo Timelli (eds), *Quant l'ung amy pour l'autre veille. Mélanges de moyen français offerts à Claude Thiry* (Turnhout: Brepols, 2008), pp. 313–322.

61 Jean de Haynin, *Mémoires (1465–1477)*, ed. D. Brouwers, 2 vols (Liège: Cormaux, 1905–06), vol. I, p. 12.

62 See the letter of the duke of Berry and the different reactions among the members of the Estates General in J. Cuvelier *et al.* (eds), *Actes des États généraux des anciens Pays-Bas* (Brussels: Académie Royale de Belgique, 1948), pp. 108–128.

63 *Ibid.*, p. 127.

64 Commynes, *Mémoires*, ed. Blanchard, vol. I, pp. 8–9, and pp. 69–70 for Louis XI's response.

65 Vaughan, *Philip the Good*, pp. 376–377.

66 R. Cazelles, 'Une exigence de l'opinion depuis Saint Louis: la réformation du royaume', *Annuaire-bulletin de la Société d'histoire de France* (1962–63), 91–99.

67 Manifesto of the duke of Berry, 26 March 1465, in Philippe de Commynes, *Mémoires*, ed. Denis Godefroy and Abbé Lenglet du Fresnoy, 4 vols (Paris: Rollin, 1747), vol. II, pp. 438–439.

68 See Lecuppre-Desjardin and Van Bruaene (eds), *De Bono Communi*.

69 *La moralité des Trois États réformés par Raison* (Receuil Trepperel, 1484), printed c. 1510. I would like to thank Estelle Doudet for this reference.

70 J. Krynen, 'La rébellion du Bien Public (1465)', in M. T. Fögen (ed.), *Ordnung und Aufruhr im Mittelalter* (Frankfurt: V. Klostermann, 1995), pp. 81–97.

71 Letters of ratification for the Treaty of Conflans, in Commynes, *Mémoires*, ed. Godefroy and Lenglet du Fresnoy, vol. II, pp. 514–516.

72 *Ibid.*, p. 440.

73 On the idea of sovereignty in Brittany, see J. Kerhervé, 'Entre conscience nationale et identité régionale en Bretagne à la fin du Moyen Âge', in R. Babel and J.-M. Moeglin (eds), *Identité régionale et conscience nationale en France et en Allemagne du Moyen Âge à l'époque moderne (actes du colloque de 1993)*, Beihefte der Francia 39 (Sigmaringen: Thorbecke, 1997), pp. 219–243.

74 Commynes, *Mémoires*, ed. Godefroy and Lenglet du Fresnoy, vol. II, p. 542.

75 Alain Bouchard, *Les grandes croniques de Bretaigne*, III, 72, quoted in Kerhervé, 'Entre conscience nationale et identité régionale'.

76 I follow here the analysis of A. and W. Paravicini, 'L'arsenal intellectuel d'un homme de pouvoir. Les livres de Guillaume Hugonet, chancelier de Bourgogne', in Paravicini, *Menschen am Hof der Herzöge von Burgund*, pp. 143–208.
77 Ducal speech uttered on the occasion of the Estates General assembled in Bruges, 12 July 1475, in Gachard (ed.), *Collection de documents inédits*, vol. I, p. 258.
78 Speech delivered by Chancellor Hugonet, Bruges, January 1473, in Cuvelier *et al.* (eds), *Actes des États généraux*, pp. 179ff.
79 See Philippe Contamine's analysis in P. Contamine (ed.), *Le Moyen Âge. Le roi, l'Église, les grands, le peuple (481–1514)* (Paris: Seuil, 2002), pp. 421–423.
80 Pierre Cochon, *Chronique normande*, ed. C. Robillard de Beaurepaire (Rouen: A. Le Brument, 1870), p. 191.
81 See M. Kempshall, *The Common Good in Late Medieval Political Thought* (Oxford: Oxford University Press, 1999).
82 B. Gaïti, 'Les inconstances politiques', *Politix* 56 (2001), 17–42.
83 Commynes, *Mémoires*, ed. Blanchard, book V, p. 19, on the fiscal tyranny of bad kings.

4

The jewels in the crown

In a treatise ordered by Mary of Burgundy, soon after the death of her father Charles the Bold, to prove her legitimate rights to her inheritance, Jean d'Auffay explains how the dukes of Burgundy had obtained each of their territories, one after the other, and how these lands were naturally and legally theirs. Nonetheless, he could not avoid confessing that he was walking a political tightrope, claiming that he did not want to damage the kingdom of France:

> I do not want to consider the right of the Crown nor to support the English cause, because, against them, I am a good Frenchman.[1]

We would do well to remember that this lawyer in the service of Charles the Bold and his daughter, a former advocate of the Parlement of Malines and a native of Artois, is one of those whom historians have labelled as 'defectors' (*transfuges*) to the French camp. A little time after the negotiations which led to the Treaty of Arras in 1482, Jean d'Auffay gave in to the siren song of the French king and, after having received lands near La Bassée, joined Louis XI's camp. Nevertheless, it would be a mistake to imagine that behind these words he was already preparing to go over to the enemy. In this text, Jean d'Auffay apologised in conventional fashion for his rough language and lack of experience before going on to present his firm objective to defend, in law and by inheritance, the possessions of the heiress of Burgundy in the service of Mary and Maximilian and against the encroachments of the king of France. The declaration quoted above instead expresses a widespread feeling, one which we have already encountered without considering it in detail, which was shared by many nobles close to the prince. When this native of Artois revealed his deepest feelings, he said that he was not

Burgundian, but French. This attraction to the kingdom of his birth was largely shared by the duke's subjects, including the princes themselves, who, whatever their attitude towards the French Crown, never ceased to refer to it. From this natural link to a kingdom which, like a family, they could love or hate but never escape, the dukes inherited considerable power, but also a major handicap in their quest for sovereignty. As jewels in the French Crown, the dukes gained prestige and prominence from their position, but it also made it difficult for them to escape from their setting and to shine in their own right.

The children of France

Paul Bonenfant said of Philip the Bold that he never acted except 'as a prince of the *fleur-de-lys*', and that the policies of Philip the Good were those of a French prince.[2] The positions of the different specialists of the principality of Burgundy are well known, as are those of the schools of historians which were founded in their wake. The partisans of the Pirenne-Vaughan school argue that the Burgundian princes were very conscious that their political policies broke with their French origins, whilst others, such as Joseph Calmette, Eugène Desprez and Édouard Perroy in France, or Johan Huizinga in the Low Countries or Paul Bonenfant in Belgium, believed that the princes remained viscerally French and that their mentality made it impossible for them to conceive of constructing a sovereign, national state.[3] What can we add to all the ink that has been spilt analysing in detail all the dukes' diplomatic negotiations in which they asserted or denied their attachment to the House of France? In these learned discussions, arguments accumulate and sometimes contradict one another. Philip the Bold, who, as we have seen, spent more time in Paris than anywhere else and who was a prime mover behind French diplomacy, also had Waleran of Luxembourg declare before the Estates of Brabant that the arrival of his family in this territory would permit him and his son to have the same power as the kings of France or England.[4] John the Fearless, who was recognised as natural lord of his northern lands, and whom Vaughan presents as an independent diplomatic actor, weakened his position in these same lands in 1411 by sending letters supposedly written by Charles VI to raise troop levies in Ghent.[5] There seems no reason to doubt that these letters were genuine. In any case what seems most important about them is the elevated style which skilfully sought to convince the people of Ghent that the projected military campaign was not to be undertaken in the name of the duke of Burgundy and count of Flanders, but in that of the king of France. The Flemish were to serve not their immediate lord, but their sovereign, Charles VI.

When we consider events together, breaking through the historiographical specialisms which tend to sacrifice a general overview to the details of particular incidents, we can see that less than three months before Philip the Good founded the order of the Golden Fleece on 10 January 1430, the same duke had been granted, on 13 October 1429, the governance of Paris and the surrounding *bailliages*, hoping to regain thereby the pre-eminent place which he aspired to play in the kingdom of France. The Treaty of Arras of 1435 would deny him it once again. But Philip the Good applied incessant pressure on the French Crown, and when in 1448 Charles VII contested his right to adopt the style, assumed by the dukes of Brabant, of ruling 'by the grace of God', the Burgundian duke, in alliance with Charles of Orléans, whose release he had just secured, demanded that Charles VII summon them both to take part in the decisions of the government. Torn between his love for France and his dislike for its king, which reached its peak with the arrival of the Dauphin Louis in the Burgundian lands in 1456, Philip both continued to expand his territories and looked back nostalgically to a time when the duke of Burgundy had dominated the French royal council.[6] His project of going on crusade under the French banner confirms the power of this unrequited but sincere affection.[7] Charles, his son, absorbed these tensions and humiliations, and although the events of 1465 ended in the renewed submission of the House of Burgundy, as we have seen, Péronne and 1468 marked a new kind of policy removed from any relationship of feudal vassalage. It thus took more than a hundred years for these ties to loosen; ten years was not enough to create new ones.

But simply lining up all these political choices in a list conceived to serve as arguments for and against the construction of a Burgundian state risks leading us into the academic error of confusing the end of the story with the end of history. To understand the dukes' attitude, we need to return to principles which were still fundamentally active at the end of the Middle Ages, those of a House (*Maison*), of a dynasty, of a family, of patrimony, of honour. The project of constructing a state was not on the agenda; that of reinforcing a princely House was much more important.

Family matters

There was nothing incongruous or unproductive about the dukes of Burgundy drawing on their French blood to establish their authority. Behind this deep and lasting attachment to the king of France lay the fact that the dukes thought of the affairs of France as family matters and that serving the king was their supreme honour.

Although the fifteenth century is often considered a crucial moment in the foundation of bureaucratic states, it remained the case that political relationships did not yet function independently from private ties, and that the former were still imagined in terms of a model based on relations of kinship. From the style of Philip the Bold, which underlined that he was the son of the king of France, to the proclamations of Louis XI to his cousin Charles, whom he addressed as a brother, the language of kinship structured political relationships.[8]

Since the 1980s, medievalists have produced many high-quality studies of the links between kinship and power either in the context of royal houses or amongst the rural nobility and the urban bourgeoisie.[9] Nonetheless, the study of the later Middle Ages has only recently been touched by this development, thanks largely to the work of Michel Nassiet.[10] Indeed, the continuity of dynastic structures between the central Middle Ages and the sixteenth century makes it possible to imagine the exercise of authority in a framework, that of fidelity to a lineage in the broad sense of a cognatic kinship structure, which is markedly different from that of justice and governmental institutions, even if it does not explain everything about late-medieval kingship. Arguments in terms of broad horizontal kinship or ancient vertical kinship continually provided resources for the legitimation of power. This rhetoric was not only to be found in court chronicles, which never tired of demonstrating, by means of more or less legendary and sometimes chaotic genealogies, that the dukes of Burgundy were the worthy heirs of the Foresters of

Flanders, of the dukes of Brabant, of the dynasty of Hainault and so on.[11] Burgundian propaganda, whose subtlety we have already considered, never failed to link the power of their dukes to their place in a broad and high-quality kinship network.

In the *complainte* compiled after the death of John the Fearless (1419), its author invoked the great, noble figures of the duke of Burgundy's family, showing their broad spread throughout Europe. He listed them, one by one, like the alabaster figures around the ducal tombs: John's son, the count of Charolais; his mother, the countess of Flanders; his sisters, Catherine, duchess of Austria, Margaret, wife of William of Bavaria and countess of Hainault, and Mary, duchess of Savoy by her marriage to Amadeus VIII; his brothers, Antoine, duke of Brabant, and Philip, count of Nevers, who lamented from beyond the grave; his nephew Philip of Saint-Pol; and his daughter Margaret, wife of the duke of Guyenne.[12] In this conventional *complainte*, we can see the importance of marriage alliances created by the skilful matrimonial policy of Philip the Bold, which Richard Vaughan uses to argue that the father of the dynasty was consciously engaging in state construction, but which above all suggest the need to reconcile neighbouring powers by the traditional means of the exchange of women.[13]

Kinship with the House of France

It is clear that the first two dukes of Burgundy always asserted their authority through their kinship with the French monarchy. This stance not only served to provide political resources in struggles amongst the princes of the *fleur-de-lys* but also allowed John the Fearless to justify his actions by asserting that his ultimate goal was to defend the interests of a suffering king whose relative he was and whose power he thus sought to support. John the Fearless even argued in terms of the 'present good of the king', portraying himself as the humble servant of the latter in the Hesdin manifesto of 25 April 1417, which he sent into the distant territories of the Mâconnais and Auxerrois.[14]

The policies of the first dukes of Burgundy were constantly marked by the loud and forceful insistence on the blood of France which ran in their veins. The texts of lamentation which followed the death of the dukes up to Philip the Good provide further powerful examples. In her *complainte* on the death of Philip the Bold, Christine de Pizan invited all the people of France to weep for the good duke, uncle of the king.[15] This poetic vein was still very much evident in 1467, when the author of a *complainte* on the death of Philip the Good had the dying duke call on Louis XI and Charles of Charolais to live in peace and friendship:

> Adieu noble king of the French
> And all those of the *fleur-de-lys*
> Peace, riches and honour enough
> God of Paradise will grant you.
> Alas! be certain friends
> One to the other, without discord
> And if one of you has enemies
> The other is wrong to preserve them.[16]

This consciousness of common origins was not swept aside by John the Fearless's murder on the bridge at Montereau. The dukes' English alliance was never an alliance of hearts, and we should remember that, after the death of John the Fearless, Philip did not immediately throw himself into the arms of England. Burgundian propaganda was always careful to explain that the Treaty of Troyes was the unavoidable consequence of Philip's need to avenge himself for his father's murder. Indeed, as Paul Bonenfant long ago demonstrated, in the deliberations which followed the episode at Montereau, the counsellors of the young duke, including Henry Goethals, Athis de Brimeu and John de Roubaix, first thought to press Philip's rights to the crown of France after the death of Charles VI. The crown seemed within reach for a duke who had just been appointed lieutenant general of the kingdom. It was only under threat that Philip the Good abandoned his pretensions, when Burgundian ambassadors who were sent to Mantes on 26 and 27 October 1419 reported that the king of England would make war until death if Philip the Good dared to claim the crown.[17] Moreover, we must remember that the Burgundian alliance with Henry V was concluded with the assent of Charles VI and Queen Isabeau, who dissociated themselves from the dauphin.[18] As 'first vassal and liege man of the Crown of France', Philip accepted the English proposals, but only by 'the licence and leave of the king of France'.[19] We should also note that the Burgundian influence at the French court did not evaporate immediately after the assassination of John the Fearless, but rather after 1422, when Philip realised that the English promises were leading nowhere and that he had little influence on the government of France. In the years that followed, up to the Treaty of Arras, the alliance with England was not the most harmonious, and attempts at rapprochement with Charles VII punctuated Franco-Burgundian relations with repeated moments of hope and disappointment. How far such emotional manipulation could go is clear from Louis XI's request to his representatives in Rheims to offer the keys of the city to Philip the Good because, he said, he thought of him as his father and owed him everything.[20] Of course, this declaration was not at all sincere, but it did work within a system of rhetoric based on the invocation of traditional family loyalties.

This fundamental social link was to be found at every level of power, from the favours of the *bailli* Jean Parmentier to his family around Douai, from the client networks of the great court princes to the dukes themselves. Fidelity was above all something one owed to one's kinsman. Burgundian political construction thus followed the hazards of hereditary transmission. In 1361 King John II recovered the duchy of Burgundy as a close kinsman of Philip of Rouvres, duke of Burgundy, and by inheritance. In the same way, he granted it to his son, Philip the Bold, not as an appanage, but as a fief, being more concerned with rewarding a beloved son than with the possible future division of his kingdom.[21] There is no contradiction between Philip the Good's determination to gain new territory by conquering Hainault and his intention, expressed in his will, to divide his lands between his three sisters in the case of his death without heirs. Once again, kinship alone guided his choices. Indeed, he justified his involvement in the succession to Hainault by the fact that he was a cousin of John IV of Brabant and of Jacqueline of Bavaria, which legitimised his military intervention and his rights of inheritance. As for the will of 1426, there is little difference between the arrangements he made there and those generally to be found amongst the nobility.[22] If Philip the Good had died without an heir, his eldest sister, Margaret, countess of Richmond, would have received the duchy of Burgundy; Mary, duchess of Cleves, would have had the title of countess of Flanders and Namur; Anne, duchess of Bedford, would have inherited, along with Hainault, Holland and Zeeland, the county of Artois (as was indeed stipulated in her marriage contract); and finally Agnes, countess of Clermont, would have received a number of lordships as well as the county of Burgundy. Philip was not culturally inclined to think of his lands as an indissoluble whole, even if in the clause dealing with his death without direct heirs he attempted to arrange matters so as to preserve groups of lands 'so that my said land of Burgundy should be and remain joined together as it has been for a long time'.[23] As Philippe Godding notes, building on the remarks of Jean de Terre Vermeille, 'there was not yet, as in France at the same time, a concern to maintain the territorial integrity of the state'.[24] The latter was guaranteed only by the birth of his legitimate son Charles, which enabled Philip to modify his will in 1441, putting in place a council of thirteen to act as the regents of lands which, now that he had a male heir, would remain together. The re-establishment of political divisions was thus imaginable on the basis of a culture which favoured the identification of family and patrimony rather than a separation between prince and state.

This privileged link with France was a central regulating principle in the court practices described by Eleonore of Poitiers in a little book under the title rendered by Jacques Paviot as 'Estates of France' (and not 'The Honours of the Court'), and was reinforced further by the honour of this double peerage for the duchy of Burgundy and the county of Flanders.[25]

The dukes, peers of France

When John II granted the duchy of Burgundy to Philip the Bold, he made him a peer of France. As Philippe Contamine reminds us, the institution of the peers of France, which drew on Carolingian epic legend, 'shows clearly enough the feudal and aristocratic character of the French monarchy, but also the will of that same monarchy to bring together all the different components of the kingdom of France in the last centuries of the Middle Ages'.[26]

The honour of the double peerage

Some readers might be surprised by the choice of the quotation which follows, but the importance of the institution of peerage as it is described in the Act of Courtrai of September 1297 remained relevant for the Valois dukes of Burgundy:

> It pertains to the honour and glory of kings and of kingdoms that remarkable men should be placed at the head of pre-eminent offices to direct the affairs of royal power, that renowned persons should be preferred for illustrious dignities, that they should rejoice in their names thus emblazoned with magnificent honours, that the cares of government should be lightened by the presence of comparable helpers and that by the strength of peace and justice the foundations of all kingdoms might be preserved more profitably thanks to a more efficient administration.[27]

This passage asserts that the king of France could count on the unfailing support and aid of his peers. When Charles V inherited the crown, the *Livre du sacre* transcribed the peers' oath, by which they swore to be good, loyal and obedient to the king of France and his successors, a not dissimilar promise to that which Philip the Bold was supposed to have extracted from his sons on his death bed. It has to be said that the association of the honour of a peer of France with the rights claimed in the *Coutumier de Bourgogne* at the end of the fourteenth century considerably reinforced the position of the duke of Burgundy with regard to the king, since in this text the duke became an irreplaceable buttress of the monarchy: 'The land of Burgundy makes the lord of it foremost peer of the king of France.' As the first peer of France, he was the one who must intervene to decide in any potential conflict between the king and the other peers.

This privileged position evidently provided material for the dukes' political arguments according to their needs and ambitions. In 1415 John the Fearless affirmed that his title of doyen and peer was the 'first prerogative, nobility and dignity which by reason of lordship should be in the kingdom after the Crown'. In 1419, in the midst of deliberations concerning the appropriate attitude to take to the pretensions of Henry V over the kingdom of France, some counsellors reminded the young duke 'that by reason of being doyen of the peers of France', he ought to summon the peers and the Estates to consider 'the case of the king and how the business of the kingdom should be disposed'.[28] In 1445, in order to impose his authority over his own nobility, during a chapter meeting of the Order of the

Golden Fleece in Ghent, the duke, according to Olivier de la Marche, was preceded by two sergeants-at-arms 'carrying maces emblazoned first with the arms of the king of France and then with his own'.[29] As tensions mounted and Charles VII sent Richard Olivier de Longueil, bishop of Coutances, to Philip the Good to remind him of his duties to the Crown, his homily insisted on the 'closeness of lineage' between the duke and the king, on his status as a vassal and on the necessity of loving the king and serving him as a peer of France, as duke of Burgundy and count of Flanders.[30] Although the editor of that text believes that the invocation of lineage, of peerage and of the position of a subject and vassal was relatively unimportant in a speech which aimed to prove the necessity of absolute obedience to the king, it seems to me that, on the contrary, the ambassador's discourse proceeds in a traditional fashion by accumulation in order to convince. The crown of France supported by the twelve peers of France is worn by a king to whom 'firstly, my lord [Philip the Good] and the other princes should be joined and thus united together in friendship and perfect union'. After having been developed at length, the duke's qualities are invoked twice more in the conclusion, first in a full and then in a simplified form.

Although, as Philippe Contamine notes, the moral and political force of such a discourse tied, or at least tried to tie, the duke of Burgundy to the kingdom,[31] I am not sure that this would necessarily have displeased him, or that he really wanted to pursue an independent course.

1461: year of disappointed hopes

As George Chastelain tells it, it was in 1461, with the death of Charles VII and the consequent end of any residual enmity over the death of John the Fearless, that Philip the Good enjoyed his finest hour.[32] The duke was full of hope. The oath he took for his lands in the kingdom of France demonstrated that the exemption from homage obtained from Charles VII in the Treaty of Arras of 1435 was not a purely political move, but was also the symptom of a personal animosity.[33] All through the triumphal procession of the new king of France, Philip played a pre-eminent role. His escort was of a magnificence typical of the Burgundian dukes. The keys of the city of Rheims were delivered into his hands. The last to leave the king in his lodgings, he was the first to meet him again on the morning of his consecration. In royal attire, as the doyen of the peers, Philip entered the cathedral with the holy ampoule of coronation oil. As the master of ceremonies, he stripped the king to the waist to prepare him for unction, then dressed him again in the clothes of the *fleur-de-lys*. The twelve peers of France guided the king to the throne and then, when all the others withdrew, the duke of Burgundy remained with him as the coronation proceeded.[34]

Over these few days Philip repeatedly affirmed his French identity, by the gifts he gave to Louis XI, by the financial support he provided for this ceremony, by his renewed declarations of friendship and by his submission to royal sovereignty, but also by the proximity he sought from his eminent kinsman. He had put 'his heart and his will' into this demonstration.[35] This makes it easier to understand the extent of Philip's disappointment with Louis XI's attitude in the months that followed. Back in Paris at the end of August 1461, we might say that Philip had at last reached the end of his search for lost time, he who had wandered 'in the forest of long waiting'.[36] The duke of Burgundy could renew the link to his past, to his youth. How else can we interpret the passage in Chastelain's chronicle where, tired of waiting for his horse to go to a tournament, Philip, who was by then sixty-five years old, jumped on to his niece's hackney and paraded with her through the streets of Paris, which rang with pleasure at the sight of a prince who was so faithful to chivalric culture.[37] Refusing to stay at the Hôtel de Saint-Pol, he instead stayed at the Hôtel d'Artois, which was then in a pitiful state but stood in the middle of the central Halles quarter. Burgundian magnificence returned to Paris as Philip laid on the kind of sumptuous banquets which had been organised at the time when the *Ménagier de Paris* had compared the different princely tables of the city. The duke hosted a memorable joust and enchanted the Parisian evenings with light, dancing, music and wine. Chastelain continued to play on the theme of family reunion, asserting that the nobles assembled in Paris saw in Philip 'the honour of France, ... the most redoubtable strength of the kingdom'.[38] But lost time proved elusive. Louis abandoned his uncle and his cherished illusions, offering a few prestigious posts to Burgundian lords with the aim of winning them over in the future, and prepared himself for the cynical exercise of exclusive power.

A number of things are worth noting here. First, it is clear that, for the third duke of Burgundy, after years of civil war and of extreme tensions with the kingdom of France, after decades of unprecedented territorial conquests, which made the Great Principality of Burgundy the most flourishing principality of Europe, Philip's attachment to the Valois Crown was still as strong as ever. His dream remained that of his father and his grandfather: to occupy the first place by the king's side, the better to serve and to be acknowledged as the most powerful of the feudal princes of the Crown of France.[39] Of course, one might object that the story told above is too reliant on the work of Chastelain, a Francophile writer if ever there was one, who does not hesitate to exaggerate the facts to suit his purpose. But we should not forget that Chastelain does not simply express his own personal opinion in his chronicle. Rather, as when he criticised the attitude of Charles the Bold when he cursed Louis XI before the French ambassadors at Saint-Omer, he stands as the spokesman of a broader group, of 'political society'. The Burgundian chronicler speaks, on this occasion, with his master's voice, which was not, for that matter, isolated. His writing projects the hopes, the ambitions, the disappointments of a prince who is still described as much in the prologue of Chastelain's chronicle as in his political works as the 'honour of the world and the ornament of France'.[40]

Real or imagined, the events which Chastelain describes express the natural allegiance of Burgundy to France which existed before Charles the Bold rejected it and before Mary of Burgundy, in her distress as an abandoned heiress, supplanted it with the *foy de Bourgogne*.[41] Yet, as sharp as change had been under Charles, the strength of old fidelities could still be felt. Ancient reflexes co-existed with the temptations of the new. Thus at the time of the War of the Public Weal, in Dijon, a number of inhabitants thought that Charles was acting truthfully, which might give the illusion of a duke recognised as an independent prince capable of defending Burgundy as a sovereign state against anyone who might attack it. Yet the argument they advanced suggests otherwise. The Burgundy which these men defended went no further than the limits of the duchy itself, not those of the duke's wider principality. Charles was in the right in making war against the king because he acted in agreement with the other peers to distance Louis XI from the temptation of tyranny:

> [He] did not blame the king, but the twelve peers and lords of the royal blood of France complained of him, and wanted to tell him that he did not govern the kingdom of France in the way he had promised.[42]

This was why, just as Jean d'Auffray had no desire to damage royal interests, so the people of Dijon were clear that 'we do not want to make war on the king nor to take what is his nor to do any ill'.[43] Similarly, when battles raged across the Burgundian lands between 1470 and 1475, a wine-maker declared, 'My lord of Burgundy does too many things; no good will come of it and none can come of it, because despite appearances, he is subject to the king of France.'[44] It was difficult in these circumstances for Mary of Burgundy to make a convincing riposte to the letters of Louis XI, which had reminded Dijon as early as 9 January 1477 that it pertained to the kingdom and the Crown. When the young princess wrote to the president of the duchy and county's Parlement, Jean Jouard, as she did as early as 23 January, asserting once more that ducal Burgundy was not an apanage, he simply suppressed the letter.[45] In a way, the fact that this territory brought with it the peerage of France condemned it to remain part of the kingdom, never to escape from the 'zone of lineal obligations' defined by Marc Bloch. Although the declaration of the customs of Burgundy, in which 'The land of Burgundy makes its lord into a peer of the king of France', placed the duke of Burgundy in a community of equals with the king, it also consecrated as natural the relationship between the duke and the kingdom.[46]

The perilous power of the peerage was well understood by the dukes of Brittany, leading them gradually to put it to one side as they asserted their sovereignty. As early as 1336, the duke of Brittany claimed that he was superior to the other peers because his territory had not been split off from the kingdom but was itself a former kingdom. Although the Treaty of Guérande of 1381 re-established John IV as a duke and peer, Peter II, at the time of the inquiry of 1455 into the 'royal rights and ancient usages of the country of

Brittany', explicitly refused the dignity of a peer, which he considered less as an honour than as an additional means of putting him under pressure.[47]

The dukes of Burgundy certainly knew how to take advantage of their French cultural heritage. Yet these borrowings from the administrative and political models of the French kingdom spread through the whole territory a set of usages which led Chastelain to declare that Philip the Good was an 'ornament of France', and this guided the pen of Eleonore of Poitiers when she honoured the 'estates of France' at the court of Burgundy and allowed one of Duke Charles's officers in the territory around Namur to justify his conduct by the words: 'this is the usage in France'.[48]

'The most illustrious and splendid house of the lord and duke of Burgundy'

Before turning to the delicate question of sovereignty, we need to deal with one last concept which could potentially have contributed to the construction of a political abstraction and worked as a unifying force in the Burgundian lands. For although the dukes of Burgundy were princes of the blood and peers and vassals of the king of France, they were also at the head of the House of Burgundy, an expression often employed by the historians of the principality and which we will use here too.

A House of Burgundy issuing from the House of France

If we follow the criteria established by Claude Lévi-Strauss, a 'house' can be defined as an abstract entity, possessing a domain composed of material and immaterial goods, perpetuated by transmitting a name, a fortune or titles. This transmission is held to be legitimate either because it passes through a direct line or a 'fictive' one. In either case it is expressed in the language of alliance and kinship. A material or spiritual inheritance can be associated with the house, a dignity, illustrious origins, symbols, power, riches and so forth.[49] All these criteria perfectly fit the reality of the power of the Valois dukes of Burgundy. The term 'house' (*maison*) might thus be thought to provide a practical solution to denote the territorial complex centred on its princes. Yet recent work by Jean-Marie Moeglin has suggested we need to be careful of the semantic ambiguity inherent in this expression and the interpretative slippages which this encourages. For if 'house' (*domus*) was a term employed to denote a lineage, a family of the upper aristocracy, it could also be used to denote the existence of a political entity linking a chief, a territory and a community of inhabitants. When German chroniclers invoked the *Haus zu Bayern* or the *Haus zu Österreich*, they evoked an organic unit, a community of responsibilities linking the prince and its inhabitants, the result of a long evolution in which the title of the prince is in some ways incidental.[50] If we compare this with the Burgundian sources, we see that the term 'house' appears only late on in the works of court encomiasts. Thus in the prologue to the *Mémoires* of Olivier de la Marche, the writer adopts a genealogical approach which seeks to explain to the young Philip the Fair the exceptional character of his double descent:

> For by way of introduction, I intend to show you from which houses you are descended and by the same means how you have succeeded to many of their lordships.[51]

The work of *memoria* was at the heart of this writer's approach. It is important to note that he is always careful to associate lordships with the house, proving thereby that the former was not identical to the latter. In a more lyrical tone, but in the same spirit, Jean Molinet evoked 'the most illustrious and splendid house of the lord and duke of Burgundy, magnificently founded on the summit of the mountains'.[52] The description of ducal origins which he associates with this term and which, once again, returns to the common, French, trunk proves that, for Molinet, living at the end of the rule of Charles the Bold, the name of House of Burgundy designated only the particular excellence of a lineage. Moreover, Philip the Bold was not the only one to have been raised in the garden of the *fleur-de-lys*, since 'the four pillars (i.e. the four dukes) descend from the lily field by direct line of royal propagation'.[53]

It has to be said that Chastelain led by example. When the term 'house' appears in the prologue of his chronicle – it is the 'sacred French house' (*sacrée maison françoise*) that is in question – Chastelain asserts that he wants to tell the story, not of the individual glory of the prince, but of 'the sacred French house of which he is a part and of which he knows that he has received all its dignity and splendour'.[54] For him, the house also meant the restricted circle of the court, of family extended to include friends and well-wishers. This can be seen in the *Hauts faits du duc Philippe* when he refers to the divisions which 'at the end of his days entered his house for petty reasons'. Chastelain explains that Philip was able to contain these divisions, and so preserve his family, holding together 'the pillars of his house and estate and the roof of his edifice without ruin'.[55] The same meaning is found in the *Advertissement au duc Charles* when, disabused by Louis XI's broken promises, Chastelain can think of no better way of preserving his prince's territories, and preventing the House of Burgundy from being trodden down by the hatred of the French, than a change of generation in the kingdom of France.[56] The recurrent image of a family equated with a building supported by sturdy pillars allows Chastelain to bring in the vocabulary of destruction.

Nonetheless, we should be wary of jumping to the conclusion that he wanted to suggest thereby a territory or a community of subjects which would occupy this edifice. This terminology is not to be found in treaties of alliance, for example between Charles the Bold and the duke of Brittany, the king of Scotland or the count palatine of the Rhine, which were concluded on every occasion between two princes, even if their aim was to protect lands, subjects and lordships.[57] In a large number of chanceries at the end of the Middle Ages, the adoption of the formula *inter reges et regna* ('between kings and kingdoms') made it possible to go beyond a personal alliance to include territories and their people in these treaties, even if the latter were still founded on friendships between princes.[58] In the case of Burgundy, however, the atomisation of the principality made it impossible to include such a phrase, and instead made it necessary to distinguish between different subjects, lands and lordships, sometimes even reciting the litany of territories in Burgundian obedience without the term 'house' being used. In some of these texts it is even specified, for example, that the agreement was made between, on the one hand, the count of Charolais and the territories under the authority of his father and, on the other, the king of Scotland.[59]

We might have expected this language to become more precise in the work of someone like Guillaume Hugonet. However, although

Hugonet's political thought is particularly subtle, a certain ambiguity remains. In his famous speech delivered at Bruges in January 1473 to the Estates, which had been summoned to provide support for a large army, Hugonet spared no pains to establish the reciprocal links between the prince and his subjects. In his argument, the House of Burgundy was invoked to remind his audience that the duke's lands had been brought together without violence under the same glorious name of the House of Burgundy.[60] Recalling, like Chastelain, the division and the discord that the presence of the dauphin Louis had caused this house, his speech becomes more political when the duke's territories are linked with it, when they are invoked as the foundation of the power of this noble house.

In the absence of a mystical body, a powerful dynasty

In Hugonet's harangue, this territory takes on a structuring political dimension for all subjects only in the expression '*chose publique*, rightly and naturally submitted to the excellent and resplendent House of Burgundy', a house whose family name apparently did not have enough power to unite its disparate components.[61] Time was needed to build the loyalty of a people and to lead it to feel a sense of belonging to a political entity which took in all these different territories. Because the Great Principality of Burgundy did not have a very long history, it was not yet possible to make claims such as those made by an officer of the Parlement of Poitiers in 1420 in his *Réponse d'un bon et loyal François* ('Reply of a good and loyal Frenchman') for whom the Crown and the kingdom of France could not be transferred to Henry V of England because, amongst other reasons, the honour of the *fleurs-de-lys* was not only that of the royal family but also that of the three Estates of France.[62]

Thus, just as the kings of France reinforced the idea of their dynastic lineage by establishing their eternal resting place at the abbey of Saint Denis, so the Burgundian family sought to strengthen its power through the notion of a dynasty manifested in their last resting place, the Chartreuse de Champmol. But the renown of the Crown of France remained even when the literary tradition of allegory made it possible to separate France from its ruler, giving it political autonomy, as in the *Tragicum argumentum* of François de Montebelluna (1357), when the author addresses France in the context of the capture of John II, saying: 'The king's capture, O France, engenders your perpetual shame, his perpetual glory.' The strictly dynastic vision of the Burgundians, by contrast, left no place for a house in a sense which might tend towards a 'transpersonal reality', as Jean-Marie Moeglin puts it,[63] which could compete with the symbolic power of the Crown.

If the concept of the common weal or *chose publique* could take on this role for Charles the Bold or his counsellors, the superior reality which it needed to embody was not so obvious, even for someone like George Chastelain. Indeed, the two texts which Chastelain composed on the deaths of Charles VII and Philip the Good show how the House of Burgundy continued to be imagined from a strictly dynastic point of view. Whilst the king's funeral dramatised 'the mystery of the perpetuity of a single political body', that of the prince simply marked the transfer of power from one natural body to another. The recent work of Estelle Doudet, based on a close comparison between *La mort du roi Charles VII*, written in 1461, and *La mort du duc Philippe, mystère par maniere de lamentacion*, composed on the orders of the townspeople of Valenciennes for the formal entry of Charles the Bold into Mons in 1468, demonstrates with great subtlety the absence of a *corpus mysticum* in Burgundian ideology.[64] In the play dedicated to Philip the Good, the author shows the human race (represented by Les Hommes) searching, between earth (La Terre) and heaven (Le Ciel et Les Anges), for the absent body of the duke, whose disappearance endangers the political stability of the principality. The question of dynastic continuity is central in this text. In *La mort du roi Charles VII* (1461), by contrast, the mystical body of France provides continuity without any need for Louis XI to be introduced to guarantee the survival of the kingdom. Yet in *La mort du duc Philippe* it is the presence of the heir which fills the political vacuum left by the death of the prince:

HEAVEN

God has ordained another
To reign as well as he.
For a man who is lacking,
The world will not go to nothing;
When one goes, another comes.
...
Thus one comes from father to son.[65]

As Estelle Doudet notes, 'although the principality is ruled by legitimate and powerful dukes, Burgundy, an area of multiple and sometimes contradictory identities, was not embodied in a political body'.[66] In these circumstances, and after the foregoing discussion of their vigorous attachment to feudal principles, it might seem odd to return to the desire for sovereignty. Nonetheless, the Burgundian principality once more provides us with an apparent paradox in the quest for the superior authority to be found by acquiring undisputed sovereignty. Already half-expressed under Philip the Good's rule, often confused with a taste for royal majesty, it became an explicit objective only for the last 'pillar of the family'.

Sovereignty and the temptation of unlimited power

When Charles the Bold came to Saint-Omer on 24 April 1469 to perform the acts and pronounce the words which necessarily accompanied a Joyous Entry, the town archives recorded the abruptness with which he replied to the magistrates who had come to hear the confirmation of their privileges, with Charles stating simply that he would have these privileges inspected now and in the future by his chancellor. This was not the only occasion on which he showed such an attitude. I have considered elsewhere how the tone changed in the oaths exchanged between Charles and his towns in the course of the inauguration ceremonies at the start of his rule. From modification of the Douai text, which inverted the order of precedence, to the insult paid to the citizens of Mons, whose town clerk the duke cut off in mid-recital with an impatient 'That's enough!', it was obvious that the new duke wanted to free himself from the mutuality inherent in the exchange of rights and duties of a feudal type which might limit his power.[67] This new approach was also seen in the speeches delivered by Charles or his counsellors to assemblies of Estates which affirmed, occasionally but forcefully, an unfulfilled desire for sovereignty.

Another Burgundian will-o'-the-wisp?

Every historian of the Burgundian principality has, at one time or another in their career, had to deal with the delicate question of

Burgundian sovereignty, often from the restricted point of view of the ambitions of Charles the Bold. Amongst them, A. G. Jongkees, W. P. Blockmans and Werner Paravicini have contributed to the substantial file on what looks suspiciously like a Burgundian will-o'-the-wisp, such is the level of contradiction and hesitation around what was supposed to be an ultimate goal of the duke.[68] Indeed, the most recent publication on the question seems to show, through the accumulation of evidence of the recurrence of this notion at court, in the Burgundian administration or in Charles's thinking, that we are here dealing with an unformed ideology, fragile in its foundations until the relatively late date of 1473.[69] The letters written in Charles's own hand, the extracts from accounts and from the proceedings of the Estates, the oaths and so forth seem to follow a distinctly uncertain trajectory.

Let us take a few steps back. In the absence of a clear definition before Jean Bodin, the notion of sovereignty, like many key concepts from this period, must be understood in relation to other principles of government such as majesty, *lèse-majesté*, authority and the perception of authority. The last of these raises two problems already. The first problem is a matter of semantic ambiguity; the second concerns the position of the dukes of Burgundy with regard to other rulers. In other words, how did they envisage the sovereignty which should have made them subject to the king of France and the emperor? How did they construct an alleged sovereignty which established them as ultimate lords in the eyes of their own subjects? To simplify struggles for symbolic power which can often be disconcerting in their subtleties, it is best to deal with the evidence one step at a time.

Before Jean Bodin formulated a theory of sovereignty based essentially on the power to legislate and the capacity to enforce the law without being subject to it, such famous principles as *Princeps legibus solutus est* ('Prince is not bound by the law') and *Quod principi placuit legis habet vigorem* ('What pleases the prince has the force of law'), although not fully active, nonetheless provided resources for authority which, if not fully consistent, were at least occasionally effective.[70] If the first mark of sovereignty is 'the power to make law to all in general and to each individually without the consent of one greater, nor equal, nor lesser', then the creation of the Parlement of Malines in 1473, with the aim of removing the duke's subjects from the procedure of appeal to the Parlement of Paris, appears to have been the first true manifestation of sovereignty by the dukes of Burgundy.[71] The idea was not entirely absent before this date, but, like the term 'house', it had exhibited a semantic ambiguity. For many men of the end of the Middle Ages, the word 'sovereign' was not restricted to the language of law but simply denoted the superiority of any leader, whether this meant the head of a military unit, a local administrative official, a prince or a princess.[72] It is this which explains how the marshal of Burgundy, Thiébaud de Neufchâtel, could address Isabella of Portugal in 1445 as 'his most feared and sovereign Lady' ('sa tres redoubtée et souveraine Dame').[73] This term of address, which is to be found in Chastelain, Olivier de la Marche and the correspondence of urban magistrates of the Franc of Bruges and even of Ghent, was used in both the duke's northern and southern lands. But was the political potential of this adjective ('sovereign') fully realised at the moment it was used? The answer cannot be categorical, for the simple reason that medieval society cannot be imagined as a monolithic block with a uniform level and type of education. It is clear that in 1467, when the king of France and his lawyers waxed indignant at the absence of the formula which implied the duke's acceptance of royal sovereignty, the word was charged (for them) with all the inheritance of Roman law developed since at least the thirteenth century.[74] But when the marshal of Burgundy used it to address the princess, it seems reasonable to imagine that this was intended simply as an honorific term, one which sought to underline the prestige of the duchess in the eyes of her servant. Outside the circles of jurists and eminent counsellors, the formula could simply denote a superior power without being concerned with the potential it had to subvert royal majesty. This was not so, however, for princes who, tempted by this crucial card in the game of European state construction, flirted for a long time with this denomination, before finally throwing in their hand.

Even Charles the Bold was hesitant. On 19 June 1467, when he announced the death of his father to the king and promised his good will to him in the future, the duke addressed Louis XI as his 'redoubted lord' (*redoubté seigneur*), but did not explicitly refer to the king as his sovereign, even though he signed himself 'Your most humble and most obedient subject Charles, duke of Burgundy and of Brabant'. The form of this letter shocked the king, who had it filed carefully in the royal archives, probably for use later as proof of the duke's *lèse-majesté*. We might have imagined that Charles would have cut his links with the king of France by denying his status as vassal to his lord. Yet in the autograph letters which follow, the terms of address are unstable, as for example on 2 July 1467, when Charles returned to the following form of address: 'To my most redoubted and sovereign lord my lord the king' ('A mon tresredoubté et souverain seigneur monseigneur le roy'). There is no need to return here to the list of such examples cited by Werner Paravicini; it is enough to remark that in his relations with Louis XI, the reference to royal sovereignty seems most often to be an index of the duke of Burgundy's varying mood, to be located once more in the register of personal relations. Just as Philip the Good had succeeded in avoiding giving homage to Charles VII for personal reasons, whilst still recognising the sovereignty of the king over part of his lands (as was made clear by his letters to the people of Ghent during the revolt of 1447–53), so Charles continued until 1473 to maintain a double relationship with Louis XI, oscillating between submission and rebellion. That said, the use of a formula close to that deployed by Philip the Good after 1435 should not make us think that history was simply repeating itself. The development of political ideas in the restricted circles of the prince's counsellors pushed him in another direction. As Guillaume Hugonet made clear in his address at Bruges in 1473, we need 'to make a distinction between the times and the people involved' ('entre le temps et les personnes').[75]

Charles the Bold and the model of the king's justice

The year 1473 incontestably marks a fundamental break in Charles's relations with the French king. The creation of the Parlement of Malines on the model of the Parlement of Paris, with the aim of ending the latter's position as an ultimate appeal court in the duke's lands, could be interpreted as a crime of *lèse-majesté*, since the king's sovereignty was necessarily judicial.[76]

The conquest of a monopoly of justice to the detriment of the king of France was a firm and recurrent objective of Charles the Bold. The desire to become a fount of justice was a central trait of his personality. We have seen that from the moment of his arrival in power, the duke reformed his public audiences, introducing sessions that lasted for hours and were stuffed full of Biblical readings and Roman law. Charles wanted to impose his power both by the sword and by the laws which he would originate and which he would enforce. The image on the Montpellier manuscript, which is difficult to date but probably comes from his reforming years, shows a bearded individual between a warrior and a judge, illustrating the *Imperatoriam maiestatem* of Justinian, by which imperial majesty receives the ornament of arms and is armed with laws (see Figure 1).

The message was clear: the prince, advised by his chancellor and his council, supported by his own virtues, must guarantee peace and justice and thus respect the will of Christ.[77] The quest for legitimate authority passed through this full exercise of justice. This could lead to notable excesses, such as the summary trial of the bastard of la Hamaide. It also meant that the desire to bring order to all the lands of his principality would be a significant theme of his rule. As the preamble of the ordinance of Thionville which founded the Parlement of Malines put it: 'Union and civil concord can be maintained by only justice, which is the soul and spirit of the public weal [*chose publique*].'[78] In this text, inspired by Cicero, Lactantius and Saint Augustine, Charles himself was to dispense justice, exercising it in all his territories in the name of God, because he answered to God alone. This aim formed part of a governmental programme which sought to establish the unity of his lands through the accessibility of his justice to all and its validity in all of his territories. We would not be wrong in seeing a clear claim to sovereignty here. This foundational document styles the duke as 'Charles by the grace of God, duke of Burgundy, of Lothier, of Brabant, etc.', without reserving the clause 'by the grace of God' for the duchy of Brabant alone. He explained that he did his duty 'by obligation to Almighty God', and that the creation of this 'sovereign court' did nothing more than to recall to this obedience lands and subjects which 'pertained and pertain' to him. Olivier de la Marche makes clear that the purpose of this decision was to break off from the kingdom of France, glossing the text to the effect that the king of France had broken the Peace of Péronne, thus freeing the duke from all fidelity and homage.[79]

The jewels in the crown 145

Figure 1 Image of power in the Montpellier manuscript, fifteenth century

The episode at Péronne enabled the duke of Burgundy to force Louis XI to concede that his Great Council would no longer hear appeals from Charles's subjects, and the Four Members of Flanders were no longer constrained by procedures which linked them to the Parlement of Paris. By declaring that this treaty had been extracted under duress, Louis XI himself triggered the clause which freed the duke from royal sovereignty if this sworn peace agreement was broken. Charles condemned the king's perjury as early as 12 November 1471, ordering his subjects in his southern lands to cease any appeal to the Parlement of Paris. Nevertheless, although in this document Charles overtly declared his break with the king of France, assuming the title 'duke by the grace of God', no ideological defence of this position was advanced. Instead, a practical explanation was given: war and the risks which Burgundians travelling to France might experience were advanced as the reason for the ban on appeals.[80]

The competition between royal and princely jurisdictions

The judicial sovereignty which the duke had so long desired was seen first and foremost in judicial practice. Nevertheless, as Serge Dauchy has demonstrated, it should be noted that despite the large number of Flemish appeals to Paris (more than 1,600 between 1320 and 1521), a latent tension existed between the two authorities, as can be seen in the poor enforcement of judicial sentences within the county.[81] Parisian decisions often became lost in the mists of the north, and royal bailiffs and sergeants were often met with bad faith or even categorical refusals to execute a judicial order. This was seen, for example, in 1455, when Martin Le Coq addressed the Council of Flanders at Ypres demanding 'obedience and assistance', only to be met with the reply that 'they were forbidden by the chancellor of Burgundy to obey any order of the king or of the court here' (i.e. of the royal court). Indeed, there was no need to wait for the Burgundian period for Denis de Guisy, a royal sergeant, to be attacked by the lord of Dixmude in 1355 and forced to eat his letters of commission, including the seals. It should be remembered that the king of France's sovereignty was faced with strong territorial constraints. When the number of appeals doubled after 1450, Philip the Good had, it is true, repeatedly tried to restrict the activities of the Parlement of Paris. The royal ordinance of 1445 authorising the suspension of appeals against the decisions of the courts of the Four Members of Flanders for nine years might be thought to have provided further proof of a desire to contest royal sovereignty. But it can be interpreted only as part of a triangular relationship between the Flemish towns, the Burgundian prince and the king of France.

Indeed, it would be more appropriate in this context to invoke not the prince but the princess of Burgundy, since it was Isabella of Portugal who carried out all the negotiations at Chalons, which also considered the ransom of René of Anjou, the ratification of the Treaty of Arras by a number of princes including the dauphin and the evacuation of the fortress of Montbéliard.[82] On the point of renewing hostilities with England, Charles VII did not want to prolong tensions with the duke of Burgundy, and Isabella took advantage of the king's relatively weak position to assert her demands with authority. Yet the documents produced by these diplomatic encounters also demonstrate that the ducal couple had no intention of contesting royal prerogatives, and the duchess was always careful to make this clear. When we read these texts, it might seem surprising to see the duchess of Burgundy explaining in intricate detail how Flanders was not a territory like any other, how customs were there defended with vigour and how it was often necessary to come to an accommodation with their sometimes surprising habits. The duchess thus behaved less like a spokeswoman for ducal authority than as an advocate of local urban customs: although these are usually presented as the worst enemy of Burgundian state formation, they were in fact an essential contributing factor to its strength. It was in her role as a power-broker, not of the prince, but of the Four Members, that she received a reward of 40,000 *saluts* for her efforts.[83] It is tempting to conclude that Isabella had skilfully manoeuvred against royal sovereignty in Flanders by hiding behind the privileges of the Flemish towns, which could prove very dangerous for both the king and the duke in the event of a renewal of the war with the English.[84] It is useful to remember that as early as 1431 the duchess had already served as an important intermediary between the duke and his restless subjects, and was well rewarded for her services.

We should also note that in this diplomatic game, as Serge Dauchy has shown, the Parlement of Paris was not just an instrument to be manipulated by the king, serving to impose his authority in the lands of his vassal, but was instead effective precisely because of its reputation for impartiality, which insulated it from direct political manipulation.[85] Progress was difficult, and advances were often immediately followed by reverses. Royal courts were quite capable of asserting their jurisdiction in Burgundian lands, as is shown for example by a royal letter addressed to Philip the Good on 6 October 1450, summoning the duke 'to the sessions of our next Parlement of Sens and of Champagne' to settle the case of one Jean Buret, a Dijon merchant.[86]

In the final analysis, it seems that if royal sovereignty was reduced by Charles VII's favour to the Four Members in temporarily suspending appeals, the recognition of Flemish claims to special treatment also damaged the duke's authority in his own territories, since when Flemish towns escaped royal jurisdiction they also imposed their customs on the duke. What is more, the well-paid services of the duchess show once again how anachronistic it is to see the undeniable development of an administrative system as the marks of a 'state', conceived of as an autonomous and depersonalised institution. In the end, ducal sovereignty could be affirmed only in opposition to the king of France or the emperor. It remained to demonstrate the legitimacy of that sovereignty to the subjects of the duke's own territories. The abolition of the Parlement of Malines as soon as Charles the Bold was known to be dead shows that, even if the principle of a central court was not completely rejected, since Philip the Fair would re-establish it in 1504, the duke's judicial sovereignty had not yet become engrained in the mentalities of his people. One way in which it might have been is our next subject, the performance of the duke's majesty through princely magnificence.

Princely majesty: between performance and 'judicial sanctuary'

From the first century BCE, Roman law raised majesty to inviolable sanctity: 'Damaging grandeur by reducing it became a crime.'[87] This legislation was a turning point in the history of majesty, since from that time onwards, it no longer developed solely in the domain of political ideas but became moored to judicial practice, becoming an institution in the sense that it existed not only in words but also in deeds. This starting point being established, we must now distinguish once again between the multiple meanings of the word 'majesty', which might otherwise lead us into confusion.

The *maiestas* of a being derived ultimately from its status as *maior*, its superior character, which put it in the pre-eminent place in a hierarchy. This was what enabled it to claim a certain dignity, an *auctoritas*, a *gravitas* understood as the quality of that which is of greater weight. Thus whereas sovereignty is binary (one either has it or one does not), majesty can be reckoned by degrees, even if, in the Middle Ages, the introduction of a divine element restricted the circle of those who might possess it.[88] Since majesty was difficult to identify, it was often preferable to approach it by means of that which damaged, attacked or injured it. In French, the operable verb was (and is) *léser*, from the Latin *lædere*, meaning to hurt, injure or do wrong to. When majesty was invoked, it was often in the context of a crime which endangered it and thus made it explicit, like a photographic negative. This invocation of judicial practice, legitimate as it is, should not lead us to forget that majesty is also what makes it possible to elevate the person who possesses it and so to establish a political distance from the people, following the model of the *roi très chrétien*, the most Christian king of France.[89] Three fundamental ideas taken from the theologico-political thinking of the Old Testament modelled the ideal of majesty: the chosen people, sacred kingship and the perpetual alliance between God and his people. Unable to fulfil completely the criteria of divine election, the dukes of Burgundy could nonetheless nourish the appearance of it. In the field of appearance, understood at the Burgundian court as a means of rule, majesty took different forms, as circumstances dictated, in order to reinforce the princes' symbolic power. Majesty was also an ostentatious art, and the dukes of Burgundy knew how to put themselves on display. They sought to use the magnificence which they mastered so well to acquire the appearance of majesty.

We have already noted how Burgundian propaganda made liberal use of clothing, precious metals and ceremonial sophistication to indicate the exceptional character of every public appearance of the prince. Yet the use of certain distinctive markers suggests a deliberate search for majesty. The dais of majesty, the raised platform with steps, for example, was a way of marking ducal exceptionality, one which Charles definitely used as early as 8 January 1469, when he received the submission of the townsmen of Ghent at Brussels. Court chroniclers describe this magisterial stage topped with the ducal throne, which lent the prince the aura of royalty. The duke's *regalia* included the ring which, like the duke of Savoy's ring of Saint Maurice, symbolised the mystical marriage of the duke of Burgundy with the duchy's subjects.[90] But whereas the dukes of Brittany tried to replace their circled diadem with a closed crown as a sign of their sovereignty, the dukes of Burgundy once more only gave the illusion of a crown, wearing a headpiece decorated with pearls and precious stones, one version of which was seized by the Swiss Confederates at the battle of Grandson in 1476 and sold to Basel in 1504 for the extraordinary sum of 47,000 florins.[91] The effect must have been particularly successful, for example when Charles took possession of the duchy of Lorraine two hours after nightfall on 18 December 1474, all the better to use the contrast of shadow and light to create the illusion, through the reflected shine of gold and jewels, that he was wearing a crown.[92] Yet the crown was still only a fake, even if the jewels were genuine.

Much ink has been spilt on the accessories of the Burgundian spectacle state. Turning the pages of exhibition catalogues, or registers of accounts, helps us to understand how such magnificence might inadvertently humiliate the emperor and his entourage, as it did in the case of the meeting at Trier which we will consider shortly. Majesty was not only displayed to excess when it was deployed in gold braid, jewels, sumptuous tapestries or flamboyant suits of armour, or in a court protocol which regulated the merest details of service at table.[93] And the prince's words were also not as carefully controlled as one might imagine. As Ernst Kantorowicz reminds us, majesty must be cloaked in mystery, and silence is often necessary to bring out the iconic dimension of power.[94] Yet here again the dukes of Burgundy hesitated between spontaneity and protocol. After John the Fearless, who appeared on the town belfry of Bruges in 1407 with a list in his hand of those to be exiled but without saying a word, and Philip the Good, 'who spoke little' and then only in a considered manner, we come to Charles the Bold, who never ceased to increase the distance between himself and his subordinates but who did not hesitate to dress down the crowd gathered on the Vrijdagmarkt in Ghent in 1467, insulting copiously all those who dared to defy his authority. It is difficult to detect the development of a sense of superior dignity which might make the prince ration his words.[95] Indeed, this is nothing particularly specific to the duchy of Burgundy. Louis XI, whose loose tongue is decried by Thomas Basin, was quite willing to admit that his ill-considered words had often cost him dearly. Charles the Bold's extensive education, all those counsels in the art of rhetoric distilled from Cicero, was not always put to good use, even if the duke was careful to perfect his speeches to the Estates, just as the kings of Navarre or Aragon polished their addresses to the *Cortes*. Nevertheless, in contrast with certain monarchs like Robert of Anjou, whose numerous sermons enabled him to fulfil the medieval ideal of a king as a form of *imitatio Christi*, an incarnation of the Word of God, Charles never ceased to undermine the ideal of princely eloquence as a synonym of wisdom and just measure, ignoring the lessons of the treatises which served as the basis of his education. Without even mentioning the famous episode in which Louis XI amused himself by having his enemy's gesticulations imitated by the seigneur de Contay, hidden by a curtain, it has to be admitted that the chroniclers themselves saw the verbal caprices of their master as an evil portent, a sign of government without wisdom ('And in saying these words, thinking to please the king, the said Louis de Ceville started to imitate the duke of Burgundy and to stamp his foot and to swear by Saint George').[96] For we should not forget that rhetoric is useless unless it is founded on the authority which arises from a political community with shared, stable customs.

Majesty was also promoted by the ideal of the crusade, which structured the relations between the dukes and their subjects, the nobility and their fellow European rulers. The possibilities of a movement which had been marked by a series of broken promises did not tempt Charles the Bold as much as his predecessors, but it did permit Philip the Good to become the fifteenth century's knight of Christ and to seize an honour fit for kings. The aspiration to save the Holy Land from the Turkish menace, endlessly repeated but never fulfilled, allowed Philip to equip his embassies with a magnificence worthy of a king when he travelled to Regensburg in 1454. It was this privileged position that enabled Enguerrand de Monstrelet to say that Burgundian embassies eclipsed French envoys when they were received abroad, as in 1459 at Mantua, when Pious II granted them the signal honour of sitting on the bench of cardinal deacons, one normally reserved for kings in person.[97] When he received the bloody banner of the legates of Calixtus III at The Hague in the autumn of 1455, Philip the Good made the ideal of the crusade into another highly respectable element of his prestige.

The exercise of princely grace, often considered a marker of majesty, or even of sovereignty, was found in other manifestations of authority which were more concrete than symbolic. After all, from 1438 at the latest, ducal letters of remission granting pardon included the formula 'by the grace of God', whilst the notion of the ruler's good pleasure in expressions such as 'thus it pleases us that it be done' also affirmed the image of the duke's omnipotence.[98] Of course, the prince was not the only one in the Low Countries to exercise the power of grace: the officers of princely and seigneurial justice exercised it in much the same manner. That is why it is more interesting to consider these documents from an anthropological than from a judicial point of view. The grant of grace reveals the nature of ties of power, showing how those subjected to the duke's justice were very sensitive to the personal character of their relationship with their lord.[99] Granting remission thus did not necessarily transmit a message of strict sovereignty (since officers could also make such grants), but instead reinforced the affective bonds between the prince and his subjects in the fashion of the *benevolentia* displayed by a forgiving father to his sinful subjects, not necessarily with intimacy but with reverence.

Sovereignty put to the test of lèse-majesté

The signs of the duke's majesty were to be found everywhere in his principality. But did this consciousness of his superior position in the hierarchy of men also support the affirmation of his supremacy in the hierarchy of institutions? The primary line of enquiry is once again that of *lèse-majesté*, which allows us to identify, by what it was believed to threaten, that 'greatness constituted in judicial practice [*droit*] by its very inviolability' described by Yan Thomas.[100] Once again, outrages against the prince and the public weal are not lacking in the Burgundian principality. The duke's officers, the court nobles, the king's agents, the prince's subjects and towns all disobeyed, betrayed or damaged the sacred boundaries which protected the exercise of ducal authority. Yet here also, the variety of responses to this panoply of insults shows that the consciousness of 'statehood' which historians have sought to project into the minds of fifteenth-century men is simply an illusion created by a modern habit of seeking to separate power and the agents of power.[101]

Whereas in the kingdom of France the trial of Jacques Coeur made it possible to identify financial malpractices as coming under the heading of *lèse-majesté*, the same was not true in the Burgundian lands, where officers guilty of embezzlement often managed to escape lightly. Pierre de Monterbaut, receiver general of Philip the Bold, was pardoned the fine imposed by the Chamber of accounts for his last period of office in 1397. Augustin Isbarre, who supported Henry V's strong currency whilst criticising the duke's own coinage in Flanders by means of libellous pamphlets in 1422, ought to have been punished 'in body and goods', but was finally condemned only to a fine of 5,000 *écus d'or*, half of which was paid back to him by Philip the Good in 1423. The famous Guy Guilbaut, whose career was a model of social climbing, was accused by the Dijon master of accounts, Jean Bonost, of having embezzled the treasure of John the Fearless and of continuing to steal from Philip the Good. Yet in a report addressed to Chancellor Rollin subsequent to an inquiry at the Lille Chamber of accounts in 1426–27, all Bonost could do was to protest at how the receiver general's misdeeds were automatically pardoned by the duke.[102] Bonost did not stop there, but went on to warn central authority of the scale of the thefts of Roland du Bois and Guérin Sucquet, masters of accounts respectively from Flanders and Artois, before receiving threats from them.[103] It was by bringing this case into different courts, first urban then royal, that the commission of inquiry managed to bring an end to the abuses, leading to Robert du Bois's official removal on 15 October 1428. Many other cases could be cited. One was that of Martin Cornille, receiver general of all finances from 1444 onwards and commissioner of the financial reform which Philip the Good wanted to effect in 1447, who was imperilled by the Vauderie of Arras but was still active in 1465 after a career marked by peculation of all kinds.[104] Another was Jan van den Driessche, magistrate of the Council of Flanders, who was banished from the ducal lands in 1456. He appeared in the service of Louis XI, having served the count of Saint-Pol, and was probably expelled for fraud, corruption or even high treason. Yet another was the father of Philippe de

Commynes, Colard II de La Clite, *souverain bailli* of Flanders, who was the subject of a report of 362 folios, compiled in 1440 and containing 698 complaints of corruption and embezzlement, but who was finally removed from office only in March 1454.[105]

The Burgundian archives abound with similar cases which prove that corruption was endemic at court and in the ducal administration, a veritable cultural phenomenon.[106] Yet what interests us here is how uninterested Philip the Good was in the resolution of these affairs. It would probably be an exaggeration to say that the energetic efforts of Charles the Bold and his mother to verify the accounts of Roland Pippe led to the latter's suicide in 1462.[107] But what is certain is that the order and regulation which Charles sought to impose contrasted strongly with Philip the Good's indulgence, reputed as he was for being slow to react with rigour ('tardif à extresme rigueur').[108] Without wandering too far from our subject, we can observe that the intention to punish always proceeds by degrees, with the possibility of the strictest sanction being kept in hand, even though the real nature of authority and its expression usually results in a less serious punishment. Thus, just as the prince in his anger first threatened the bourgeois of Ghent with the destruction of their city, and then with destroying its walls, before finally simply closing two of its gates, so the ducal ire first put Jan van den Driessche under the threat of death, before commuting his sentence to one of perpetual banishment. It is easy to imagine how the prince would first behave like a king whose majesty was offended, before selecting punishments which were more appropriate to his status and to the politico-cultural context of his territory.

That said, the civil war had stimulated some significant ideological developments. John the Fearless constantly flirted with the idea of invoking the crime of *lèse-majesté*, first in his defence of the crime perpetrated against Louis of Orléans, then in his accusations against Jean de Montaigu, grand master of the household of Charles VI, who was suspected of 'stealing the royal treasure'. The felony of Louis de Chalon, count of Tonnerre, gave the duke the opportunity to return to these arguments the better to appropriate them. During the winter of 1406–07, the count abandoned his wife and seduced and abducted Jeanne de Perellos, an Aragonese maid of honour of Margaret of Bavaria, with whom he had two illegitimate children. John the Fearless rendered judgement against the guilty man, imprisoning him and seizing his goods in March 1407. Subsequently reconciled with the duke for a few years, the count later joined the Orléans faction on the pretext that John the Fearless had not restored all his lands.[109] On 18 July 1413 the Parlement of Dole exiled the doubly unfaithful lord, declaring all his lands forfeit for the crime of *lèse-majesté*. Rendered within the imperial territory, this sentence and its justification did not impinge on the dignity of the king of France. Moreover, it was in the duke's absence that his status was thus asserted, since it was Margaret of Bavaria who was charged with defending her lands against the count of Tonnerre and his new Orléanist friends. The duke returned to his lands in the south only in 1414, by which time the battle was over. Nevertheless, similar ideas were also making headway in the north. In a letter of commission appointing Philip, count of Charolais, as governor of his northern lands in his absence, John the Fearless granted him full powers, excepting certain specified matters, in the manner of a royal grant.[110]

Under Philip the Good, the duke's hesitations slowed the progress of the concept of *lèse-majesté*, which only flourished under his son. Of course, the episode of the *Grande Vauderie* and the war with Ghent, without forgetting the hunt for sodomites, have led some to identify a desire to impose consistency within Philip's principality.[111] But, as we have seen, the duke kept his distance from events at Arras; even in the manifesto published against Ghent, the expression *lèse-majesté* is not to be found, and 'the repression and pursuit of the sodomites at Bruges owed more to the search for authority in the Flemish towns than to a long-term preoccupation'.[112] The crime of *lèse-majesté* was thus invoked only on a case-by-case basis, without any overarching plan. This does not mean that this concept was not present. Indeed, as Jonas Braekevelt's work has revealed, it was even relatively old. There is not much point in attempting to establish the date of its emergence since, like many medieval concepts, it came to prominence, disappeared, lost its force with time, lent princely discourse a nuance spreading doubt and ambiguity and was then promoted with vigour once more under Charles the Bold. Before being constructed as a means of justifying opposition to the kingdom of France, the concept of *lèse-majesté* was still part of a feudal model of submission to the French king as lord. Thus on the eve of his marriage to the heiress of Flanders, Philip the

Bold promised that, if Flanders came into his possession, he would, as a peer of France, defend the king's privileges.[113] As a peer of France, one profoundly attached to the Crown, Philip the Bold, like John the Fearless, did not attack the interests of the king of France when he invoked (relatively rarely, it has to be said) the concept of *lèse-majesté*. Under Philip the Good, the term seems to have taken two separate paths. In the presence of the king or in the context of a direct threat to royal interests, the duke of Burgundy was always careful not to hurt the king of France, although in the diplomatic negotiations of 1451 which we have already discussed, Charles VII reminded his vassal of his duties of complete obedience. Whilst the manifesto condemning Ghent for its revolt does not use the term *lèse-majesté*, the Latin text of the Peace of Gavre of 1453 does include it.[114]

Invoked only timidly in the dukes' relations with the king of France, *lèse-majesté* was regularly employed in the disturbed political context of the double monarchy, to restrain local privileges or to repress rebellious towns. Thus in a letter of commission addressed to Jean de Bourgogne in 1434, naming him governor of the lands *de par-delà*, the duke authorised him to accord letters of remission except in the case of *lèse-majesté*. Philip the Good also invoked the concept when punishing the rebels of Ghent in 1440. And whereas in 1431, he recognised the judicial privileges of Wervicq except in 'privileged cases to which the great princes are accustomed and must be cognisant', in 1463 terminological hesitations disappeared when he applied exactly the same restrictions to the town of Menin, stipulating this time 'excepting and reserving to us the cognizance, judgement and punishment of the crime of *lèse-majesté*'.[115]

But this progression, which was generally quite discreet and did not lead to direct confrontation with French sovereignty, took a distinctly different turn when Charles the Bold invoked the notion of *lèse-majesté* to justify the arrest and summary execution of Jean Coustain, to condemn the people of Liège as rebels in 1464, to have the men of Ghent summoned to Brussels in 1469 to 'cry mercy' and to describe Bruges rebels in the Estates General of 12 July 1475. The legitimacy acquired through the term's use in such legal contexts made it available as a weapon to attack the king of France. Just as Louis XI used it to stigmatise the count of Charolais in the affair of the bastard of Rubempré, so Charles deployed it in turn to position himself politically as the equal of the king.[116]

Yet if the *crimen laesae majestatis* was now used as a means of breaking from dependence to a superior sovereign, belatedly but undeniably affirming Burgundian sovereignty in foreign policy, did this mean that this institutionalised majesty was also conceived of as a potential integrative force throughout the entirety of the principality?[117] It would be wrong, of course, to deny a certain degree of majesty to the dukes of Burgundy, placing them, for example, below the dukes of Brittany but above the dukes of Savoy. Far away from this ranking of pride and honour, the assertions of princely majesty at Cassel, in a Latin text addressed to Ghent, in the privileges of the inhabitants of Menin or in the context of the Parlement of Dole were not enough to unify the dukes' entire territory. After all, if this adaptable notion could be used by Charles the Bold to sanction the men of Ghent, only for the same concept to be deployed against him by Louis XI for conspiring with the English or the duke of Brittany, in the end it was always the king who came out on top. Indeed, even if René of Anjou was the living proof that a crown alone was not enough, it was in his battle for a royal title that Charles the Bold might have found a solution to the spatial, cultural and political dispersal of his principality.

The man who would be king

Let us say straight away: Charles the Bold, during his short rule, did try to secure a crown. The strength of this symbol in the kingdom of France, capable of uniting men against the enemy and accustoming them to the idea of a political abstraction more powerful than the man which embodied it, might make us think that Charles was acting along the right lines and that the political construction he was determined to go ahead with was conceived with rigour and good sense. Nevertheless, a more detailed analysis shows that, in this enterprise, Charles the Bold was above all pursuing his own personal ambitions and that he sought a crown not as the symbol of the unity of his peoples and his lands but to guarantee his sovereignty. In other words, Charles was more interested in ridding

158   *The illusion of the Burgundian state*

himself of the uncomfortable costume of the vassal than in donning the mantle of royal majesty which might serve to unify his lands. The negotiations at Trier demonstrate this clearly.

Trier or frustrated hopes

The scene would have made a good opening for a chivalric romance: on the banks of the Moselle, in the pale light of early morning, close by the abbey of Notre Dame aux Martyrs, a group of knights tried in vain to halt the imperial barge and to persuade Frederick III to accord a final interview to the duke of Burgundy. During the night of 24–25 November 1473, after weeks of feasts, banquets and negotiations, the emperor had decided to slip away from Trier, where Charles the Bold had been trying to persuade him to grant him a crown. 'But alas! How changeable and variable in a few instants [are] human desires!'[118] Thomas Basin was well placed to comment on this change of policy, whose precise causes will probably never be known. Historians have given numerous interpretations of these events, presenting this failed meeting as a key moment in the disappointments of Charles the Bold, even seeing it as the first link in the long chain of sufferings which would end with his defeat and death at the battle of Nancy.[119] It has to be said that this reverse sums up both the prince's ambitions and his personal and political faults, as well as the cultural differences which constantly worked against him. As we have shown, Charles was the first of the Burgundian dukes to break with the House of France, but he had not turned his back on the ideal of power which it embodied. For a prince in the Middle Ages, the ultimate mark of power and authority resided in a royal title. Shaped by a chivalric culture which accorded perfectly with the structuring rules of feudalism, Charles thought to receive this honour from his suzerain lord and emperor, Frederick III of Habsburg, even though, as the reports of the Italian ambassadors bear witness, Charles showed a profound contempt for the emperor and paid no attention to the imperial judicial hierarchy.[120] German customs in general were ill-understood by the Burgundian chroniclers, who mocked the rustic manners of the imperial court and condemned the emperor as indolent, passive and unworthy of his office. For Olivier de la Marche, an elective monarchy was by definition of lesser value.[121] Under these conditions, this meeting, however magnificent it might have been, could only fail for want of a sufficiently solid diplomatic foundation.

Charles had come to Trier on 30 September with a perfectly clear objective, namely to seize the crown of the king of the Romans. Accompanied by 250 courtiers and an army of 6,000 soldiers, he used the first week of the meeting to display his wealth and power. Yet one anecdote reveals much about Charles's unconscious attitude. When they arrived outside Trier, the duke's entourage realised that his sumptuous coat, embroidered with twenty-three large rubies, 1,400 large pearls and 3.7 ounces of gold, had been left fifty kilometres behind in Luxembourg. The duke immediately ordered that the convoy come to a halt. Nothing could be done to convince him to appear before the emperor without this coat, not even the arrival of the archbishop of Trier. Once his coat was eventually brought to him, Charles put it on with no other protection and set out in the pouring rain, forbidding the other members of the court from taking shelter. He had paid nearly 38,819 *livres* of Flanders (or the annual wages of 555 masons) for this magisterial piece of goldsmith's work, created by Gérard Loyet, and he was not about to lose the opportunity to show it off. This unprecedented display of riches was rounded off with all the paraphernalia of the Burgundian court: display cabinets, reliquaries, precious tapestries, sumptuous banquets with breath-taking entertainments and so on and so forth. The desire to display royal dignity was more than obvious, but it ultimately served to humiliate the emperor and to offend the prince-electors, who, when they saw all this magnificence, 'were disconcerted by it'.[122]

Charles entered into negotiations on 7 October, the day after the feast given by the Burgundians at the abbey of Saint Maximin, where they were staying. He had been encouraged since 1469 to claim the crown of the Romans by Sigismond of Tyrol, from whom he had bought Alsace and the county of Ferette. Now private sessions began at Trier, punctuated once a week by public declarations. Then, probably exhausted by the emperor's delaying tactics, the duke of Burgundy made four public demands, most notably to be recognised as the heir to the lordship of Guelders, before threatening to leave on 31 October. The emperor and the princes finally agreed to recognise his rights to the Guelders inheritance, but the discussions concerning the crown remained lively. A kingdom of Frisia or Burgundy was suggested, but under no circumstances was Charles to become king of the Romans. All in all, Trier was a fiasco for Charles, and the emperor's response to all the duke's splendour was a discreet yet contemptuous departure.

Petra Ehm has rightly stressed the cultural divisions between the two delegations and the 'diplomatic gaffes' which lined up like the pearls on Charles's costume.[123] The duke of Burgundy and his entourage completely neglected the prince-electors, with the exception of Frederick of Wittelsbach, the count palatine of the Rhine, whom Charles tried to reconcile with his enemy Frederick III. From the moment of his first entry into the town, at masses and public audiences, the duke always snubbed them by taking the place of honour next to the emperor. Similarly, Charles's ermine collar was longer than that on the electors' robes. Only the archbishops of Mainz and Trier were placed to the right of the emperor during the banquet of 7 October, no doubt in recognition of their ecclesiastical dignity, whereas the envoys of the margrave of Brandenburg were degraded in the order of precedence. Finally, Charles only interacted with one party, the emperor, which once more betrays his still very French political assumptions. Even if Charles was the enemy of the king of France, his origins, his education and his milieu had formed a political theory which knew little of elective practices. Power was conquered by deeds of arms, by marriage, by money and by the authority symbolised by a crown given by a superior authority if it could not be inherited. This was how Charles saw things: he was little interested in German political norms.

Although election was not unknown in fifteenth-century France, ducal Burgundy was closer to the political thought of Eustache Deschamps, for whom 'By succession / It is better for any region / To have a lord by marriage / And to descend by lineage' than to that of Nicole Oresme, for whom 'personal election is better than election by lineage'.[124] Charles thus completely neglected the princes of the Empire. He omitted to a gift to the German electors, something he never failed to do when writing to the English or Italian courts in support of his demands. The only exception here was of the count palatine, who was no help, and the archbishop of Mainz, to whom he had promised some money in 1469 if he were to be elected as king.[125] Charles's counsellors were unfamiliar with German affairs and stressed their attachment to French culture in opposition to

Antoine Haneron or Peter von Hagenbach, who wanted to bring Burgundy closer to the Empire but whose voices did not carry the most weight. All in all, it was not very surprising that the duke's ambitions were met coldly and that all he managed to secure was his investiture as duke of Guelders.

Indeed, the unreflective and incoherent nature of Charles's pretensions to the title of king of the Romans was constantly apparent. He made his intentions clear in the orders he sent to Peter von Hagenbach at the start of 1473, explaining that he wanted to trade the marriage of his daughter, Mary, to Maximilian, son of Frederick III, for the crown of king of the Romans. He would then assume this title until the death of Frederick III, at which point he would become emperor, passing on his royal crown to Maximilian. This, according to the duke of Burgundy, was the surest means to ensure the continuity of the imperial title in the Habsburg family.[126] Thus Charles the Bold seems to have been more concerned with the success of the House of Austria than with the fact that, as he had only a daughter, his own political edifice was itself exposed to the fragility of female succession. This plan could very well have appealed to Frederick III, whose attachment to the House of Austria was evident in his motto A E I O U (*Austriae Est Imperare Orbi Universo*) ('It Falls to Austria to Rule the Whole World'). But the throne's hereditability, which the emperor wanted and which was envisaged by the duke as the only route to a legitimate title, was confronted with a very real political obstacle, namely the power of the electors, who would never have pardoned Frederick for selling off the Empire for a marriage whose fruits could benefit only the House of Austria.

Charles was one those border princes, like Mathias Corvin in Hungary or Georges Podiebrad in Bohemia, who threatened the Empire. The expressions *deutsche Lande* or *Alemanica natio* became more common in official documents after 1430, underlining that it was the German language, the *deutsche Zunge*, which unified this nation whose political will extended even beyond the borders of Germany.[127] All in all, the leadership of the Empire pertained to Germany or, as Albrecht Achilles put it, 'the emperor must not be a non-German'. In these circumstances, Charles became nothing less than a 'Grand Turk of the West' for the Germans, and

Frederick III joined forces with the Swiss, with results which are well known.[128]

A crown for which kingdom?

What, though, were the foundations and the repercussions of this quest for a royal title within the duke's own territories? It seems that, for Charles, the kingdom was less important than the fact of having a crown.[129] At Trier, no fewer than three titles were envisaged, those of king of the Romans, king of Frisia and king of Burgundy. Although, as we have seen, the duke's imperial ambitions made little sense and can be most easily ascribed to Charles's hubris, the last two seem to fit Burgundian territorial reality better.[130] But here once more, historiographical myths die hard. Thus, despite the magisterial work of Paul Bonenfant, modern historians still often characterise the final ambitions of the dukes of Burgundy in terms of a desire to reconstruct the 'ancient kingdom of Lotharingia'. This is despite the fact that, as long ago as the 1930s, the Belgian historian repeatedly demonstrated that this formula was late and probably a caprice of a Brabantine official, without Philip the Good being particularly convinced of its pertinence. It will thus be useful to summarise once again the principal arguments in his complex case.[131]

The first mention of the creation of a kingdom in the Burgundian territories dates from 1447, but the evidence indicates that it was not Philip the Good who instigated this project but rather the imperial chancellor, Gaspard Schlieck. The Burgundian prince responded cautiously, instructing his ambassadors, Henri de Heesel and Adrien Van der Ee, to be as discreet as possible, 'since one can well imagine that there would be great danger in pursuing and formulating such great things, without first knowing if they can be brought to the desired end, and that it would be shameful to be refused in such as case'.[132] If, for his part, Frederick III already wanted to bring together the Houses of Austria and Burgundy and to protect the rights of his family in Luxembourg, Hainault, Holland and Zeeland, then Philip also wanted to take advantage of this opportunity, not just to gain the title of king of Brabant or of Frisia but to acquire a crown which would unite the entirety of his lands in the Empire. There was thus a considerable distance between the creation of a vassal kingdom of Brabant proposed by Frederick III and the foundation of a vast kingdom independent of the Empire which Philip the Good was seeking. This difference of aims put an end to the negotiations which Philip had hoped to keep secret. All he kept from this project was a mark of esteem, which allowed him to retort to the French ambassadors on 4 November 1464: 'I would like everyone to know that if I should have wanted, I might have been king.'[133]

As for the expression 'kingdom of Lotharingia', which appears at this date, it seems to be related to the political culture of Brabant. Van der Ee was secretary of the Brabantine chancery and was thus very familiar with the Lotharingian traditions of that duchy. Reference to the kingdom of Lotharingia sometimes came up, as in 1460, when the duke had to defend the fiefs in the Empire which Frederick III was contesting, on the pretext of descent through the female line. Philip thus invoked the memory of a kingdom of Lotharingia which possessed a *jus brabantium* recognising succession in the female line. The resurrection of the kingdom of Lotharingia was thus not an ultimate objective, essential to the policy of Philip the Good or even of Charles the Bold.[134] When the latter entered Nancy and formulated his speech to the Estates on 27 December 1475, he was content with his intermediary position 'between France and Germany' but made no mention of the ancient kingdom of Lotharingia.[135]

The invocation of a kingdom of Frisia was thus not essential to the policy either of Philip the Good or of Charles the Bold. It is true that J. R. Veenstra has shown how Frisian myths fed into a courtly literature which was held in high esteem at the court of Burgundy.[136] The perpetual privilege allegedly obtained by the Frisians from Charlemagne defined the liberty of this territory and could provide ideological ammunition for the dukes' claims to sovereignty. But the composition of the *Livre du roy Rambaux de Frise et du roy Brunor de Dampnemarche* in the middle of the fifteenth century is best situated in the context of the broader grouping of chronicles, genealogies and romances which served to insert the dukes of Burgundy naturally and legitimately into the lineage of the lords of the territories they had recently conquered.[137] When the kingdom of Frisia was mentioned by Jean Germain in an address to the Council of Basel, or by the pen of Olivier de la Marche, it served once more to reinforce ducal majesty, rather than to lay the foundations of a kingdom uniting the Burgundian territories. For, contrary to what Veenstra asserts, I do not think that we should speak of a 'long process' when we invoke the royal policy of the dukes of Burgundy.

It is true that the idea of a kingdom of Burgundy was more important for Charles the Bold, who made repeated allusions to the sacred dignity which he dreamed of finding. Where his predecessors had insisted on the blood of France which ran in their veins, Charles claimed that his blood was nobler than the king of France himself:

> ... taking nobility as the French take it, that is to say from Charlemagne, saying that he was descended in direct line, and without interruption from the stock of the said Charles, which the king of France was not at all because of the usurpation of Hugh Capet.[138]

The *Chronique des royz, ducs, comtes et autres saintes personnes de la tres noble maison de Bourgogne* goes even further than Philip the Good's policy of legitimising his territorial claims by making his *scriptoria* pump out material demonstrating a common past uniting him and his people of Hainault, him and his people of Holland, him and his people of Brabant and so on. The *Chronique des roys de Bourgogne* was indeed written to underline the superiority of Burgundy over the kingdom of France. From the marriage of Clovis and Clotilde, a Burgundian princess to whom the former owed his conversion, to the deeds of Girard de Roussillon, everything demonstrated the greatness of a kingdom which 'the kings of France had usurped'.[139] This chronicle undoubtedly reinforced Charles's pretensions. They were affirmed again, somewhat cryptically but nonetheless publicly, on the occasion of his entry into Dijon on 25 January 1474, demonstrating that the imperial rebuff had not sapped the duke's morale. Whilst Chastelain still presented the dynastic succession as a simple transmission of power from father to son, Charles dreamed of being a king, invoking

> The kingdom of Burgundy which those of France usurped for a long time and made a duchy, which all subjects must regret, and said that he had in himself things which it pertained to no one but him to know.[140]

It is clear that this little chronicle of Burgundian kings could have provided material to support claims to the title of king, or even to justify new conquests in Switzerland, Savoy or Angevin Provence, whilst at the same time rejecting French interests.[141] A genealogical roll created at the beginning of Charles's rule, which shows how, thanks to his links with the royal Houses of France and England, the new duke of Burgundy could claim such exceptional origins, says much the same thing.[142] Yet here again, the seemingly self-evident conclusion that the duke deserved a crown remained simply an idea in Charles's head. After all, the real question for present purposes is less the identification of the analogues and the origins of this kind of writing than assessing the reception of this idea. Did this desire to acquire a crown meet with a favourable response in the Burgundian territories? Did it have enough symbolic potential to unify all of this region? To return to the subject we have just raised, it does not seem that the Burgundians of the duchy were particularly moved by the allusion to an ancient kingdom of Burgundy. The figure of the king remained French, even if the *foy de Bourgogne* had some partisans. The weakness of 'Burgundian' sentiment is betrayed by the examples alluded to above of those who rallied to the French king, by the weakness of the Dijon Rebellion or *mutemaque* of 1477, despite the assassination of Jean Jouard, and by the rapid conversion of ducal officials such as the same Jouard, president of the Parlement of Burgundy, who was supported by Louis XI after his submission, and Jean Gros, the ducal secretary and *audiencier* of the Chamber of Accounts, who was named chief clerk of the Parlement of Burgundy by the king. Much stronger than any putative Burgundian patriotism was the desire to avoid conflict and the destruction of war.[143]

History always favours the victor. But aside from the universal desire for peace and security, the absence of a strong and immediate attachment to a dynasty whose history corresponded with that of a people inevitably weakened the Burgundian political project. In the north of the duke's territories, for example, it is difficult to imagine that the idea of a crown of Frisia appealed to the people of Holland, who were more used to massacring kings than to rallying to their side. The memory of Count William II, king of the Romans, killed in 1256 by the proud Frisians, described as unspeakable barbarians by the chronicles of the period but celebrated in the *Livre du Roy Rambaux*, had been reinforced by the death of William V, also slaughtered at the hands of the Frisians in 1345.[144] After all, Brabantine erudition had first infiltrated the chancery to affirm the privileges which allowed people of Brabant to create the charter of the *Blijde Inkomst* of 1356, guaranteeing the indivisibility of the duchy and protecting it from the appetites of foreign monarchs. Flanders, used to being ruled by foreign families, did not hesitate to acclaim Edward III as king of France in the Vrijdagmarkt of Ghent in 1340 to save its trade with England and always called on the king of France, against the duke of Burgundy, when its privileges were threatened. In other words, the Burgundian crown envisaged primarily by Charles the Bold was the product of the ambitions of a single man, not those of a people.

That said, the end of the Middle Ages was a propitious time for holding forth on the virtues of kingship. On the theatre stage, in political treatises and in 'mirrors for princes', all kinds of authors added a few lines portraying monarchy as a sublimation of the collective interest, their works being less an expression of devotion to the king than a theoretical analysis of the functions and purpose of the royal office. Yet the French-style royal model which obsesses so many historians was not necessarily the one which most inspired the people of Besançon, Antwerp or Ghent. Although the ultimate accolade for any medieval ruler was to be a king, it is salutary to recall, as John Watts does, that kingship was not a form of rule that was spontaneously accepted but rather a structure, a tool of government which did not automatically deliver effective power over the people under its authority.[145] The crown which René of Anjou inherited in 1435 did nothing to resolve the problem of the *Kumulativreich* of which he was the head.

In 1527 the Emperor Charles V charged his counsellor Louis de Praet with the project of raising the Low Countries to the status of a kingdom. One year previously, thanks to the Treaty of Madrid, the emperor had obtained from Francis I the renunciation of the latter's claim to sovereignty over Flanders and Artois. The young emperor's objective was to go beyond the personal relationship which alone linked his states to one another, to overcome differences of language and customs by uniting his northern territories on the French model, to reinforce his sovereignty there and, to that end, to re-establish in the Great Council of Malines a parlement as in the time of Charles the Bold. Yet this idea came to nothing, probably because the war with France meant that Charles V had no interest in antagonising his subjects and raising discontent against him.[146] This project originated for reasons of internal policy but was brought to nothing by foreign policy which, as always, was bound up with complicated relations with the kingdom of France, both as a model and an enemy. Although this unification project seemed self-evident to the rulers of these territories, the people's reticence shows how, even at the start of the sixteenth century, kingship was still not a familiar structure for them. Two decades later, in 1548, the Circle of Burgundy, which defined the northern geopolitical zone in the lands of the Habsburg Empire, was no more successful in convincing them. Common feeling, a common culture, an attachment to a common honour which needed to be defended, all this was lacking. We shall now turn to the Burgundian wars, the conquests which they permitted and the desertions which endlessly undermined them, demolishing in one round of cannon blasts the myth of 'Burgundianisation'.

Notes

1 Bibliothèque municipale de Lille, ms 625. For an introduction to this manuscript, see K. Daily, 'Jean d'Auffray: culture historique et polémique à la cour de Bourgogne', *Le Moyen Âge* 112:3 (2006), 603–618.
2 Bonenfant, *Philippe le Bon*, pp. 23, 118.
3 See the Introduction of this book.
4 J. Froissart, *Chroniques*, ed. J. Kervyn de Lettenhove (Brussels: Académie de Belgique, 1867–77), vol. XIII, pp. 342–345.
5 R. Vaughan, *John the Fearless*, 2nd edn (Woodbridge: Boydell and Brewer, 2002), p. 250.
6 It should be underlined that the increase in the extent of the dukes' lands was neither regular nor predetermined. Lands could come into their hands or could be given away. For example, in 1422 Philip the Good declared that he would give to his sister Anne, the wife of the duke of Bedford, his county of Artois if he died without any children. See Schnerb, *L'État bourguignon* (Paris: Perrin, 1999), pp. 177–178.
7 Paviot, *Les ducs de Bourgogne*, p. 146.
8 For some sixteenth-century examples, see B. Haan, *L'amitié entre princes: une alliance franco-espagnole au temps des guerres de religion (1560–1570)* (Paris: PUF, 2011).
9 The literature on this topic is abundant; see, for example, A. Guerreau-Jalabert, 'Sur les structures de la parenté dans l'Europe médiévale', *Annales ESC* 36 (1981), 1028–1049.

10 M. Nassiet, *Parenté, noblesse et États dynastiques (XVe–XVIe siècles)* (Paris: Éditions de l'EHESS, 2000).
11 On this topic, see below, Chapter 7.
12 *Complainte sur la mort de Jean sans Peur* (1419), in A. Leroux de Lincy (ed.), *Chants historiques et populaires du temps de Charles VII et de Louis XI* (Paris: A. Aubry, 1852).
13 See C. A. J. Armstrong, 'La politique matrimoniale des ducs de Bourgogne de la Maison de Valois', *Annales de Bourgogne* 40 (1968), 5–58 and 89–139.
14 B. Léthenet, 'Le manifeste de Hesdin et ses réponses dans l'Auxerrois/Mâconnais (1417–1435)', *Bulletin du Centre d'Études médiévales de l'Auxerrois* 14 (2010), 2–15. The manifesto, edited by Urbain Plancher, underlined the common lineage of the king and John the Fearless: Plancher, *Histoire générale et particulière*, vol. III, doc. 303.
15 'Complainte de Christine de Pizan sur la mort de Philippe le Hardi' (Royal Library of Belgium, ms. no. 7217), ed. in A. Leroux de Lincy (ed.), *Recueil de chants historiques français depuis le XIIe jusqu'au XVIIIe siècle* (Paris: C. Gosselin, 1841), p. 292.
16 'Complainte sur la mort de Philippe le Bon' (1467), in Leroux de Lincy (ed.), *Chants historiques et populaires*, pp. 147ff.
17 P. Bonenfant, 'Du meurtre de Montereau au traité de Troyes', in *Philippe le Bon, sa politique, son action*, pp. 306–309.
18 The Dauphin Charles was behind the murder of John the Fearless at Montereau and had to leave the court and create his own party. Both Charles VI and Isabeau of Bavaria agreed to the Treaty of Troyes (21 May 1420), disinheriting their son Charles in favour of Henry V and his heirs. See A. Curry, 'Two Kingdoms, One King: The Treaty of Troyes (1420) and the Creation of a Double Monarchy of England and France', in G. Richardson (ed.), *'The Contending Kingdoms': France and England (1420–1700)* (Aldershot: Ashgate, 2008), pp. 23–42.
19 Monstrelet, *Chronique*, vol. III, p. 362.
20 Chastelain, *Chronique*, vol. IV, book VI:1, ch. VI, p. 47: 'Car leur contoit que son royaume il le tenoit de luy et de sa vertu, et que c'estoit son père et son salut …'.
21 The text of this gift to Philip is edited in U. Plancher, *Histoire générale et particulière*, vol. III, doc. 315. The heraldic discourse is clear on this point, as the coats of arms of Philip the Bold are quartered and not broken. See F. Salet, 'Histoire et héraldique: la succession de Bourgogne de 1361', in *Mélanges offerts à R. Crozet* (Poitiers: Société d'Études Médiévales, 1966), vol. II, pp. 1307–1316.

22 P. Godding, 'Le testament princier dans les Pays-Bas méridionaux (12e–15e siècle): acte privé et instrument politique', *Revue d'histoire du droit / Tijdschrift voor rechtsgeschiedenis* 61 (1993), 217–235.
23 Testament of Philip the Good, 4 July 1426, ADNord, B 456/15.507.
24 Godding, 'Le testament princier', p. 226, n. 53, in which he quotes Jean de Terre Vermeille, who asserted in 1419 that the king could not include the kingdom in his own legacy ('le roi n'a jamais pu, et ne peut, faire de testament au sujet du royaume').
25 Eléonore of Poitiers, *Les États de France (Les honneurs de la cour)*, ed. J. Paviot in *Annuaire-bulletin de la Société d'histoire de France* (1998), 75–135, at p. 93. This book is entitled 'Estates of France' and not 'Estates of Burgundy', even though it deals with the court of Philip the Good.
26 P. Contamine, 'Essai sur la place des "XII pairs" dans l'*ordo* de la royauté française à la fin du Moyen Âge', in C. Carozzi and H. Taviani-Carozzi (eds), *Hiérarchies et services au Moyen Âge* (Aix-en-Provence: Presse de l'Université de Provence, 2001), pp. 53–70.
27 Archives nationales, Paris, J 178 B, no, 57, quoted in *ibid.*, p. 57.
28 *Mémoire consignant, à l'intention du conseil du duc de Bourgogne, les arguments pour ou contre l'acceptation des conditions de paix du roi d'Angleterre* (Arras, end of October 1419), ed. in Bonenfant, *Du meurtre de Montereau*, pp. 310–314.
29 La Marche, *Mémoires*, vol. II, book I, ch. XV, p. 87.
30 See the edition of this speech in A.-B. Spitzbarth, 'De la vassalité à la sujétion: l'application du traité d'Arras (21 septembre 1435) par la couronne', *Revue du Nord* 85 (2003), 43–72.
31 See Contamine, 'Essai sur la place des "XII pairs"'.
32 Chastelain, *Chronique*, vol. IV, book VI:1, Proesme, pp. 5–22.
33 This oath is edited in Commynes, *Mémoires*, ed. Godefroy and Lenglet du Fresnoy Lenglet-Dufresnoy, vol. II, no. VII, pp. 344–345.
34 Chastelain, *Chronique*, vol. IV, book VI:1, ch. IX, p. 59.
35 *Ibid.*, vol. IV, book VI:1, ch. IX, p. 63.
36 W. Paravicini, 'Le temps retrouvé? Philippe le Bon à Paris en 1461', in W. Paravicini and B. Schnerb (eds), *Paris, capitale des ducs de Bourgogne* (Ostfildern: Thorbecke, 2007), pp. 399–477.
37 Chastelain, *Chronique*, vol. IV, book VI:1, ch. XXXVIII, p. 137.
38 *Ibid.*, vol. IV, book VI:1, ch. IX, ch. XXVIII, p. 113.
39 I follow the analysis of Werner Paravicini in 'Le temps retrouvé?', p. 439: 'Son espoir n'était pourtant pas d'évincer le roi, ni d'exercer le gouvernement effectif de la France, mais de jouer le premier rôle auprès du roi en toute loyauté'.

40 Chastelain, *Epistre au bon duc de Bourgogne*, in *Œuvres*, vol. VI, p. 165.
41 This rallying cry, used by Mary of Burgundy, signified faith and fidelity to Burgundy.
42 A. Leguai, 'Dijon et Louis XI', *Annales de Bourgogne* 17 (1945), 35.
43 *Ibid.*
44 *Ibid.*, p. 106.
45 Plancher, *Histoire générale et particulière*, vol. IV, doc. 269.
46 See P. Saenger, 'Burgundy and the Inalienability of Appanages in the Reign of Louis XI', *French Historical Studies* 10:1 (1977), 1–26, at p. 15, n. 58.
47 See J.-C. Cassard, 'Pairie de France et barons de Bretagne: plasticité et vacuité des mythes historico-politiques', in *Vérité poétique, vérité politique: mythes, modèles et idéologies politiques au Moyen Âge. Actes du colloque de Brest 22–24 septembre 2005* (Brest: Université de Bretagne occidentale, 2007), pp. 59–76.
48 P. Gorissen, 'Caractères généraux de l'aide namuroise de 1473', in *Études d'histoire et d'archéologie namuroises dédiées à Ferdinand Courtoy* (Gembloux: Société Archéologique de Namur, 1952), vol. II, pp. 572–573.
49 See Claude Lévi-Strauss's thoughts in 'Histoire et ethnologie', *Annales ESC* 38:6 (1983), 1217–1231.
50 J.-M. Moeglin, 'Les dynasties princières allemandes et la notion de Maison à la fin du Moyen Âge', in *Les princes et le pouvoir au Moyen Âge. Actes du colloque de la SHMESP (Brest-1992)* (Paris: Publications de la Sorbonne, 1993), pp. 137–154.
51 La Marche, *Mémoires*, vol. I, book I, prologue, pp. 7–17.
52 Molinet, *Chroniques*, prologue.
53 *Ibid.*
54 Chastelain, *Chronique*, vol. I, book 1, prologue, p. 12.
55 Chastelain, *Déclaration de tous les hauts faits et glorieuses aventures du duc Philippe de Bourgogne, celuy qui se nomme le grand duc et le grand lyon*, in *Œuvres*, vol. VII, p. 218.
56 *Ibid.*, vol. VII, p. 308, 'Advertissement au duc Charles sous fiction de son propre entendement parlant à luy-mesme'.
57 All the treaties of alliance concluded in 1465 are edited in Commynes, *Mémoires*, ed. Godefroy and Lenglet du Fresnoy, vol. II, pp. 422, 440, 461, 468, 470, etc.
58 F. Autrand and P. Contamine, 'Remarques sur les alliances des rois de France aux XIVe et XVe siècles. La forme et le fond', in L. Bély (ed.), *L'Europe des traités de Westphalie – esprit de la diplomatie et diplomatie de l'esprit* (Paris: PUF, 2000), pp. 83–110.

59 Commynes, *Mémoires*, ed. Godefroy and Lenglet du Fresnoy, vol. II, p. 461.
60 Cuvelier *et al.* (eds), *Actes des États généraux*, p. 180: '... par la conjonction des pays, faicte par droiture de legitime succession, sans violence ou tirannie aucune, soubz le tres heureux et tres renommé nom, la tres redoubtée puissance droituriere et tres debonnaire seignourie de ceste tres victorieuse et tres glorieuse maison de Bourgogne ...'
61 *Ibid.* For a discussion of these problems, which were inherent to dynastic order, see J.-M. Moeglin, 'Entre 1250 et 1350: système des états et ordre dynastique', in Hoppenbrouwers, Janse and Stein (eds), *Power and Persuasion*, pp. 4–25.
62 N. Pons (ed.), *'L'honneur de la couronne de France'. Quatre libelles contre les Anglais (v. 1418–v. 1429)* (Paris: Klincksieck, 1990), pp. 122–133.
63 Moeglin, 'Les dynasties princières allemandes'.
64 Doudet, 'Présence du corps absent'.
65 Chastelain, *La mort du duc Philippe*, in *Œuvres*, vol. VII, pp. 263–264.
66 Doudet, 'Présence du corps absent', p. 29.
67 Some more examples in Lecuppre-Desjardin, *La ville des cérémonies*, pp. 56ff. and 141–148.
68 See W. P. Blockmans, '"Crisme de leze magesté". Les idées politiques de Charles le Téméraire', in J. M. Duvosquel *et al.* (eds), *Les Pays-Bas bourguignons. Histoire et institutions. Mélanges André Uyttebrouck*, special issue of *Archives et bibliothèques de Belgique* (1996), pp. 71–81.
69 See W. Paravicini, '"Mon souverain seigneur"', in Hoppenbrouwers, Janse and Stein (eds), *Power and Persuasion*, pp. 27–48 for the examples which follow.
70 On these two phrases from the *Digeste*, see A. Rigaudière, '*Princeps legibus solutus est* (Dig. I, 3, 31) et *Quod principi placuit legis habet vigorem* (Dig. I, 4,1 et Inst. I, 2,6) à travers trois coutumiers du XIIIe siècle', in *Penser et construire l'État*, pp. 39–66.
71 See Jean Bodin's definition of sovereignty in *Les six livres de la République*, 6 vols (Paris: Fayard, 1986), vol. I, chs 8 and 10, at p. 306.
72 We should remember that in the thirteenth century, sovereignty simply referred to the superiority of a man over a group of people. This is exactly what Philip de Beaumanoir was thinking when he wrote: 'chascuns barons est souverain en sa baronnie'. For this phrase and a clarification of this word, see M. David, *La souveraineté et les limites du pouvoir monarchique du IXe au XVe siècle* (Paris: Dalloz, 1954).
73 Paravicini, '"Mon souverain seigneur"'.

74 Some catalogues of royal rights existed at the end of the Middle Ages and were used to defend kings' prerogatives. See J. Krynen, 'Notes sur Bodin, la souveraineté, les juristes médiévaux', in *Pouvoir et liberté. Études offertes à Jacques Mourgeon* (Brussels: Bruylant, 1998), pp. 53–66.
75 Cuvelier *et al.* (eds), *Actes des États généraux*, p. 188.
76 For analogies between the Parlement of Malines and that of Paris, see J. Van Rompaey, *De Grote Raad van de hertogen van Boergondïe en het Parlement van Mechelen* (Brussels: Palais des Académies, 1973).
77 For a full explanation of this image, see W. Paravicini, 'Le parchemin de Montpellier, une image troublante du règne de Charles le Téméraire', *Journal des Savants* (2010), no. 2, pp. 301–370.
78 Ordinance of Thionville, December 1473, ed. in A. Anselmo *et al.* (eds), *Placcaerten ende ordonnantien van de hertogen van Brabandt* (Brussels and Anvers, 1648–1774), vol. IV (1724), pp. 321–328.
79 La Marche, *Mémoires*, vol. I, book I, ch. XXIV, pp. 132–133.
80 Order cancelling the appeal to the Parlement of France, Saint-Omer, 12 November 1471, in E. Champeaux (ed.), *Les ordonnances des ducs de Bourgogne sur l'administration de la justice du Duché*, special issue of *Revue Bourguignonne* (Dijon and Paris, 1907), pp. 194–196.
81 See R. C. Van Caenegem, 'Les appels flamands au Parlement de Paris au Moyen Âge', in *Études d'histoire du droit privé offertes à P. Petot* (Paris: Lib. générale de droit et jurisprudence, 1959), pp. 61–68. The examples that follow are taken from S. Dauchy, 'Souveraineté et justice. L'exécution des arrêts et jugés du Parlement de Paris en Flandre aux XVe et XVIe siècles', *Les épisodiques* 5 (1991), 1–15.
82 On the role of the duchess in these negotiations, see M. Sommé, *Isabelle de Portugal, duchesse de Bourgogne. Une femme au pouvoir au XVe siècle* (Lille: Presses du Septentrion, 1998), pp. 404–408.
83 The agreement was renewed in 1457 (the duchess was compensated again for her intervention) and then in Péronne in 1468.
84 According to B. Schnerb, M. Sommé and S. Dauchy, it was sign of the assertion of the sovereignty of the Burgundian state. See Schnerb, *L'État bourguignon*; Sommé, *Isabelle de Portugal*; and S. Dauchy, 'Le Parlement de Paris et les Pays-Bas bourguignons', *Revue d'histoire du droit* 61:3 (1993), 367–373.
85 See Dauchy, 'Le Parlement de Paris et les Pays-Bas bourguignons'.
86 Plancher, *Histoire générale et particulière*, vol. IV, doc. 152.
87 See Y. Thomas, 'L'institution de la majesté', *Revue de synthèse* 4:3–4 (1991), 331–386, who introduced the concept of 'judicial sanctuary' (*sanctuaire juridique*).

88 This topic has yet to be thoroughly explored by historians. See J. Chiffoleau, 'Dire l'indicible. Remarques sur la catégorie du *nefandum* du XIIe au XVe siècle', *Annales ESC* 45:2 (1990), 289–324. See also the introduction to J.-P. Barraqué and B. Leroy, *La majesté en Navarre et dans les couronnes de Castille et d'Aragon à la fin du Moyen Âge* (Limoges: Presses Universitaires de Limoges, 2011).

89 On the inspirational power of the Biblical model, see A. Graboïs, 'Un mythe fondamental de l'histoire de France au Moyen Âge: "le roi David" précurseur du "roi très chrétien"', *Revue historique* 287:1 (581) (1992), 11–31.

90 The golden ring with a ruby worn by John the Fearless on his portrait was bought by his father Philip the Bold and given to the monks of Saint-Bénigne. During the duke's inauguration ceremony as the head of the Burgundian duchy, the abbot of Saint-Bénigne placed the ring on his finger to symbolise the political union between the lord and his lordship. See Schnerb, *Jean sans Peur*, pp. 139–140.

91 For the appearance of this golden headpiece, see the proposed reconstruction illustrated in *Splendeurs de la cour de Bourgogne. Charles le Téméraire (1433–1477)* (Antwerp: Fonds Mercator, 2008), pp. 270 and 277–278.

92 For other examples of this kind, see Vaughan, *Charles the Bold*, pp. 169–171.

93 See W. Paravicini, 'Die zwölf "Magnificences" Karls des Kühnen', in G. Althoff (ed.), *Formen und Funktionen öffentlicher Kommunikation im Mittelalter* (Stuttgart: Thorbecke, 2001), pp. 319–395.

94 See e.g. E. Kantorowicz, 'Mystères de l'État. Un concept absolutiste et ses origines médiévales', in *Mourir pour la patrie et autres textes* (Paris: Fayard, 2004), pp. 75–103.

95 See É. Lecuppre-Desjardin, '"Et le prince respondit de par sa bouche"': Monarchal Speech Habits in Late Medieval Europe', in J. Deploige and G. Deneckere (eds), *Mystifying the Monarch: Studies on Discourse, Power, and History* (Amsterdam: Amsterdam University Press, 2006), pp. 55–64 and 244–247.

96 Commynes, *Mémoires*, ed. Blanchard, vol. II, p. 278: 'Et en disant ces parolles, pour cuyder complaire au Roy, ledict Loys de Ceville commença à contrefaire le duc de Bourgogne et a frapper du pied contre terre et a jurer saint George.'

97 On this episode, see Paviot, *Les ducs de bourgogne*, p. 155.

98 On the act of remission as a royal prerogative, see C. Gauvard, *'De Grace especial'. Crime, État et société en France à la fin du Moyen Âge* (Paris: Publications de la Sorbonne, 1991).

99   M. Nassiet and A. Musin, 'Requérir le pouvoir. L'exercice de la rémission et la construction étatique (France-Pays-Bas)', *Revue historique* 314: 1 (661) (2012), 3–26.
100 Thomas, 'L'institution de la majesté'.
101 The analysis of the case of the *Coquillards* above has already underlined a certain lack of political cohesion. See Chapter 3.
102 For these and the examples that follow, see J.-B. Santamaria, 'Crimes, complots et trahisons: les gens de finances du duc de Bourgogne Philippe le Bon à l'ère du soupçon (v.1420–v.1430)', in *L'envers du décor*, pp. 91–113.
103 On Roland du Bois, see J.-B. Santamaria, 'Un maître prévaricateur à la Chambre des comptes de Lille sous Philippe le Bon: Roland du Bois', in Paravicini and Schnerb (eds), *La face noire de la splendeur*, pp. 421–448.
104 For the Vauderie of Arras, see above, Chapter 3, pp. 96–102.
105 On these three corrupt officers, see H. Kruse, 'Les malversations commises par le receveur général Martin Cornille à la cour de Philippe le Bon d'après l'enquête de 1449', *Revue du Nord* 310 (1995), 283–312; J. Dumolyn, 'Jan van der Driessche/Jehan de la Driessche, un fonctionnaire flamand au service de Louis XI', *Revue historique* 309:1 (641) (2007), 71–90, and M. Boone, 'Philippe de Commynes et le monde urbain', in J. Blanchard (ed.), *1511–2011. Philippe de Commynes. Droit, écriture: deux piliers de la souveraineté* (Geneva: Droz, 2012), pp. 201–224.
106 On this topic, see W. Blockmans, 'Patronage, Brokerage and Corruption as Symptoms of Incipient State Formation in the Burgundian-Habsburg Netherlands', in A. Maczak (ed.), *Klientelsysteme im Europa der frühen Neuzeit* (Munich: Oldenbourg, 1988), pp. 117–126, who notes that 23 per cent of the privileges granted by Mary of Burgundy in 1477 concerned the fight against corruption.
107 Even if Rolan Pippe was far from innocent, he was psychologically vulnerable. See W. Paravicini, 'Un suicide à la cour de Bourgogne: Roland Pippe', in Paravicini and Schnerb (eds), *La face noire de la splendeur*, pp. 385–420.
108 Chastelain, *Chronique*, vol. IV, book VI:1, ch. LXXXII, p. 261.
109 On this case, see P. Gresser, 'Inconduite et trahison d'un prince sous Jean sans Peur: le cas de Louis de Chalon, comte de Tonnerre', in *L'envers du décor*, pp. 57–72.
110 Cauchies (ed.), *Ordonnances de Jean sans Peur (1405–1419)*, doc. 227, pp. 376–377.
111 At that time a veritable hunt for sodomites began in Bruges. See M. Boone, 'State Power and Illicit Sexuality: The Persecution of Sodomy

in Late Medieval Bruges', *Journal of Medieval History* 22 (1996), 135–153.
112 This and the reflections that follow are inspired by two unpublished dissertations. I would like to thank the authors for their permission to make use of them. M.-H. Méresse, 'L'expression de la lèse-majesté dans la principauté de Bourgogne de Philippe le Hardi à Charles le Téméraire (1363–1477)', unpublished MA thesis, University of Lille, 2010, and J. Braekevelt, '"Un prince de justice". Vorstelijke wetgeving, sovereiniteit en staatsvorming in het graafschap Vlaanderen tijdens de regering van Filips de Goede (1419–1467)', unpublished PhD thesis, University of Ghent, 2013.
113 U. Plancher, *Histoire générale et particulière*, vol. III, doc. 307, p. 22, Péronne, 12 September 1368.
114 Gachard (ed.), *Collection de documents inédits*, vol. II, p. 145.
115 Braekevelt, '"Un prince de justice"'.
116 Blockmans, '"Crisme de leze magesté"'.
117 The question of dependency to a superior sovereign had already been raised by the Ghibelline Alberico de Rosate on behalf of the Visconti, concerning their obedience to the emperor. See M. Sbriccoli, *Crimen laesae maiestatis. Il problema del reato politico alle sglie della scienza penalistica moderna* (Milan: Giuffré, 1974), p. 215.
118 Basin, *Histoire de Louis XI*, book I, ch. VIII, pp. 173–183.
119 P. Ehm, *Burgund und das Reich. Spätmittelalterliche Außenpolitik am Beispiel der Regierung Karls des Kühnen* (Munich: Oldenbourg, 2002).
120 See the letter of the ambassador Panigarola to Galeazzo Maria, 31 May 1475, in E. Sestan (ed.), *Carteggi diplomatici fra Milano sforzesca e la Borgogna* (Rome: Istituto Storico Italiano per l'età moderna et contemporanea, 1985–87), vol. I, no. 304, pp. 515ff.
121 On the negative opinion of Burgundian court chroniclers concerning the Empire, see M. Zingel, *Frankreich, das Reich und Burgund im Urteil der burgundischen Historiographie des 15. Jahrhunderts* (Sigmaringen: Thorbecke, 1995).
122 On this show of riches and the Germans' humiliation, see Paravicini, 'Die zwölf "Magnificences" Karls des Kühnen'.
123 P. Ehm-Schnocks, 'L'empereur ne doit pas être un non-Allemand. Charles le Téméraire, Frédéric III et l'Empire', in S. Weiß (ed.), *Regnum und Imperium. Die Französisch-deutschen Beziehungen im 14. und 15. Jahrhundert* (Munich: Oldenbourg, 2008), pp. 235–248.
124 See Contamine (ed.), *Le Moyen Âge. Le roi, l'Église, les grands*, pp. 315–322. On the evolution of French thought concerning election, see G. Lecuppre, 'Ordre capétien et confusion germanique. La compétition

royale dans les sources françaises au XIIIe siècle', in M. Aurell (ed.), *Convaincre et persuader: communication et propagande aux XIIe et XIIIe siècles* (Poitiers: CESM, 2007), pp. 513–531.

125 Ehm, *Burgund und das Reich*, pp. 261–284.

126 J. Chmel (ed.), *Aktenstücke und Briefe zur Geschichte des Hauses Habsburg*, 3 vols (Vienna: Akademie der Wissenschaften zu Wien, 1854–58), vol. I, pp. 32–34.

127 For a clarification concerning the evolution from Empire to *Heiliges Römische Reich deutscher Nation*, see F. Rapp, *Le Saint Empire Romain Germanique d'Otton le Grand à Charles Quint* (Paris: Seuil, 2000), pp. 292–304.

128 See C. Sieber-Lehmann, 'Der türkische Sultan Mehmet II und Karl der Kühne, der "Türk im Occident"', in F. R. Erkens (ed.), *Europa und die osmanische Expansion im ausgehenden Mittelalter* (Berlin: Duncker & Humblot, 1997), pp. 13–38.

129 Italian ambassadors reported that Charles the Bold constantly changed his mind about what he wanted, much to the annoyance of Frederick III. See Vaughan, *Charles the Bold*, p. 153.

130 On the cultural imaginary of the kingdom of Friesland in the fifteenth century, see A. G. Jongkees, 'Het koninkrijk Friesland in de vijftiende eeuw', in *Burgundica et Varia* (Hilversum: Verloren, 1990), pp. 27–47.

131 P. Bonenfant, 'État bourguignon et Lotharingie', in *Philippe le Bon*, pp. 351–363; P. Bonenfant, 'Le projet d'érection des États bourguignons en Royaume', *Le Moyen Âge* 45 (1935), 10–23.

132 Instruction given to Adrien Van der Ee, 22 October 1447, in E. Birk (ed.), 'Actenstücke, Herzog Philipps von Burgund Gesandtschaft an der Hof des römischen Königs Friedrichs IV. in den Jahren 1447 und 1448 betreffend', in J. Chmel (ed.), *Der österreichische Geschichtsforscher* (Vienna: Akademie der Wissenschaften zu Wien, 1838), vol. I:2, pp. 231–271, at p. 254.

133 Du Clercq, *Mémoires*, vol. IV, book V, ch. XV, p. 80.

134 On the limits of Philip the Good's ambitions, see R. Stein, 'Recht und Territorium. Die lotharingischen Ambitionen Philipps des Guten', *Zeitschrift für historische Forschung* 24 (1997), 481–508.

135 A. Calmet, *Histoire de Lorraine* (Nancy: A. Leseure, 1757), vol. VII: *Preuves*, col. 83.

136 See J. R. Veenstra, '"Le prince qui se veult faire de nouvel roy": Literature and Ideology of Burgundian Self-Determination', in Boulton and Veenstra (eds), *The Ideology of Burgundy*, pp. 195–221.

137 On historical thought in Burgundy, see É. Lecuppre-Desjardin, 'Maîtriser le temps pour maîtriser les lieux. La politique historiographique bourguignonne dans l'appropriation des terres du Nord au XVe siècle',

in D. Bohler and C. Magnien Simonin (eds), *Écritures de l'histoire (XIVe–XVIe siècle). Actes du colloque du Centre Montaigne, Bordeaux, 19–21 septembre 2002* (Geneva: Droz, 2005), pp. 371–383.

138 Philippe Wielant, *Recueil des antiquités de Flandre*, in *Recueil des chroniques de Flandre*, ed. J.-J. De Smet (Brussels: Hayez, 1865), vol. IV, p. 55.

139 British Library, Yates Thompson MS 32, fol. 6. For more details about this chronicle, see G. Small, 'Of Burgundian Dukes, Counts, Saints and Kings (14 C.E.–C. 1500)', in Boulton and Veenstra (eds), *The Ideology of Burgundy*, pp. 151–187.

140 H. Chabeuf, 'Charles le Téméraire à Dijon en janvier 1474. Relations officielles avec introduction', *Mémoires de la société bourguignonne de géographie et d'histoire* 18 (1902), 81–349, at pp. 291–292.

141 When Charles the Bold realised that there was no hope for his ambitions in the east, he decided to expand his conquests to the south. To this end, he began marriage negotiations with Ferdinand I, king of Naples. See J. Calmette, 'Le projet de mariage burgondo-napolitain en 1474 d'après une acquisition récente de la Bibliothèque nationale', *Bibliothèque de l'École des Chartes* 72 (1911), 459–472.

142 C. Bauer-Smith, 'Mapping Family Lines: A Late Fifteenth Century Example of Genealogical Display', in D. L. Biggs *et al.* (eds), *Reputation and Representation in Fifteenth-Century Europe* (Leiden and Boston: Brill, 2004), pp. 123–144. According to the author, the manuscript is dated between 15 July 1467 and spring 1468.

143 A. Leguai reached the same conclusion in 'Dijon et Louis XI', p. 262.

144 On the death of William II, count of Holland, see G. Lecuppre and É. Lecuppre-Desjardin, '*Anno 5. Regni sui a Frixonibus occiditur in glacie*. Perceptions de la mort pathétique de Guillaume, comte de Hollande et roi des Romains (1256)', *Revue du Nord* 93 (2011), 833–849.

145 John Watts, *The Making of Polities: Europe, 1300–1500* (Cambridge: Cambridge University Press, 2012), p. 68.

146 J. Richard, 'Du cercle de Bourgogne, et que ce n'est qu'un nom', *PCEEB* 13 (1971), 74–81.

5

Awake, Picards and Burgundians!

> Awake, you Picards, Picards and Burgundians,
> And find a way to have a good fight,
> For see how the springtime is also the season
> To go to war to deal out some hard blows.
>
> Someone talks about war who does not know what it is;
> I swear by my soul that it's a piteous enterprise,
> And that many a man-at-arms and noble fellow
> Has there lost his life, his robe and his cap.
>
> Where is the duke of Austria? He is in the Low Countries;
> He is in lower Flanders with his Picards,
> Who pray him night and day that he should lead them
> Into upper Burgundy to conquer it for him.
>
> Goodbye, goodbye, Salins, Salins and Besançon,
> And the town of Beaune, there where the good wines are;
> The Picards have drunk them, the Flemish will pay for them,
> Four Flemish pence the pint, or they will be well beaten.[1]

A song or a poem can be worth a thousand words of prose. In this text, the author admirably describes the diplomatic situation at the moment of its composition. He presents the violence and the sufferings of war. He also describes the divisions between the different Burgundian lands, which were also divisions between men. This song is difficult to date precisely, but it was probably composed between 1477 and December 1482, that is between the start of the French invasion of the Burgundian territories and the Peace of Arras. Its four stanzas might be enough to convince us of the fine reputation of the ducal armies, whose soldiers, and especially the Picards and the Burgundians, were feared for their warlike character and their fierceness in combat. We might also note that when the 'Burgundians' were invoked at the end of the fifteenth century, it was not necessarily the inhabitants of the duchy that were referred to, but fighting men from both Burgundies (the county and the duchy), who had more than adequately proved their mettle in Charles the Bold's wars.

As we read on, however, it becomes clear that despite the bellicose tone, which was quite appropriate for this kind of composition, violence, the pain of loss and the shadow of death are also invoked. This reminds us that war was not a simple tactical exercise, and that the price to be paid was heavy both for combatants and for civilian populations who, very often, were uninterested in the stakes at hand and wanted only peace. Finally, the context shows that in the aftermath of the death of Charles the Bold, as his principality was attacked by the troops of a king of France determined to conquer or reconquer all the territories bordering his kingdom, a form of political consciousness emerged that we might be tempted to characterise as 'national'. The identification of a common enemy brought out the contours of a space constituted by the rejection of the invading French, when it became necessary to fight together.[2] That said, the space in question was still not unified, and the Burgundian soldier prays Maximilian to abandon Flanders and to come and save Burgundy with its good wines, which the troops would drink at the expense of the Flemings. The jump is brutal from a common enemy to the competing interests of the duke's subjects. It makes explicit a twofold reality: first that of the Burgundian armies, which were mainly formed of soldiers from the *pays de par-delà* and Picardy, and were paid for by Flemish taxes; and second the total lack of solidarity between the northern and the southern lands.

War, which is so important in the process of identification with a state, mobilised and inspired men throughout this period. Yet the series of defeats provoked by Charles the Bold's projects finally destroyed this vast political entity, which had been accumulated more by clever acquisitions and fortunate marriage alliances than by military conquest. Does the principality of Burgundy provide a counter-example to the principle according to which war fosters the emergence of a state? The question is worth considering, since, as we shall see, Burgundian failures did not result from a lack of organisation but more from limitations in their overt objectives. Waging war and doing it well was one thing, but convincing a sceptical population of the justice of its prince's cause was quite another.

'War is a very perilous heritage'

The dukes of Burgundy constantly raised troops. War in the Middle Ages in general, and in this period in particular, was a phenomenon inherent to the rise of states.[3] In a schema which is now well understood for the kingdoms of England and France, 'almost continual warfare could only stimulate certain aspects of the process of state construction', including both the establishment of a regular fiscal structure and attempts to convince subjects involved directly or indirectly in long-term military operations of the latter's rightness.[4] Over the long term, the discourse which asserted the necessity of defending the state helped to shore up its foundations, despite the sacrifices of money and men that war demanded, even as legislative innovation, the call for reform and for justice gave the king's government an ever greater role in the lives of his people. In other words, to quote Emmanuel Le Roy Ladurie, 'Long-term balance is reached only through tragedy.'[5]

The monarchies of France and England were not the only ones to benefit from the positive consequences of waging war. The Italian communes also developed to the rhythm of hatred, rivalry and conflict, feeding their prosperity and their identity with the blood shed on the field of battle or in the streets. War in this context stimulated a competitive dynamic in which certain political entities triumphed over others, not always in the same way, and also fed tensions that the Peace of Lodi between the Italian city-states in 1454 did not succeed in eliminating entirely. War did not bring an end to recurrent skirmishes, to fratricidal enmities, to the existence of numerous minor powers like the principality of Mantua or the republic of Lucca, but it did considerably simplify the map of the Italian states.[6] Similarly, if in Catalonia peace was essential for the establishment of social and economic structures, the war and the spirit of the Reconquista had created a concept of power and its exercise which was specific to the Iberian peninsula.[7] In short, the primacy of war, understood in all its multiple and changing forms, was repeatedly affirmed in the different trajectories of the governments of Europe in this period. The Great Principality of Burgundy ought also to be included in this field of enquiry, if only to add some nuance to the familiar association between war, taxation and the affirmation of the state.

The north: a land in arms

Despite Raymond van Uytven's efforts to qualify the famous remark of Commynes concerning the exceptional riches of the Burgundian territories, it has to be said that Commynes's designation of the territory as the 'promised lands' does still seem to be a good description of the duke's principality.[8] Of course, all such judgements are relative, and periods of crisis were felt just as intensely in these territories as elsewhere. But the principality as a whole did not experience the same economic slowdown as in the nearby kingdom of France, where the war against the English, the passage of the great companies and the exactions of the *écorcheurs* contributed, as is well known, to the disruption of local production and even the ruin of certain territories.[9] When we consider the major wars of the end of the Middle Ages – the Hundred Years War, of course, but also the dynastic quarrels in Castile, the Hussite wars, the succession crises in the duchy of Brittany and the kingdom of Naples, the naval rivalries between Genoa and Venice and so on – the principality of Burgundy seems to be lucky in its 'marginal' position. Yet this does not mean that the noise of war was not heard there as elsewhere.

The Burgundian lands were regularly at war, even though the prince's lands were never united in a fight to the death with a common enemy. That much can be shown by considering the conflicts between the dukes and their rebellious subjects, the struggles between the Burgundians and the Armagnac clan, the involvement of the dukes in the succession of Hainault, Guelders or Luxembourg, or their clashes with the king of France or the emperor. As a result, the principality had to adapt to the paradox that whilst it was never really at the heart of the great European conflicts, it nonetheless suffered from the effects of the wars in which its prince was involved.

Thus, although the most disastrous episodes of the Hundred Years War did not take place in their country, the duke's subjects were not spared by war: far from it. The revolts of the Flemish towns, for example, were localised, but could have serious consequences for the surrounding countryside. The streets of the Flemish towns saw a certain number of skirmishes and even full-scale battles between the dukes and their restless subjects. Mills destroyed, villages burned to the ground, towns sacked (as Aardenburg was by the men of Ghent in 1452) and populations displaced: these were the sordid counterpart to the battles and the political ideology of muscular opposition in the Flemish towns. Without going as far as Guy Bois, who described the economic and demographic disaster on the Caux plateau around 1435 as a 'Norman Hiroshima', a number of studies have shown how Flanders suffered the consequences of the revolts of Ghent against Louis de Male (1379–85) and Philip the Good (1450–53) and of the civil wars between the towns and Maximilian of Austria (1488–92), even without taking into account the damage caused by more limited conflicts whose consequences, although more difficult to estimate, were no less real for all that.[10] To take some examples: the farms of the abbey of Saint Peter of Ghent around Alost, Oudenaarde and in the Waasland were abandoned for a number of years as a result of the war of 1379–85. In 1492 the area around Ghent, from the river Scheldt to the frontiers of Hainault, was more than 85 per cent deserted. The figures for rental contracts of agricultural holdings around the towns give some impression of the relative violence of these conflicts. Whereas it would take more than twenty-five years for their level to return to normal after the revolts against Louis de Male and Maximilian, seven years were enough to remedy the economic consequences, at least, of the conflict with Philip the Good which occurred in a mid-fifteenth-century economic context more favourable to recovery. Often threatened with destruction for their lack of obedience, the great and good towns of Flanders were always spared, the prince preferring to demonstrate his power of destruction at the expense of their neighbours, as at Dinant in 1466 and at Liège in 1467.[11]

Flanders was not the only part of the duke's lands to be touched by war. Further south, the disruption of cereal production and transport directly hit the supply chains of cities like Bruges and Ghent. Artois and Gallicant Flanders (the broad area of predominantly French-speaking Flanders centred on Lille, now split between France and Belgium) suffered from the passage of all kinds of men-at-arms.[12] On the news of the arrival of royal troops at Artois in 1414, Lille decided to open the lock gates on the upper Deûle, flooding the surrounding lands, and a ducal mandate addressed to the *bailli* on 18 July ordered the imprisonment of any villager who tried to divert the water. Both in 1411 and in 1414, Lille was particularly exposed to the passage of Flemish militia, who camped in the region before joining the ducal army at Douai.[13] In addition to farms, religious houses were not spared, as can be clearly seen in the disturbed history of the abbey of Mont Saint Eloi. This house was situated, unfortunately for its monks, on the old Roman road running from Arras to Thérouanne, and was thus regularly 'visited and frequented' by soldiers.[14] Much the same can be said of Arras, whose population resisted Louis XI and which, after numerous revolts, was first severely damaged before finally being emptied of its population and renamed 'Franchise'.[15]

The list goes on of those areas, from Frisia to the limits of the Cambrésis, which were exposed to the consequences of these more or less distant conflicts. Although conflict abated in relative terms between the peaks of violence which marked the first half of the fourteenth century and the second half of the fifteenth, this region remained a transit zone for troop movements, whatever their origin.

The south: brigands on campaign

In the duke's southern lands, the damage wrought by wars near or far was probably less intense than in the north, but there was still more or less continuous disruption. What is more, the duke's ducal and comital lands, repeatedly ravaged by disease, famine and troop movements, did not have a reputation for being particularly rich.[16] Charles the Bold himself said of Burgundy: 'and there is no money, it feels like France!'[17] On the edge of civil conflicts and the Anglo-French war, the Burgundian lands, which had suffered from the presence of mercenary companies until 1375, had to deal once more with the presence of undisciplined soldiery, now called *écorcheurs* because they were reputed to strip their victims down to their shirt, from 1435 until 1445. As happened with the great companies of the fourteenth century, soldiers demobilised after the Treaty of Arras ravaged areas from Hainault to the Languedoc until the dauphin, Louis, following the example of Bertrand du Guesclin, exported this violence abroad, to wars in the principality of Basel.

The two Burgundies were on the front line, even before the arrival of underemployed royal troops. From 1429 onwards, Charles of Bourbon was the French lieutenant general for matters of war for all lands which had been conquered or were to be conquered on the near side of the Seine. Allied with the Castilian *condottiere*, Rodrigue de Villandrando, he applied systematic pressure on the western frontier of the duchy of Burgundy. Despite the truces agreed by the two brothers-in-law after the assembly at Pont-de-Veyle and its promise of peace in 1434, the troops paid no attention to the agreement between their leaders, and the peace between the king of France and the duke of Burgundy gave no respite for local populations. Instead, 1435 brought a new wave of violence by the under-occupied soldiery. A number of historians have argued that Louis XI was not necessarily displeased by the damage caused by his men, whatever official condemnations he might have issued. We might also note that before the military ordinances of 1445, the king must have tolerated customs of war which permitted soldiers to take their reward from the land in the absence of regular wages. The troops described as *haussaires* by Olivier de la Marche, but more generally referred to, as we have seen, as *écorcheurs*, carved up Burgundy and made a number of incursions into lands further north from their bases in Champagne.

There is no space here for a detailed account of the movements and the exactions of the *écorcheurs*.[18] We need only recall that these very mobile troops created the same climate of terror in both the north and the south. It was not only in the Auxerrois and the Mâconnais that the *écorcheurs* were active. In Hainault, between 1437 and 1445, they followed in the wake of groups of adventurers who had threatened the population during the rule of Jacqueline of Bavaria. They appeared in Hainault during the winter of 1437–38 and in Burgundy in March and April 1438, for example, following no orders whilst taking advantage of the available opportunities for pillage. A group from Normandy under the command of Antoine de Chabannes and Gauthier de Bron devastated Picardy and the Cambrésis before establishing a base close to Solesmes. The *écorcheurs* were also active in the region of Quesnoy and the Avesnois before looking for juicier prey at Meaux, which they besieged in June 1439. They then established themselves once more in Champagne, from where they would soon attack Hainault once again. If some of these men left to serve the king in his campaigns of re-conquest in lower Normandy, others remained to devastate the church of Liessies in January 1440 or the area around Etrœungt near Avesnes, which was also attacked by the men of Louis of Luxembourg, count of Saint-Pol.[19] At the same time, raiding continued in the duchy and the county of Burgundy. Philip the Good, like all the other major nobles of this period, had to deal with bands of pillagers who, we should not forget, had sometimes also served in his own armies. In the end, bags of money were more effective than official declarations in dealing with the groups of armed men holed up in the lands of their enemies or their former masters. In 1435 the duke paid La Hire a significant sum of money in exchange for the return of Breteuil-en-Beauvaisis. The same year, Philip paid Perrinet Gressart 1,700 francs for the delivery of Marcigny, as well as an annual subsidy of 333 *livres*, 2,800 *livres* for ceasing all aggression against the duke of Bourbon and finally 4,000 francs to abstain from any fresh incursion.

These bands of brigands, whose violence respected no frontier, reveal the reality of brute force in the hands of great magnates who had little interest in notions of 'state' or sovereignty. After the relative calm of 1441 and 1442, it was the turn of the church of the village of Forest to be pillaged, before the *écorcheurs*, moving towards the Thiérache, once more ravaged the Avesnois.[20] As transit zones between Champagne, where the *écorcheurs* were based, and Normandy, where they were regularly called upon to fight in the king's wars, Picardy, Artois and Hainault were spared only when the Dauphin Louis led them on his campaign of autumn 1444.

Finding an outlet for the fury of war

In this climate of ubiquitous violence, which pushed rural populations to defend themselves and so to become accustomed to fighting, local urban authorities did what they could. This was the case both in Burgundy, where the men of the council and of the Chamber of Accounts in Dijon, the marshal and the municipal authorities all acted in the absence of the duke, and in the north, where, even when the duke was present, it was the *baillis* and the urban authorities who sought to protect local security. The *bailli* of Hainault, Jean de Croÿ, regularly promulgated measures to organise resistance. In

1440 he even created a kind of mounted police force of about thirty men which was to patrol the borders of his territory, in the hope of counteracting the enemy's high level of mobility. The prince's officers also attended to urban security arrangements, the state of fortifications, the maintenance of garrisons and the preparations of towns in case of a siege. This was perhaps why the *écorcheurs* kept to raiding in the open countryside.

Both in the north and in the south, the consequences of war were serious and long-lasting. The atmosphere of generalised tension was made worse not only by genuine dangers but also by rumours which caused localised panic. In a culture where news travelled slowly and where oral transmission remained central, the terrible reputation of the *écorcheurs* was enough to create a climate of fear and insecurity. In this way, several dozen armed men in Vervins became thousands in the stories told of their adventures at Bavay, fifty-five kilometres to the north. Then, by contagion, the nearby duchy of Brabant and county of Flanders began to fear the arrival at the town gates of this unstoppable company of brigands. Yet if the violence was difficult to control, the enemy was also difficult to identify, with serious consequences for the construction of a common identity. Worse still, the duke of Burgundy's troops were feared just as much by the civilian population. At Mons in the duchy of Hainault, for example, on 8 May 1441, the municipal council decided to take protective measures against the very men who were supposed to save them. Complaints were received that at Rouvres, near Dijon, mounted troops in the service of the governor of Burgundy were causing as much damage as the *écorcheurs*. Mâcon, Talant, Auxonne, Nuits-Saint-Georges, Pontailler and Beaune repeatedly refused to open their gates to the troops of the governor, Jean de Fribourg, whilst further north, the men of the count of Étampes, lieutenant general of the ducal army, were feared as much as those of the *routier* captains.[21]

Moreover, if people could never be sure whether rumours of soldiers' barbarity would turn out to be justified, the new and increased fiscal pressure which followed them was in many ways a more certain threat. To maintain troops and equipment, and when necessary to buy the brigands off, the duke repeatedly asked for money: 12,000 *livres* from Valenciennes in 1438, 10,000 from the Estates of Hainault in 1440, 50,000 in 1444 and so on. In the duchy of Burgundy, the Estates assembled fifteen times in ten years and granted more than 80,000 *livres*. All in all, when we consider the years 1435–45, as Jean-Marie Cauchies has done, taking into account not only the pressures of war and taxation but also the appalling weather and the bad harvests and epidemics which accompanied it, it is clear that the epithet 'promised lands' needs to be very seriously qualified.

The devastation caused by war did not stop there. In the south, skirmishes more numerous than outright battles made the duchy and the county into a theatre of constant warfare, wearing down the population. A few decades later, the famous Burgundian wars against the French monarchy took place over three periods carefully described by J. Robert de Chevanne: from 6 January to 4 April 1471, from 15 June to 3 November 1472 and from 30 April to 13 September 1475. But warfare did not cease abruptly at the end of each of these offensives, nor did the attendant pillage, arson, rape, murder and kidnapping.[22] The Nivernais, for example, whose lord Jean de Bourgogne was in disgrace with Charles the Bold, suffered continually from 1471 to 1475. Elsewhere, where reinforcements were late in arriving, doubts spread and with them disorder. When Louis XI demanded the return of Auxerre to his allegiance in January 1471, riots broke out in the town between pro-royalists and pro-Burgundians, until finally, under pressure from the ducal garrison which had arrived on 20 January, the town authorities refused the king's offer, leading to immediate attacks on the surrounding vineyards. The defenders were even ready to sacrifice certain lands in order to protect themselves, at the expense of inhabitants to whom it mattered little whether they lost their goods to their lords or to the enemy.[23] In the Charolais, the accounts of Semur-en-Brionnais record the decision to burn the lower town to make the site more defensible against the troops of the duke of Bourbon in 1471.[24] In 1472, whilst the protagonists concentrated their forces in the north, the defence of the Burgundian frontiers fell to the communal militias of the Mâconnais, who soon proved just as predatory to the local population. During 1475 the western frontier of the duchy was breached, and all of the upper valley of the Saône in Burgundian allegiance was ravaged. Charles the Bold, well aware of what was going on, nonetheless preferred to send his troops to Lorraine.[25]

The population of the lands of the princes of Burgundy could certainly have joined their voices to those of people of the kingdom who, in Alain Chartier's *Quadrilogue invectif*, called on a personified France to bear witness to their sufferings: 'Look, mother, look, see and consider my most painful affliction.' Chroniclers like Enguerrand de Monstrelet and Jean Molinet excelled themselves in bemoaning the miseries of the 'povre peuple' ('poor people'), who suffered the worst of all.[26] For although these episodes of war did not last long, we should not forget that a 'burned and destroyed' land took twenty years or more to become economically viable again. Everything is relative, and the price to pay could be more or less heavy. But these few examples show how the dukes' lordships were not spared by warfare. War was far from unknown, and we might then think that it ought to have led, according to a logic which appeals to theorists of the construction of the 'modern state', to the rise of a political consciousness linked to the creation of a system of regular taxation and to the development of national feeling, or at the very least of a feeling of belonging to a community. Instead, the principality's brutal schism after 1477 shows the failure of this political construction. What went wrong in this chain of cause and effect? One way to approach this question is through a simpler one: for whom, and for what, did the dukes order the raising of troops?

Wars of honour

At the heart of the propaganda scattered hither and thither in the France of Charles VI and Charles VII, the enemy was clearly identified. The French must rise as a single man to chase the English from their land.[27] Artisans, labourers, officers, knights, priests, women and children were all united by their common destiny, suffering under the yoke of the invader, which should in turn inspire them to fight or to pay for the preservation of the kingdom. The kings of France, much like the dukes of Brittany, went to war on the basis of their land, their lords and their subjects.[28] How does this compare with the arguments which the dukes of Burgundy mobilised to raise troops and money? At the risk of repeating ourselves, it is worth examining how the dukes' deep attachment to the kingdom of France, considered in the previous chapter, influenced the methods which they used.

In the name of the king of France

When John the Fearless issued a military summons in January 1414, he was careful, as he often was, to accompany it with a manifesto setting out his excellent reasons for going to war. After the Cabochien riots, he left Paris and thereafter returned to the capital only to defend his interests there. But even though on 10 February 1414 he was declared a 'rebel to the king', the Burgundian prince still used the now traditional argument that he was acting to protect the king of France. In a letter addressed to the towns of Picardy, he wrote that he needed the support and assistance of his faithful friends in Amiens and elsewhere to protect the king and the common good of the kingdom.[29] The language and the arguments used were always the same, whether they were addressed to the Four Members of Flanders in the hope of receiving monetary aid, to the knights of Artois or to the townsfolk of Amiens, Mâcon or Dijon. Even if the situation had changed since his father's day, and John the Fearless no longer had the prerogatives that Philip the Bold had enjoyed at the court of France, Burgundian troops were always raised with the ostensible purpose of aiding the king and kingdom and thus defending the honour of the prince.

This rhetoric, which had now become more or less obviously false, was based on that of the first Valois duke of Burgundy. Philip the Bold, who was considered to be a better diplomat than soldier, had nonetheless been named 'captain general of all the troops and castles of the kingdom' by Charles V, one month before the king's death. He took charge of a number of campaigns, including one to reconquer Poitou (1370–72); one mounted against a number of castles in English hands around Calais (September 1377); another to help his father-in-law, the count of Flanders, against the revolts which hit the county between 1379 and 1385; and another which sought to protect Brabant against the pretentions of the duke of Guelders, William of Jülich, between 1397 and 1399.[30] Yet even when he raised taxes in the duchy of Burgundy to pay troops fighting in Flanders, Philip insisted that this was done 'for the wars [*le fait de guerre*] of my lord the king'.[31] It was thus natural for John the

Fearless to adopt this formula and to summon his troops 'for the great affairs touching the good of my lord the king and his kingdom',[32] whether serving God on the crusade to Hungary in 1396, fighting against English troops in Flanders in 1405 or going to Paris to oppose the Orléanist party, with or without royal approval.

The closeness of the duke of Burgundy to the Crown even had consequences for the organisation of his armies, as we shall see in more detail in a moment. For the time being, we can observe that when Margaret of Bavaria summoned troops for her husband in 1417, she ordered that the men be paid according to the usage of the kingdom of France.[33] Similarly, we might cite the ambiguous position of the marshal of Burgundy, who swore an oath with his hands clasped in those of the duke, but who continued, as Olivier de la Marche makes clear, to consider himself to be a marshal of France. He exercised the privileges of this function as defined by the charter of 1361, by which John the Good 'recognised the marshal's exclusive competence in the context of the duchy of Burgundy'.[34] The marshal of Burgundy acted in the name of the king, yet the oaths that he swore bound him to defend the duke and his lands. Nonetheless, the language of his oath did not distinguish his office from a simple lieutenancy, as it did in Savoy, for example, where the equivalent oath suggested a form of service which went beyond a personal relation and set him on the road to becoming one of the great officers of state.[35]

In the name of the king of France and of England

With the crisis caused by the murder of John the Fearless on the bridge at Montereau, Philip the Good was obliged to defend a number of his territories at one time or another. Despite his reputation for nonchalance and negligence, Philip nonetheless fought a number of battles. After the alliance with the English, war was now waged against the dauphin's troops, but still for the defence of the honour of the kings of France and England. At Mons-en-Vimeu in 1421, where Philip was knighted by John of Luxembourg, the battle was celebrated at length by the ducal chroniclers as a Burgundian victory. Yet the brains behind these operations had been Henry V, who gave the orders, and it was Charles VI who paid troops who were engaged 'in the service of the king of France'.[36] It certainly cannot be said that Philip fled the field of battle. We find him after the battle of Cravant in the front line defending his lands in the Mâconnais in 1424. Yet here again the strategy adopted came from the English. Philip's expeditions into the kingdom of France were now motivated exclusively by the promise of substantial financial rewards. The duke of Burgundy answered the call of the duke of Bedford and besieged Compiègne in 1430, but that he was far from acting independently became clear when he sent the king of England a bill for 113,075 francs and 2 *sous*.[37] By this time, strictly Burgundian military activities were focused towards the north of the duke's domains, notably in the disputed territories of Jacqueline of Bavaria, the mercurial heiress of the counties of Hainault, Holland and Zeeland, who left her Brabantine husband only to return with a new one, Humphrey, duke of Gloucester, and at the head of an army.[38] It was of course to protect his own interests that Philip took the side of her abandoned husband, John IV of Brabant, but it was in the latter's name that Burgundian troops joined the Brabantine forces. In 1425 Philip sent his messengers to all the *bonnes villes* of Hainault to announce his military support for John IV,[39] and when he threatened Humphrey of Gloucester, he emphasised his indignation at the insult to his cousin's honour.[40]

John the Fearless had already led his army in defence of the honour of his brother-in-law John III of Bavaria against the revolt of the *Haidroits* (citizens of Liège). It was when fighting against them at the battle of Othée in 1408 that he won his sobriquet 'the Fearless'. Philip now followed his father's example, engaging in a war of conquest in Holland, initially in the name of the duke of Brabant. After the latter's death on 17 April 1427, Philip continued in his own name, ostensibly to defend the interests of his inconsistent cousin. He was willing to recognise her as duchess of Bavaria and countess of Hainault, Holland and Zeeland in the Treaty of Delft of 1428, but on condition that she named him as her heir and as the governor of her lands. The years between 1425 and 1428 were thus very active, being punctuated by battles culminating in that of Brouwershaven on 13 January 1426, which marked the victory of the Burgundians supported by the militia of Dordrecht, The Hague and Delft.

In the name of the duke of Burgundy and his family

Honour, first that of the king, then that of the prince, was always central to the arguments adopted by the dukes of Burgundy to justify their actions. For example, after the rupture with England, when Philip decided to lay siege to Calais in 1436, he once more called on his Flemish subjects to defend the king's honour. Yet on 8 March 1436, in a speech delivered in the duke's name and in his presence by Collard de La Clite, the sovereign-bailiff of Flanders, to an assembly of the deans, sworn officers and burgesses of Ghent, the introduction of a number of nuances suggested a subtle change of tone. Whilst the sovereignty of the king of France was still respected, the *bailli* used figures of rhetoric and economic arguments to unite the people of Flanders behind their prince and the interests of his patrimony. The duke's spokesman began with an emotional appeal to his audience, insisting on the fact that the duke had summoned them 'for a thing which touches [him] much at heart'. He then insisted that the duke was a conciliatory prince who honoured the undertakings which he had made to his sovereign, acting in the name of the peace concluded between the king of France and himself at Arras. It was thus that he had decided to act once more, for the love of a people impoverished and maltreated by war, on the pope's command and 'for compassion for the crown of France'. Collard de La Clite laid the blame squarely on the English, who not only had insulted the duke and spread unrest in Holland and Zeeland, but had also started to 'kill a certain number of Flemings' and to attack their boats. And what better way was there to defend Flemish commercial interests than to try and retake his 'paternal inheritance which is the town of Calais'?[41] Starting with his duty as a vassal to defend the crown of France, the *bailli* moved on to arguments much more likely to appeal to the burgesses of Ghent, namely Philip's unceasing concern for the economic security of his Flemish people, even if that meant recalling more or less dubious moments of glory, as when he called upon them to show the same loyalty to him as their predecessors had done to John the Fearless at Pont-à-Choisy or at Hem-en-Vermandois.[42] Abandoning the duke would ruin their reputation and condemn them to dishonour. This is the reason why, in a final passage which has remained famous, Colard de La Clite appealed once more to their emotions to make sure that they remembered the strength of the personal bonds between the subjects and their prince, warning any ill-disposed listener:

> And because some might say that he would be happy with silver, it is not so, for he loves more your service than what a million in gold would give him.[43]

Solidarity with the Crown of France, love for the people of Flanders, concern for economic prosperity, each element of this speech adds a more 'patriotic' tone to the traditional arguments through appeals both to the emotions and to economic considerations which would have been quickly understood. Nonetheless, although the war to be fought against the English was undertaken for Philip's honour, the conquest of Calais and the pacification of this important commercial area, the results, as we shall see, show that the tacit contract between the duke and his Flemish subjects was far from secure.

When Philip's ambitions moved towards the territories of Luxembourg, he once again presented himself as a dutiful knight. In the speech he delivered in the presence of ambassadors from Saxony and in the words recorded by Olivier de la Marche, the duke appeared simply as a noble prince, moved by the plight of his aunt, Elisabeth von Görlitz, a poor, defenceless widow.[44] Speaking after his chancellor, in the presence of the representatives of Wilhelm of Saxony at Florange on 26 October 1443, Philip the Good presented arguments in an epic and a human register, promising to protect with his own body a member of his family threatened by her weak, female condition.

As Olivier de la Marche makes clear, the duke had decided to raise troops and to lead these Burgundians and Picards into Luxembourg in order to crush the ambitions of Wilhelm according to 'the agreement made between the duke and the duchess his aunt ... under her title and cause'.[45] Philip thus took up arms in the name of noble values, by 'duty of lineage' and with God's help. In the event, his campaign met with few difficulties, and the taking of Luxembourg by the Burgundian *écheleurs* ('ladder-men') put a temporary halt to the ambitions of the young lord of Saxony. For Richard Vaughan, the speech delivered at Florange was a perfect piece of hypocrisy. Yet one might reply that even if the intervention in Luxembourg was not purely altruistic, it nonetheless involved a kind of action which was more in line with courtly ideals than with a Machiavellian pragmatism. We might simply note that the war in Luxembourg was once more fought in the name of the duchess and not for the defence of the Philip's principality, even if, in practice, this was its actual result.

In the name of an impoverished community

A few years later, the revolt of Ghent led Philip the Good into a long conflict with his own subjects. Before examining the nature of the arguments developed against this rebellion, let us consider a speech delivered to the authorities of this town in 1447, in which Philip asked for a salt tax or *gabelle* and revealed his desire to establish permanent taxation. What interests us here is the account which Philip presents of the immediately preceding years, in which he had gone to war often and spent much.

Always comfortable in an emotional register, Philip reminded his audience of the circumstances of his arrival in power and the spirit of revenge in which he had embarked on many perilous battles. In this light, the military operations in the aftermath of the assassination of John the Fearless were now presented under the sign of filial devotion (avenging his father's murder) and as the necessary defence of territories threatened by the enemy, even though Philip the Good had sent out summonses to the nobles at the time 'in order to accompany him in the service of the king' and to maintain his position within the kingdom.[46] Similarly, the English incursions which followed the ratification of the Treaty of Arras, and which Philip had attempted to stop in the name of the defence of his honour and that of the king of France, were now presented above all as dangers which the good duke had wisely opposed with God's help and for the love of his Flemish lands. It was likewise for the protection of his lands in Brabant and Flanders that he had now engaged in conflicts in Luxembourg, at his great personal expense. In a nutshell, his urgent need for continuous and stable revenues was justified simply by his desire to protect his subjects, himself and his lands – with an interesting change of order putting the well-being of his subjects before that of the prince.[47]

Such speeches were of course adapted to the context in which they were delivered, and history was written and rewritten as particular needs dictated. When Ghent refused the duke's requests, matters quickly deteriorated, and after years of confrontation and provocation, war was declared.[48] The manifesto of 1452, composed at Brussels on 31 March and addressed to all the duke's subjects, now forcefully summoned all the men of the duke's territories to live or die for their prince in defence of his lands against the treacherous rebels:

> Thus we pray and require insistently all our good and loyal subjects ... on the faith, loyalty and obedience that they owe us, that they should take to heart our right, cause and quarrel in this case, which is so just, reasonable and favourable, and help, assist and serve us in it, each one himself and according to his estate and vocation, and to live and die with us in it, as we hope that they will do, as good and loyal subjects must do with their lord and prince against the said [men] of Ghent ... who are only looking for evil and the destruction of the land.[49]

This was a powerful appeal, finally freeing itself from the rhetoric of honour, familial solidarity and the duty of a vassal to the king of France and instead bringing together in a sacred union the faithful subjects of the duke threatened by men whose 'tyrannies, cruelties and inhumanities'[50] menaced the land. We might see here a positive development, the coming to consciousness of a community, were it not for the fact that the enemy to be destroyed was actually a group of the duke's own subjects. The right tone was finally found, but it was applied only to an alliance against one member of the Burgundian body politic. This paradox was difficult to resolve, and the plethora of reasons advanced for fighting within the principality did not succeed in creating unanimity.

It should be remembered that, in the second half of the fifteenth century, the dukes, whose land-hunger is not in doubt, were careful to hide their game. It was as saviours of Christendom, of the king, of betrayed brothers-in-law, of an irresponsible cousin or of a suffering widow that the dukes presented themselves, and such arguments proved effective in assisting the very real expansion of their principality. Nevertheless, it is difficult to detect any signs on the ground of the consequent development of a consciousness of a community. Indeed, one might ask whether such a result was ever envisaged by the duke. Nothing seems less certain.

An emperor's conquests

When Charles the Bold made his debut in the area of military action, we might have expected that the decisions of this impetuous duke of Burgundy would mark an immediate change of direction. But the Burgundian obsession with France proved difficult to shake off. It was once more as the saviour of the kingdom of France, this time from the tyranny of its own sovereign, that Charles justified his first actions.

Charles received the command of the Burgundian army when he was count of Charolais, leading it to the battle of Montlhéry in 1465, which was thought of as a victory by both sides. By this point in the argument, we can easily imagine that the young heir's ambitions would push him towards perspectives other than the duty of a vassal or the friendship between princes who were interrelated in so many ways. But chivalric rhetoric remained powerful. In 1472 it was the death of the king's brother, the duke of Guyenne, which provided the excuse to break the truce and go on campaign on 4 June. On the pretext that Charles of France had been assassinated by Louis XI, he presented himself 'as the avenger of this murder, insofar as God will give him the power' in all the letters which he sent to his towns, raising a violet banner inscribed with the words 'Vengeance! Vengeance!'[51]

Charles the Bold: a life of battles

It is, though, clear that Charles the Bold's accession marked a radical break in Burgundian policy. He marched through the ten years of his rule as prince to the rhythm of battles which were presented to his people by his propaganda as being fought for the common good. This was the man who replied to his mother, Isabella of Portugal, when she tried to persuade him not to fight in person on the field of battle in his war with Ghent, that it was better for him and his people to die young than to be seen as a lord without courage.[52] On the French front, after the War of the Public Weal and the battle of Montlhéry (1465), Charles took up arms in 1471, starting a cycle of violence which led to appalling atrocities at Nesle, Montdidier and Roye in June 1472. Picardy and Burgundy would suffer from the attacks of French armies on a number of occasions until 1477 and for some time after the duke's death. In his northern lands, which he closely monitored, Charles sacked Dinant in 1466, defeated Liège at Brustem on 28 October 1467 and razed the city to the ground. In 1473 he received the submission of the inhabitants of Guelders after the taking of Nijmegen. He would later force the duke of Lorraine, René II, to accept a protectorate by military means, in a first step towards the annexation of this territory. The revolt of Alsace, which had been purchased from Sigismund of Austria in 1469, took him east in 1474, before the dispute between the archbishop of Cologne and the burgesses of the town gave him the chance to support the prelate and thus to intervene in lands in the Empire. Cologne's resistance, supported by imperial forces, was harder to overcome than that of Liège, and the duke took Neuss only in 1475. Diverting his troops southwards, he had other wrongs to avenge before thinking of Provence. In particular, he wanted to deal with the French, with the men of Lorraine and with the Swiss who had ravaged his lands during the siege of Neuss. He easily conquered Lorraine in November 1475, before turning his attention to the importunate Swiss peasants who had sacked the Franche-Comté. We know what happened next: the Burgundians had to withdraw in haste at the battle of Grandson on 2 March 1476, leaving an exceptional booty for the Swiss Confederates. Charles then stubbornly rallied what remained of his army, leading it to the disastrous defeat of Morat on 22 June, before turning around and returning to Lorraine. This time, René II, with the support of the Swiss and the men of Alsace, brutally ended Charles the Bold's dreams of glory before Nancy on 5 January 1477. Charles's reign was thus packed with battles, sieges and armies continually on the march.[53]

Propaganda ideals and military realities

To gain the means to achieve his ends, Charles needed more and more money. The figures determined by historians tell us much about the duke's appetites. They also explain the reticence of the towns, who in ten years gave Charles the equivalent of forty-five years of taxation under Philip the Good.[54] This constant need for money produced a number of striking speeches, including that delivered at Bruges to the deputies of the Estates assembled from 12 to 14 January 1473, which is worth attending to in detail.

In this impressive speech, Chancellor Hugonet developed an argument of striking political maturity, given what we have heard above, in the hope of raising the substantial sum of 600,000 crowns to pay for a powerful army to fight against Louis XI. The chancellor based his request on a series of introductory arguments drawn from classical authors including Cicero, Aristotle, Lactantius and even Xenophon, whose *Cyropedia* had been translated for Charles's court by Vasco de Lucena. The chancellor asserted that, from the moment a people needed a superior principle to govern them, it was best for them to be placed in the hands of a single prince. For the public weal to flourish, the interests of the prince must be those of the people and vice versa. The chancellor was very clear on this point, which he presented as conditioning the success of any warlike enterprise. For, in the end, the prince's war was the business of all, because it was in the name of the people and for the defence of his lands that the latter risked his life and his patrimony:

> If war or hostility is raised against subjects, the prince cannot say that the war is not his [i.e. that it does not affect him], as he is the one who is principally ordained to protect his subjects. If war is raised or violence made to the prince, the subjects also cannot say that it is not theirs [i.e. that it does not affect them] nor consider it restricted to the prince ...[55]

The reciprocity which makes war into a common enterprise runs through this speech, in which the enemy of the prince – clearly identified this time – is also the enemy of the people. Hugonet used a political language, a vocabulary, which the town representatives would have understood and which had the potential to convince them. How could they not react when the chancellor reminded them that the prince was assembling his troops to protect his people from falling 'into servitude to the king and the French'[56] and so to safeguard their liberties?

The reasons for war put forward in 1473 were radically different from those which had been repeated over and over again by each duke since Philip the Bold. It is not only historians who have noticed this: Hugonet himself was conscious of the change of register. He headed off criticism by pointing out that Philip the Good's wars had been less expensive because they were waged in alliance with the king of England or with other princes. Charles now fought his own wars, in his own name and for his own people: at least, the speech is constructed in a way which suggests this argument. Should we see it as proof of a political ideology shared by the chancellor, the prince and their audience?[57] Nothing could be less certain: what did the latter retain of the ideal of the public weal and of the almost ontological bond which ought to link the prince to his people?

In the immediate aftermath of this address, the audience, no doubt intimidated by the solemnity of the occasion, had little possibility to express themselves.[58] But in the discussions between the town representatives and their fellow citizens on their return home, the lofty political ideal admirably presented by the chancellor is nowhere to be found. The most important piece of information, and the one which was the subject of most debate, was the amount of money which had to be collected in order to satisfy the prince's needs once again. In Saint-Omer, Bethune, Ypres and Douai, the king of France's threats and the necessity to defend the frontiers were invoked in one form or another.[59] Elsewhere, however, the debate never went beyond economic matters. What is more, the unanimity called for by the chancellor was less obvious than a concert of voices which, if they were not quite discordant, were at least individualised. Each community replied to this stirring speech in favour of the defence of the *res publica* and the common good with an agreement in principle linked to specific demands, which ranged from the simple reduction of military service to the confirmation of judicial privileges. In Hainault, for example, the grant of military aid was even made conditional on the recognition of the sovereignty of the court of Mons.[60]

A conquering prince overreaches

The reception of Guillaume Hugonet's address soon showed that his main political argument had not struck home. The same political thought, presented with subtlety and taste by the chancellor, was wielded in a far more brutal and down-to-earth fashion by a prince guided by his obsession with results. When Charles the Bold spoke after his chancellor, he demanded two things: first, that his subjects should hold themselves ready and in arms to assist him; and second, that effective punishments be put in place to punish the deserters who were sapping his army.⁶¹ The duke's words grew harsher as defeat followed defeat, whether he was addressing a chapter meeting of the Golden Fleece or an assembly of Estates.⁶² We can recall the duke's reply to the Four Members of Flanders in May 1470 on the subject of an *aide* of 12,000 *écus*, in which Charles began insulting the Flemish: 'and you have such fat and hard Flemish heads, and you always want to persist in your hardness and your bad opinions'.⁶³ When Charles summoned the deputies of Flanders on 12 July 1475, on his return from the siege of Neuss, he accused them of being responsible for this reverse. The cowards had abandoned him before Neuss and in Picardy, just as he had feared in 1473, thus giving 'courage to the enemy' and committing the crime of *lèse-majesté* by their desertion.⁶⁴

The duke was not always so brutal, and it would be unfair to consign him to a position of cynical haggling removed from any diplomatic consideration. The severity he used when addressing the population of his northern lands, especially the Flemish, apparently disappeared when he talked to his subjects in the south, who were, as has been said, exposed to far less pressure. On 13 July 1476 the Milanese diplomat Panigarola wrote to his duke from an assembly of the two Burgundies which had been summoned to Salins after the defeat by the Swiss at Morat. Charles the Bold, he reported, was using every emotional argument he could to convince the Burgundians to pay for the defence of their lands.⁶⁵ Charles always used the same excuses, explaining his defeat by the ill-will of some of his men and following this up with dark evocations of the fate of women and children at the hands of the German and French armies if the Estates refused to pay. Yet he also said how much he would be a good lord for them, better still than he had already been and ready to live and to die for his people.⁶⁶ This theme of the good prince's paternal desire to make every sacrifice for his lands and for his subjects recurs throughout his speeches. With Charles, however, his choice of words did not hide the extent of his ambitions. The prince's war fever now led him into an imperial temptation.

Much has been written on Charles's reading and how he was raised on the great deeds of Roman emperors and on the epics of Alexander and Cyrus. Philippe Contamine puts it perfectly when he wonders whether it might be better to class Charles the Bold as being above all motivated by the spirit of conquest, rather than including him amongst 'the promoters or founders of the modern state'.[67] His taste for conquest is also found in speeches delivered to the Estates. In 1473 Hugonet cited Julius Caesar's *Commentaries*. In 1476, speaking after the president, Jouard, Charles evoked the personality of Octavian, the future Augustus, who despite his defeat by Pompey's son returned to become the ruler of Rome and of the world.[68] Charles was haunted by the desire to match these exceptional men, to avoid their vices the better to equal their military genius.[69] Richard Vaughan long ago demonstrated, on the strength of the duke's numerous excesses, the reality of his impetuous and egocentric character.[70] Charles's immoderate nature is well attested. Yet if we go further and start to analyse his military strategies, tactics and rapid manoeuvres in detail, we return to the same idea: his lust for empire.

We have already seen that at Trier, Charles was so concerned to obtain a crown that he was ready to allow his territory to come under the Empire's influence. The same concern guided his military actions. When his troops could have joined those of Edward IV and finally defeated his enemies, he turned his back on his English ally, advancing into the Empire instead. Repelled on that side, he turned his attention to Provence, which he hoped to obtain from René II. En route for the new object of his ambitions, he lost Alsace but then stopped to retaliate against the arrogant Swiss, comforted in his decision by the need to attend to his interests in Savoy. All of this is well known, but it is worth adding that the propaganda which accompanied these erratic and ruinous manoeuvres was itself based on an incoherency. For whilst Charles was mobilising all his military resources in support of the conquests which would raise him to the status of emperor, his arguments were based on the defence of his lands. In the ordinance promulgated at Abbeville in July 1471, the army was to be assembled 'for the good, security and defence of his lands, lordships and subjects'.[71] Every declaration in the duke's name followed this line, even though his subjects knew perfectly well that 'war' was a synonym for additional taxes, devastation and lost profits. Charles the Bold's actions were thus in constant contradiction with his expressed intentions. The troops which he presented as a defensive force were in reality an instrument of conquest. Just before his death, the mask slipped in an ordinance, issued from his camp before Lausanne in June 1476, which declared that the good order which the battle captains enforced would permit them 'to have and to acquire honour and good fame throughout the whole world'.[72] Charles's ambitions cut him off from a people whom he deliberately distanced from his dreams. He took their wealth and the lives of their men, giving them only fallacious war propaganda in return. His speeches for war were certainly ill-constructed or at the very least ill-adapted for the circumstances. What of the infrastructure which supported his military action?

The power of the Burgundian armies

It would be wrong, with the benefit of hindsight, to judge the Burgundian armies as another weakness in Burgundian 'governance'. It is certainly not this aspect of 'state building' in the principality which should be put in question. The military apparatus established by the first three dukes and modernised by the last had nothing to envy in the other armies deployed on the European stage. It might have been possible to deal with this matter only briefly, were it not for the fact that it reveals new paradoxes which lead us on to new questions, namely that the more the military machine was modernised the more the defeats accumulated. For Philippe Contamine, the more cosmopolitan composition of the army which emerged from these reforms should not be blamed for the final debacle, which was mainly the result of strategic errors.[73] For Bertrand Schnerb, the paradox is only a superficial one, since the reforms which Charles wanted to put in place necessarily led him to act on ambitions whose extent unfortunately destroyed the apparatus which had been constructed to support them.[74] For others still, such as David S. Bachrach, there is no case to answer, since Charles's reforms did not constitute a genuine military revolution.[75] For Bachrach, the ideas of Hermann Heimpel, who regarded the military ordinances as 'the victory of the values of the state over chivalric values', and of Bertrand Schnerb, who considered that the Burgundian state manifested itself in this armed force and in a military society devoted to the prince and the common weal, should be subject to criticism.[76]

So is it possible to establish a link between military reform and state construction?

Armies to fight a war

The title of this section might seem like a pleonasm. Nonetheless, it helps us to get to the heart of the matter and to raise an essential question. Did the dukes of Burgundy, and medieval rulers in general, intend to turn their armies into a means of forming national consciousness?

It would seem that the primary objectives of every duke were to win battles and to provide themselves with the means to do so. Until the reforms of Charles the Bold, the summons of the host took place on the basis of the feudal system, assembling all those who held fiefs and rear-fiefs, but also 'all those who were accustomed to bear arms'. The armies also included volunteers from allied principalities, who were hired by contract, and mercenaries who offered their services to the highest bidder. Service in the feudal host was normally unpaid when it took place in the vassal's country of origin, but the dukes of Burgundy also used a system of paid military service with fixed daily wages just like that of the kings of France and England.[77] It was thus the nobles, French-speaking for the most part, who provided the army officers, whilst the dukes themselves were happy to take the role of commander-in-chief. The captains of the army were designated by the duke. The marshal of Burgundy, whose title, unlike that of the marshals of other counties and duchies in the Burgundian principality, was no mere formality, took the duke's place when he was absent.[78] Amongst these troops, an increasing number were archers, rising from 12 per cent under Philip the Bold to about 70 per cent during the English alliance under Philip the Good. At the same time, the growing importance of ever more elaborate artillery brought with it the recruitment of foreign specialists, such as Roland and Jacques of Majorca under Philip the Bold, and the creation of the office of 'warden and master of the artillery', whose first holder, Germain de Givry, was appointed in 1414.[79] The towns also sent men on occasion or were required to provide artillery, as in the case of Malines. In July 1467 Charles sent numerous letters to the magistrates of Ypres, Bruges, Le Franc and Cassel, amongst other towns, asking for pikemen and infantry. The repetition of the duke's demands and the resulting comments found in the registers of Ypres show the difficulties the duke encountered when he made requests which were felt to be both very onerous and very odious ('zeer lastich ende odieulx') by the Flemish townspeople.[80] Effective enough for the dukes' occasional requirements, the army was unchanged until the eve of the War of the Public Weal.

When Charles the Bold took over his Great Principality, he turned to a general reform of its finances, justice, the court and the army. To my mind, Charles appears more as a great administrator than as a subtle strategist in his military ordinances. The duke nevertheless did attempt to resolve a major weakness in the Burgundian armies, one whose consequences he had suffered at Monthléry, namely the troops' dispersal and their slow movement.[81] On the opposing side, the king of France could count on a royal guard composed of a thousand Scots and Frenchmen, a few dozen cannon, a 'national' infantry, a militia of free archers, free crossbowmen and free hand-cannoneers, one of whom was recruited per parish (i.e. per 16,000 men), holders of fiefs and rear-fiefs, occasionally reinforced by additional forces including Spanish light cavalry, and especially the ordinance companies created in 1445–46, which numbered 10,000 or so professional troops. Charles thus sought to remedy his lack of a standing army by paying his men 'household wages' (gaiges mesnagiers) from 1470; that is, he paid them wages to stay at home, in their households, ready for action. Then, after having obtained a tax from the Estates of Flanders to support permanent companies of 1,000 lances in defence against the French threat, Charles drafted his first military ordinance, on 25 July 1471 at Abbeville, to regulate 'the action, conduct, government, way of living, accommodation, dress and so forth' ('le fait, conduite, gouvernement, manière de vivre, de logis, habilement et autrement') of the new permanent troops, named 'ordinance companies' in the French manner. This text, completed with an ordinance issued at Bohain on 13 November 1472, established the chains of command and the organisation of 1,250 soldiers with 'three mounted archers, one hand-cannoneer, one crossbowman and a pikeman on foot' for each man-at-arms. At the abbey of Saint Maximin, Trier, in November 1473, Charles increased the number of companies to twenty-two, which would have provided him with 20,000 men, as many as the king of France had. Their organisation was now defined more precisely: each company consisted of a hundred lances, subdivided into four squadrons of twenty-five lances, and each squadron was divided in its turn into five chambers of five lances. The vocabulary marked a new departure from French practice, taking on the subtleties of the Italian military world with its squadrons (escadres, in French, from the Italian squadra), and the conducteurs at the head of each company like Burgundian-style condottiere.

Without entering into the detail of these ordinances, it should be noted that Charles's army was governed by the nobility and that troops composed of men owing feudal military service were still very important. The duke ordered inquiries to make the most of the men he had. In an order addressed to the bailli of Dole, issued from The Hague on 13 October 1469, for example, he had divided his feudal troops into five categories according to their physical abilities, ranging from those who were 'strong and fast' to the 'frail and aged'.[82] The inquiries ordered by the duke in each of his territories enabled him to establish legislation covering all of them, which also suggests the existence of a political approach capable of going beyond individual cases, establishing in this case a standard for the number of armed men to be summoned according to the economic potential of each fief. These ordinances were intended to make the raising of troops fairer but also, and above all, to allow them to be mustered more quickly. For this reason we should stress that despite the creation of ordinance companies, the feudal element of the army was still very significant under Charles the Bold. According to the calculations of Bertrand Schnerb, on the basis of the presentation of arms in the two Burgundies and the account of the war treasurer for the Low Countries in 1472, feudal service yielded 16,746 men-at-arms (5,365 in Burgundy and 11,381 in the north), as against 8,400 combatants from the duke's permanent forces.[83] We can thus conclude that, even if its social composition was more heterogeneous under Charles than under his great-grandfather, the leadership of the army stayed firmly in the hands of the nobles in the north and in the south. As we shall see, this was not without consequences for the duke's choice of tactics.

The recruitment of mercenaries has often been taken to be particularly characteristic of Charles's rule. Yet if the names of Troylo da Rossano, Pierre and Antoine de Lignana, Jacques Galeotto and

Cola di Monforte are all associated with the campaigns of the last Valois duke of Burgundy, his predecessors had also made considerable use of foreigners to serve in their ranks.[84] In this he was no different from other European princes. The French and the English armies both included foreigners known for their professionalism, who were hired by the highest bidder. However, there is one point of contrast which ought to attract our attention. Whereas the English, after the success of Joan of Arc, sought to anglicise their forces for fear of treason, Charles the Bold, who persistently blamed his failures on the treachery of his men, opened up his army, as his defeats multiplied, to Italians, Germans, Englishmen and Savoyards.[85] Indeed, the Italians were not the only ones to fight for the duke of Burgundy. English troops, despite George Chastelain's denunciation of their pride, violence and lies, nonetheless acquitted themselves well at the siege of Nijmegen in July 1473 and under the leadership of Sir John Middleton in 1475.[86]

A military revolution or readjustment?

Did Charles the Bold's remodelling of his armies constitute a military revolution? Was it a sign of the consciousness of a Burgundian state? A few questions and answers should help us to understand what exactly was going on.

Firstly, was the structure of the duke's army fundamentally different from what had come before? If we put to one side the ordinance companies, the bulk of his forces remained the same. But the addition of mercenaries and the permanent availability of his soldiers undoubtedly resulted in a change in the nature of his army and a modernisation of his military resources. Secondly, were his troops more mobile as a result? Apparently not, as a number of tragicomic anecdotes suggest. When John the Fearless gave siege to Vellexon in 1409, no one could find the master of artillery, because he had yet to turn up. In 1472 Charles had already crossed France's frontier and burned Nesle, before the troops from Burgundy had mustered at Brazey, Perrigny-sur-l'Ognon, Gourdon, Montsaugeon and elsewhere, far away from the action.[87] Thirdly, were the troops more energetic in their response to the duke's requirements? The urban militia of the northern lands were not the only ones to chafe at orders for mass military summonses. At the time of the great war of 1472, the government of the two

Burgundies had to issue repeated summons to both vassals and rear-vassals. Indeed, on 8 February 1474, the duke issued a grand ordinance addressed to the *bailli* of Dijon and to all the men of Burgundy, in which he publicly ticked off his tenants-in-chief and sub-tenants who had responded very late, or even not at all, to his appeals, and hoped that in the future they would react more quickly. Finally, did the increasing number of foreign soldiers threaten the cohesion of his forces and contribute to their defeat? It would seem decidedly unfair to draw this kind of conclusion, on the pretext of the treachery of the count of Campobasso before Nancy or the tensions between the representatives of different nations. Admittedly, that the highest salaries went to foreign professionals must have caused a certain amount of jealousy, and the duke's intimates apparently did not appreciate this 'company of foreign folk', if we are to believe that Jean Molinet faithfully represents what was said at the time.[88] But the direct incorporation of the latter into the Burgundian armies had unified wage scales, and the heavy losses suffered by foreign mercenaries in the Swiss campaigns are enough to demonstrate their fidelity to the last.[89]

There was probably no military revolution under Charles the Bold, but rather a readjustment which allowed him to adapt his military resources to new rhythms of warfare and new objectives. There was certainly no birth of a Burgundian state consciousness in a reform introduced by Charles at the service of his personal ambitions alone, despite the borrowings of the language of the duke's ordinances from Vegetius, with their insistence on the preservation of the public weal.[90] It is worth insisting on the point that his armies were first and foremost organised to win battles. Their achievements and their failures nonetheless reveal more than their military potential and its limits.

The military ordinances of Charles the Bold: order and suspicion

Charles is widely regarded as both the most warlike duke of Burgundy and the one most interested in military matters. The traditional picture of him is that of a man in a hurry, always on horseback, keeping his armour on for hours and leaving the field to compose military ordinances. In short, when he was not making war, he was writing about it. During his brief rule, he produced an exponentially increasing range of orders, letters of commission certainly, but also, and above all, ordinances which provoked the admiration of his contemporaries from the moment of their publication, for example on the part of Panigarola, who copied out that of 1473 for his Sforza master.

The specificities of Charles the Bold's ordinances

The texts produced between 1471 and 1476 were part of a long tradition, one harking back to the text composed by Philip the Bold on the occasion of his departure for Hungary on 29 March 1396.[91] Philip the Good also sought to correct the indiscipline of his troops in an order addressed to the *bailli* of Dole on 27 March 1438.[92] The ordinances of Abbeville (June 1471), Bohain (13 November 1472), Saint Maximin of Trier (November 1473) and Lausanne (June 1476) present an array of decisions, sanctions, banning orders and restrictions which suggest both constant dissatisfaction and increasingly desperate activity on the part of the duke.[93]

If we compare these ordinances with those produced in the entourage of the king of France in the same period (the ordinance of Montils-lès-Tours, April 1467; the ordinance of Amboise, 13 May 1470), what strikes us is how laconic the latter are, with formulas like 'the good pleasure of the king, by the advice and deliberation of many princes ... and people of our great council', 'to the honour of the king and the good of his kingdom and the relief of his good and faithful people', in contrast with Charles the Bold's more elaborate rhetoric. Charles's ordinances are studded with the famous phrase 'on pain of incurring my indignation'; they declare decisions to have been taken personally (the ordinances were made 'by my lord the duke of Burgundy'); and they justify the duke's actions 'by the keeping, surety and defences of our person, estate, lands, lordships and subjects'.[94] We should notice in passing that Charles presents himself as an individual defending his own person and not, like the king of France, in terms of the title he held. Louis XI's ordinances are relatively brief, and they only refine or repeat some of the articles of the foundational ordinance of Loupy-le-Châtel. We should also note that, all through the fifteenth century, kings and princes had to deal with the disorder caused by their own troops, legislating ceaselessly to stop pillage and violence against the local population. But whereas this theme almost entirely dominated the French texts, Charles went further, regulating in detail the chain of command, his troops' equipment, their accommodation, their pay, their leave, the role of each type of soldier in battle, the principles of loyalty and so on. However, one recurrent concern, absent from Louis XI's ordinances, prevails in the ducal ordinances: the fight against desertion.

Order and rule in military matters

In all of Charles the Bold's texts, what is particularly apparent is his love of seeing 'matters well ordered, ruled, controlled and well maintained', as he put it.[95] Moreover, when we compare the ordinances of his household with those of his army, what quickly emerges is the coherence of approach in these two areas. Careful attention was paid in the one to the hierarchy of the household, from the chamberlains who obey the first amongst them, and in the other to the *conducteurs* who are given charge of four squadrons each. In both kinds of ordinances, we find a similar depersonalisation of relations and the development of written petitions. At court, as on the field of battle, this rigorous order was maintained by penalties paid not only by the guilty party, but also by the man who was responsible for him, encouraging denunciation. It can also be seen that the relationships between levels of this pyramid of duties were each articulated by an oath. Finally, the moral order which can be discerned in the household ordinances, for example in the ban on the feast of fools being celebrated by its clerical members, finds its echo in the military ordinances forbidding drunkenness, whores, games of dice and blasphemy.

This comparison of the prince's different ordinances could be carried further to demonstrate Charles's veritable obsession with planning in every domain. Nevertheless, before these texts seduced the princes of Europe, who quite rightly came to see them as a set of exemplary administrative protocols, the duke's extreme rigour shocked his own entourage. The nobles' dissatisfaction and the lassitude of the towns have already been invoked. Charles's obsession with order even enabled the jurist Philippe Wielant, in a double portrait of father and son, to contrast the two once again in these words:

> Duke Philip put order in his deeds and had a very well-run household, whereas the duke Charles often turned his estate to superfluities and useless expenses.[96]

Yet whilst the order described in theory in these ordinances was close to perfection, its application in real life was more problematic. What we see instead is a theory ill-adapted to practice, forms of practice which resisted structure and a structure which gave in to the force of circumstances and the unforeseen. How after all could one bind together a band of men ready to die in battle on the basis of practices of denunciation? How could men be expected to abandon the familiar pastimes of soldiery (gambling, blasphemy, drink) to satisfy the honour of the House of Burgundy and the duties of their prince to the Almighty? How could an army of nearly twenty thousand men be made effective on so many fronts and in so little time?

The chronic disjuncture between the duke's ideas on the one hand and the constraints of his milieu and his time on the other explains in part his failures and on occasion the desertion of men who ended up by fleeing almost without fighting at the battle of Grandson.

Desertion in the mirror of the ordinances

Of course, desertion was not a problem unique to Burgundian armies.[97] From the end of the thirteenth century, the kings of England had to face this danger, which dogged, for example, Edward I's campaigns in Scotland. Even Henry V's successes in France did not put a stop to desertion.[98] In Valois France in 1351, John the Good alluded to this problem in one ordinance and tried to counter it by using the same methods as Charles the Bold would use later: more regular troop inspections, the swearing of oaths which bound men not to leave their company and the compilation of registers of identified absentees. In 1374 the problem was still there, and any soldier who left the ranks of the army was supposed to be denounced to the war treasurer. Deserting meant endangering both the king and his subjects, thereby threatening the public weal, but with time and the multiplication of military offices, the royal armies came to be more effectively controlled. In the Great Principality of Burgundy, although this phenomenon is most apparent in the last years of Charles's rule, it was not new for all that. During the campaigns of the Bien Public, of Dinant and of Liège, Duke Philip and his son sent out orders and letters deploring the desertion of men-at-arms, which worsened when the booty was sufficiently plentiful to allow soldiers to return home with full pockets.[99] The penalties imposed on those who quit the army without leave were graduated, ranging from the death penalty to simply being returned to the ranks. The ordinances of Charles the Bold once more allow us to track his state of mind. In 1471 no penalty was to be imposed; it was simply asked that guarantees be required in the case of leaves of absence. At Bohain in 1472, the duke left the punishment of the guilty to the discretion of the *conducteur*, promising his pardon to those who returned within eight days and ordering the civil authorities to cooperate. In January 1473 he reminded a meeting of the Estates General at Bruges of the need to punish those who deserted from his army. In the ordinance of that November, he ordered that the *conducteurs* should take care of 'criminal punishment, corporal or otherwise at their discretion, by the sole notification of the justice of the place where he was taken and apprehended'.[100]

With the acceleration and multiplication of Charles's campaigns, the troops' morale faltered, even when these campaigns were successful. The long siege of Neuss, which lasted from 30 July 1474 to 13 June 1475, made matters worse. It was on returning from the latter that Charles, bitter with defeat, attacked the Flemings, who 'by their accustomed cowardice ... do not know how to do anything in due time, which redounds to their or other people's profit'.[101] But Flanders was only one example of a more widespread phenomenon. Jean-Marie Cauchies has shown how the men of Hainault were just as likely to 'return without licence over here' ('retournéz sans licence par decha'),[102] fleeing an interminable siege whose conditions were rather harsher than is suggested by Olivier de la Marche's account. In a letter addressed to George Chastelain, the count of Chimay describes how the noise of artillery mixed with the cries of the injured and complains of the cold and the snow, which froze men just as the fear of death froze the blood in their veins. He describes the habits of soldiers who danced and played to forget the mud, the gunpowder and the sudden disappearance of a comrade-in-arms. In these few lines, where the count of Chimay explains how the duke flew 'like a swallow' from one camp to the next, stopping one activity to begin another and haranguing his vassals so as to encourage the ordinance men, we can feel the fatigue. It is expressed through disgust at the base realities of human existence, nostalgia for the pleasures of Bruges and fear in the face of a death which arrives each day to carry off its quota of men, except when they are reprieved through mutilation.[103]

Horror and distress pushed men to desertion. It was said that at Grandson, Charles lost more men in flight than on the field of battle. In a letter from a Milanese ambassador dated 6 June 1476, it was said that the Lombards had fled when they could, that the Burgundians took refuge with the sire of Château-Guyon in Piedmont and that the duke's army was in such a dilapidated state that the soldiers were forced to beg as an atmosphere of murder and rapine took hold.[104] Charles reacted violently, ordering his lieutenant, Claude de Neufchâtel, to execute all deserters, including young men and those who were slow to rejoin the army.[105] The camp ordinance issued at Lausanne in June 1476 specified that all those who 'disobeyed his order by decamping' should be put to death. Charles reacted to his men's distress with ever greater rigour. This ordinance also suggests a fifteenth-century prince who feared that defeat would inevitably fall on a camp which forsook God. For the duke, this was clearly the fault of his soldiers, whose detestable behaviour had to be corrected at all costs. So, to start with, 'all whores and ribalds' should be forced from the camp, and the men should drink 'more water [i.e. as opposed to wine] so that they will be less hot'. In addition, 'detestable men who make execrable and detestable oaths against the name of God' should be tied 'to some chariot wheel ... day and night ... on bread and water'.[106] Yet this new turn of the screw changed nothing, despite identical orders sent to the *baillis* in all the duke's lands. At Morat, it was even the fourth corps of the army led by Jacques de Romont, who was presented by chroniclers as the most experienced and highly motivated of the duke's captains, who quit the field of battle and made its way safe and sound back to the Pays de Vaud. But the question of demoralisation and collective rebellion is another subject which we will deal with later.

From Commynes and Panigarolla to Jean Molinet, historians have made it their business to stress the errors of a prince who dug the grave of his own *dominium*. Still others try to rehabilitate the memory of a man whose only fault was to be on the wrong side of fortune. Desertion was of course a widespread phenomenon in all the armies of Europe, the result of such natural human feelings as fear, greed and lassitude, but in Charles's armies it also revealed a lack of confidence caused by the accumulation of defeats.

Armies without strategists?

The deliberately provocative title of this section could very well be used to describe the military career of the last duke of Burgundy, if we follow the wise counsels of Sun Tzu in his advice to the strategist: 'In war, then, let your great object be victory, not lengthy campaigns.' Although Charles the Bold could not have been aware of the theories of the great Chinese general, he had read Julius Caesar, Vegetius and especially Xenophon, and he was thus perfectly conversant with the military treatises available at the time. Together with his almost compulsive military activity, this education has earned the last duke of Burgundy his place in the pantheon of the great warriors of his day, unlucky in most of his battles, but valiant to the last.

The hubris, ubiquity and isolation of a fighting prince

The armies of Charles's predecessors were certainly not better organised than his, nor were they more conscious of the need to defend an improbable common good, but they had not exhausted themselves in ceaseless warfare. More to the point, they won, often in alliance with other military forces. Lady Fortune naturally played a role in all this, and it is no exaggeration to say, for example, that Philip the Good was lucky to have her on his side at the battle of Mons-en-Vimeu on 30 August 1421. On this occasion, things started badly when the duke's valet threw his banner to the ground and two thirds of the Burgundian army panicked and started to flee. If the Dauphinois had not decided to pursue them, the rest of the duke's army would have been unable to regroup, thus enabling Philip to win the battle. There is perhaps no need to remind the reader that the Flemish at Roosebeke (27 November 1382) were defeated by an army of royal and Burgundian troops, or that at the great battle of Othée (23 September 1408) against Liège, the battle was won by John the Fearless in alliance with William of Bavaria. At Cravant (31 July 1423), the troops of the marshal Jean de Toulongeon fought alongside those of the earl of Suffolk. At Bulgnéville (2 July 1431), the duke's armies marched under a pennon with the arms of Antoine de Vaudémont and took counsel with the English knight Thomas Gargrave,[107] and Luxembourg was taken on 21 November 1443 by the Burgundians with the assistance of the men of Elisabeth von Görlitz.

By contrast, after the War of the Public Weal, Charles often faced the troops of the king of France alone. At a time in 1469 and 1470 when the talk at the Burgundian court revolved around war, Louis XI took care never to begin any military operation without first securing the neutrality of the duke of Brittany. He also manoeuvred to assist the earl of Warwick to return to England, swapping sides in support of the deposed king Henry VI and forcing Charles's ally, Edward IV, to flee to Holland.[108] Opening two fronts, in Picardy and in the two Burgundies, Louis nonetheless ceased hostilities on 4 April 1471. This was probably, as Henri Dubois argues, because he felt isolated and did not want to risk his interests in a battle.[109] In the meantime, the fate of the House of Lancaster had been sealed for some years by Warwick's death at the battle of Barnet on 14 April 1471, the death of the Lancastrian Prince Edward at Tewkesbury on 4 May and the murder of Henry VI on 21 May. Charles the Bold's brother-in-law and ally, Edward IV, was now more secure in power than ever. Nonetheless, Charles was persuaded to accept a treaty with Louis XI, who pacified the duke of Burgundy by returning to him several places in the Mâconnais without giving up what was most important: Saint-Quentin and Amiens. Louis was in a delicate position, whereas Charles, by contrast, was gaining in power, with troops already mobilised, an alliance made with the duke of Brittany and the king of England and fresh discontent emerging amongst the princes of France. Yet nothing came of it, and the duke of Burgundy instead turned his attention to the Empire and to Lorraine.

No one could say that Charles was not aware that war was won primarily through diplomatic alliances. All these years of war were accompanied by numerous embassies which tried to make or unmake alliances on behalf of Louis XI, the duke of Burgundy, the emperor and Italian princes, amongst others. The Burgundian diplomatic situation was consolidated with treaties of alliance signed with Naples, the kings of England, Scotland, Aragon and the dukes of Savoy and Cleves. Charles, concerned to fight a just war, took the opportunity offered by the mysterious death of the king's brother to launch a series of extremely violent campaigns. With the help of contingents from Lorraine under Nicolas de Calabre and those sent from England by Edward IV, Charles opened hostilities and fought a devastating war in Picardy and Normandy, although Beauvais succeeded in resisting him. The French soon returned like for like, and Prisches experienced the same atrocities as Nesle in the war of 1472. This state of affairs, where neither side entirely prevailed, has been used by historians to argue that Charles had the advantage. Yet it must have seemed rather less advantageous to the subjects who were ceaselessly taxed for a ruinous war in which armies fought but no victor emerged.

Charles certainly mastered the diplomatic game, but he always pursued several simultaneous projects, so that rather than using truces to rest his men and regroup his forces, he instead launched further long and exhausting campaigns. After conquering Guelders and the county of Zutphen, for example, in the summer of 1473, and disappointed by the emperor's about-turn at Trier, he then made for Luxembourg, which he had bought from Sigismond of Austria in 1469 and which had been suffering under the rod of Peter von Hagenbach. In the spring, after the formation of the League of Constance, the region had risen in rebellion, and Hagenbach had been decapitated on 9 May 1474. When Charles sent his troops to avenge his *bailli*, almost all the princes of the Empire came to the aid of Alsace.[110] Instead of settling the question of Alsace once and for all, Charles changed his mind again. Suspicious of the count of Montbéliard, he had him seized by Claude de Neufchâtel and Olivier de la Marche. This act was not without its consequences, since the town of Montbéliard refused to surrender, despite the threat to the life of its lord. Little progress was made. Charles thus decided to move his men once more so as to come to the aid of the bishop of Cologne – since for him the surrender of that town was essential in order to defend Alsace and to chastise the rebels and their Swiss allies. His strategy of dealing with one front by opening up another could easily be confusing, and it never ceases to puzzle historians. Conscious that his attack on upper Alsace risked encouraging the whole Holy Roman Empire to rise against him, thus weakening his position in the east, Charles lit a third fire by stoking the embers of the Hundred Years War, encouraging Edward IV's pretensions to the crown of France.[111]

So, to return to this broad-brush survey of Charles's campaigns, it can be said that whilst Charles entrenched his men in the camp at Neuss for nearly a year (from July 1474 to June 1475), he was still considering future strategies which had nothing to do with the battle he was currently engaged in but which prepared those to come. This recurring disassociation between immediate events and long-term strategy, this refusal of the present, this constant flight forwards, forced Charles into notable errors. When the English ambassadors tried to persuade him to abandon this siege and come to the aid of their monarch, who was ready to arrive in Normandy with 35,000–40,000 men, Charles replied with a dilatory formula, promising that he would be ready whilst stubbornly remaining in the shadow of Cologne.[112] When he finally left Neuss to greet Edward at Calais around 13 July 1475, his honour salved by the treaty arranged by the papal legate which made it possible to avoid declaring who was the victor and who the vanquished, he came without an army. It is thus easy to understand the disappointment of the king of England and his readiness to conclude the Treaty of Picquigny with Louis XI on 29 August.[113]

The clock stops, the clock accelerates

The siege of Neuss, the twelfth great deed of Duke Charles according to Chastelain, was a turning point in Burgundian military history. On the Burgundian side, the clock had stopped, or only advanced to the rhythm of a 'what if', whereas on the side of his enemies it had definitely sped up. The emperor organised a *Reichskrieg* against Charles as best he could. The Swiss Confederates allied with Sigismund, and the towns of the upper Rhine launched a first attack in the county of Burgundy at Héricourt, in reprisal for the atrocities committed by Stefan von Hagenbach, Peter's brother. The Burgundians moved to Héricourt, and it was the armies of the marshal of Burgundy, Jacques de Savoie, count of Romont, backed by Lombard troops, which sought in vain to relieve the town. Héricourt fell on 14 November 1474. More than 1,600 Burgundians died in battle, and eighteen Italian mercenaries accused of sodomy were taken to Basel to be burned to the honour of 'God Almighty, the Christian faith, and all the Germans'.[114] Charles was too busy digging mines, organising archers, draining the rivers around Neuss or receiving ambassadors from Milan or Hungary, as part of one utopian scheme or another, to be too worried by this defeat. Had he paid more attention, he might have realised that the periphery is often a weak spot, and that in reality it was not the towns in Flanders, which were still paying for all this, but rather those of Alsace and Switzerland which constituted the greatest threat to his position.[115] For although the duke of Burgundy, through his zigzagging, changeable, risky and sometimes incomprehensible strategies, did not manage to unite his subjects behind him, he did succeed in uniting his enemies against him, helping to create a 'German nation' conscious of its identity in the face of Charles, the Grand Turk of the West.[116]

The duke's next moves were just as over-complicated, although he now spent much time reassuring allies who were starting to lose faith in him, even if he had no intention of pausing in his projects. The Treaty of Soleuvre with France, which established a nine-year truce starting on 13 September 1475, showed that Charles was no longer focused on his ancestral homeland and demonstrated once again that the war propaganda which justified taxation by stigmatising the French enemy was no more than rhetoric. Although Louis XI was still his personal enemy, the duke's ambitions now took him eastwards. Hardly had he raised the camp at Neuss than he assembled his men to go and conquer Lorraine. The success of this campaign was mitigated, as we have seen, by the fact that Charles was less concerned to satisfy his men and consolidate his position than to salve his honour by crushing the Swiss. Burgundian diplomacy worked to deprive them of French and imperial aid. Charles was now convinced, as he himself put it, that nothing could resist military discipline and courage.

At Grandson, as at Morat and at Nancy, failure came not from diplomatic strategy but from tactical and human errors: the inappropriateness of the army he had assembled for the terrain and the lack of attention paid to hungry and exhausted soldiers. This is why, if we look at military strategy from the point of view of the alliances undertaken by the duke and all the diplomatic activity which lay behind them, it is difficult to fault the considerable efforts of the Burgundian ambassadors.[117] But when we turn to military strategy, it is surprising to find Charles preferring heavy cavalry to infantry – even though after Grandson he learnt the lessons of this humiliation and reinforced the latter. It is just as difficult to understand why, at the camp at Lausanne, he decided to replace his longbows, with their fast and easy fire, with crossbows, which were certainly more powerful but ten times slower. Once more, the literature on the subject is plentiful, and there is no lack of historians to point out that, by adopting a system of four armed corps at Morat, Charles isolated the lines of his army, who were thus rendered incapable of providing support for one another, or that the ever-inflexible duke deployed an army ill-adapted to the terrain on which the battle was fought.[118]

Reconnoitring the field of battle was not unknown at the Burgundian court. In 1436 Philip the Good ordered a 'map [*patron*] of the situation of the town of Calais' to be made, and in 1466–67 Charles sent two officers to Neufchâteau in Lorraine to reconnoitre the banks of the Meuse.[119] Yet this did not stop the Burgundian troops from being carried away by their own momentum, meeting their fate in the lake at the battle of Morat, as we see in the miniatures of Diebold Schilling, or from meeting a coalition of the Swiss with the men of Lorrain and Alsace on 5 January 1477 in much reduced numbers, with disastrous results.

Questions of logistics further complicated the use of the ever-multiplying taxes which the duke of Burgundy had imposed, to the great discontent of his subjects. As the song went, 'the Flemish will pay' but at what pace? How to make sure that the money arrived in time? How to victual an army which was constantly moving and far from its base? The Italian mercenaries who crossed the Alps to bring aid at Grandson were already fatigued when they arrived, and those from the north were not keen to come to the 'market of great blows' ('au marché à horions'), as Jean de Haynin describes it.[120] Once they arrived, the army's masters were afraid to pay the soldiers for fear that they would seize the opportunity to return home.

The military ordinances: a mirage of efficiency

In the end, Charles did indeed try to link the Burgundian military apparatus to his authority. From this point of view, the ordinances were a masterpiece of the dramatisation of ducal power of a familiar Burgundian kind. 'A document is a monument', to quote Jacques Le Goff, and that of 1473 had nearly sixty-one articles, as against ten in the largest grand ordinance of the French monarchy.[121] This text was copied out so that each *conducteur* could have a copy of it. The script was large and the binding luxurious, and the miniature on the frontispiece represented the duke sitting on a dais of majesty during the investiture ceremony of the *conducteurs* (see Figure 2). Kneeling before the duke, they received the very same ordinance from his hands along with the baton of command. As the ordinance specifies, the ceremony included an oath on the Holy Evangelists by which each head of company agreed to serve the duke 'well and loyally'.[122] By demanding an identical oath from the heads of each squadron, by naming one squadron leader out of four (the three others being chosen by the *conducteurs*) and by creating commissars and officers who acted directly in his name within the army, the duke exerted his control at every level, putting his mark on every level of the chain of command. On the other hand, the widespread use of *condottieri* and of foreign soldiers in general tended to suggest the duke's desire to professionalise his troops and to depersonalise the relationship between soldiers and their captains. Thus, although what would once have been known as 'Philippe de Chaumergis's company' now had no other name than '19th company', it was not so easy to escape from the feudal reflexes which tied fighting men to their lord and led them to fight for his honour and theirs. After all, it was to defend his honour that the originator of this elaborate schema embroiled himself in conflict first at Neuss, then at Grandson, then at Morat and finally and fatally before Nancy. Might it be possible that the difficult relationship between the old model, based on the duke's vassals, and the new one, involving professionals, caused numerous problems at the moment of battle? I leave this question for specialists of military history to consider.

The structure of techniques, the human machinery which Charles tried to construct was at once too rigid, too brutal and, again, ill-adapted to the values based on close relationships shared by most of the men who lived at that time and in that region. War in Burgundy certainly did not accelerate state formation. The taxes negotiated with his subjects made their way into his coffers without too much difficulty. More problematic is the question of whether we can say

Figure 2 Military ordinance, 1473

that the last of the Burgundian princes succeeded in uniting people behind his ambitions, either in the army or in the general population. Can we say, for example, to adopt the language of sociologists, that the political construction undertaken by the dukes of Burgundy allowed Charles to obtain a Weberian monopoly of legitimate violence? To achieve such a result, the dukes of Burgundy would have had to get past the sheer territorial and ideological variety which we invoked in the first half of this book (see e.g. Chapter 3) and which was still to be found even within the ducal armies. To achieve such a result, they would have had to find a way to legitimate violence which was expressed in the prince's wars, and not in the wars of a federation of peoples united around a common good.

If war provides a particularly favourable context in which to observe and evaluate the nature and strength of a political structure, this is no doubt because it makes it possible to test the relations between a prince and his subjects. In the rest of this chapter, we will consider the fissures of the Burgundian bloc from three final points-of-view: on the ground, at the moment of battle; in the opinions of townsmen and the minor nobility; and finally in its long-term impact. We have already seen how Charles the Bold managed to unite Germany against him; we will now see how his grandfather achieved much the same result with England.

The siege of Calais (1436): The 'Good Duke Humphrey' versus 'Phelippe ... Capiteine of cowardise'

Great was the anger of the English in the aftermath of the Treaty of Arras.[123] The reconciliation between the king of France and the duke of Burgundy was experienced as a betrayal. The delegation of Burgundian diplomats sent to London to announce the new political situation received such an icy reception that the Golden Fleece King of Arms was in fear for his life. The theatricalisation of the wound inflicted on the king of England and his people by Philip the Good reached its peak in a meeting of the royal council, when the young Henry VI began to weep in indignation at the unpardonable attitude of this friend of fifteen-years' standing.[124]

Philip the Good's about-face provoked a wave of national solidarity in England. The two rival factions headed by Humphrey, duke of Gloucester, and Cardinal Beaufort were reconciled, and Parliament, having heard the arguments of Bishop John Stafford, granted the taxation necessary to raise an army. Although the English people were tired of the French war, an attack against their own kingdom was considered differently. The accompanying propaganda was careful to transmit the picture of a king betrayed by his ally and a country insulted, stigmatising the felony of Philip the Good and insisting that Calais belonged to England. To lose it would be the worst dishonour and shame that the kingdom could suffer.[125]

Insulted monarchs ready to fight

The English army quickly assembled. On 29 October 1435 Gloucester was made the new captain of Calais by indenture, *chevauchées* started to sack the territories of Philip the Good, and a propaganda campaign was launched in the duke's lands, especially in Zeeland, where the king of England insisted on the long friendship he shared with the merchants whose prosperity relied on the good relations endangered by the behaviour of their new lord.[126] This strategy was anticipated well in advance by one of the duke's counsellors who had been opposed to any military aggression against Henry VI. In a memorandum addressed to Philip the Good, composed at the end of 1435, Hue de Lannoy had foreseen this propaganda war and the consequent weakening of the duke's forces. He counselled the duke to bind all his territories to fight in a common alliance with him and not to treat separately with each of them.[127]

Philip the Good had no patience with such English insults, and in the course of January 1436 he turned to a military solution. It was thus the duke who, ready to assemble 16,000 men to defend his honour, sent letters of defiance to Henry VI on 19 February 1436, although war was already on everybody's mind.[128] He summoned the Four Members of Flanders to Ghent for 8 March and presented them with his plans and his demands: money and men to take Calais. The Flemish agreed, but on condition that they would be accorded new privileges, notably that they would be granted the Calais wool staple. The king of England was perfectly aware of this situation, since one of his spies attended this assembly and passed on precise information as early as 26 March. This report was also attached to all the letters summoning troops which Henry VI sent to the towns, nobles and religious houses.[129]

It is thus clear that the Calais garrison had considerable time to prepare for the siege which finally began on 9 July. The duke was already at Gravelines on 25 June, but he had managed to assemble only twenty-four ships by the end of that month.[130] Jean de Hornes and the commander of la Morée very quickly lost control of the situation and were unable to establish a blockade of the port. Everyone felt betrayed: the people of Bruges, by the incompetence of the military authorities; and the duke, by the rapid dispersal of his Flemish subjects. As soon as the latter understood that there was no more hope of help from the sea, 'they decided to break camp and return to their country', whilst some of them even thought to kill 'some of the duke's officers [*gouverneurs*]'.[131] Philip knew that nothing could stop them leaving and decided to depart himself. He brought an end to the siege of Calais on 28 July, thus founding a reputation for cowardice in English songs which mocked the Flemings, whose name was supposed to derive from the 'flemed men' or fleeing men who first populated Flanders and whose lord was nothing but a 'Capiteine of cowardise'.[132]

Autopsy of a Burgundian debacle

The siege of Calais was a terrible defeat for the duke of Burgundy. In the days that followed, according to Olivier van Dixmude, the English armies ravaged the Flemish coastline and made a number of incursions into Picardy. It was Duchess Isabella of Portugal who was charged to take matters in hand, whilst Philip took the road to Artois.[133] For Jean de Wavrin, the cause of these reversals was linked to the failure of the blockade of Calais. Historians who have considered these events have identified a number of other causes: the incompetence of the *sénéchal* of Brabant, Jean de Hornes; the slow arrival of men and war supplies, whereas the English had been sitting in readiness, fully informed of the arrival of the Burgundian army, for six months; the poor weather conditions; the absence of coordination between the forces on land and sea; and the lack of sufficient finances. If this latter point might be qualified, there was another one which escaped nobody's attention outside the walls of Calais: the disunity amongst the Flemish troops and their rapid withdrawal. The same Hue de Lannoy, after this defeat, drove his point home, arguing that the duke should make peace with England immediately, so precarious was the Burgundian position.[134]

Although, according to Monstrelet, it was the cowardly Flemish who abandoned their lord, chronicles in Flemish qualified this easy simplification. In truth, the prince's error lay once more in a misunderstanding of the socio-economic realities of the mid-1430s in Flanders, which ultimately led to the great revolt of Bruges. In the midst of a serious crisis in the cloth industry, Bruges was in conflict with its out-port, Sluys, and with the *châtellenie* of the Franc in its hinterland. Before going to Calais, the Bruges contingent had waited for five hours for troops from Sluys who never appeared, further exacerbating existing tensions. In the *Excellente cronicke van Vlaenderen*, preserved in MS 437 of the Bruges Municipal Library, the author insists that the men of Bruges were ashamed when Ghentish troops decided to decamp, presenting the former as loyal men whose reasons for discontent were just.[135] Although Monstrelet asserts that 'there were often great alarums in the host of these Flemings, since for very little they were stirred up and took to arms', neither he nor Wavrin understood the reasons for these scuffles.[136] As for the English, they took advantage of the general disunity of their opponents to insult the enemy and pull together against a disparate army, whose flight was interpreted as a sign of lack of courage in the face of a fearsome English force. The loss of nerve of the Flemish and the duke of Burgundy, more than their actual retreat, fed numerous texts, which drew attention to the treachery of the duke of Burgundy and mocked the barbarity of the men of Bruges and Ghent – fierce as hinds before a hunter – whilst at the same time celebrating the courage of the good Duke Humphrey of Gloucester and especially the English identity of the town of Calais, which had so admirably defended itself.[137] In this affair, which consolidated Lancastrian propaganda amongst the English but degenerated into a revolt on the Flemish side, Philip the Good set out on a war for the defence of his honour, a war of knights whose causes were not understood by an urban population preoccupied by economic crisis. Cultural misunderstanding and a lack of *esprit de corps* were thus the cause of this military disaster.

Town burgesses and field knights

The affront was certainly severe for Philip the Good. The siege of Calais was a humiliation, and the chronicles which narrate this event are full of words evoking shame and honour endangered, lost or offended.[138] Yet the prince, contrary to what the chronicles in French imply, was not the only one within the Burgundian camp who was sensitive to these questions of reputation, since they also ranged Ghent against Bruges.

The noble deeds of knightly princes

Much recent work by medievalists has stressed that honour in the Middle Ages was an ideal of physical and moral fulfilment which could be adapted to anyone's estate, noble knights or communal militiamen.[139] As Arlette Jouanna put it, honour, though difficult to define, 'is in a way the fruit of a meeting between an act and a public'.[140] From this point of view, at the siege of Calais the meeting was a failure and honour was trodden underfoot. On the Flemish side, the men of Bruges were offended first by the lateness of the men of Sluys, then by the words of the captain of the out-port, Roland van Uutkerke, who called them *meuytmakers* ('rebels'), then by the men of Ghent who mocked their failed attack on Calais's Boulogne gate. On the prince's side, Philip was presented by Enguerrand de Monstrelet as a man who constantly sought to save his honour against the insults of the English and against threatening subjects who did not seem to respect his authority at all or to understand how important his honour was to him.

We might imagine that, following this fiasco, Philip would have complained that his attack had failed and that the enemy had seen the weaknesses of his army. Yet in a letter which he probably sent to the count of Richemont, he was more concerned that the feudal contract which bound him to his men had been broken, and it was the failure to keep a promise, imperilling his honour as a knight on the field of battle, which troubled him profoundly.[141] Philip was a knightly prince, one who needed a theatre of war to display the virtues that won him renown. The model of the chivalric hero, shared by all the European courts of this period but especially prized in the principality of Burgundy, powerfully shaped behaviour, so much so that even a few decades ago it still troubled historians who could see it only as an evident archaism. From this point of view, the remarks of Johan Huizinga, published in 1919, are all the more pertinent, as he invited scholars to consider the permeability between romantic ideal and historical actions. This permeability did not just characterise the end of the Middle Ages, as when it inspired Charles VI, who was determined to march to Roosebeke in 1382, but continued into the early modern period, as in 1590 when Henry IV of France invited his men at Ivry to follow his white plume on the path to victory and honour.[142] The chivalric ideal is no longer considered to be a feudal relic, inimical to the construction of an authoritarian, monarchical state, which means that the absolutist French state of the sixteenth century might be thought of as also feudal in nature.[143]

In a fifteenth-century world in which fiction and reality were powerfully intermingled, the heroes of romance and chivalric biography adapted Arthurian models to create characters like Jean de Saintré or Jacques de Lalaing. One was imaginary, the other real, but both were men of their time, demonstrating that the Burgundian court should not be seen as an embalming jar in which princes were preserved in permanent contrast to their own time.[144] The words, the deeds, the ceremonies, the dream of crusade all formed part of a codified system which had to be perpetuated, not in order to take refuge in a dated imaginary world, but rather to reinforce a particular, contemporary social position. That said, the behaviour of knights on the field of battle can sometimes be surprising, taking on a chivalric glimmer which we find in the deeds of Gilles de Chin or Lancelot of the Lake.[145] Olivier de la Marche, the 'writer-knight', made no bones about portraying the ancestors of Philip the Fair as paragons of virtue who were able to bear comparison with the Nine Worthies, slipping from an account of a tournament to the assembly of men on the road to war as if the two were exercises of a fundamentally similar nature.[146] Princes thus went to war joyfully and received letters of defiance with pleasure. Charles the Bold at Neuss seems to have been happy to receive the herald Lorrayne who informed him of the entry of his master René II into the war 'of fire and blood' against the duke, his lands, his subjects and his allies. Charles replied to this message: 'Herald, I have heard and listened to the declaration of your charge, by which you have given me reason for joy [*matiere de joye*].'[147]

The anecdotes which accompany these tales of battles and sieges can be disconcerting for the modern reader, to whom they can give the impression that making war is also playing at making war. For example, during the siege of Arras in the summer of 1414, both those 'without' (i.e. the men of the Orléans party) and the knights 'within' (i.e. the men of the duke of Burgundy) took advantage of a pause in the action to organise a tournament (*béhourt*) in the mines dug by the besiegers, with as a prize a diamond worth 100 *écus* which the count of Eu was supposed to give to his lady. A few days later, lances were broken once more to pass the time, and the enemies banqueted together at the end of the tournament.[148] We should not forget that Philip the Good, duke of Burgundy, was nonetheless a noble who liked to pray as much as to be entertained. When messengers brought him news of the fall of Luxembourg, the duke, some thirty-five kilometres away at Arlon, did not immediately leap into the saddle but instead went to hear mass, telling those who complained: 'If God has given me victory, he will keep it for me.'[149] The chivalric behaviour which included taking oaths, made famous by the Banquet of the Pheasant, also motivated military leaders who, with their weapons in hand, still thought of their honour in these terms. It is easy to mock Charles the Bold, who decided not to cut his beard after defeat at Grandson, but what should we say of Edward I, who refused the surrender of those besieged at Stirling until he had demonstrated a new siege engine, the Warwolf, before an audience of noble ladies, or of Henry, duke of Lancaster, who, when forced to abandon the siege of Rennes in 1356, nonetheless negotiated to have his banner fly a few minutes over the city walls, in order to accomplish his vow and so avoid dishonour, despite his failure to take the town?[150]

Chivalric virtue, self-esteem, the concern to protect one's reputation and to accomplish one's Christian duty: these were all principles which defined the attitudes of men who looked for glory in the context of a just war. Because killing, in the end, is not a game, and the many offers of duels made by Philip the Good to his adversaries were not just acts of a propaganda 'which strongly recalls a political pamphlet' – to quote one interpretation, this time a little too hasty, of Johan Huizinga – but serious challenges seriously made. In 1425 Philip invited his opponent Humphrey of Gloucester, the suitor of the countess of Hainault, to resolve the matter of Jacqueline of Bavaria by a duel, 'to avoid the shedding of Christian blood and the destruction of the people, for whom he had compassion in [his] heart'.[151] In 1436 the two enemies met, and this time Gloucester took the initiative to propose a duel, although here Monstrelet was careful not to suggest any ethical motive for the challenge. Just before the Luxembourg war, the duke of Burgundy once more proposed to settle a quarrel which set him against the duke of Saxony by combat 'hand to hand ... in the presence of the emperor, ... to bring an end to the danger to so many people'. Combat was refused this time on the grounds of the youth of Wilhelm of Saxony.[152]

This means of resolving conflicts, which generally did not see words turned into deeds, might seem to be simply insincere. Yet the rhetoric which accompanied such offers does reveal something else about chivalric scruples around the act of killing. We now know that most chivalric biographies take care to distance noble deeds of war from the dire consequences which might flow from them and so to avoid staining the valorous image of the protagonist with the blood of his victims. The prince, similarly, by offering to sacrifice himself to save the people from the outrages of war, invokes not only the secular repertoire of chivalric values but also the Christian ethic which asked the good prince to show mercy.[153] Of course, if we remember the words of John the Fearless at Othée, ordering his men to spare none of the rebellious *Haidroits*, or still worse the massacre at Nesle, after which Charles the Bold was said to have congratulated his men for having done 'good butchery', we might doubt the sincerity of these preliminary formulas which offered the sacrifice of the prince alone to bring an end to conflict.[154] But we can go further to place these offers of a duel, and these letters of defiance which seek to establish the legitimacy of the conflict to come, in the context of a long process which enabled these princes to assemble all the arguments necessary to present them as being, in any future confrontations, on the side of what was right, good, just and so pleasing to God.[155] In the same way, the main preoccupation of Philip the Good when he reneged on the Treaty of Troyes and made peace with the king of France at Arras in 1435 was to defend his soul against any mortal sin: making sure that the wars they embarked upon were just was essential for these men haunted by their salvation.[156] The honour of the prince and of his knights had an ethical, religious and contractual basis which made the giving of their word, in the sight of God and defended valiantly, the essence of noble action in combat.

The temptation of 'living nobly'

Were these noble principles familiar to the urban militias who abandoned their prince before Calais? How might simple soldiers react when, in 1406, after having worked for months, assembling thousands of men and engines of war, cutting down 32,000 oak trunks in the forest of Saint-Omer and so exhausting it for forty years, John the Fearless finally decided to turn back, cancelling his expedition against Calais?[157] How was it that the burgesses of Ghent or Auxerre always gave a favourable answer to requests for men, money and *matériel* from a prince concerned to defend his honour or that of his king or of one of his relatives? Honour, as we have already observed, was a powerful motivating factor throughout medieval society. The urban populations of the north, moreover, who were particularly to blame for these military debacles, were especially sensitive to questions of pride and esteem. Many recent studies have shown how far 'living nobly' was a value which allowed each individual in search of social advancement to mark his place in the social hierarchy by means of his dress and public self-presentation. Wealthy burgesses rivalled noble courtiers with their rich clothing; their marriages with men or women of higher rank than themselves were celebrated magnificently with food and entertainment, the purchase of fine houses and fiefs and sometimes even, as in the case of Pierre Bladelin, the foundation of a town.[158] The chivalric ideal was always present. This noble ethos was seen in the spread of Arthurian names, in urban jousts, in competitions organised by fraternities of archers and crossbowmen.

Yet there was more to this than passive reception: chivalric culture was entirely assimilated into urban culture. The desire to imitate chivalric models was always accompanied by an equally strong desire to mark the specificity of urban identity.[159] In 1411, before the departure of the troops of John the Fearless for the Vermandois, it took no less than five weeks to find a solution between the rival claims of the Franc of Bruges and the men of Ypres to march at the head of the ducal army. After deliberating with the counsel of the Four Members of Flanders, John the Fearless finally delivered an order to the effect that they should each head the army on alternate days. The dukes worked hard to unite all their troops under a single banner. The cross of Saint Andrew gradually became the 'recognisable ensign of the Burgundians' ('l'ensaigne congnoissable des Bourguignons'), in the ducal army in which all 'faithful, subjects, and others' had to wear this emblem which first signified adhesion to a party, then to an army.[160] Yet the banners of the towns of Flanders still identified different groups of militia, who were feverishly obsessed by the idea that their standard might be overtaken by those of militia from different towns. The power of such symbols of identity is shown, for example, by an incident in the town of Ghent itself on 26 February 1453, in the midst of the war against Philip the Good, when the dean of the oil merchants was condemned by the college of deans for refusing to take part in the military parade with his banner. The dukes meanwhile made sure to order that the ducal banner would always be the first one to be raised, as John the Fearless did at Bruges on 25 April 1407, or that the arms of the county of Flanders would appear on the banners of the trade guilds, as Philip the Good did at Ghent in 1430.[161] The honour of the militia was almost expressed in the same register as the honour of the prince, although as with the ideal of the common good, everyone worked in the service of their own aspirations, often resulting in a dialogue of the deaf which had ultimately disastrous consequences.

The honour of the militiaman, used to jousts and other military pastimes; of the burgess, doing business and carefully cultivating the signs of his social advancement by accumulating the marks of 'living nobly'; or of the towns who brought their economic rivalries with them when they joined the ducal armies: all of these were very different from the honour of the prince, which found its expression in a privileged place in the royal council, in territorial expansion, in vengeance or even in the quest for a crown. As the Four Members of Flanders pointed out in numerous altercations with Charles the Bold, their honour resided in the unequalled quality of their industry, in their ability to trade. The Bruges rhetorician Anthonis de Roovere, in his *Van pays en oorloghe*, a dialogue between peace and war, summed up perfectly the two different positions. Peace proclaimed that 'Whereas I make commerce grow / You [War] chase industry from the land.'[162] It would be difficult to put it better.

The absence of common enemies

Of course, the sudden collapse of the Burgundian armies on various occasions did not derive from a single cause. Exhaustion, fear and loss of confidence in a leader who racked up setbacks and yet continued to pursue the same course no doubt explain the rout at Grandson or the retreat of the entire company of Jacques de Romont in the thick of the action at Morat. The same causes led to the same effects at Nancy after the defection of the count of Campobasso, which was also motivated by personal humiliation. As Olivier de la Marche puts it, after repeated defeats, 'the prince could get little obedience".[163] Nevertheless, such factors more readily explain desertion than the sudden collapses which, from John the Fearless to Charles the Bold, dogged Burgundian military action.

Time-serving

When the Flemish militia abandoned John the Fearless, just after he had put Ham to siege and was about to take Montdidier in September 1411, they argued that they 'had served the time, term and space that their lord had required of them'.[164] In other words, they had done the required service in the host and, whatever the prince's motives might be, whatever the urgency of the mobilisation or the closeness of a fresh victory, there was no question of them serving a single day more. According to Enguerrand de Monstrelet, when the duke tried to keep them, the militia captains lost their temper, threatening to send him 'his only son, count of Charolais', who was then staying at Ghent 'chopped into pieces' unless he allowed them to leave.[165] In 1436 the Flemish troops started to complain, considering themselves betrayed by their prince's advisers. The duke pleaded his case in vain, arguing that if they retreated, great shame would come to him and to them, but the Flemings stood their ground, leaving the ranks without waiting for an escort.[166] The prince's honour mattered little. Later, it was the tardy arrival of soldiers which provoked a kind of freeze-frame of the action just as Philip the Good was winning victory on victory around Ghent in the week of 7 July 1453. In a letter to Sire Antoine de Croÿ, governor of Luxembourg, the duke of Burgundy wrote that, after the attacks on Schendelbecque and Pouques, as he arrived before Courtrai, and much to his great displeasure, his army had ground to a halt for want of paid soldiers.[167] The victorious military leader found that he was forced to bring a sudden halt to his progress, and we must imagine that his rousing speeches to the troops fell on deaf ears.

Mutual ignorance

Later, Charles the Bold would repeatedly try to stimulate the honour of his subjects, notably by comparing them to the faithful and grateful subjects of France. In a letter sent to the magistrates of the Franc of Bruges on 19 December 1470, he railed: what honour would there be in Flanders if its inhabitants let themselves be trodden underfoot by French troops?[168] But a few years later, after many defeats and disillusionments, Charles's judgement, so often clouded by stubbornness and a refusal to listen to counsel, was surprisingly clear when he explained the rout at Morat. Those of the north had no interest in the quarrels of the south and considered that the difficulties of the people of the duchy had little to do with them. So whilst the subjects of the duchy and the county of Burgundy offered men and money to guard the borders against France, Lorraine and Germany, those in the north felt concerned neither by these French quarrels nor by disorders in the southern lands. All that interested them was to keep the peace in their own country.[169] Similarly, when the duke had asked for men and money to defend Lorraine, he observed that those in the north refused and that, as a result, they should be held responsible for the 'danger in which those in our said land of Lorraine now find themselves'.[170]

In these letters, chronicles and addresses to Estates General, it becomes clear that war was not a unifying factor within the vast territorial complex of the Great Principality of Burgundy. Indeed, on the occasion of his ceremonial reception as duke of Brabant, the Estates made it clear to Philip the Good that the duchy would not participate in his wars in France or around Liège, and nor would they participate in any conflict against their will.[171] The affairs of the north were quite separate from those of the south. The brawls within the army between Burgundians and Flemish were the perfect reflection of this lack of common interest. The enemies at the gate at the end of Charles the Bold's rule were no enemies of the Flemings, any more than those of Philip the Good had been in 1436. For the Flemings, the English remained essential economic partners. The absence of common enemies no doubt hindered the political construction of this principality. Thus, although we can certainly point to the large number of mercenaries used by Charles the Bold as a symbol of weakness, this was a result less of the mercenaries' actions on the ground than of the fact that such mercenaries filled the gap left by subjects who felt less and less concerned by the wars of a prince who no longer inspired confidence. It is no accident that on Charles's death, the 'Great Privilege' granted by Mary of Burgundy in spring 1477 proclaimed, amongst other things, that henceforth no declaration of war could be made without the agreement of the Estates General.[172] Without such consent, the subjects of the duke of Burgundy were no longer bound to serve nor to interrupt their commercial activities with the country against which the duke might have declared war. The Estates officially distanced themselves from conflicts begun by their princes and thus in some way took on part of the monopoly of legitimate violence which had constantly been directly or indirectly contested.

This discussion of the wars of the dukes of Burgundy has led us through a range of cases, bringing to our attention a military machine which was becoming better and better organised and which was sometimes effective and sometimes deficient. We have considered a series of measures, undertaken in a spirit of political experimentation, which were not experienced or thought out at all as steps on the road to the construction of the 'modern state' but were rather adopted as a means to achieve specific ambitions, such as territorial expansion or the conquest of a title. We have seen, in a multiplicity of contexts, a society which was certainly capable of organising itself but which equally certainly failed to create a sense of common life. This was partly a matter of a space which was too large, too varied, too extended in terms of distance but also in terms of different perceptions of time. The example of Neuss, where Charles the Bold held up his army, the better to accomplish the future conquests he planned whilst his enemies sped up their movements and turned the attention to the periphery of his lands, already shows how far the conjuncture of different perceptions of time could be dangerous. In a society subject to the same prince from the coast of Frisia to the vineyards of the Mâconnais, war and conflict constituted an important test which broke the rhythm of the everyday, violently projecting men and women into an accelerated time in which the rhythms of work, trade and family life were subjugated to the time of a prince in search of glory and memorable deeds.

The reference to figures of the past and to almost universal values in late-medieval and early modern societies can sometimes be a source of misunderstanding and can even lead to the construction of a fresh paradox. Why was it that a society which was sensitive to the deeds of the great and to questions of honour proved incapable of uniting around these models and defending its values? To resolve this seeming contradiction, it helps to recall the difference between the 'field of experience' and the 'horizon of expectations'. The temporal order thought of as ideal was subject to wide variations within the same period and in the same region. The merchant's time, indexed to the promise of future profits and guaranteed by peace, was not the same as the prince's time, haunted by dreams of glory and recognition.[173] War could have repaired divisions if particular interests could have been subsumed, if it had been waged in the name of a common interest, in a spirit of common enterprise, that of a federation if not of a nation.

That said, the experience of the principality of Burgundy was not unique. After all, in the fifteenth century the kingdom of England had just as much trouble when raising taxes for a war which no longer concerned the king's subjects. In that country, one generally considered to be a perfect example of the development of the 'modern state', was war really such as powerful catalyst, a tool of progress destined to rid the kingdom of its medieval archaisms, as has often been claimed? Impoverished and destabilised, the kingdom collapsed into a civil war which slowed growth and threatened to relegate England to the rank of a second-order power.[174] The Great Principality of Burgundy, by amplifying effects observed elsewhere, is an important test case. If we take each element in isolation, as historians have done in analyses pre-structured by various criteria supposed to define the 'modern state', we are left only with shifting judgements of relative success or failure. Only by taking them all together can we see the limits of this model.

Notes

1 'Réveillez-vous Piccarz', BnF, ms. fr. 12744, ed. G. Paris and A. Gevaert in *Chansons du XVe siècle* (Paris: Defirmin-Didot et Cie, 1875), pp. 140–141.
2 As early as 19 January 1477, Louis XI declared that his intention was to reclaim the heritage of Charles the Bold ('réunir, remettre et réduyre a la coronne et seigneurie de France les contez de Flandres, de Bourgoigne, Ponthieu, Arthoys et autres terres et seigneuries que nagaires tenoit et occupoit feu Charles, de son vivant duc de Bourgoigne'). J. Vaesen and E. Charavay (eds), *Lettres de Louis XI, roi de France* (Paris: Renouard, 1883–1909), vol. VI, pp. 115–117.
3 This idea is mainly derived from C. Tilly, *Coercion, Capital and European States, AD 990–1992* (Cambridge, MA, and Oxford: Wiley-Blackwell, 1992). 'C'est un très périlleux héritage que guerre' is a quotation from Jean Gerson and is also the title of an article by P. Contamine in *Vingtième siècle: revue d'histoire* 3 (1984), 5–15.
4 See, for example, the observations of R. W. Kaeuper, *War, Justice and Public Order: England and France in the Later Middle Ages* (Oxford: Clarendon Press, 1988), pp. 104ff.
5 E. Le Roy Ladurie, 'L'histoire immobile', *Annales ESC* 29:3 (1974), 673–692: 'L'équilibre long n'est atteint que dans la tragédie.'
6 On the Italian military experience, see the comprehensive overview in E. Crouzet-Pavan, *Renaissances italiennes (1380–1500)* (Paris: Albin Michel, 2007), pp. 211–227.
7 A. Rucquoi, 'Genèse médiévale de l'Espagne moderne: du pouvoir et de la nation (1250–1516)', in J.-P. Genet (ed.), *Genèse de l'État moderne. Bilans et perspectives* (Paris: CNRS, 1990), pp. 17–32.
8 R. van Uytven, 'La Flandre et le Brabant: terres de promission sous les ducs de Bourgogne?', *Revue du Nord* 172 (1961), 281–317.
9 The devastation of war of course being accentuated by epidemic disease, the decline of the climate and famine, as is well known.
10 E. Thoen, 'Oorlogen en platteland. Sociale en ekonomische aspekten van militaire destruktie in Vlaanderen tijdens de late middeleeuwen en de vroege moderne tijden', *Tijdschrift voor geschiedenis* 91 (1978), 363–378. For the Pays de Caux in Normandy, see G. Bois, *La crise du féodalisme* (Paris: Presses de Sciences Po, 1976), p. 299.

11 On the link between princely authority and urban destruction, see M. Boone, 'Destroying and Reconstructing the City: The Inculcation and Arrogation of Princely Power in the Burgundian Netherlands (14th–16th Centuries)', in M. Gosman *et al.* (eds), *The Propagation of Power in the Medieval West* (Groningen: Egbert Forsten, 1997), pp. 1–33.

12 For numerous examples of war ruins in the Calais area and the county of Artois, as well as a map of devastated villages in 1472 and 1475, see A. Bocquet, *Recherches sur la population rurale de l'Artois et du Boulonnais pendant la période bourguignonne (1384–1477)* (Arras: Commission Départementale des Monuments Historiques, 1969), pp. 62–63.

13 G. Blieck, 'Une ville close face à l'éminent péril: Lille en Flandre en 1411 et 1414', in G. Blieck *et al.* (eds), *Les enceintes urbaines (XIIe–XVIe s.)* (Paris: CTHS, 1999), pp. 297–311.

14 B. Schnerb, 'Un monastère dans la guerre: l'abbaye du Mont-Saint-Éloi (fin XIVe–début XVe siècle)', in P. Contamine and O. Guyotjeannin (eds), *La guerre, la violence et les gens au Moyen Âge* (Paris: CTHS, 1996), vol. II, pp. 101–117.

15 W. Paravicini, 'Terreur royale: Louis XI et la ville d'Arras, avril 1477', *Revue belge de philologie et d'histoire* 89:2 (2011), 551–583.

16 P. Gresser, *Calamités et maux naturels en Franche-Comté aux XIVe et XVe siècles* (Besançon: Éditions Cêtre, 2008).

17 Response to the Four Members of Flanders about an *aide* of 120,000 écus, May 1470, in Gachard (ed.), *Collection de documents inédits*, vol. I, p. 220.

18 For more information about this kind of soldier, see J. de Fréminville, *Les écorcheurs en Bourgogne (1435–1445)* (Dijon: Imp. de Darentière, 1888). The examples that follow are taken from M. Canat de Chizy, *Documents pour servir à l'histoire de Bourgogne* (Chalon: Dejussieu, 1863), vol. I, pp. 267–296, 372–485.

19 J.-M. Cauchies, 'Les écorcheurs en Hainaut (1437–1445)', *Revue belge d'histoire militaire* 20:5 (March 1974), 317–339.

20 All these town and villages were located in the county of Hainault.

21 Philip the Good, at Douai on 3 July 1438, fined disobedient towns. Auxonne was even stripped of her privileges. See Vaughan, *Philip the Good*, p. 95.

22 See J. Robert de Chevanne, *Les guerres en Bourgogne de 1470 à 1475. Étude sur les interventions armées des Français au duché sous Charles le Téméraire* (Paris: Picard, 1934).

23 Ypres also burned her suburban area to resist the English army in 1382.

24 Chevanne, *Les guerres en Bourgogne de 1470 à 1475*, p. 81: 'Compte de Semur-en-Brionnais du 1er octobre au 30 septembre 1471', fol. VIv: 'La basse ville fut brûlée et destruite par doubte du siège que Mgr de Bourbon vouloit mectre devant lesdiz chastel et ville de Semur.'
25 See above, 'An emperor's conquests?'
26 J. Dumolyn, '"Le povre peuple estoit moult opprimé": Elite Discourses on "the People" in the Burgundian Netherlands (Fourteenth to Fifteenth Centuries)', *French History* 23:2 (2009), 171–192.
27 We will return to the question of national feelings in Chapter 7, but we note for the moment some examples of French national feelings in N. Grévy-Pons, 'Propagande et sentiment national pendant le règne de Charles VII: l'exemple de Jean de Montreuil', *Francia* 8 (1980), 127–146.
28 On Britanny and the declaration of war between Henry VI and John V in January 1426, see P. Contamine, 'Serments bretons (8–15 septembre 1427)', in J.-C. Cassard *et al.* (eds), *Le prince, l'argent, les hommes au Moyen Âge. Mélanges offerts à Jean Kerhervé* (Rennes: PUR, 2008), pp. 123–132.
29 Monstrelet, *Chronique*, vol. II, p. 424.
30 On the war of Guelders, see S. Boffa, *Warfare in Medieval Brabant (1356–1406)* (Woodbridge: Boydell & Brewer, 2004), pp. 38–42.
31 ADCO, B 2293, fols 1–2b.
32 J. de La Chauvelays, 'Les armées des trois premiers ducs de Bourgogne de la maison de Valois', *Mémoires de l'Académie des sciences, arts, belles lettres de Dijon* 6 (1880), 19–335, at pp. 85ff.
33 *Ibid.*, p. 250.
34 B. Schnerb, *'L'honneur de la maréchaussée'. Maréchal et maréchaux en Bourgogne des origines à la fin du XVe siècle* (Turnhout: Brepols, 2000), p. 97.
35 A comparison can be made with G. Castelnuovo, 'Les maréchaux de Savoie au bas Moyen Âge', in C. Sorrel (ed.), *La société savoyarde et la guerre (XIIIe–XXe siècle). Actes du XXXVIe Congrès des Sociétés Savantes de la Savoie (Montmélian, septembre 1996)*, Mémoires et Documents de la Société Savoisienne d'Histoire et d'Archéologie 100 (Chambéry, 1998), pp. 91–99.
36 Vaughan, *Philip the Good*, p. 17.
37 For the detail, see M. Gachard, *Rapport sur différentes séries de documents concernant l'histoire de la Belgique conservées à Lille* (Brussels: M. Hayez, 1841), pp. 362–363.
38 On a woman whose eventful life has caused much ink to be spilt, and for synthesis of the events of this period, see A. Janse, *Een pion*

voor een dame. Jacoba van Beieren (1401–1436) (Amsterdam: Balans, 2009).
39 ADN, B 7995, fol. 43.
40 Monstrelet, *Chronique*, vol. IV, ch. 26.
41 This speech is recorded by Jean Lefebvre de Saint-Remy in his *Chroniques*, ed. F. Morand (Paris: Renouard, 1876–81), vol. II, pp. 374–381.
42 We will see that Flemish soldiers abandoned the field, and their prince.
43 Saint-Remy, *Chroniques*, vol. II, pp. 374–381, at p. 380.
44 Elizabeth von Görlitz (d. 1451) married successively Antoine, duke of Brabant (d. 1415), one of the brothers of John the Fearless; and John of Bavaria (d. 1425), former bishop of Liège, governor of Holland, who was also the brother of Marguerite of Bavaria, the mother of Philip the Good. On Philip the Good's speech to the Saxon ambassadors, see L. P. Gachard, *Analectes historiques*, 2nd series, VI (1858), vol. XI, pp. 202–204. These events are related in La Marche, *Mémoires*, vol. II, book 1, chs X, XI, XII, pp. 5–50.
45 La Marche, *Mémoires*, vol. II, book I, ch. X, pp. 1–23.
46 On Philip the Good's reasons as expressed by Henri Goethals at Arras on 19 October 1419, see Bonenfant, *Du meurtre de Montereau*, p. 189 ff.
47 See the text in *Dagboek van Gent van 1447 to 1470*, ed. V. Fris (Ghent: C. Annoot-Braeckman, 1904), vol. I, pp. 57–68.
48 On the events of this conflict, see Haemers, *De Gentse opstand*.
49 Manifesto of Philip the Good against the people of Ghent, 31 March 1452, in Gachard (ed.), *Collection de documents inédits*, vol. II, pp. 96–111, at p. 110.
50 *Ibid.*
51 On this banner, see P. Murray-Kendall, *Louis XI* (Paris: Fayard, 1974), p. 282.
52 The battles of Ruppelmonde (1452) and Gavre (1453) were his two first military exploits.
53 For details of these events, see Vaughan, *Charles the Bold*, *passim*.
54 M. Mollat, 'Recherche sur les finances des ducs Valois de Bourgogne', *Revue historique* 219 (1958), 258–321.
55 Text edited in Cuvelier *et al.* (eds), *Actes des États généraux*, pp. 179ff.
56 *Ibid.*
57 In the study of the common good that I wrote with Jan Dumolyn I show how the same words could be used to express different political ideas. See J. Dumolyn and É. Lecuppre-Desjardin, 'Le Bien Commun en Flandre médiévale: une lutte discursive entre princes et sujets',

in Lecuppre-Desjardin and Van Bruaene (eds), *De Bono Communi*, pp. 253–266.
58 On the general atmosphere in this kind of assembly, see G. Small and J. Dumolyn, 'Parole d'État et mémoire "collective" dans les pays bourguignons: les discours prononcés devant des assemblées représentatives (XVe–XVIe siècle)', *PCEEB* 52 (2012), 15–28.
59 Cuvelier *et al.* (eds), *Actes des États généraux*, pp. 191, 193, 194.
60 Details of these privileges in *ibid.*, pp. 202ff.
61 *Ibid.*, p. 188.
62 During the Estates General of May 1470, Charles the Bold insulted the deputies of Flanders when they quibbled about the *aide* of 120,000 crowns he had requested. According to him, they were Flemish blockheads, persevering in their stupid and bad opinions: 'et avez vous testes flamengues si grosses et si dures, et voulez toudis perseverer en vous duretez et mauvais oppinions …' See Gachard (ed.), *Collection de documents inédits*, vol. I, p. 221.
63 *Ibid.*
64 Speech delivered by the duke to the deputies of Flanders at Bruges, 12 July 1475, *ibid.*, pp. 249ff.
65 F. de Gingins la Sarra (ed.), *Dépêches des ambassadeurs milanais sur les campagnes de Charles le Hardi*, 2 vols (Paris and Geneva, 1858), vol. II, p. 354.
66 P. Ehm-Schnocks and H. von Seggern (eds), *Recueil du Fay. Die Briefsammlung des Claude de Neufchâtel zur Geschichte Karls des Kühnen 1474–1477 (1505)* (Ostfildern: Thorbecke, 2003), p. 155.
67 P. Contamine, 'L'armée de Charles le Téméraire: expression d'un État en devenir ou instrument d'un conquérant?', in M. Vaïsse (ed.), *Aux armes, citoyens! Conscription et armée de métier des grecs à nos jours* (Paris: A. Colin, 1998), pp. 61–77: 'Peut-être faut-il placer la figure du Téméraire dans la galerie des grands conquérants plutôt que dans celle des promoteurs ou des bâtisseurs de l'État moderne', p. 61.
68 Gingins la Sarra (ed.), *Dépêches des ambassadeurs milanais sur les campagnes de Charles le Hardi*, vol. II, p. 217.
69 On the place of Alexander the Great in the ideology of Charles the Bold, see C. Blondeau, 'Les intentions d'une œuvre (*Faits et gestes d'Alexandre le Grand* de Vasque de Lucène) et sa réception par Charles le Téméraire', *Revue du Nord* 83 (2001), 731–752.
70 Vaughan, *Charles the Bold*, p. 184: 'Charles the Bold, then, was egocentric, and absolutist or at any rate authoritarian.'
71 Ordinance of Abbeville, June 1471, ADCO, B 16, fol. 231; ed. in F. Delpu, 'Une réforme militaire en Bourgogne à la fin du Moyen

Âge: l'ordonnance de Saint-Maximin de Trèves (novembre 1473)', unpublished master's thesis, University of Lille, 2012, p. 155.
72 De la Chauvelays, 'Les armées des trois premiers ducs de Bourgogne', p. 297.
73 Contamine, 'L'armée de Charles le Téméraire'.
74 Schnerb, *L'État bourguignon*, p. 274.
75 D. S. Bachrach, 'A Military Revolution Reconsidered: The Case of the Burgundian State under the Valois Dukes', *Essays in Medieval Studies* 15 (1998), 9–17.
76 H. Heimpel, 'Karl der Kühne und der Burgundische Staat', in R. Nürnberger (ed.), *Festschrift Gerhard Ritter* (Tübingen: R. Nürnberger, 1950), pp. 140–160; Schnerb, *L'État bourguignon*, p. 262.
77 For what follows, see de la Chauvelays, 'Les armées des trois premiers ducs de Bourgogne'; J. de la Chauvelays, *Mémoire sur la composition des armées de Charles le Téméraire dans les deux Bourgogne, Mémoires de l'Académie des sciences, arts, belles lettres de Dijon* (1878), pp. 138–169.
78 On this military office, see Schnerb, 'L'honneur de la maréchaussée'.
79 See also M. Depreter, *De Gavre à Nancy (1453–1477). L'artillerie bourguignonne sur la Mémoire sur la composition des armées de Charles le Téméraire dans les deux Bourgognevoie de la 'modernité'* (Turnhout: Brepols, 2011).
80 Sections of this correspondence between the prince and his towns can be found in Gachard (ed.), *Collection de documents inédits*, vol. I, pp. 154–160.
81 In 1465 in Montlhéry, as in 1467 in Brusthem, the armies of the duchy and county of Burgundy arrived too late. See de la Chauvelays, *Mémoire sur la composition des armées de Charles le Téméraire*.
82 *Ibid.*, pp. 150–151.
83 See B. Schnerb, 'Le recrutement social et géographique des armées des ducs de Bourgogne (1340–1477)', *Cahiers du Centre de recherches en histoire du droit et des institutions (guerre, pouvoir, principauté)* 18 (2002), 53–67.
84 For a portrait of one of these mercenaries, see B. Schnerb, 'Troylo da Rossano et les Italiens au service de Charles le Téméraire avec deux pièces justificative', *Francia* 26:1 (1999), 103–128. On the English soldiers in the Burgundian army, see L.-E. Roulet, 'Présence et engagement des combattants anglais à Grandson et à Morat', *PCEEB* 35 (1995), 107–122.
85 A. Curry, 'The Nationality of Men-at-Arms Serving in English Armies in Normandy and the *pays de conquête*, 1415–1450: A Preliminary Survey', *Reading Medieval Studies* 18 (1992), 135–163.

86 E. Doudet, 'De l'allié à l'ennemi: la représentation des Anglais dans les œuvres politiques de George Chastelain, indiciaire de la cour de Bourgogne', in D. Couty et al. (eds), *Images de la Guerre de Cent Ans. Actes du colloque de Rouen, 21–23 mai 2000* (Paris: PUF, 2002), pp. 81–94.

87 De la Chauvelays, *Mémoire sur la composition des armées de Charles le Téméraire*, pp. 225ff., and for what follows, pp. 247ff.

88 Molinet, *Chroniques*, vol. I, pp. 61–62.

89 G. Soldi-Rondinini, 'Condottieri italiens au service de Charles le Hardi', *PCEEB* 20 (1980), 55–62.

90 C. Allmand, 'Did the *De re militari* of Vegetius Influence the Military Ordinance of Charles the Bold?', *PCEEB* 41 (2001), 135–144.

91 Plancher, *Histoire générale et particulière*, vol. III, doc. 420.

92 The text is edited in E. Champeaux (ed.), *Ordonnances franc-comtoises sur l'administration de la justice (1343–1477)*, special issue of *Revue Bourguignonne* (Dijon, 1912), pp. 134–135.

93 I am using here Delpu's unpublished thesis, 'Une réforme militaire en Bourgogne', and particularly his critical edition of the military ordinance of 1473.

94 We should stress that according to specialists in military history, Charles was probably advised by men-at-arms in the definition of such rules, even if he appears as the only author in the final document. Regarding the role of counsellors at the court, see M. A. Arnould, 'Le séjour bruxellois de Charles le Téméraire pendant l'hiver 1467–1468', *Annales de la Société royale d'archéologie de Bruxelles* 58 (1981), 27–50.

95 This comparison is based on the 1473 military ordinance and on Paravicini, 'Ordre et règle'.

96 Wielant, *Recueil des antiquités de Flandre*, p. 55.

97 There are some points of comparison in C. Allmand, 'Le problème de la désertion en France, en Angleterre et en Bourgogne à la fin du Moyen Âge', in J. Paviot and J. Verger (eds), *Guerre, pouvoir et noblesse. Mélanges en l'honneur de Ph. Contamine* (Paris: Presses de l'Université de Paris Sorbonne, 2000), pp. 31–41.

98 It is important to note that wages were half-paid before the departure of the troops, so encouraging the desertion of soldiers.

99 See J.-M. Cauchies, 'La désertion dans les armées bourguignonnes de 1465 à 1476', *Revue belge d'histoire militaire* 22:2 (1977), 131–148.

100 Cuvelier et al. (eds), *Actes des États généraux*, p. 181.

101 Gachard (ed.), *Collection de documents inédits*, vol. I, p. 221.

102 Cauchies, 'La désertion dans les armées bourguignonnes', pp. 131–148, at p. 140.

103 Letter ed. in Haynin, *Mémoires*, vol. II, pp. 182–184.

104 Dispatch from Fr. Petrassanta to the duke of Milan, 6 June 1476, in Gingins la Sarra (ed.), *Dépêches des ambassadeurs milanais*, vol. II, pp. 221–222.
105 Ehm-Schnocks and von Seggern (eds), *Recueil du Fay*, p. 151.
106 The ordinance of 1476 is edited in de la Chauvelays, 'Les armées des trois premiers ducs de Bourgogne', pp. 297ff.
107 B. Schnerb, *Bulgnéville (1431). L'État bourguignon prend pied en Lorraine* (Paris: Economica, 1993), pp. 75–76.
108 On upheavals during the Wars of the Roses and their consequences on the conflict between French and Burgundians, see Vaughan, *Charles the Bold*, pp. 59ff.
109 Dubois, *Charles le Téméraire*, p. 264.
110 On these events, see Vaughan, *Charles the Bold*, pp. 261–311.
111 In the Treaty of London (25 July 1474), it was expected that the king of England would arrive in France on 1 July 1475 and, with the help of 1,000 Burgundian soldiers, take the French crown, leaving the Champagne area to Charles.
112 See the dispatch of Panigarola, 23 May 1475, in Vaughan, *Charles the Bold*, p. 349.
113 On this occasion, Louis XI signed a seven-year truce with the king of England.
114 *Die Berner-Chronik des Diebold Schilling (1468–1484)*, ed. G. Tobler (Bern: Druck und Verlag von K. J. Wyes, 1897–1901), vol. I, p. 136.
115 Note that during winter 1474, Mathias Corvin and Charles the Bold made plans to share the Empire between them.
116 On the idea of nation, see Chapter 7. For the moment, I would cite C. Sieber-Lehmann, *Spätmiterlalterlicher Nationalismus. Die Burgunderkriege am Oberrhein und in der Eidgenossenschaft* (Göttingen: Vandenhoeck & Ruprecht, 1995).
117 We should note that Louis XI also got into trouble, especially during the War of the Public Weal. But, unlike Charles, he knew how to wait.
118 See the works of C. Brusten, especially *L'armée bourguignonne de 1465 à 1468* (Brussels: Éditions Fr. van Muysewinkel, 1953).
119 J. Paviot, 'Les cartes et leur utilisation à la fin du Moyen Âge: l'exemple des principautés bourguignonnes et angevines', *Itineraria* (2003), 201–228.
120 See *Les mémoires de messire Jean de Haynin et de Louvignies*, 2 vols (Mons: Hoyois, 1842), vol. I, p. 37.
121 J. Le Goff, 'Documento/monumento', in *Enciclopedia* (Turin: Einaudi, 1978), vol. V, pp. 38–47.

122 Arts. 59, 60 and 61 from the ordinance of 1473.
123 Quotations in the subheading from D. Grummit, *The Calais Garrison: War and Military Service in England, 1436–1558* (Woodbridge: Boydell & Brewer, 2008), ch. 2.
124 Monstrelet, *Chronique*, vol. V, pp. 190–194: 'Et meismement, le josne roy Henri print en si grande desplaisance, que les larmes luy saillirent hors des yeulx ...'
125 Grummit, *The Calais Garrison*, ch. 2.
126 Monstrelet, *Chronique*, vol. V, pp. 206–209.
127 C. Potvin, 'Hue de Lannoy (1384–1456)', *Bulletin de la Commission Royale d'Histoire*, fourth series, 6 (1879), 117–138.
128 ADN, B 571, no. 15666, letter ed. in M.-R. Thielemans, *Bourgogne et Angleterre. Relations économiques et politiques entre les Pays-Bas bourguignons et l'Angleterre (1435–1467)* (Brussels: Presses Universitaires de Bruxelles, 1966), pp. 437–438.
129 Documents which prove this information had been leaked can be found in A. Doig, 'A New Source for the Siege of Calais in 1436', *English Historical Review* 110:436 (1995), 404–416.
130 On the composition of the army see M. Sommé, 'L'armée bourguignonne au siège de Calais', in P. Contamine, C. Giry-Deloison and M. Keen (eds), *Guerre et société en France, en Angleterre et en Bourgogne (XIVe–XVe siècle)* (Lille: CHRENO, 1991), pp. 197–219.
131 Monstrelet, *Chronique*, vol. V, pp. 252–253.
132 'Mockery of the Flemings' (1436), in R. H. Robbins (ed.), *Historical Poems of the XIVth and XVth Centuries* (New York: Columbia University Press, 1959), pp. 83–86; 'On the Duke of Burgundy', in T. Wright (ed.), *A Collection of Political Poems and Songs Relating to English History from the Accession of Edward III to the Reign of Henry VIII* (London: Longman, 1859–61), vol. I, pp. 148–149.
133 Sommé, *Isabelle de Portugal*, pp. 388–389.
134 Document ed. in J. Kervyn de Lettenhove, 'Programme d'un gouvernement constitutionnel en Belgique au XVe siècle', *Bulletin de l'Académie Royale de Belgique*, second series, 14 (1862), 218–250.
135 J. Dumolyn and É. Lecuppre-Desjardin, 'Propagande et sensibilité: la fibre émotionnelle au cœur des luttes politiques et sociales dans les villes des anciens Pays-Bas bourguignons. L'exemple de la révolte brugeoise de 1436–1438', in É. Lecuppre-Desjardin and A.-L. Van Bruaene (eds), *Emotions in the Heart of the City (14th–16th Century)* (Turnhout: Brepols, 2005), pp. 41–62.
136 Monstrelet, *Chronique*, vol. V, p. 249.
137 On this propaganda, see A. Doig, 'Propaganda, Public Opinion and the Siege of Calais in 1436', in R. Archer (ed.), *Crown, Government*

and People in the Fifteenth Century (Stroud: Alan Sutton, 1995), pp. 79–106.
138 See Dumolyn and Lecuppre-Desjardin, 'Propagande et sensibilité'.
139 Regarding the medieval concept of *fama*, see C. Gauvard, 'La fama, une parole fondatrice', *Médiévales* 24 (1993), 5–13.
140 A. Jouanna, 'Recherche sur la notion d'honneur au XVIe siècle', *Revue d'histoire moderne et contemporaine* 15 (1968), 597–623.
141 M.-R. Thielemans, 'Une lettre missive inédite de Philippe le Bon concernant le siège de Calais', *Bulletin de la Commission Royale d'Histoire* 115 (1950), pp. 285–296.
142 See B. Deruelle, 'Pour Dieu, le roi et l'honneur. Ethos chevaleresque, mérite et récompense au XVIe siècle', *Hypothèses* (2008), no. 1, 209–220.
143 On this point, see A. Boltansky, *Les ducs de Nevers et l'État royal, genèse d'un compromis (ca. 1550-ca. 1600)* (Geneva: Droz, 2006).
144 For a better understanding of the closeness between the chivalrous heroes of the fifteenth century and the new values of the Burgundian court, see M. Szkilnik, *Jean de Saintré. Une carrière chevaleresque au XVe siècle* (Geneva: Droz, 2003).
145 There are numerous examples in E. Gaucher, *La biographie chevaleresque. Typologie d'un genre (XIIIe–XVe siècle)* (Paris: Champion, 1994).
146 On the fascination of chivalrous ideals in the works Olivier de la Marche, see J. Devaux, 'Le culte du héros chevaleresque dans les Mémoires d'Olivier de la Marche', *PCEEB* 41 (2001), 53–66.
147 J. Schneider (ed.), *Lorraine et Bourgogne (1473–1478)* (Nancy: Presses Universitaires de Nancy, 1982), pp. 55–57.
148 Regarding these entertainment during wartime, see Schnerb, *Jean sans Peur*, pp. 507–510.
149 La Marche, *Mémoires*, vol. II, book I, ch. XII, p. 40.
150 All these examples are presented in M. Prestwich, *Armies and Warfare in the Middle Ages: The English Experience* (New Haven, CT: Yale University Press, 1999), pp. 300–301.
151 Monstrelet, *Chronique*, vol. IV, p. 219.
152 La Marche, *Mémoires*, vol. II, book I, ch. XI, p. 34.
153 K. Oschema, '"Si fut moult grande perte …": l'attitude paradoxale de l'idéologie chevaleresque envers la mort (XVe–XVIe siècles)', *Francia* 31:1 (2004), 95–120. I broadly follow his analyses even if I prefer to insist on the role of Christian ethics in chivalrous duty.
154 F. Viltart, 'Exploitiez la guerre par tous les moyens! Pillages et violences dans les campagnes militaires de Charles le Téméraire (1466–1476)', *Revue du Nord* 380 (2009), 473–490.

155 On these letters of defiance, see C. Gauvard, 'Le défi aux derniers siècles du Moyen Âge: une pratique entre guerre et vengeance', in B. Guenée and J.-M. Moeglin (eds), *Relations, échanges, transferts en Occident au cours des derniers siècles du Moyen Âge. Hommage à Werner Paravicini* (Paris: Académie des Inscriptions et Belles Lettres, 2010), pp. 383–401.
156 On the intervention of Hugues de Lusignan and Nicolas Albergati with the aim of appeasing the worried duke of Burgundy about his broken pledge, see J. G. Dickinson, *The Treaty of Arras 1435: A Study in Medieval Diplomacy* (Oxford: Clarendon Press, 1955), p. 174.
157 Details on this failed expedition in Schnerb, *Jean sans Peur*, pp. 193–202.
158 Literature on this topic is abundant; see, for example, W. Blockmans and A. Janse (eds), *Showing Status: Representations of Social Positions in the Late Middle Ages* (Turnhout: Brepols, 1999); W. De Clercq, J. Dumolyn and J. Haemers, '"Vivre noblement": Material Culture and Elite Identity in Late Medieval Flanders', *Journal of Interdisciplinary History* 38:1 (2007), pp. 1–31.
159 É. Lecuppre-Desjardin, 'La ville: creuset des cultures urbaine et princière dans les anciens Pays-Bas bourguignons', in Paravicini (ed.), *La cour de Bourgogne et l'Europe*, pp. 287–302, at p. 292.
160 B. Schnerb, 'La croix de Saint-André, "ensaigne congnoissable" des bourguignons', in D. Turrel *et al.* (eds), *Signes et couleurs des identités politiques du Moyen Âge à nos jours* (Rennes: PUR, 2008), pp. 45–55.
161 P. Arnade, 'Crowds, Banners, and the Marketplace: Symbols of Defiance and Defeat during the Ghent War of 1452–1453', *Journal of Medieval and Renaissance Studies* 24:3 (1994), pp. 471–497.
162 Anthonis de Roovere, *Van pays en oorloghe*, in *De gedichten van Anthonis de Roovere*, ed. J. Mak (Zwolle: W. E. J. Tjeenk Willink, 1955), p. 377, lines 171–172, viewed in Digitale Bibliotheek voor de Nederlandse Letteren, https://www.dbnl.org (accessed 2016).
163 La Marche, *Mémoires*, vol. I, book I, ch. XXIV, p. 141.
164 Monstrelet, *Chronique*, vol. II, p. 183.
165 *Ibid.*, p. 185.
166 *Ibid.*, p. 254.
167 Letter from Philip the Good dated 13 July 1453, in Gachard (ed.), *Collection de documents inédits*, vol. II, pp. 131–132.
168 Letter from Charles the Bold, 10 December 1470, in L. Gilliodts van Severen, *Coutumes du Franc de Bruges*, 2 vols (Brussels: F. Gobbaerts, 1879–80), vol. II, p. 379.
169 Letter from Charles the Bold, written at Salins, 22 July 1476, ed. in Ehm-Schnocks and von Seggern (eds), *Recueil du Fay*, pp. 154–157.
170 *Ibid.*

171 P. Godding, *La législation ducale en Brabant sous le règne de Philippe le Bon (1430–1467)* (Brussels: Académie Royale de Belgique, 2006), p. 18.
172 A. Sablon du Corail, *La guerre, le prince et ses sujets. Les finances des Pays-bas bourguignons soys Marie de Bourgogne et Maximilien (1477–1493)* (Turnhout: Brepols, 2019).
173 These remarks draw on F. Hartog, *Régimes d'historicité. Présentisme et expérience du temps* (Paris: Seuil, 2003), which discusses terms used by R. Koselleck ('champ d'expérience' and 'horizon d'attente'). See also the use of these 'différentiels de temps' in P. Boucheron, *Léonard et Machiavel* (Paris: Verdier, 2008).
174 On the English decline, see G. Lecuppre, 'De l'ennemi séculaire au serviteur ingrat: regards croisés d'historiens sur les royaumes de France et d'Angleterre au temps de Commynes', in Blanchard (ed.), *1511–2011. Philippe de Commynes*, pp. 165–177.

6

Measuring and imagining: reflections on territorial consciousness

After his arrival in Nancy on 30 November 1475, Charles the Bold decided to summon the Estates of Lorraine to meet a few days later. On 18 December he addressed them in the following manner, after first reassuring them of his intentions:

> This is the country [*pays*] that I wanted most, I am now in the middle of my lands, free to come and to go; ... be assured that you will find me a good prince, you know that I am held in awe, I have the power to keep you well, since I am now stronger between Germany and France than before, all fear me, they know that I am powerful.[1]

Despite the complete indifference with which this declaration was received, according to the dialogue transcribed by two secretaries of René II, the duke of Lorraine – the silence was broken only by cries of agreement paid for by the lords of Bièvre and Olivier de La Marche – it leaves no doubt about the duke's pleasure in resolving the problem of his non-contiguous territories.[2] Charles's satisfaction with his success in overcoming this difficulty draws attention to how much of a handicap the dispersal of his lands really was. There is no doubt of the duke's geostrategic aims. This speech confirms Commynes's opinion that the 'Lorraine enterprise' was, from the duke of Burgundy's point of view, the only way to establish a 'passage from Luxembourg to Burgundy' so that 'all his lordships should be joined together'.[3] Charles talked 'as if he had books before his eyes', but he also acted as if he had cards in his hands. We have already considered the almost academic approach of this man, isolated in his theories, detached from the men who were for him no more than unavoidable factors that had to be taken into account in his power games. In the context of the present chapter, this extract from his speech at Nancy serves to pose the question of the measure of space and of the emergence of geopolitical consciousness in this vast, constantly evolving and more or less strictly demarcated territory, which remained difficult to unite under one name, one symbolic system or one approach to government. As we have seen, attempts to impose the same practices in all these different places repeatedly clashed with the diversity of the duke's lands, their multi-polarity and the accumulation of different lands and countries, the list of which is as impressive as it is impossibly diverse. By considering how this territorial complex was perceived by the men of the time, we will attempt to show how far a vision of a territory accumulated through a series of marriages, legacies and conquests predominated over that of a space considered as the foundation of a united community.

'My lord's countries': spatial realities

According to one witness questioned in 1452, Henriote de Vergey, lady of Fontaine-Française (Côte d'Or), who died in 1427, claimed that when she sat down, she was in the kingdom of France, but when she put her feet on the ground, she was in Burgundy.[4] 'Whoa there! Let's not go any further! The kingdom stops here!' exclaimed a French royal sergeant on the banks of the river Sensée between Artois and Ostrevent in 1448.[5] During a fiscal inquiry in Walloon Flanders in 1449, an inhabitant of Attiches complained that a certain rich man known as Mahieu le Terrier claimed to have a house in the Empire and that as a result he refused to pay the *taille*.[6] We could extend the list of complaints, witness statements, demands and inquiries which, directly or indirectly, suggest the limits of what we could almost describe as a 'pointillist' territory. Between long lists of titles, and with an overall view stretching from the fogs of Frisia to the constantly contested Mâconnais, we will, in what follows, attempt to describe how the space of the Burgundian territorial complex was perceived.

Limits, frontiers, marches

The dukes of Burgundy continually expanded their territories, and here is not the place to retell the well-known story of their successive conquests. One consequence of this appetite for lands and lordships was an extremely mobile frontier, or rather the existence of a variety of frontiers which were either secure or vulnerable according to the events of each particular period.

It can be said immediately that official texts, charters, ordinances, letters and mandates give very few details about the concrete structure of the lands of the duke of Burgundy. Nor is their terminology definitively fixed. Sometimes 'marches' are referred to, as in the instructions given by the Burgundian envoys to England who had to complain of the losses suffered by the duke's subjects 'as much in the marches of Burgundy as in Picardy'. Sometimes 'frontiers' are invoked, as when the same text deplores the presence of thousands of enemies 'in various places on the frontiers of these countries of Burgundy and of Charolais'.[7] Sometimes it is 'limits' that are at issue, for example in the meeting organised between the representatives of the dukes of Savoy and Burgundy in September 1427. It must be admitted that such demarcations were more nebulous than linear, that they were adapted to the particular spheres of influence, mechanisms and ambitions which they expressed. The Burgundian losses which had to be deplored in order to secure compensation concerned a large band of territory which it made sense to describe as a 'march'. Hostile forces were spread across a long front, threatening the integrity of a country protected by its frontier. Finally, efforts to establish peaceful relations between Savoy and Burgundy were facilitated by the definition of a 'limit' which made it possible to determine rights and profits.

We can remark in passing that the word 'frontier' appears only rarely in chronicles, except in that of Jean Molinet, who, during Maximilian's wars, refers to the frontier to be defended as being constituted by Saint-Omer, Aire-sur-la-Lys, Lille, Douai and Valenciennes: the 'five towns on the frontier'.[8] In the treaties which established new rights and the transfer of territories, we see the same geographical inconsistency. On the occasion of the marriage of Marguerite de Male and Philip the Bold, when the wedding presents included the return to Flanders of the castellanies of Lille, Douai and Orchies, Charles V declared simply that he gave the said towns and castellanies in perpetual inheritance with the revenues which were attached to them, without precisely specifying where they were.[9] When Jacqueline of Bavaria was forced to cede her lands to Philip the Good in 1433, we can note the same absence of details.[10] These documents of course gave only an overview of the situation. In other contexts more precision was needed, as when, in pursuance of this ordinance, Philip granted the countess lands to meet her needs in a way which shows a good knowledge of the different lordships of the ceded counties.[11] Yet overall, the concrete elements found in these treaties refer more to a landscape of rights and revenues than to a well-defined geographical entity.

Space understood in terms of legal rights

The duke's territory was above all an accumulation of rights. When the king of France granted the towns of Roye and Montdidier to Philip the Good on 6 May 1420, precisely the same privileges and revenues were listed in each.[12] A careful reading of the materials collated by Urbain Plancher in his *Histoire générale et particulière de la Bourgogne* suggests such spaces took concrete form only when there were interests to be defended. In 1422, when Philip the Good decided that the best way to provide 'good justice' to the inhabitants of the *bailliage* of Aval was to divide it in two, he listed all the towns and castellanies which would allow an equitable division.[13] In 1427, when tax assessments were revised following wars in the county of Charolais, the inquiry had to be precise, and Philip the Good ordered his tenants to make an exhaustive declaration of their goods.[14] Yet the work of the inquisitors, who did, it is true, actually visit the scene of their inquiries, seems to have been limited to putting questions to taxpayers, rather than making an assessment on the basis of their own direct observation. In the household assessments in the Burgundian lands, such as the fiscal inquiry of 1449 in Walloon Flanders, the commissioners did appear in person and sometimes went from door to door, but they still usually followed declarations made under oath.[15] There again, little information is given about the limits of the different taxable areas.

Sometimes the geographical imagination emerged from the fog of these vague descriptions to cite a natural phenomenon which made it possible to fix or to contest specific boundaries. This was the case for rivers, which were more permanent elements of the landscape than hedges, ditches or copses. The Somme thus provided a convenient punctuation mark between different territories. The

Saône on the other hand was a zone of permanent dispute, as we shall see in a moment, to which princely and royal inquisitors made repeated visits to establish the lord's rights. It will be seen that, as Bernard Demotz put it in his discussion of the frontiers of Savoy, 'the surest source of information is that of financial documents which, more than more or less elaborate treatises, show incontestably where the prince's authority comes to an end'.[16] Contestation, infractions and external threats led to moments of crisis which made it necessary to measure the prince's territory.

Known boundary markers

In the period we are dealing with, the county of Flanders belonged to the dukes of Burgundy; the rights of the different castellanies which defined its administrative contours were in their hands, and fiscal receipts made their way to the Chamber of Accounts at Lille. In general, as Paul Bonenfant remarked, 'in those areas where the population was dense, the frontier must have been determined earlier and with greater precision'. The extent of a territory could be marked by planting trees, hedges or batons topped with straw known as 'brooms' (*escouves*), by digging ditches, placing boundary markers or setting up stone crosses. For Bonenfant, this explained the relative scarcity of problems over jurisdictional limits in this area.[17] In the north, the dukes thus inherited territories which had already been the object of early delimitation, thanks notably to the 'public measurers' to be found in the country as well as in towns.[18] As a result, the boundary markers between the county of Namur and the duchy of Brabant could be surveyed in 1385, and Philippe de Saint-Pol was able to fix 'frontier poles' with inscriptions in Latin, French and German in 1430, with the aim of protecting the neutrality of his duchy in the war between Liège and the Burgundians.

Yet causes for litigation remained. The fiscal inquest held in Walloon Flanders in 1449 showed how the limits of a castellany or a *bailliage* could become a very concrete element in the life of inhabitants who were very much aware of the subtleties of the dimensions of their *domaine-ressort*, since this could allow them to escape from taxation. We might consider, for example, how one Perceval de le Court of Néchin took advantage of his position on a frontier to escape taxation, or at least to pay as little as possible, by disassociating his place of residence from his rent-bearing lands.[19] This game of frontiers was certainly exhausting for the fiscal commissioners of 1449, although perhaps the palpable tension in these texts was also due to the pressure which the king of France was applying to the ducal lands.

The attack on enclaves in the 1440s

We should not make the mistake of concluding that because official texts were particularly terse and give very little detail about the boundaries of the Burgundian lands, these boundaries were not known on the ground. Indeed, it was perhaps because the lands under the authority of the duke of Burgundy were in general clearly identified that attacks on the duchy's frontiers tended to occur in those places which had posed a problem for a long time. The events on which the following discussion is based are well known in a different context, but have not, as far as I know, been considered as a whole, even though some of them were compiled in a list of recriminations drawn up by Philip the Good in preparation for the meetings at Rheims and Châlons between March and May 1445.[20]

Disputes in the Haute-Saône

Jean Richard has explored and explained the ever-increasing threat posed by the king of France to the Burgundian lands on the west of the Saône. The lands in question were made up of isolated pockets which, although they were part of the 'country of Burgundy' and thus observed Burgundian customs, did not recognise ducal authority. By the Treaty of Arras of 1435, the king retained these enclaves but at the same time permitted Philip the Good and his heirs to appoint officers there and to raise aids and *gabelles*.[21] However, from 17 March 1442, the royal administration became more aggressive, forbidding the duke's men from raising aids in the castellanies of Bèze and Tilchâtel and initiating inquiries on the ground. Subsequent meetings at Châlons in 1445 and at Paris in 1448 did not make any progress. In 1451 the royal administration even went back on the Treaty of Arras. In 1468, after the sequestration of Louis XI at Péronne, Charles the Bold incorporated these enclaves into the duchy, and in 1477 the king re-established the rights of royal enclaves which now found themselves amongst royal *bailliages*.[22] A lasting solution would have to wait until the Treaty of Cateau-Cambrésis of 1559, which resolved the matter and simplified the map.

Opposing attitudes and opposing languages clashed in the continuing dispute between Charles VII and Philip the Good over these lands. On one side, the royal commissioners often used delaying tactics, avoiding meetings and hiding behind a discourse which limited the definition of an enclave to a pocket of royal authority in Burgundian territory. On the other, numerous means were mobilised to prove the duke's legitimate rights.[23] Legal materials were collected into two fat registers compiled between 1446 and 1447. Royal officials took their stand on the defence of royal sovereignty, whereas the Burgundians wagered their cause on the reality on the ground, on the lived experience of the inhabitants of these lands and their history. Indeed, whereas the king's men argued simply in 1452 that 'the river Seine separates and delimits the kingdom of France and the county of Burgundy', the partisans of the duke developed their learned discourse on the basis of an historical argument founded on the existence and antiquity of the kingdom of Burgundy.[24]

Quarrels in the Tournaisis

Royal incursions were not limited to the controversial frontier on the upper Saône. More modestly, but still in the same spirit, the ordinance of inquiry delivered by Charles VII on 28 January 1449 to determine the jurisdiction of the lordships from Le Val to Mouscron and from La Rousselerie to Herseaux also reveals the activities of royal officers in a region which oscillated between royal Tournaisis and the county of Flanders.[25] Indeed, thanks to the improvement of relations between Charles VII and Philip the Good, the king could now take the moral high ground by ordering four commissioners drawn from the two parties to resolve questions of jurisdiction and sovereignty raised by acts of violence perpetrated by the king's men against local inhabitants.

It was the complaints of subjects who had been taxed twice, in the context of the castellany of Courtrai and of the *bailliage* of Tournai, which alerted the duke to the activities of royal officials. This took place after Philip the Good's complaints of 1445 against

Charles VII's questioning of his lordship in the castellanies of Lille, Douai and Orchies. It is clear that on the ground, when controversial questions of feudal rights were raised, words were followed by deeds.

The recurring problem of Ostrevant

Our final example takes us a few miles from the Tournaisis, to the borders of Ostrevant. In this territory, the former Frankish *pagus*, bordered by the Schelde, the Scarpe, the Sensée and the Tringuige, was the object of a long controversy. In 1257 Louis IX had passed judgement in the *Dit de Péronne*, assigning Ostrevant to Hainault and the Empire, but this did not prevent Philip IV from claiming sovereignty over it once more at the end of the thirteenth century.[26] Two different interpretations of the situation came face-to-face in this struggle, as in the quarrel in the Haute-Saône. Just as, for the royal commissioners, the Saône provided a clear frontier between France and the county of Burgundy, the latter lying in the Empire, so the Schelde separated the Empire and the kingdom of France in the land of Ostrevant. For the ducal officers, what mattered were recent feudal arrangements, namely the enfeoffment of the lordship of Bouchain to Hainault, which put the limit on the Scarpe and the Sensée.[27] The debate went on and on. Between 1445 and 1448, Philip the Good had a list of his prerogatives drawn up by assembling numerous archival documents, notably those to be found in the castle of Quesnoy. He also made use of the direct testimony of the inhabitants, who reported their customs, stating to whom they paid taxes and which officers visited them, or noting the existence near a bridge on the Scarpe at Douai of a copper marker indicating the boundary between France and the Empire. The Burgundians' conclusion was categorical: Ostrevant was not part of the kingdom of France.

For Jean-Marie Cauchies, this episode proves that Philip the Good was seeking sovereignty. This hypothesis should not be rejected out of hand, but it must be noted, in the light of the incidents mentioned earlier in Tournaisis and Haute-Saône, that the duke's attitude came in reaction to a royal attack from multiple directions which targeted the jurisdiction of contestable regions that weakened the kingdom's borders. In Louis XI's letters of 3 October 1464, which postponed currently active cases concerning the kingdom's borders for a further twelve years, the summary of the situation there presented makes clear the systematic action which Charles VII had previously taken in order to affirm the limits of his kingdom.[28] These letters also invoked the case of the counties of Alost and Waas, which were situated to the west of the Schelde but fell in that part of Flanders situated in the Empire. Their geographical position was difficult to contest, but in a number of legal cases which adversely affected inhabitants of that area who had appealed to the Parlement of Paris, Philip the Good was obliged to defend his interests and sovereignty, with supporting documentation to hand, in 1458 and again in 1462.[29] Here again, tensions persisted until the Treaty of Madrid of 1526 definitively detached Flanders and Artois from the jurisdiction of the Parlement of Paris.[30] In all these cases, the duke was motivated not by the idea of defending the borders of his lands but by his desire to defend his honour and right.

These examples combine with recent studies of frontiers to demolish the received idea that a concern to precisely delimit territories did not exist in this period. Nevertheless, we need to underline – and this is a particularity neither of the dukes of Burgundy nor of the period – that the acquisition of lands and opportunities for expansion undoubtedly preceded the development of theories concerning the nature of a territory and the necessity to make it coherent. This does not of course mean that no ideology of territory yet existed, however preliminary. In France, the argument was adapted to the variety of the lands in question, and their geographical spread could be used to reinforce the *potestas* of the kingdom through its diversity.[31] Whilst in ducal Burgundy allusions to the ancient kingdom of the Burgundians occasionally served the argument for full ducal sovereignty, in the Dauphiné the same kind of argument enabled Matthieu Thomassin to assert that since Vienne was the necropolis of the kings of Burgundy, and since the kingdom of Burgundy had been absorbed by the kingdom of the Franks, then this region was a natural addition to the French kingdom.[32] History was once more put to service to support the establishment of authority and to define borders in retrospect. Moreover, it was, as we shall now see, the same order of priorities (prove one's rights, then re-establish contested limits) which guided the cartographic activity ordered by the dukes.

Maps as proof

The medieval period is not known for the abundance of its maps. It was not until the sixteenth century that general plans were available for many areas of western Europe.[33] Nevertheless, recent studies building on the work of François de Dainville have drawn our attention to early attempts to portray geographical space.[34] The Burgundian territorial complex was also committed to paper or parchment in different forms at a number of key moments and on a limited scale. The examples are not numerous, but they do exist. They confirm the idea that the desire to map emerged from a specific aim, whether military, economic or legal. Laurence Moal puts it well when she says that 'maps serve as preliminaries, not as conclusions'.[35]

Representing points of view

A number of episodes in Burgundian military history led to the depiction of strategic landmarks in support of defence or attack. Between 1422 and 1423, expeditions to the Holy Land inspired Ghillebert de Lannoy to accompany his narrative with five maps of the new port of Alexandria and of the ports of Acre and Saïda amongst others. Similarly, before the siege of Calais, Philip the Good ordered two painters, Jean de Husteneuve and Colin des Prez, to prepare 'a map of the situation' ('un patron de la scituation') of the town. Likewise, during the siege of Neuss in 1474, Charles the Bold ordered a map giving a plan of the town and showing the situation of the Burgundian forces at each gate.[36] The dukes were far from being the only ones to take this kind of initiative. In 1436, for example, in the brief war between the Burgundians and the English, the town of Saint-Omer ordered the painter Yvain du Molin to depict the position of the enemy in the surrounding area.[37] It is in Saint-Omer, too, that we find the famous topographic roll dating from around 1470, which represents in more than three metres the course of the river Aa from Saint-Bertin Abbey to Blendecques, as

Figure 3 Roll of the river Aa, from Saint-Bertin Abbey to Blendecques, c. 1470

part of a court case concerning mills on the river.[38] The judicial aspect of these commissions is obvious, classing them alongside those representations of particular points of view with a judicial purpose which were already developing in the thirteenth century, some time before the Italian lawyer Bartholus of Sassoferato and his 'tiberiads' of 1355.[39] A number of good examples come from ducal lands, such as that of Heuilley and Talmay realised in 1474 or those undertaken at Amiens, Douai or Antwerp.[40] The Antwerp panorama is certainly impressive, measuring some 5.20 metres in length. Yet the view of the Schelde commissioned by the town in the context of a confrontation with Charles the Bold in 1468, which was followed by a colour version which was less precise but more aesthetically pleasing, was still the result of the same objective: to defend the rights of the towover the toll-booths on the river (see Figure 3).

Maps in the footsteps of the merchant and in the hand of God

In all of these representations of different viewpoints, places are often shown along the direction of travel, as with the first map of Flanders, dated to 1452, which was inserted into an Italian version of the chronicle of Flanders (see Figure 4). This map follows the trajectory of a foreign merchant who took to the stretch of water

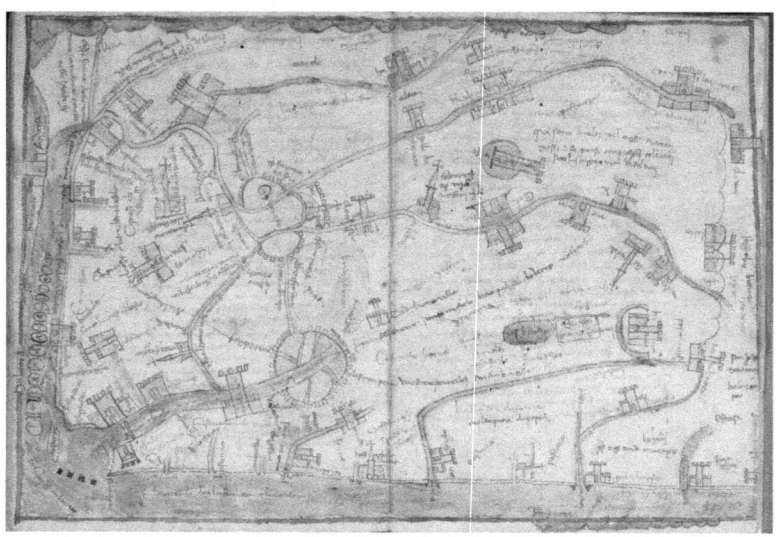

Figure 4 Map of Flanders, from an Italian version of the *Kroniek van Vlaanderen*, 1452

called the Zwin with the aim of conquering the markets of its hinterland.[41] The cartographic approach became more subtle with time and could sometimes take on a more rational dimension. That said, the progression towards precision and abstraction was not continuous or linear. A little before his death in 1538, Gilles van der Hecken, a member of the priory of Les Sept Fontaines, executed on paper what is considered to be the first map of the duchy of Brabant, inscribed within two concentric circles, the outer one 14 cm in diameter (see Figure 5). A colour code distinguishes watercourses in grey and dry land in green, and the names of towns are shown with coloured labels in grey, yellow or orange to mark the hierarchy between them. Neighbouring principalities are identified in the inner circle whilst the outer circle marks the points of the compass and the most important towns in each direction. In this round *mappa mundi*-type map, the frontiers of the duchy are of course not marked.[42] Sergio Boffa has linked the realisation of this map with the list of towns and franchises of the duchy which accompany it, because the painting was placed at the beginning of

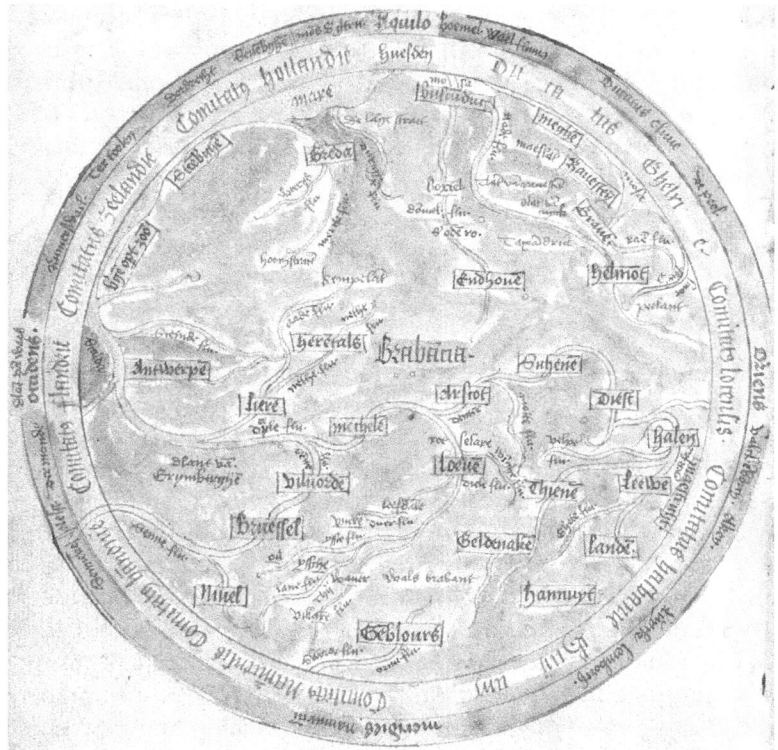

Figure 5 Map of Brabant by Gilles van der Hecken, c. 1535

the *Oppida Brabantie cum villis liberis atque pagis seriatim descripta*.[43] We also need to recall the obsession with roundness in cosmological thought which allowed this clerical cartographer to link the duchy, earth and heaven.[44] But when we compare this round map with the work of Jacob van Deventer from the same period, we are confronted once more with the problem of attempting to force history into convenient periodisations and the difficulty of building models. The reality and the figuration of this reality by these two men took very different forms, even though they both submitted their work to the duke of Brabant in almost the same year. For one, the harmony of the cosmos and the honour of the land of Brabant based on the excellence of its imagined proportions dominate. For the other, a map must portray a territory with the greatest possible accuracy on the basis of land surveys. In the same way, frontiers were lived differently by a prince at the head of his army and a simple peasant trying to escape from heavier taxation. The way frontiers were fixed on a map most certainly depended on the political ideal which was being pursued.

Geography through listing

Pierre Le Baud, Anne of Brittany's almoner, drafted a second version of his history of the Bretons between 1498 and 1505. At the beginning of this new text, he replaced the narrative of mythical genealogies with a geographical representation of Brittany.[45] This desire to imagine a territory first, before telling its story, can already be detected in Burgundy in an inquest of 1455 concerning ducal rights in which one witness based the superiority of the duchy on its singleness and wholeness: 'This country of Burgundy is a whole country, without any thing enclaved within it which is not part of the government of the said country.'[46] During the same period, around 1493, Olivier de la Marche compiled his *Mémoires* with the didactic aim of edifying and educating the young Philip the Fair.[47] He proposed to prepare the young prince for his future duties by teaching him how noble his lineage was, issuing from an exemplary genealogy, by showing him how his estates had legitimately descended to him and, finally, by describing the memorable events of his time. The second part of this demonstration might have led to a description of these territories, but the author instead limited himself to describing the marriages and annexations which occurred under the four Valois dukes and under Maximilian of Austria.

Turning from this work by a 'writer knight' to that of a respected jurist such as Philippe Wielant, we might have expected to find a slightly different understanding of territorial realities. It is true that several of his chapters distinguish between towns and urban districts in terms of their privileges and size. Yet he describes Flanders crudely when it comes to evoking the origins of the county, before leaving its new extent up to the imagination as he provides a list of modifications brought by marriages listed one after the other.[48] So, without ever invoking a precise geographic depiction, even though such descriptions often provided resources for argument concerning litigation over frontiers, the jurist ends his narration by once more extrapolating the greatness of the Burgundian territory from the number of marriages and inheritances which led to such an exceptional accumulation of lands.

Inheritance, lineage and the accumulation of titles were thus at the heart of discussions of the Burgundian lands by two men from very different intellectual backgrounds. Their understanding of the Burgundian territories reflected in both cases a culture of the list but also expressed a perception of the regions from which the dukes drew their power, which was more feudal than territorial.

Enumerating one's identity

The first contact of many students with the history of the principality of Burgundy is the discovery of the astonishingly long list of the duke's titles, a further example of the 'infinity of lists' discussed by Umberto Eco.[49] In the first exercises of palaeography or in the first readings, few forget this accumulation of status, which contemporaries themselves often brought to an exhausted close with 'etc.'. In the Great Privilege Charter of 1477, Mary of Burgundy imposed her authority after a recital of her titles which reminds us that she was:

> Mary, by the grace of God duchess of Burgundy, of Lothier, of Brabant, of Limburg, of Luxembourg and Guelders, countess of Flanders, of Artois, countess palatine of Burgundy, countess of Hainault, Holland and Zeeland, of Namur and Zutphen, margrave of the Holy [Roman] Empire, lady of Frisia, of Salins and of Malines.

As Robert Stein has shown, the style which the duchess inherited from her father did not reflect any geographical reality, but was rather an accumulation of titles, an issue to which we shall return in a moment.[50] For the time being, we need simply note that these lists were an intellectual tool which served to celebrate a whole territory even though its general contours were hard to identify. This use of a list was still the most widespread mode of expression for anyone who wanted to represent the image of any territory.[51] Studies of the geographic perceptions of medieval people are now numerous and often ascribe a significant role to subjectivity.[52] It was not that medieval people lacked notions of circumscription, localisation and orientation, but rather that their system was focused on social norms rather than on universalised markers.[53] This is the key to understanding medieval geographical thought. Also helpful is Paul Zumthor's remark, along similar lines, that 'space in the Middle Ages was a field marked with sites heavy with positive, stable and rich meaning.' The sources continually bring this way of thinking, which I have elsewhere described as a 'linear conception of space', to our attention when they assemble rigorous lists to concentrate the attention on intangible entities.[54]

Lists as landmarks

This form of geographical writing had nothing specific about it and could be applied as easily to Burgundy as to Flanders or elsewhere, and it was used by many different social groups. Lists of toponyms are thus found in the writings of ducal administrators who sought to establish the extent of the territories under their financial administration in the form of series, whose order can sometimes be perplexing. Take, for example, the receivers of the castellany of Douai and Orchies. Their account book of 1399–1400 follows a zig-zagging stream of consciousness, leaving a trail including multiple diversions and about-turns, clearly following some logic other than that to be found in the field and privileging the hierarchy of different townships or simply habit.[55] Similar lists also fed the *compendia* of heralds of arms, such as the list of the duchies and counties holding from the king of France in MS français 1968 of the Bibliothèque nationale de France, which also includes a precise hierarchical list of the said towns under each of the duke's duchies, counties and lordships.[56] This was probably conceived as a manual, and was no doubt compiled to facilitate memorisation. When the scribe mentions the title of 'duke of Lothier', he notes that there was no town in that territory, as he might well do, since this was a purely honorific title. Similarly, he takes the time to evoke the marquisate of the Holy Roman Empire, pointing out that this was 'an imperial dignity without land'. The understanding of territory which this exemplifies depends on titles and no doubt draws on older sources that are more or less well understood.

Moving beyond the court and its institutions, we might cite an anonymous satirical poem from the end of the fourteenth century, which lists, like a litany of saints, fifty-eight places, including forty-two towns. For each place, a distinctive characteristic is ascribed to its inhabitants, associated with their trades, the food they eat, their pastimes or their morality. In the long list of towns in the *Properheden van den steden van Vlaenderen* ('Features of the Flemish towns'), we find the 'Heeren van Gent' ('Ghent M'Lords), the 'Speerbekers van Rijsele' ('Lille Lancers'), the 'Cabelliau heters vander Nieuport' ('Nieuport Cod Eaters'), the 'Vechters van Cassele' ('Cassel Brawlers') and so on.[57] We see once again that space was understood through lived experience, gaining meaning from the men who lived in it. But this cognitive procedure was also an inheritance of classical and early medieval learning. We should not forget, as Pierre Gaultier-Dalché reminds us, that *mappae mundi* were the graphic equivalents of lists.[58] This practice above all expressed a way of thinking which gave the highest value to accumulation, compilation and repetition. Moreover, the plan of the duchy of Brabant cited above was composed by a man who also had a plan of Brussels made which has been regarded as a kind of 'mapping list'.

Arguments over lists at the Council of Basel

In this context it is not surprising to find arguments which sought to convince by making use of lists to assert the legitimacy of a particular authority. At the Council of Basel in 1433, in the famous argument over precedence which occupied the Burgundian delegates for more than a year, they used figures and interminable lists to defend the superiority of their master, first and foremost against the envoys of the prince-electors and then, after 19 March 1434, against the delegates of the duke of Brittany.[59] Jean Germain, bishop of Chalon, the head of the Burgundian delegation, defended the pre-eminent place of the duke on the basis of *origo*, *nobilitas* and *potentia*. The duke's Trojan and Carolingian origins, his kinship with the royal dynasties of England and Cyprus, and finally the possession of four duchies and fifteen counties provided support for this demonstration. Yet the emperor replied by accusing the duke of hubris, like a bird flying too high in the air, asserting that he was, at the highest, only fifth or sixth in rank within the House of France, and the delegates of the prince-electors sheltered behind the Golden Bull in order to affirm their pre-eminence with regard to the emperor. As for the recriminations of the Breton envoys, they were supported by the intervention of Philippe de Coëtquis, archbishop of Tours, who observed that the duke of Brittany had never been the vassal of the duke of Normandy, and that he was superior in dignity to the duke of Burgundy, as was demonstrated by an appropriate list of the riches of Brittany.[60] This remark was too much for Jean Germain, who declared that the archbishop was a 'mortal enemy of the House of the duke of Burgundy'. A few days later, Gaspard de Pérouse, the representative of Burgundian interests, formulated a new reply which once more raised the stakes. The duke of Burgundy was of superior dignity since he had great duchies, great counties, lordships and domains, not to mention populous towns, hundreds and thousands of soldiers and the thousands of pounds raised from the salt produced at Salins. Examples abound which show that, amongst the humblest as amongst the greatest minds of the age, the list remained an important tool to evoke a space and the power associated with it, putting it into an ideal order.

Art in the service of synthesis

That said, a simple list might also be followed by a more general survey which showed some attempt at synthesis. The nature of the examples which follow might at first seem surprising, but we should not forget that the prince's entertainments were always packed with political discourse. Thus it is said that Master Chiquart, cook to the duke of Savoy, Amadeus VIII, contributed to the main sweet course of a grand banquet given on the occasion of the succession of the new duke in 1416 by producing 'a colossal pastry which presented a relief map of the Estates of the new duchy'.[61] The court of Burgundy showed no less imagination when it came to illustrating the reasons behind a banquet through games, images or cookery. During a tournament at La Fontaine des Pleurs in 1450, for example, a dessert course made at the lodgings of the bishop of Chalon represented the town of Chalon, its churches, its belfry with its clock tower, its houses, its wall and the tower on the bridge on the Saône towards Saint-Laurent.[62] The technique of the relief map was thus an established culinary possibility. On the other hand, when

Charles the Bold celebrated his marriage to Margaret of York at Bruges in July 1468, he did not seek to demonstrate Burgundian territorial weight and hence power through a relief map representing this space in three dimensions but, once again, through a list of lordships represented by thirty vassals:

> First the tables were set as if for dinner; but they were far wider, and on the said tables there were thirty ships, each one bearing the name of one of the lordships of my said lord of Burgundy, amongst which there were five duchies and fourteen counties; and the others were the lordships of Salins, Malines, Arcle and Bethune, which are great and noble lordships.[63]

The ships, loaded with meat, were painted with gold and azure and with the arms of the said lordships, whereas each mast-top bore the arms of Charles the Bold. The heraldic spectacle did not stop there, since thirty great pastries were also placed on the tables, topped with castles which each bore 'the arms and the name of one of my lord's good towns'.[64] Olivier de la Marche concludes by declaring that the power of the duke of Burgundy was thus demonstrated by his thirty principalities and lordships and his thirty unrivalled towns.

This desire to mark the immensity of a territory through a heraldic composition clearly interested Charles the Bold. Some years later, on the occasion of a solemn entry into Ghent on 6 May 1472, in the presence of the ambassadors of Rome, Naples, Venice and Brittany and the envoys of Frederick III, the duke commissioned a great assemblage of his personal arms surrounded by the escutcheons of his different territories. This imposing object was constructed by Hugo van der Goes, who had already been called upon for the duke's wedding at Bruges. It was to be suspended from the Bruges Gate, showing Charles's arms surrounded with the collar of the Golden Fleece. The escutcheons of each lordship were carried by heraldic animals, on a field of Burgundian *briquets* and of daisies, the duchess's flower.[65] We have no more details, although this work can be compared to another which was exhibited for the marriage of 1468, in which two lions held Charles's helm and arms, whilst an archer distributed white wine and a mounted crossbowman red wine, surrounded by shields representing some of Charles's other possessions.[66] In short, it is clear that Charles was more and more attached to the diffusion of this kind of heraldic assemblage as a means of summarising his territorial power, even though, *pace* Robert Stein, the number seventeen was not yet associated with this means of symbolizing power, as the following section will show.[67]

The numerical imagination

Historians have recently searched for a number, a symbol, an expression which might make it possible to identify the appearance at the Burgundian court of a form of political communication driven by some kind of will to synthesise, some kind of desire to unify. It is true that when we examine practical sources, letters of remission, speeches to assemblies of Estates or ducal ordinances, it can be seen that the princes constantly invoked the extent of their possessions by the complete style of their title, which on its own declared 'the extent of [their] power'.[68] The most frequent expression was always in the plural: 'the lands and lordships of our lord'. The land or *pays* remained the measure of reference, but what topographic reality did it represent?

The Great Principality: an accumulation of pays

It is certainly extremely difficult to define the contours of a *pays* or country. The word could be used to denote the immediate lived space occupied by a peasant from the Thiérache or as as a generic term for the different territorial entities in the principality of Burgundy or the kingdom of France. Thus at the Estates of Tours in 1484, France was presented as a sum of different *pays*: 'France, Guyenne, the Bourbonnais, Rouergue … and all the other *pays* of the kingdom, each in its place'.[69] This is how this designation should be understood when it appears in official Burgundian texts – as the countries (*pays*) and lordships which make it possible to denote the Burgundian territorial mosaic. But whereas, during the same Estates of Tours, the memorandum presented by the representatives of the French king used the formula 'kingdom and Dauphiné' or 'Kingdom, Dauphiné and adjacent countries [*pays adjacens*]' to denote, by its exterior limits, the coherence of the French territorial entity expressed by the language of 'kingdom', the principality of Burgundy never reached this level of synthesis.[70] In other words, the kingdom of France, just as much as the Great Principality of Burgundy, was made up of an accumulation of *pays*, of lands and towns, but the challenge of unification, and of detachment from a level of reference which was primarily linked to the person of the ruler, was met only in the first case.

We might think that a first step towards unity had been taken by this young principality from the two-fold division, often used by historians, between the *pays de par-deçà*, the 'country over here', and the *pays de par-delà*, or 'country over there', as the two geographical groups formed by the lordships of the north and of the south were known. Yet such a view would fail to grasp the true sense of these words, which Pierre Cockshaw examined as long ago as 1974.[71] *Par-deçà* is nothing more than an expression indicating proximity, whereas *par-delà* denotes a physically more distant space. A familiar vagueness and familiar difficulties are found in the application of these terms. Thus when, on 5 May 1404, the Chamber of Accounts at Douai learnt of the death of Philip the Bold, it decided that 'the officers of my said lord being over here [*par deçà*] will undertake their office as they did formerly'.[72] As one is always south of something north and vice versa, the secretary of the Chancery of Brabant wrote in 1446 to the officers of the Chamber of Accounts at Lille asking it to find letters which were available only over here (*par deçà*) in the Brabant archives as copies. In short, even though, just like the 'Burgundian state', these terms provide historians with a convenient term of art, *pays de par-deçà* and *pays de par-delà* do not refer to any particular political construction in contemporary sources but are quite simply expressions of the physical location of a place in relation to another. As for the expression *pays-bas* or 'low country', the *lage landen bij de zee*, we should note that this expression appears under the Habsburgs only to distinguish their new lands closer to the sea from their earlier possessions (*vorlande*) such as the Tyrol, Bavaria and so forth.[73] The only possible conclusion is that no overall expression existed to denote all the lands belonging to the duke of Burgundy. The title of king might have made it possible to bring everything together, but in the absence of this supreme dignity, the language of community did not emerge, except in the evocation of the common good, whose limits and ambiguities we have already explored.

A symbolic number?

In his work on the origins of 'Burgundian national sentiment', Robert Stein concentrated his attention on one number, with a strong symbolic power, which might at last have expressed a desire to bring these different territories together: the number seventeen. This was held by contemporaries to be the number of lands held by the Burgundian dukes. Yet, as Stein quite rightly points out, following the warnings of Johan Huizinga, it is better not to try and identify precisely which lands lie behind this figure.[74] We should remember that in Christian culture from the book of Wisdom to Saint Augustine, creation is good because it is founded on number. Measurement and enumeration were amongst the most important ways of expressing moral values whose precision was the guarantee of rightness. Seventeen is, for example, a symbolically important number in the *De arithmetica* of Boethius, and also in the *rithmomachia* or number battles fought by monks since the eleventh century. It is thus not surprising that medieval authors used this number when writing about the seventeen Christian kingdoms on whom the balance of the world must rest, since seventeen peoples and nations were present on the day of Pentecost in the Acts of the Apostles (Acts 2: 7–11). As with lists, we must agree with Huizinga that the number seventeen was not a preoccupation not merely of the educated but also of the ordinary people, who gave it a prominent place in their songs as in their stories. In the little ditty 'Nachtwacht heeft u nog boeven gezien? / Ja mijnheer, wel zeventien' ('Watchman, have you any villains seen? / Yes sir, a good seventeen'), the reply is more evocative of a symbolic mass than of a precise number. The same can be said in the elaboration of the myth of the 1,700,000 clock towers of the kingdom of France, where the number at the head of a line of zeroes serves once more to suggest an uncountable multitude by means of a finite figure.[75]

However, whereas the number seventeen enjoyed undeniable success in the modern period, especially in the 1570s, under the medieval dukes of Burgundy it did not provide a way of denoting all the duke's lands or even his northern lands. Although it is true that this number appears in 1466, in a play performed before Charles of Charolais which presented Philip the Good as 'Philip, our noble and powerful prince, / lord of seventeen powerful lands', it re-emerged only in 1485 in the *Dagboek der Gentsche collatie*, and in the anonymous chronicle of Liège which noted at the death of Charles the Bold that seventeen countries were not enough for this prince.[76] Moreover, seventeen was not the only number to be used in connection with the prince's lands. We have already mentioned the thirty lands carried by the ships at the banquet of 1468, the four duchies and fifteen counties of Jean Germain, the fifteen titles of Philip the Good in 1460 and the eighteen used by his son in 1475 and by his granddaughter Mary of Burgundy. Seventeen seems to have been a symbolic number more appreciated in Brabant than at the Burgundian court. Certainly, in Robert Stein's demonstration, it is clear that the duchy of Brabant was the real centre for the diffusion of the symbolism at work in Van Boendale's chronicle from 1334, in the *Van menych simpel* of 1466 and, finally, in the 'Lofsang van Brabant' ('Anthem of Brabant') composed by the Calvinist Jan van der Noot, who in 1578 referred to Brabant as 'the principal head of all the Low Countries … the sixteen other provinces'. Brussels very early on sought to promote its image as a capital, an issue to which we shall return in a moment.[77] It must be admitted that the fifteenth-century principality had not found its golden number and continued to express both its power and its dispersed nature through the plurality of its lands and titles.

A rich harvest of titles

It would seem that, at the end of the Middle Ages, princes conceived of the area or space of their power by, above all, declaring their titles to their possessions, as the first part of this chapter has shown. The Great Principality of Burgundy was in no way a political construction in contradiction with the ideals of the time. It was characterised not by the fact that it was composed of a sum of different territories but by chronic incompleteness and by the difficulty of finding a federating motif which might identify all of them. After all, the kingdom of France was a political construct which actually gained strength from the diversity of the lands of which it was composed. In his writing, the Saint-Denis chronicler Michel Pintoin distinguishes between the love of the country and the love of the kingdom, following a logic which leads to a feudal geography of duchies, counties and castellanies, whereas the *patria* remains the particular region of one's birth. Others, however, like Eustache Deschamps, who deplored the state of the kingdom in his *Complainte du pays de France*, showed a different way of thinking, which did take France to be the country, the *patria*, of origin.[78] It is difficult to disagree with Philippe Contamine that 'the kingdom of France was indeed fundamentally constituted and structured by assemblage or rather by juxtaposition within a space, which was moreover quite precisely defined on the ground of "countries" [*patriae*] to which both public institutions and collective reflexes corresponded'.[79] Following Léonard Dauphant, I would add that the regnal state had constructed a history of a territorially defined France which still respected regional specificities and that 'the nation France became conscious of itself at the same time as its diversity'.[80] Plurality was thus not necessarily a handicap for political construction. The same tools of the representation and expression of the same diversity were available to the king of France, the duke of Anjou or the duke of Burgundy, to name but a few. Nonetheless, behind the use of similar means of representation there were different political ambitions.

An 'emblematised space'

Heraldry makes it possible to observe the ideological divide between the kingdom of France and the Great Principality of Burgundy. Perfectly adapted to express both an accumulation of lands and titles and an exceptional pedigree, it consequently enjoyed great success in the fifteenth century. In this period, the appearance of mottos and short phrases could be used to express the individuality of those who chose them whilst conserving in their arms their claims to lineage, to rank, to title and to honour. The Burgundian court was at the forefront of this trend in both the invention and the regulation of heraldic protocol, which was guaranteed by heralds of arms.[81] The dukes certainly made great use of this means of symbolising power, leaving their mark on the palaces they occupied, on their books and on their clothes, but also in the open space of their territories. In official ceremonies as in everyday life, the prince's symbolic presence was expressed through his arms, enabling him to display and to project his power. As Laurent Hablot emphasises, this was a 'construction of emblematised spaces [*construction d'espaces emblématisés*], intended to dramatise [*mettre en scène*] the prince and his power'.[82]

Numerous studies have shown this dissemination of the princely sign throughout the duke's territories. The princely arms served as markers which expressed the association of lord, land and allegiance, whether in the case of the official plaques imposed by Philip the Bold in 1373 in the lands of his vassal Hugh of Vienne, whose fief had just been seized for breaking homage, of the stained glass windows installed on the order of Philip the Good in the main churches of Lille, or of the boundary markers which enabled the inhabitants of lands in Burgundian obedience to know whether they were in the kingdom or in the duchy. Yet when we consider the second term of the dialectic between heraldry and territory, the conclusions are less clear. Coats of arms marked territory in a very concrete manner, but did they express a geographical understanding of this power space? In other words, did these figurative heraldic creations carry out the role played by *mappae mundi* earlier in the Middle Ages and so form a pictorial equivalent to the list? The question is worth asking, even if we must answer it with considerable caution.

Heraldry as the expression of a political ideology

Coats of arms were considered above all to be signs of belonging to a lineage and so were a form of representation closer to genealogy than to geography. According to Michel Nassiet, coats of arms are markers of lineage; thus to refer to coats of arms, as used to be done, as a sign of lordship is an imprecise use of language. Nevertheless, 'the territory is [also] a fief associated with a sovereign whose arms and whose name it shares'.[83] Philip the Bold thus bore the arms of a lineage (the broken arms of the Capetian-Valois) quartered with the arms of a lineage associated with a fief (those of the first House of Burgundy, which had become the arms of the duchy). Each heraldic shield thus symbolised the territories to which the dukes had rights. In the frontispiece of the *Champion des dames* of Martin le Franc, we find the same association of dynastic and territorial emblems (see Figure 6).[84] Placed above Philip the Good, who sits on a dais of majesty, we see his own arms surrounded by

Figure 6 Philip the Good surrounded by his coats of arms. Martin Le Franc, *Champion des dames*, 1440

two shields which mark his French descent and fourteen shields representing his territories (the duchy of Burgundy, duchy of Brabant, county of Flanders, etc.). In this miniature, as in others, dynastic and territorial emblems are mixed, as if to remind us that lords and lordships were intrinsically linked. The representation of lineage and its implantation in a particular land cannot be dissociated from one another, so that geographical reality is understood through the lord's feudal and familial possessions. We see something similar in the lexical field of the family, which was not limited to heraldry but also made it possible to express the reality of a territory and of the connections and the hierarchies which composed it. For Michel Pintoin, for example, Paris was the mother of the towns of the kingdom, whereas Saint-Denis was the 'beloved daughter of the mother of the towns of the kingdom'.[85]

It would seem that this taste for heraldic emblems, constructed to assemble around the prince all his titles which were also his possessions, is proof of a perception of a territory as the consequence of the logic of titles to which it corresponds. In other words, a feudal understanding of the space of power is more pertinent here than a topographical one. This is what explains the presence of the duchy of Lothier in Mary of Burgundy's list of lordships, even though this dignity did not correspond to any territory. In this principality, despite considerable creative effort, heraldry still served an ideology which celebrated the plurality of the spaces within which its master's power was wielded. In this way, the prince's coats of arms constantly became more complex as new territories were acquired or conquered, without, however, ever using any of the symbols which were readily available – the cross of Saint Andrew, the *briquet* or the Golden Fleece – to unify them. This was not the result of the intrinsic limits of this kind of representation by colours and motifs but rather of a political thought which was not yet marked by a desire to bring a community together.

This difference of usage is illustrated, for example, by the frontispiece of the 'Treatise establishing the rights of Louis XI over the duchy of Burgundy' in MS français 5079 of the Bibliothèque nationale de France, which provides a particularly interesting example of the use of heraldry in the new conception of the state current in France at the end of the fifteenth century (see Figure 7).[86] This manuscript, which is attributed by Paul Saenger to Michel de Pons, general

274 The illusion of the Burgundian state

Figure 7 'Treatise establishing the rights of Louis XI over the Duchy of Burgundy', late fifteenth century

prosecutor in the Parlement of Paris, was apparently drafted some time between 1479 and the Treaty of Arras of 1482, in reply to the treatise of Jean d'Auffay on the rights of Mary of Burgundy. The iconography is greatly marked by the royal political project and by its legal justification. It presents the king on his throne, his feet on a lion, a symbol of strength and justice, holding the sceptre and the Hand of Justice (part of the French royal regalia). He is accompanied by four virtues. On his right, Reason and Rectitude (*Droiture*) hold four heraldic shields: those of the duchy and county of Burgundy, and the lordships of Auxerre and Mâcon. A parchment emerges from their mouths on which is written 'These four shields we present to you of which the lordship comes to you.' On the left, Justice and Truth (*Vérité*) declare, 'By justice they are due to you, for truth has so ordained it.' Another statement issues from the royal crown: 'My spouse and protector, these four lands [I] present to you which pertain to you and to me.' Lower down, Mary of Burgundy raises her arms in the direction of the shields, whilst the king's advocate answers her: 'My young lady, do not come closer, for you have no right to them.' This suggests two things. On the one hand, the contested Burgundian lands are presented using the coats of arms which correspond to the titles which characterise them, with heraldry serving to evoke these territories concisely. On the other, Michel de Pons defends royal prerogatives through the model of the mystic marriage which united, for example, each bishop to the Church. For him, thanks to the influence of the writings of Lucas de Penna, an indissoluble bond united the Crown, the king and the royal domain. As a result, it is not the king who speaks, but the Crown of France which calls upon its husband, reminding him that he must not lose the lands which pertain to him in the name of the moral and political union between the king and the *chose publique*.

If we compare this political image with the great heraldic assemblage ordered by Charles the Bold, we can see that no such mystical invocation of the state was apparent in this representation of the power and authority of the duke of Burgundy (see Figure 8). The coats of arms of the different ducal possessions were placed under the protection of Saint Andrew and Saint George, whilst two lions supported the coats of arms of Charles the Bold, with his motto beneath it: *Je l'ay emprins* ('I undertook it'). Once more, we are dealing with a representation which linked each territory to the

Figure 8 Copperplate with the symbols of power of Charles the Bold, after 1472

Measuring and imagining 277

person of its prince, individualised by his motto, and not a political figuration which presented each as the parts of a Burgundian *chose publique* defended by a prince who nonetheless regularly manipulated this concept in his different political interventions. Indeed, it was during the rule of this duke that the only allegory of Burgundian power appeared in which a reference to some kind of state may be discerned, namely the Montpellier manuscript considered above.

'My Lord's lands' were thus still attached to the titles associated with them without this leading to a general view or synthetic representation which a geographic mapping of these places would have made incontestable. Diversity and multiplicity were put into order but persisted nonetheless.

From the Parisian reflex to the dream of Nancy

Let us return to the quotation which opened this chapter and which seems to suggest that, for Charles the Bold, Nancy was a capital in the making which would allow him to align the territory over which he ruled with a town at the centre of his lands. Indeed, the only real attraction of this choice was the fact that Nancy was at an almost equal distance from his northern and his southern lands. This decision once more demonstrates how the last duke of Burgundy reasoned without any concern for the human element of his schemes.

A multi-polar entity without a capital

Whether it was his settled will or a careless whim, the idea marked a radical change of approach. Charles did not use the term 'capital', but he did invoke a series of characteristics which come close to the definition recently proposed by historians for whom a capital is a 'town occupying the first hierarchical rank and where the state and the government reside in a fixed manner'.[87] Charles announced that he wished to reside in Nancy, enlarge the town and, one might suppose, beautify it, to hold his 'estate' (*estat*) there and to summon to it the representatives of all his lands, thus finally centralising his territories. This speech alone could be used as proof that before 1473 to 1475 the Burgundian state did not exist in the head of the princes of Burgundy. It was only Charles who advanced the idea of a single central town from which he would control a territory which might to that extent be thought to be united. Before him, the dukes of Burgundy never affirmed the superiority of one town over another. The problem identified by Patrick Gilli remains: 'how to imagine the idea of a capital, which presupposes the organic unity of a group of territories, when the words are lacking even in the mouths of rulers to express the unity of domination?'[88] The dukes of Burgundy, as we have often seen, had no conception of this kind of unity, and so a capital was impossible to find. Yet, to take up the concerns of Richard Vaughan, cited in the Introduction, can we conceive of a state without a capital? Or even, to again borrow one of Charles Tilly's questions, did not the very extent of the urban network in the duke's northern lands act as a brake on the development of a state?[89]

If we must look for a capital for the Burgundian princes, we should certainly first look where they placed their coats of arms.[90] In what follows, I will consider in outline matters which have already been well studied by historians who have shown, with the figures to hand, how the dukes' ceaseless movement itself constituted a form of government, a choice of political dynamic incompatible with the designation of a single capital.[91]

Of course, Dijon has long been presented as the capital of the Valois dukes of Burgundy, through an unacknowledged slippage which assimilates the whole of the dukes' territories to the duchy alone. Yet although Louis XI was quite ready to recognise Dijon in 1479 as the 'principal town' of the duchy which now belonged to him, it was nonetheless very much a secondary destination for the dukes and duchesses who went there to die and to rest for eternity.[92] From this point of view, Dijon, whose claim to be the dukes' capital is the central theme of a volume of essays which appeared in 2007, also shows above all the attachment of these descendants of King John II to the kingdom of France and its rituals.[93] There is no need to repeat how far the Chartreuse of Champmol served as a Burgundian Saint-Denis. It is enough to point out that the dukes very rarely stayed there and that Charles the Bold got round to organising his ceremonial entry to the town only in 1474, seven years after his accession.

It is important to consider here the work of Florence Berland on the presence of the two first dukes and their court in the capital of the kingdom of France. On the basis of itineraries and accounts it has been possible to prove that Paris was the favourite place of residence for Philip the Bold and his son, at least before the latter was expelled from the city by force. Yet to conclude from this that Paris might be considered the capital of all the Burgundian territories would be a grave error. After all, Paris, in the late-fourteenth and early fifteenth centuries, was establishing itself above all as the king's town. The dukes of Burgundy represented only one princely house amongst others, and the 'cumulative dynamic' which served to promote the emergence of a capital over the long term worked in this case in favour of the kingdom. It is true that John the Fearless paid particular attention to the Hôtel d'Artois, but the capital of a great principality could not be limited to a single town quarter. Although Paris was of capital importance for both Philip the Bold and John the Fearless, it was not their capital. The study of Burgundian investments in Paris, of court residence and of the dukes' itineraries shows how the dukes of Burgundy, just like those of Orléans, Berry, Anjou and the rest, were princes of the blood who behaved as such and who had to stay close to the Crown if they wanted to enjoy the advantages of their status. When Philip the Bold came to Paris, he returned to the bosom of his family, and although the bonds of kinship were less straightforward for his son, all the energy the latter expended to correct his estrangement from the court shows his desire to take his place amongst the circles of the great and to be close to the royal treasury.[94] Moreover, when they were not in Paris, the two first dukes were careful not to go too far, preferring Arras and Lille to Bruges, for example. The situation changed with Philip the Good, who, on the one hand, expanded his territory and, on the other, turned away, although probably against his will, from the French sphere of influence. Dijon gained little from this new state of affairs, but as conquests accumulated, increasing the choice of possible residences, and princes and princesses continued to travel around right up to their deaths, Lille and its Chamber of Accounts, Bruges and its pleasures and Brussels in particular started to receive the court for longer periods. The game changed once more under Charles the Bold, who, even though he wanted to move both his new Parlement and the Chamber of Accounts to Malines by the Thionville ordinances of 1473, nonetheless thought of Nancy as a possible seat for his government.

In sum, the dukes were in constant motion, a capital was impossible to find, their spending on building projects was relatively restrained, and their style of governance was definitively based on itinerancy.

Capital cities

Let us reconsider this issue in relation to Richard Vaughan's arguments. Was the absence of a capital a handicap to the development of Burgundian government, as Vaughan claimed? It must be admitted that historians have had difficulty in freeing themselves from deceivingly comfortable modes of thought, which seem all the more natural when the historian in question is French. The coincidence of territory, nation, state and capital city, which works for the French kingdom, has provided and still provides an important element in many people's political assumptions. It seems reasonable to imagine that when Richard Vaughan criticised the work of the dukes and their council, it was this same model which underlay his analysis. Yet, in fact, although the kingdom had indeed come to consecrate Paris as 'the true navel of France', in the words of Christine de Pizan, or as 'the royal city of France', to take up those of Laurent de Premierfait, the enthusiasm for the Parisian capital had not always been as strong in the thirteenth and fourteenth centuries as it was at the beginning of the fifteenth century.[95]

It is true that the prosopographical studies of Boris Bove have helped to correct an older, univocal vision which stressed the strong antagonisms between the king and the Parisians on the basis of chronicles which focus on moments of crisis. He shows convincingly that Parisian notables, from the reign of Philip Augustus to that of Louis XI, 'well understood the honour and the power which the role as the king's interlocutor conferred on them', and that the construction of the French royal state was also based on a two-way contract between the king and his 'good towns', of which Paris was one.[96] For Bove, Paris was thus nothing more than the theatre of national crises in which the Parisians were sometimes obliged to take sides as a result of their belonging to one patronage network or another. It seems to me, though, taking just the years 1407–19, that the power of the Burgundian party in Paris during the civil war went further than simply an involvement in a particular network.

The bitterness of Charles VII which led him to delay his entry into the capital after reconquering it from the English, the French kings' dislike for 'the town of towns', led them to develop a reflex of returning to the Loire which was finally established as a long-term phenomenon. Yet the kings' itinerancy and their installation at a fair distance from Paris was not the result of a period of weakened power; far from it. The French royal state, during the reconquest and subsequently in the consolidation of its territory and its authority, did not base itself on the capital.

This simple observation puts into perspective the importance of a 'chief town' in the development of political authority in the Middle Ages. We can go further, as Boris Bove does with regard to the ambiguities of Capetian policy towards Paris, and note that the concentration of the administration, of the archives, of the treasury and of the king's person in a single place was not without its risks. As a result, we can conclude not only that the absence of a capital in the Burgundian territories was not a sign of weakness, but even that it provided a perfectly appropriate model of governance. By making a virtue of necessity and leaving aside the element of chance, the itinerancy of the Burgundian princes and the dispersal of their instruments of power may even have provided an advantage in the construction of a Burgundian state, if such a thing had existed. The real risk of physical danger posed by setting up residence in a particular city is shown as much by the Parisian revolts as by Charles the Bold's failed entry into Ghent in 1468.[97] The loss of the Burgundian treasury at Grandson would then no longer be considered to be further proof of the duke's archaic methods, i.e. of having his riches follow him about, but would simply demonstrate the absence of mutual confidence between him and his subjects.

From a different perspective, we might also ask what use it would have been to the towns to raise one or another of them to the rank of the first city of the prince and his government. After all, as can be seen from urban registers of deliberations and municipal accounts, the presence of the king and his court was above all a financial windfall.[98] As a result, the towns did not hesitate to throw themselves into a dangerous bidding war in the hope of attracting the court to reside within their walls. In 1458 Valenciennes drew up proposals to construct a new palace in the hope of receiving Philip the Bold more often. On that occasion, the assembly made an offer of 4,000 *livres* to the duke. Yet it was turned down because Brussels and Lille were offering to construct a residence worth ten times as much. The presence of the court increased sales of all kinds and was an incontestable source of profit. But the reasons which encouraged towns to attract the prince were not all economic. In Flanders, the residence of the count in his country was also a political demand. On 31 August 1387 the representatives of the good towns of Flanders petitioned Philip the Bold either to keep residence in the country or else to ensure that a member of his family did so, specifically his son or his wife. This request was made again on the occasion of the ceremonial entry of John the Fearless into Ghent on 21 April 1405, and it was repeated with no little anxiety when Philip the Good, in the midst of his arguments with his son, announced his desire to depart on crusade in the winter of 1463–64.[99] To have the prince readily to hand gave hope of a more immediate and more affable kind of authority, cutting out the intermediaries and the courtiers keen to profit from the vicious circle of racketeering and bribery. Alternatively, from a more hostile point of view, the residence of the court opened the possibility of physically laying hands on the duke's person, or on a member of his entourage, in order to apply pressure on him or at least to gain better guarantees in the course of tense negotiations.

Yet no desire to identify a 'chief town' emerged from all these demands. In the end, this can be shown by place names. Unlike Italian cities, which are often invoked by way of comparison with the duke's northern lands, political entities in the Low Countries were not constructed around a town. Whereas in the Italian peninsula one referred to the duchy of Milan, the republic of Florence, of Genoa or of Venice, in the north the lands in question were still called the duchy of Brabant, the counties of Flanders, Holland, Zeeland and so on. In the Low Countries, history had left its mark, and the old Carolingian *pagi* continued to develop within a feudal structure which gave an important place to networks of towns, drawing strength from their economic power and their numerous privileges.

Although in the case of Brabant, Brussels certainly seems to have cultivated its pre-eminent position in the urban hierarchy, we should be wary of seeing this, as older teleological accounts did, as establishing this town as a capital in the fullness of its power as early as the fourteenth century. Claire Billen, for example, has analysed the holy legend of Our Lady of the Sablon, which can be dated to 1348, just after the secret protocols which had led John III of Brabant to give up Malines and Antwerp in the context of the marriage of his daughter to Louis de Male, count of Flanders. Billen shows how the invention of this story served to recall the indivisible association of Antwerp and Brussels through the translation of a miraculous statue of the Virgin from the former to the latter via the Schelde, and in the process to establish Brussels as the guarantor of the unity of the duchy.[100] Chroniclers of Brabant used this story to prove the sacral supremacy of Brussels. We might add that by installing this statue in the chapel of the crossbowmen's fraternity, Brussels began to establish its position, at the expense of Louvain, as 'the symbolic and warlike champion of the military integrity of Brabant'.[101] Yet this is better seen as symptomatic of competition for pre-eminence amongst towns within Brabant than as evidence of a firmly accepted 'capital' status.

Brussels certainly had larger ambitions. Much later, in the course of the fifteenth century, the town was careful to set out its dynastic heritage in theatrical performances which, from the *Van menych simpel* of 1466 onwards, attempted to establish the reliability of genealogies which successively integrated the Valois dukes of Burgundy and the Habsburg princes into the lineage of the dukes of Brabant. The *Voortzetting des Brabantsche yeesten* (1432–41), for example, which expanded by almost 30,000 lines the early fourteenth-century *Brabant yeesten* of Jan van Boendale, was clearly commissioned from Petrus a Thymo by the municipal authorities with the aim of maintaining Brussels's rank as the favourite place of residence for the new Burgundian dukes of Brabant. Yet the desire to attract the duke and his court, accompanied by architectural projects which were designed to expand and improve the gardens and the halls of the Coudenberg palace, did not cancel out an equal enthusiasm to insist on the historical and territorial coherence of the duchy of Brabant and so to prevent Brussels from being absorbed into a wider Burgundian territory. The *Vortzetting*, whose content was transmitted through public spectacles, served Brabançon supremacy more than anything else, and it is only to this extent that it might be seen as presaging a putative project to become the central kernel of the Burgundian lands.[102]

Alongside signs of Brussels's assertiveness, we need to set a careful reading of chronicle and annalistic texts across the lands held by the dukes of Burgundy, or even simple memoranda produced in the neighbouring county of Flanders. Such sources reveal the strength of urban localism and the inability to combine the multiple histories of different towns into a single regional narrative, let alone into a national one. They show no trace of any kind of history which might have made one of them into a capital of a political entity which went beyond the walls of Ypres, Ghent and Bruges. Was it then the towns of the north that stood in the way of the establishment of a Burgundian state?

Towns against the state?

It is true that the saturation of the Burgundian space with towns possessing strong cultural and political identities, and with age-old traditions of revolts against the decisions of central authority – something which is well known for Flanders but which was also the case in Brabant, Holland and even the city of Liège – might lead one to agree with the sociologist Charles Tilly when he argues that the nation-state became strongest where the urban world was weak. Tilly has indeed theorised at length how the political geography of urban commercial systems can delay the formation of the nation-state.[103] One thing is certain: in this zone of high political potential, commercial practices transformed ideas about marriage, property, exchange, religious morality and forms of association and political life.[104] But were the institutions and the political reflexes of these great northern towns incompatible with the development of the state? To answer this question, we must first define which state we are talking about.

The wealth of the towns in the service of princely policy

The model of the state with which the dukes' culture and education would most naturally have made them familiar was without doubt that of the kingdom of France. A state founded on the institutions adopted by the Four Members of Flanders, or on the constitution of Brabant, would have looked more like a parliamentary monarchy in which the prince would have been a contractual ruler rather than a king on his way to absolute power. We have already insisted on the paradox which led John the Fearless to promote in France an ideal of government which he refused to see applied in his own lands, or which encouraged Charles the Bold to demand greater power for the Estates General in the kingdom whilst reminding his own subjects that any suggestion of opposition to his authority would be met with total destruction. The inappropriateness of the ideology of the princes for the political realities of the lands which they ruled was blatant. If it is true that 'the solidity of a state regime depends on its access to economic resources but also on local and regional loyalties', it was on the side of the latter that the ducal political enterprise was at fault.[105] Following the French royal model, the dukes tried to establish permanent taxation; on the English model, they launched numerous projects aiming to tax imports as varied as wool sacks, salt and barrels of herring.[106] Taxes and aids, subject to a process of negotiation which annoyed the dukes, applied differently in different areas: *fouages* (a direct tax on households) applied to the duchy of Burgundy, to Hainault, Luxembourg and the county of Namur; taxes distributed on the basis of local inquests applied in Walloon Flanders; whilst in Flemish-speaking Flanders, impositions were based on the 'Transport', which put more than a third of the burden on the towns of Bruges, Ghent and Ypres, which, in turn, put pressure on the small towns around them. The important things to note here are that princely taxation, which was not unified, remained reliant on urban finances, and that attempts to rationalise it clashed with the interests of local elites.[107] But if we move away from the means of raising taxes and from moments of conflict, which were certainly endemic but which always worked out in the prince's favour, we find that the ducal coffers were constantly filled, making the dukes of Burgundy if not the richest in western Europe then probably the 'second richest in the west' behind the kingdom of France, at least before the catastrophe at Nancy.[108] It was, moreover, only as late as 1476, when the Estates General of the northern lands considered recent fiascos and the risks to come, that they refused to finance new wars. The legendary splendour of the dukes of Burgundy, which in a society of display was fundamental for any political power which wanted to have influence in international diplomacy, was incontestably filled by the fountain of plenty provided by the towns of the north, once the French royal treasury had ceased to be available.[109] Thus the towns' riches contributed largely to the development of Burgundian political power.

For what common good?

Yet the commercial dynamism which created these urban networks, whose existence long preceded the arrival of the dukes of Burgundy, had fed a political ideology which was very distant from ducal ambitions and which inevitably led to significant conflicts of interest. Thus whereas in the north, peace, free trade, judicial autonomy, a strong and stable currency and low taxation were the very basis of the common good, the defence of the prince's honour and his lust for new conquests led to a heavy tax burden and to war which was justified in turn by the need to defend the common weal of which the dukes were the guarantors.[110] As a result, the 'regional and local loyalties' which were supposed to support the development of the state do not seem to have been available to the dukes of Burgundy, in whose discourse the common good had failed to shift from one paradigm to the other in a way which might have allowed individuals to identify themselves not only with the community of the town but also with an over-arching state.

It would be wrong to think that towns had no concern for the wider community. We have already seen how the delegates of the Estates had done all they could to reconcile father and son in 1463. When the rumour spread that Philip the Good wanted to entrust the government of his lands to the king of France with the lord of Chimay as governor, or when it was said that Holland and Zeeland would be placed under the protection of the king of England, their members raised the alarm. The duke had to make denials in such circumstances on four separate occasions.[111] But, there again, the interests of the large towns encouraged them to try to guarantee continuity of trade, which was the only real aim of their diplomatic activity whether internal or international.[112] Consequently, they were capable only of forming temporary alliances based on a sense of community which was geographically unstable and limited in duration.[113] Moreover, the princes could take advantage of the lack of solidarity between towns across borders to weaken them when necessary. The war with Ghent shows that the composite structure of the Great Principality allowed the dukes to suppress rebel subjects, since the people of Holland, Brabant, Artois and so forth provided troops and arms for Philip the Good, but it also demonstrates the absence of links between all these territories. This urban self-interest can even be seen within a single *pays*, that of Flanders, when the people of Ghent provided reinforcements for the duke against the rebels of Bruges in 1437. Urban political ideology was not totally absent, but it had difficulty going beyond the city walls of the 'little fatherland' or *petite patrie* to create a wider collective consciousness.

Towns as petites patries?

Those historians who have given a central position to a monopoly of taxation, justice or warfare as a measure of state progression all retain, more or less directly, the starting criteria defined by Max Weber, Norbert Elias and Charles Tilly with regard to legitimate violence. Thus Wim Blockmans, in his first studies of the relationship between urban powers and central authority, insisted that 'states are institutions which are relatively autonomous, centralised and differentiated whose agents claim to control with greater or lesser success the most important means of violence in a territory'.[114] Yet the mastery of legitimate violence as the criterion which defines the state seems to constitute a circular argument, since here it is the state which recognises itself as legitimate, legitimising its legitimacy. The state cannot simply be that coercive force which decides alone on its rights. Because it presupposes universal acceptance, the state is opposed to feudalism; because it has by definition the capacity to create ties, state power alone has the possibility, as an authority which transcends all others, to assure the transformation from monopoly to universality. This is, in the end, the 'miracle of the state', i.e. its ability to dispossess, to monopolise and then to redistribute. Pierre Bourdieu sums this up when he says that there is no 'physical capital without the simultaneous or preliminary accumulation of symbolic capital', that is to say moves to stimulate or nourish participation and acquiescence.[115]

Towns had abundant institutional tools which encouraged an old habit of political debate. But if the means for political action were not lacking, their aims remained those of their time and their context, namely the defence of economic interests, a *modus vivendi* in these territories since the first manifestations of visible and readable urban identities at the beginning of the twelfth century. The logic of the owner, jealous of his economic prosperity – which was in the end the same as that of the prince who wanted to preserve his patrimony – did not evolve in the direction of openness and unity. To cite just one example, in the context of the Bruges revolt in 1488, the rebels drafted a petition based on a politico-moral discourse which was founded on the stability of the coinage and the free circulation of merchandise, within which the prince was seen as the guarantor of the prosperity which had been threatened by the wars of Maximilian.[116] Since the interests of the city were never subordinated to the superior interests of the state, the prince featured only in the guise of a lord in a restricted bilateral relationship. The political vitality of this economic discourse served an urban consciousness which invited the men of the north to show their fidelity to their own town, to identify with Bruges or Ghent, even before feeling Flemish – even if this statement may need to be qualified in the case of Brabant or Holland.

Yet the historian who goes in search of this 'urban patriotism' promoted by economic interest rapidly encounters the lack of sources. The genre of the *laudatio urbis* or praise of the city, for example, was not particularly widespread in the towns of the north. Only a few texts, such as 'De zeven poorten van Brugge' ('The seven gates of Bruges') from the early fifteenth-century Gruuthuse manuscript or Boudin van de Lore's poem 'De maagd van Gent' ('The maid of Ghent'), summarise the themes of urban ideology spread by the members of Chambers of Rhetoric (*Rederijkers*), namely honour, fraternity and unity, along with a desire for justice and the love of liberties.[117] In van de Lore's poem, composed in 1382, at the height of the revolt of Ghent against the count of Flanders and the king of France, his verses do go beyond the ordinary themes of urban thought. The young maid, in an enclosure which represents the market square, is isolated from the rest of the world by two rivers which presumably represent the two watercourses which gird the town of Ghent: the Lys and the Scheldt. Beside her stand a litany of local saints who are in fact patron saints bearing the standards of the different crafts. The threat to the besieged town, in rebellion against its lord and suffering from starvation, incites the author to galvanise the resistance of its inhabitants. The latter must fight to live freely and so as not to suffer the effects of a centralised government which goes against the interests of the town. The conclusion brooks no compromise: 'It is better to prefer an existence free and without servitude than gold and precious stones.'[118] Boudin van de Lore's text should be located in an idealised world, in which the population of Ghent guaranteed the preservation of the common good of the city and where, to arrive at a just balance, all must free themselves from material contingencies and from a certain kind of private property as a proof of their liberty. This ideal, we should say straight away, is a long way from the popular refrains which, in poems and in plays, spent most time encouraging the lesser sort not to revolt and to avoid falling into want. Urban ideology, as developed in these texts, was essentially based on a Christian morality of *caritas*, of the fair price and of harmony, and when a text became politicised it was to denounce excesses of all kinds which would endanger social equilibrium.[119] From Jan van Boendale of Brabant to Cornelis van Everaert in Bruges, in speeches, chronicles, complaints and pamphlets, the ambitions of townspeople were focused almost exclusively on urban prosperity and on the conditions of its fulfilment.

Economic concerns were without any doubt the motor of political action in this northern region. It was economic criteria which provoked revolt against the prince when his actions threatened the immediate interests of the richest townsfolk, which motivated towns to oppose one another so as to secure a hegemonic position or to fight against a troublesome competitor, and which endangered internal order by putting too much pressure on the workers, by bleeding the surrounding countryside dry or by leading local elites to abuse their power to fill their own coffers. Yet, in a virtuous circle, economic concerns might also have led towards a kind of patriotism that crossed borders, leading to a union of towns – large and small – in the defence of a common good which might have provided a shared basis for their collective action. Within urban communities, social and local identities were much stronger than territorial identities.

Craft organisations, with their political conquests, their hold over the urban rhythms of work and holiday, over architecture through the development of infrastructure, and the presence of their emblems on rebel banners, were deeply embedded in the everyday identity of these fifteenth-century men and women of the north.[120] Public order was not just a creation of policing and the army; rather it relied on consent, and this could also take the form of the acceptance, for example, of a kind of common time. From this point of view, merchant's time was not only the best one for counting profits; it was also the one which made all the townsfolk live to the same rhythm and which could thus compete with the prince's time through the fundamental guide-marks it spread in the simple lives of men. These anthropological remarks are not a digression from our discussion of political authority but instead serve to remind us how the operation of the state also relies on these essential categories of common life.

Towns doubtless offered princes the means to realise their ambitions; they developed a vocabulary for political expression whose richness would inspire the centuries to come, but they were not inherently either an obstacle to or a support for the development of princely authority. They accompanied their lord, in the feudal context that was theirs also, in his activity of *seigneuriage* or lordship, to use the terminology of the time, by untiringly reformulating the terms of a contract divided between rights and duties, for the good of communities and the profit of individuals. Towns did not oppose the state; they gave it the resources necessary for its development in the form of taxes, of personnel trained in their schools and at university, of the soldiers provided by their militias, by their infrastructures and so on. Yet what mattered in terms of state formation was that the ways in which the towns might have adhered to a princely political ideology were too far removed from their socioeconomic and, finally, their cultural concerns. It was not because it lacked a capital that it is difficult to recognise a Burgundian state, as Richard Vaughan argued. On closer observation, this notion proves to be both anachronistic and ill-adapted to this region. Instead, what mattered was the lack of a strong alliance between the princes and their towns, on the model of a contract, or of contractualism on the Aragonese model, which preserved the specificities of each member the better to permit the state to master the whole. The idea of a nation might have provided the necessary 'glue' to permit the transformation from a territorial grouping into a federated state.

Notes

1 Calmet, *Histoire de Lorraine*, vol. VII, Documents, col. 78, no. 125. We do not know if Charles the Bold actually said the words that are here ascribed to him, but in one way or another, it reveals that his ambitions were well known.
2 *Chronique ou dialogue entre Joannes Lud et Chrétien, secrétaires de René II, duc de Lorraine, sur la défaite de Charles le Téméraire devant Nancy, 5 janvier 1477, publiée pour la première fois avec des annotations et des éclaircissements historiques nouveaux par Jean Cayon* (Nancy, 1844), p. 23.
3 Commynes, *Mémoires*, vol. I, book IV, ch. 12, p. 309.
4 For more details of this topic, see É. Lecuppre-Desjardin, 'Annexions, conquêtes, héritages: réflexions sur la perception du complexe territorial bourguignon (XIVe–XVe siècle)', in S. Péquignot and P. Savy (eds), *Déplacements de frontières et annexions dans l'Occident médiéval (XIIe–XVe)* (Rennes: PUR, 2016), pp. 141–158.
5 ADN, B 1191/15862, p. 11, quoted in J.-M. Cauchies, '"Hola! N'allons plus avant! Cy fault le royaulme!" ou l'Ostrevant entre France et Empire au XVe siècle', in S. Curveiller (ed.), *Les champs relationnels en Europe du Nord et du Nord-Ouest des origines à la fin du Ier Empire* (Calais: Colloque historique de Calais, 1994), pp. 91–100.
6 A. Derville, *Enquêtes fiscales de la Flandre wallonne (1449–1559)* (Lille: Commission Historique du Nord, 1983), vol. I, p. 49. Attiches is near Pont-à-Marcq (Nord, France).
7 Instruction to Quentin Menard and Christian Hautain, on a mission in England, 17 April 1431, in Plancher, *Histoire générale et particulière*, vol. IV, p. 84.
8 Molinet, *Chroniques*, vol. II, p. 71. According to I. Guyot-Bachy, the notion of 'frontier' was more closely associated with the idea of identity in Flanders and Hainault than in France where, at the same time, in the thirteenth and fourteenth centuries, it was more connected to the limits of lordship. See I. Guyot-Bachy, 'Eine Grenze-zwei Betrachtungsweisen. Die Grenze zwischen Frankreich und Flandern in der französischen und flämischen Historiographie', in N. Bock *et al.* (eds), *Faktum und Konstrukt. Politische Grenzziehungen im Mittelalter: Verdichtung, Symbolisierung, Reflexion* (Münster: Rhema, 2011), pp. 187–202.

9 Plancher, *Histoire générale et particulière*, vol. III, pp. 25–28.
10 The treaty of 1433 (12 April) is edited in Cauchies (ed.), *Ordonnances de Philippe le Bon pour le comté de Hainaut*, no. 55, pp. 90–95.
11 *Ibid.*, pp. 92–93.
12 Plancher, *Histoire générale et particulière*, vol. IV, pp. 6–7.
13 Division dated 24 July 1422, *ibid.*, pp. 23–24.
14 *Ordonnance pour la confection du terrier de Charolois* (12 August 1427), *ibid.*, p. LXXI.
15 See the working methodology for such documents in P. Beck, *Archéologie d'un document d'archives. Approche codicologique et diplomatique des cherches des feux bourguignonnes (1285–1543)* (Paris: École des Chartes, 2006), pp. 132ff.
16 B. Demotz, 'La frontière au Moyen Âge d'après l'exemple du comté de Savoie (déb. XIIIe–déb. XVe siècle)', in *Les principautés au Moyen Âge. Actes de la SHMESP de 1973* (Bordeaux: 1979), pp. 95–116.
17 Reflections inspired by P. Bonenfant, 'À propos des limites médiévales', in F. Braudel (ed.), *Hommage à Lucien Febvre. Éventail de l'histoire vivante* (Paris: A. Colin, 1953), vol. II, pp. 73–79.
18 For the cases of Douai, Ypres, Bruges, Ghent, etc., see A. de Smet, 'De l'utilité de recueillir les mentions d'arpenteurs cités dans les documents d'archives du Moyen Âge', in *Fédération archéologique et historique de Belgique. Annales du XXXIIIe congrès* (Tournai, 1951), vol. III, pp. 782–795.
19 These examples are taken from Derville, *Enquêtes fiscales de la Flandre wallonne*, vol. I, pp. 62–63 and 166–167.
20 Plancher, *Histoire générale et particulière*, vol. IV, docs 138 and 139.
21 For more details, see J. Richard, 'Problèmes de circonscriptions et de ressorts. "Enclaves" royales et limites des provinces. Les élections bourguignonnes', *Annales de Bourgogne* 20 (1948), 89–113.
22 See the statement of Louis XI dating from 14 March 1477, in Plancher, *Histoire générale et particulière*, vol. IV, pp. 379–381.
23 See A.-B. Spitzbarth, *Ambassades et ambassadeurs de Philippe le Bon, troisième duc Valois de Bourgogne (1419–1467)*, Burgundica 21 (Turnhout: Brepols, 2013), pp. 140–151.
24 'car le pays et nacion de Bourgongne a eu de grande ancienneté royaume qui contenoit et s'extendoit en long dès la rivière du Rhin, ... jusques à Arles le Blanc ...' ADCO, B262, quoted in J. Richard, 'Les débats entre le roi de France et le duc de Bourgogne sur la frontière du royaume à l'ouest de la Saône: l'enquête de 1452', *Bulletin philologique et historique du CTHS, année 1964. Actes du 89ème congrès de Lyon* (Paris, 1967), pp. 113–132, at p. 120.
25 Herseaux is now a part of Mouscron (Hainault, Belgium). C. Depauw, 'Les seigneuries de Le Val et de la Rousselerie à Mouscron et Herseaux

au XVe siècle', *Mémoires de la Société d'histoire de Mouscron et de la région* 8 (1986), 15–40.
26 J.-M. Moeglin, 'La frontière introuvable: l'Ostrevant', in Allirot et al. (eds), *Une histoire pour un royaume (XIIe–XVe siècle)*, pp. 381–392 and pp. 557–561.
27 Details of this quarrel in Cauchies, '"Hola! N'allons plus avant!"'
28 Plancher, *Histoire générale et particulière*, vol. IV, p. 308.
29 ADN, B 1972, fol. 75v, ed. in Spitzbarth, *Ambassades et ambassadeurs de Philippe le Bon*, p. 148.
30 On this political and legal conflict, see S. Dauchy, '*Deça l'Escault estoit l'Empire*. La compétence du Parlement de Paris en Flandre impériale', *PCEEB* 42 (2002), 75–84.
31 See L. Dauphant, *Le royaume des quatre rivières. L'espace politique français (1380–1515)* (Seyssel: Champ Vallon, 2012).
32 L. Dauphant, 'Matthieu Thomassin et l'espace dauphinois (1436–v. 1456): naissance d'un humanisme géopolitique', *Journal des Savants* (2008), no. 1, pp. 57–105.
33 On evolution in historical geography methodology, see K. Lilley, 'Geography's Medieval History: A Neglected Enterprise?', *Dialogues in Human Geography* 1 (2011), 147–162.
34 F. de Dainville, *La cartographie reflet de l'histoire. Recueil d'articles présentés par M. Mollat du Jourdain, avec L. Lagarde, M.-A. Vannereau & N. Broc* (Geneva and Paris: Slatkine, 1986).
35 L. Moal, 'Dans le royaume ou en marge? Les frontières des principautés (XIIIe–XVe siècle)', *Annales de Bretagne et des Pays de l'Ouest* 1212:2 (2014), 47–81.
36 Examples listed in Paviot, 'Les cartes et leur utilisation à la fin du Moyen Âge', 201–228.
37 See M. Boone and É. Lecuppre-Desjardin, 'Entre vision idéale et représentation du vécu. Nouveaux aperçus sur la conscience urbaine dans les Pays-Bas', in P. Johanek (ed.), *Bild und Wahrnehmung der Stadt* (Vienna, Cologne and Weimar: Böhlau, 2012), 79–97, at p. 92.
38 Bibliothèque de Saint-Omer, ms. 1489.
39 See J. Dumasy-Rabineau, 'La vue, la preuve et le droit: les vues figurées de la fin du Moyen Âge', *Revue historique* 315:4 (668) (2013), 805–831.
40 ADCO, B 263. Other examples in A. H. Huusen, *Jurisprudentie en kartografie in de XVe en XVIe eeuw*, Algemeen rijksarchief en rijksarchief in de provincien, Miscellanea Archivistica 6 (Brussels: Algemen Rijksarchief, 1974).
41 Some details of this map are given in M. Boone and É. Lecuppre-Desjardin, 'Entre vision idéale et représentation du vécu. Nouveaux aperçus sur la conscience urbaine dans les Pays-Bas', in Johanek (ed.), *Bild und Wahrnehmung der Stadt*, pp. 79–97, at p. 88.

42 Facsimile of Deventer's map in B. Van't Hoff, *De kaarten van de Nederlandsche Proviniciën in de zestiende eeuw door Jacob van Deventer* (The Hague: Martinus Nijhoff, 1941).
43 The names of 750 locations are given in the *Oppida Brabantie*. See S. Boffa, 'La première carte manuscrite du duché de Brabant (c. 1535)', in A. Dierkens, Christophe Loir, Denis Morsa and Guy Vanthemsche (eds), *Villes et villages. Organisation et représentation de l'espace*, *Revue belge de philologie et d'histoire* 89:1 (2011), pp. 95–109 and fig. 3, p. 296.
44 See K. Lilley, *City and Cosmos: The Medieval World in Urban Form* (Chicago: University of Chicago Press, 2009).
45 Pierre Le Baud, *Croniques et ystoires des Bretons*, ed. C. De la Lande de Calan (Rennes: Société des bibliophiles bretons, 1910), vol. III, pp. 7–8.
46 Quotation from Kerhervé, 'Entre conscience nationale et identité régionale', p. 220.
47 La Marche, *Mémoires*, vol. I, prologue, p. 11.
48 Wielant, *Recueil des antiquités de Flandre*, p. 33.
49 U. Eco, *Vertige de la liste* (Paris: Flammarion, 2009).
50 R. Stein, 'Seventeen: The Multiplicity of a Unity in the Low Countries', in Boulton and Veenstra (eds), *The Ideology of Burgundy*, pp. 223–285.
51 P. Boucheron, 'Représenter l'espace féodal: un défi à relever', *Espace temps* 68 (1998), 59–66.
52 See, for example, B. Cursente and M. Mousnier, *Les territoires du médiéviste* (Rennes: PUR, 2005).
53 On the perception of space thanks to a social approach, see the studies of the philosopher Michel de Certeau in *L'invention du quotidien. Arts de faire I* (Paris: Gallimard, 1980; new edn, 1990).
54 P. Zumthor, *La mesure du monde: représentation de l'espace au Moyen Âge* (Paris: Seuil, 1993), part I, 'La demeure', section 3 'Lieux et non-lieux'; Lecuppre-Desjardin, *La ville des cérémonies*, pp. 20–22.
55 See the account of Watier Painmouillet (ADN, B 4627), discussed in A. Leclercq, 'Étude environnementale de la châtellenie de Douai et Orchies à travers l'étude du compte du domaine ordinaire de l'année 1399–1400' (master's dissertation, University of Lille, 2010) and p. 45, map. For a comparable example from the Carolingian era, see J.-P. Devroey, 'Gérer et exploiter la distance. Pratiques de gestion et perception du monde dans les livres fonciers carolingiens', in P. Depereux *et al.* (eds), *Les élites et leurs espaces. Mobilité, rayonnement, domination (du VIe au XIe siècle)* (Turnhout: Brepols, 2007), pp. 49–66.

56 On this document (BnF, ms. fr. 1968), see T. Hiltmann, *Spätmittelalterliche Heroldskompedien. Referenzenadeliger Wissenskultur in Zeiten gesellschaftlichen Wandels (Frankreich und Burgund, 15. Jahrhundert)* (Munich: Oldenbourg, 2011), pp. 142–169.
57 A. Viaene, 'De Properheden van den steden van Vlaenderen', *Biekorf* 77 (1977), 129–133.
58 P. Gaultier-Dalché, 'De la liste à la carte: limite et frontière dans la géographie et la cartographie de l'Occident médiéval', in *Castrum 4. Frontière et peuplement dans le monde médiéval au Moyen Âge* (Rome and Madrid: EFR, Casa de Velàzquez, 1992), pp. 19–31.
59 On this topic, see H. Müller, *Théâtre de la préséance. Les ducs de Bourgogne face aux grandes assemblées dans le Saint-Empire*, Conférences annuelles de l'Institut historique allemand 13 (Ostfildern: Thorbecke, 2007).
60 For more details of this quarrel, see H. Müller, 'Siège, rang et honneur: la querelle de préséance entre la Bretagne et la Bourgogne au concile de Bâle', in Cassard et al. (eds), *Le prince, l'argent, les hommes au Moyen Âge*, pp. 195–205.
61 M.-J. Reine, *La maison de Savoie* (Paris: A. Michel, 1956–62), vol. II, p. 293.
62 Chastelain, *Le livre des faits de Jacques de Lalaing*, in *Œuvres*, vol. VIII, ch. LXV, p. 239.
63 La Marche, *Mémoires*, vol. III, book II, ch. IV, pp. 133–135.
64 *Ibid.*, p. 134.
65 E. Dhanens, *Hugo van der Goes* (Anvers: Fonds Mercator, 1998), p. 76.
66 H. von Seggern, *Herrschermedien in Spätmittelalter. Studien zur Informationsübermittlung im burgundischen Staat unter Karl dem Kühnen* (Ostfildern: Thorbecke, 2003), pp. 273–307.
67 Robert Stein notes in 'Seventeen' that this heraldic composition showed five duchies and twelve counties, i.e. seventeen lands. But neither the *Mémoires* from Olivier de la Marche nor the *Huwelijksplechtigheden van Karel van Bourgondië en Margaretha van York* mentions this number.
68 Notes on this formula in M. Dumont, 'Essai sur la diplomatique des ducs de Bourgogne', in*Fédération archéologique et historique de Belgique. Annales du XXXIIIe congrès*, vol. III, pp. 726–739.
69 Extract from the journal of the Estates General, Tours, 1484, written by Jehan Masselin, quoted in Dauphant, *Le royaume des quatre rivières*, p. 66.
70 On the difficulty of finding a convenient term to name the whole territory, see Cauchies, 'État bourguignon ou états bourguignons'.

71 P. Cockshaw, 'À propos des pays de par-deçà et des pays de par-delà', *Revue belge de philologie et d'histoire* 52:2 (1974), 386–388.
72 *Ibid.*, p. 387.
73 On the expression *pays-bas*, see A. Duke, 'The Elusive Netherlands: The Question of National Identity in the Early Modern Low Countries on the Eve of the Revolt', *Bijdragen en Mededelingen betreffende de geschiedenis de Nederlanden* 119 (2004), 10–38.
74 Stein, 'Seventeen'; J. Huizinga, 'Uit de voorgeschiedenis van ons nationaal besef', in *Verzamelde werken*, vol. II (Haarlem, 1948), pp. 97–114, viewed in Digitale Bibliotheek voor de Nederlandse Letteren, https://www.dbnl.org/tekst/huiz003verz03_01/huiz003verz03_01_0011.php (accessed 19 July 2021).
75 P. Contamine, 'Contribution à l'histoire d'un mythe: les 1.700000 clochers du royaume de France (XVe–XVIe siècle)', in *Mélanges Édouard Perroy* (Paris: Publications de la Sorbonne, 1973), pp. 414–428.
76 All these examples and others in Stein, 'Seventeen', pp. 238–240.
77 *Ibid.*, pp. 234–235. Boendale wrote in 1334, following the *Brabantsche yeesten*, that the duke of Brabant was attacked by seventeen princes during the war of 1332–34.
78 See B. Guenée, 'Un royaume et des pays: la France de Michel Pintoin', in Babel and Moeglin (eds), *Identité régionale et conscience nationale en France et en Allemagne*, pp. 403–412.
79 P. Contamine, 'Les cadres "nationaux" de la vie politique', in *Le Moyen Âge*, p. 344.
80 Dauphant, *Le royaume des Quatre Rivières*, ch. 5.
81 M. Pastoureau, 'Armoiries, devises, emblèmes. Usages et décors héraldiques à la cour de Bourgogne et les Pays-Bas méridionaux au XVe siècle', in B. Bousmanne and T. Delcourt (eds), *Miniatures flamandes (1404–1482)* (Paris: Bibliothèque nationale de France, 2011), pp. 89–102.
82 L. Hablot, 'Le décor emblématique chez les princes de la fin du Moyen Âge: un outil pour construire et qualifier l'espace', in *Construction de l'espace au Moyen Âge: pratiques et représentation, actes du XXXVIIe congrès de la SHMESP* (Paris: Publications de la Sorbonne, 2007), pp. 147–165.
83 M. Nassiet, 'Nom et blason. Un discours de la filiation et de l'alliance (XIVe–XVIIIe siècle)', *L'homme* 34 (1994), 5–30.
84 BnF, ms. fr. 12476, fol 1v.
85 Guenée, 'Un royaume et des pays'.
86 'Mémoire établissant les droits de Louis XI sur le duché de Bourgogne', BnF, ms. fr. 5079.
87 See P. Boucheron, D. Menjot and P. Monnet, 'Formes d'émergence, d'affirmation et de déclin des capitales: rapport introductif', in *Les*

villes capitales au Moyen Âge. XXXVIe congrès de la SHMESP, Istanbul, 1er–6 juin 2005 (Paris: Publications de la Sorbonne, 2006), pp. 13–56.

88 P. Gilli, 'L'impossible capitale ou la souveraineté inachevée: Florence, Milan et leurs territoires (fin XIVe–XVe siècle)', in Les villes capitales au Moyen Âge, pp. 75–95.

89 C. Tilly, 'Space for Capital, Space for States', Theory and Society 15 (1986), 301–309, at p. 303.

90 I follow here W. Paravicini, 'Die Residenzen der Herzöge von Burgund (1362–1477)', in H. Patze and W. Paravicini (eds), Fürstliche Residenzen im spätmittelalterlichen Europa (Sigmaringen: Thorbecke, 1991), pp. 205–258, at p. 247.

91 Lecuppre-Desjardin, La ville des cérémonies, pp. 36–40.

92 Plancher, Histoire générale et particulière, vol. IV, doc. 296, p. 408.

93 Paravicini and Schnerb (eds), Paris, capitale des ducs de Bourgogne.

94 See F. Berland, 'La cour de Bourgogne à Paris (1363–1422)', unpublished PhD thesis, University of Lille, 2011.

95 For a selection of these expressions, see Contamine (ed.), Le Moyen Âge, pp. 348–349.

96 B. Bove, 'Alliance ou défiance? Les ambiguïtés de la politique des Capétiens envers leur capitale entre le XIIe et le XVIIe siècle', in Les villes capitales au Moyen Âge, pp. 131–154, at p. 140.

97 On threats to the royal person, see the recent research of Gilles Lecuppre, in particular 'Rapts royaux à la fin du Moyen Âge: le cas français', in Allirot et al. (eds), Une histoire pour un royaume (XIIe–XVe siècle), pp. 264–280.

98 This remark is contested by Peter Stabel, who does not see any economic interest in the court's presence. P. Stabel, 'For Mutual Benefit? Court and City in the Burgundian Low Countries', in S. Gunn and A. Janse (eds), The Court as a Stage: England and the Low Countries in the Later Middle Ages (Woodbridge: Boydell, 2006), pp. 101–117. Yet these benefits were not just financial in nature, since we also need to take into account how socio-political networks were activated by the presence of the court.

99 On the fears of the deputies of North during the Estates General in Bruges (winter 1463–1464), see Cuvelier et al. (eds), Actes des États généraux, vol. I, pp. 52–101.

100 See C. Billen, 'La construction d'une centralité: Bruxelles dans le duché de Brabant au bas Moyen Âge', in M. Boone and M. Howell (eds), The Power of Space in Late Medieval and Early Modern Europe. The Cities of Italy, Northern France and the Low Countries, SEUH 30 (Turnhout: Brepols, 2013), pp. 183–196.

101 Ibid., p. 190.

102 On all these topics, see A.-L. Van Buaene, 'L'écriture de la mémoire urbaine en Flandre et en Brabant (XIVe–XVIe siècle)', in E. Crouzet-Pavan and É. Lecuppre-Desjardin (eds), *Villes de Flandre et d'Italie XIIIe–XVIe siècle). Les enseignements d'une comparaison*, SEUH 12 (Turnhout: Brepols, 2008), pp. 149–164; B. Caers, L. Demets and T. Van Gassen (eds), *Urban History Writing in Northwest Europe (15th–16th Centuries)*, SEUH 47 (Turnhout: Brepols, 2019).
103 Tilly, 'Space for Capital, Space for States'.
104 On this topic, see M. Howell, *Commerce before Capitalism in Europe (1300–1600)* (Cambridge: Cambridge University Press, 2010). The author, rather than giving a teleological interpretation, explains that the society of the Low Countries organised its commerce according to values of this time, including honour, gift-giving and brotherhood, but also greed, vanity and so forth.
105 Wim Blockmans, 'Les origines des États modernes en Europe, XIIIe-XVIIIe siècle: état de la question et perspectives', *in Vision sur le développement des États européens. Théories et historiographies de l'État moderne* (Rome: École française de Rome, 1993), pp. 1–14, at p. 12.
106 On these topics, see the extensive work of Marc Boone, including *À la recherche d'une modernité civique. La société urbaine des anciens Pays-Bas au bas Moyen Âge* (Brussels: Éditions de l'Université de Bruxelles, 2010), pp. 123–149.
107 M. Boone, 'Stratégies fiscales et financières des élites urbaines dans les anciens Pays-Bas face à l'état burgondo-habsbourgeois', in *L'argent au Moyen Âge. Actes du XXVIIIe congrès de la SHMESP* (Paris: Publications de la Sorbonne, 1997), pp. 235–253.
108 J.-F. Lassalmonie, 'Le plus riche prince d'Occident?', in Paravicini (ed.), *La cour de Bourgogne et l'Europe*, pp. 63–82.
109 When Maximilian arrived in Flanders, for example, he wrote to his father saying that he had found 'the hen who lays golden eggs'.
110 On the different meanings of this expression, see Dumolyn and Lecuppre-Desjardin, 'Le Bien Commun en Flandre médiévale'.
111 Cuvelier *et al.* (eds), *Actes des États généraux*, pp. 59–95.
112 On this point, see Lecuppre-Desjardin, 'Par-delà la muraille'.
113 The same idea is developed by W. Blockmans, 'L'impact des villes sur l'édification de l'État: trois différents territoires des Pays-Bas du XIVe au XVIe siècle', in P. Blickle (ed.), *Résistance, représentation et communauté* (Paris: PUF, 1998), pp. 340–358, at p. 350.
114 Wim Blockmans, 'Princes cconquérants et bourgeois calculateurs. Le poids des réseaux urbains dans la formation des États', in N. Bulst and J.-P. Genet (eds), *La ville, la bourgeoisie et la genèse de l'État*

moderne (XIIe–XVIIIe s.) (Paris: Éditions du Centre national de la recherche scientifique, 1988), pp. 167–181, summarising ideas in C. Tilly, 'War Making and State Making as Organised Crime', in P. B. Evans *et al.* (eds), *Bringing the State Back In* (Cambridge: Cambridge University Press, 1985), p. 170.

115 P. Bourdieu, 'Cours du 21 février 1991', in *Sur l'État. Cours au Collège de France (1989–1992)*, ed. P. Champagne, R. Lenoir, F. Poupeau and M.-C. Rivière (Paris: Seuil and Raisons d'Agir, 2012), p. 317.

116 J. Dumolyn, '"Our land is only founded on trade and industry": Economic Discourses in Fifteenth-Century Bruges', *Journal of Medieval History* 36 (2010), 374–389.

117 On the common subjects of *Rederijkers*, see A.-L. Van Bruaene, *Omme betters wille. Rederijkerskamers en de stedelijke cultuur in de Zuideleijke Nederlanden (1400–1650)* (Amsterdam: Amsterdam University Press, 2008).

118 On the utopian quality of this poem, see É. Lecuppre-Desjardin, 'De la projection utopique au regret de l'âge d'or. À propos de l'idéal urbain dans les Pays-Bas bourguignons à la fin du Moyen Âge', in F. Sabaté (ed.), *Utopies i alternatives de vida a l'Edat Mitjana* (Lleida: Pagès, 2009), pp. 127–143.

119 J. Dumolyn and J. Haemers, '"Let each man carry on with his trade and remain silent': Middle Class Ideology in the Urban Literature of the Late Medieval Low Countries', *Cultural and Social History* 10:2 (2013), 169–189.

120 On the rise of guilds in Flemish towns, see Boone, *À la recherche d'une modernité civique*, pp. 29–56.

7

'Burgundianisation', or the fantasy of a Burgundian nation

Now it is time for us, at the end of this broad synthesis, to ask the key question: how far does it make sense to talk about a 'Burgundian nation' with an existence beyond that of an agglomeration of territories held by a single prince? If we look at the military action, for example, we can see that the Burgundian armies, whom we last saw in disarray in 1477, did not simply vanish at the death of Charles the Bold. After the collapse of the Great Principality of Burgundy, soldiers and communal militia in the northern lands continued, even into the seventeenth century, to march under banners marked with cross of Saint Andrew, to cries of 'Vive Bourgogne!'[1] This attachment to Burgundian military emblems was one of the last traces of what some historians of this territory call 'Burgundianisation', which, from time to time in the sixteenth and seventeenth centuries, in boundary markers, seals and sometimes in coinage, brought the Burgundian past back to life.[2] Historians of the dukes of Burgundy, who used to praise the political action of these princes, have recently been through a kind of historiographical 'detox', expressing their desire to distance themselves from this ideal Burgundy so as to re-evaluate their object of study through a systematic comparison with other European courts.[3] At the same time, we must recognise that historians are men and women of their age. As a result, the modern fear of disunity and a desire to create bonds in societies disappointed by the European model has led historians to re-examine concepts such as that of nation, which has now become the key for unifying and making meaningful a principality of Burgundy whose very essence was a diversity which was difficult to bring under control.

If historians, bedazzled by the complexity of their object of study, were to seek reassurance outside their field and to identify in what is considered a 'Burgundian' artistic style the signs of a well-established cultural community in painting or in letters, they would have to admit that identical hesitations are to be found amongst historians of art and literary scholars, who show the same discomfort when it comes to identifying a style which can be linked to a specific territory. Two recent works on 'Burgundian' literature and manuscripts bristle with scare quotes, and specialists use alternative approaches, basing their analysis not on the finished artistic product but rather on the process of production.[4] They no longer speak of a common style of 'Burgundian manuscripts' but rather refer to 'Burgundian libraries' characterised by a dominant language – French – and a preferred genre – moralising didactic texts, both histories and romances – and by production in workshops in Flanders and Hainault. Thus 'Burgundianisation', by which we mean a kind of acculturation process directed at the rest of society by the court, was limited to a fashion followed by great nobles who imitated the princely entourage. Similarly, in the field of literature, if the works produced in Burgundy swung between a French academic tradition and a desire to celebrate the ambitions of a prince, it cannot be denied that academic emulation only concerned the restricted public of the court. In short, if there was such a thing as a Burgundian style, the 'Burgundianisation' which is supposed to have led to the elaboration of 'Burgundian nationalism' encouraged by a 'national dynasty' appears to be a highly problematic notion.

To complete this picture, a study of vocabulary, of the development of the historiography and of the misunderstandings to which it has sometimes given rise seems appropriate. Once this analysis has been accomplished, an observation of the meaning of 'imagined communities' and an assessment of the usefulness of the couplet 'nation-state' in relation to the principality of Burgundy will be possible.

From 'my Lord's lands' to 'Burgundian national consciousness'

In taking up the problem of the nation and the formation of national identity, historians enter a minefield, particularly as far-right political groups continue to make progress throughout Europe. When their object of study corresponds in part to modern Belgium and the Low

Countries, where extremist parties like the New Flemish Alliance (NVA) demand the division of the country, or where the Freedom Party of Geert Wilders succeeded in 2010 in allying with the liberal government of Mark Rutte, the danger of anachronism inspired by the current situation is all the greater. This risk, though, is hardly a new one. In the wake of the development of nation-states in the nineteenth century, history has often been called upon to justify the venerable origins of this or that conviction.

Philippe le Bon: father of the nation?

The debates between German Romantics and French thinkers are well known, opposing, to put it simply, Herder's conception of an organic nation to the political legitimacy advocated by Renan. By contrast, the debates among Belgian historians, who wanted to make the Burgundian period into the cradle of their young nation, has been much less widely discussed.[5] Yet in Belgium, two seemingly opposed currents ended up reinforcing one another. On one side stood Henri Pirenne, who explained, in 1899, that the House of Burgundy had benefited from the fact that 'for centuries, the different feudal provinces on the right and left banks of the Scheldt unconsciously tended towards unity' and so contributed to reinforcing this sentiment of national unity.[6] On the other were those such as Godefroid Kurth and Paul Fredericq who maintained that the dukes behaved like tyrants and thus inadvertently promoted a national awakening for the 'spirit of Germanic liberty' which the people had been denied.[7] In short, whether as the *Conditor Belgii*, for Pirenne, or as the tyrant who unintentionally facilitated a coming to political consciousness of Germanic peoples, as Fredericq imagines him, Philip the Good stands out as the father of the Belgian nation. Thereafter, in the second half of the twentieth century, the national question faded in intensity, before re-emerging once more, drawing on a calmer political climate and on scholarly studies produced without partisan bias. Nevertheless, it is not for nothing that the question of the nation has come to exercise minds and spirits once again at a time when the risk of the division of Belgium is no longer a mere myth, and where a technocratic and bureaucratic Europe suppresses the particularities of the countries which make it up. We can draw parallels with the work of Pierre Monnet on the pertinence and usefulness of the term *patria* or fatherland in the works of German historians in the immediate aftermath of reunification, or with Denis Menjot's analysis of the evolution of Spanish historiography after the constitution of 1978 had transformed the Spanish state into a federation of regions and nations.[8] Historians cannot, consciously or unconsciously, escape the influence of their own time and their own milieu on their choice of themes.

In a work published in 2006, Jonathan Boulton and Jan Veenstra had no hesitation in appealing to the idea of national consciousness to characterise the political ideology which developed progressively in the lands assembled by the Valois dukes of Burgundy.[9] The word 'nation' is now being used once more to describe this medieval political entity, but without offering any precise definition of it. At the same time, pride of place is given to studies limited to the milieu of the great officers of the principality of Burgundy, knights of the Golden Fleece, court historians and counsellors to the prince. Yet the court had no monopoly of contemporary culture. Indeed, it is not possible to envisage the construction of the nation from the point of view of the elite alone, as if the Burgundian court had succeeded in accumulating 'exclusive symbolic capital, codified and guaranteed by the state'.[10] Only the constant dialectic between the court and the people would make it possible to identify the nation positively. Yet the absence of a theoretical or definitional structure and the narrow focus of study (i.e. the prince's court) has not prevented a number of scholars from following Boulton and Veenstra in referring to a veritable 'national Burgundian literature' or to signs of undoubted 'Burgundianisation'.[11] Deploying multiple anachronisms to postulate the unity of a territorial assemblage which took the form of an ethnic mosaic rather than a monolithic principality, this recent tendency nonetheless provokes us to reconsider the dossier of 'Burgundianisation', by which is meant a supposedly successful process of acculturation leading to the birth of a national feeling which allegedly covered the entirety of the territories under Burgundian rule.

From this point of view, the research group headed by Robert Stein and Wim Blockmans in Leiden since 2002 has concentrated its efforts on the question of the putative existence of a supra-regional identity which lay behind the unification of the United Provinces by the Peace of Utrecht of 1579.[12] Peter Hoppenbrouwers has clarified possible lines of development.[13] For him, the creation of a nation can take two routes. The first involves either the evolution of an ethnic group towards the constitution of an autonomous state or the unification of several ethnic groups as part of a political whole. The second involves the raising of the ethnic aspirations of people towards a common project, to avoid tensions between these communities and the central government. This second option was without doubt the challenge which the dukes of Burgundy had to meet. We can now examine contemporary sources to try and gauge in their vocabulary such signs as there are of a union of peoples around a common political ideal.

The meaning of 'nation' in fifteenth-century sources

Let us begin by considering a foreigner's view of this great principality, in the hope of understanding its nature. In fifteenth-century England, greatly disturbed as it was by Philip the Good's breaking of his alliance with Henry VI in 1435, the Burgundian political entity was evoked by means of its prince. A lexical study of the *Brut*, the vernacular chronicle tradition which was most widely diffused in fifteenth-century England, shows that of 226 occurrences which deal with Burgundian affairs, more than a quarter use the expression 'duke of Burgoyne' to identify the subject.[14] In this text, whilst the term 'Bourguignons' denotes fighting men in association with the 'Picards', the title 'duke of Burgundy' serves to personify power. The principality appears through the evocation of a person, the product of a House and representative of dynasty. The same observation could be made for the French chronicles which constructed political history around the person of the duke of Burgundy and in which 'Burgundian' referred first to an opponent of the Armagnacs and then to a fighting man. On the other hand, when the authors of the *Brut* evoke the duke's subjects, the Burgundian is, in fact, a 'Fleming'. Where the *Chronicles of London* prefer the term 'Duche' or 'Duchemen', different versions of the *Brut* edited by F. W. D. Brie use 'Flemish' to denote the inhabitants of lands under the authority of the duke. This is understandable given the familiarity of the English with trading partners present not only in London but also in a number of English towns. In satirical poetry in particular, the treason of Philip the Good after the signature of the Treaty of

Arras was thus refracted on to these Flemings, who were insulted as cowards along with their lord.[15] The poetic genre, however, sometimes paints a more general picture, probably because of the requirements inherent in its form. So in "On the Duke of Burgundy", the first verse refers to 'all Burgundy' ('alle Bourgoyne').[16] In a similar way, in an anonymous Latin short poem which seems to allude to an exchange of letters between Philip the Good and James I of Scotland, the last lines refer to England, Burgundy, France and Scotland.[17] That said, there is no general rule here, and another poem of the same period, 'On the Siege of Calais', refers to a list of lands that composed the Great Principalty, much as we have seen elsewhere.[18]

In the reports of the Milanese ambassadors, which readily talk about the 'Stato di Piamonte', the 'Stato di Milano', the 'Stato di Sabaudia' and so forth, and in the poems of Johannes Knebel or Hans Erhard Tüsch, to which we shall return, political commentary always refers to 'Monsignore de Borgogna', 'le duca di Borgogna' or the 'hertzog von Burgund'. German commentators, meanwhile, were careful to distinguish between the duke's 'upper' and 'lower' territories. A change is palpable, however, in 1477 when, after the death of Charles the Bold, the *Chronique scandaleuse* of Jean de Roye refers first to 'the aforesaid of Burgundy' ('ledit de Bourgogne') to introduce the duke into his narrative and then alludes to a 'party of Burgundy' ('parti de Bourgogne') opposed to Louis XI.[19] But there again the expression is only used once and in a very specific context. Political reality was only embodied by reference to a prince, with a title, whose power rested on many different territories and peoples who figure in the chronicles under their various identities as Brabantine, Hainaulter, Flemish, Burgundian and so on.

As we saw in the previous chapter, in Burgundian sources the language of 'countries and lordships' (*pays et seigneuries*) was the only one which could be used to denote the ducal lands. The word 'nation', on the other hand, appears in its classic medieval usage, namely to denote a people of the same origin and, behind that, of a common birth. We can thus see that for George Chastelain, the nation is the place of someone's birth when he refers, for example, to '[Messire] Jehan de Croy, of the nation of Picardy, and Master Jehan Lorfevre, Picard too'.[20] But 'nation' went beyond the question of ethnic origin and became politicised when he considered 'Calais, which is held by the English in France, making a front' [*faisant front*, that is both providing a frontier and standing in defiance] 'to the land [of France] and to the whole French nation'. This reference is undeniably political, allowing us to make use of a term which is often denied to us as medievalists. Indeed, it is difficult for medieval historians to take our place at the table to discuss the 'nation', since the theorisation of this phenomenon, whether in the work of Ernest Gellner, Benedict Anderson, Elie Kedourie or Eric Hobsbawm, in sociology, history or anthropology, inevitably leads to the description of a phenomenon dating from after the French Revolution.[21] Yet as R. R. Davies remarked, we have to be careful of definitions made to fit the object under study.[22] When Anthony Smith, for example, lists his criteria for defining a nation, he does so with reference to the assumptions of the present day. Some of these criteria fit the medieval period, such as a named population, a common mythology, a shared memory and the link to a historical territory, whereas others do not, such as the diffusion of mass culture, a common economy and rights and duties shared equally by the whole of this community, which necessarily exclude early modern and medieval societies from this definition of nationhood.[23] Yet, whereas certain historians use definitions derived from modern parameters to argue that medieval nations did not exist, it is not difficult to give examples of certain occasions where medieval thought did resemble the 'modern' idea of the nation, whether in the words of Chastelain concerning the kingdom of France, those used by the Scots in the Declaration of Arbroath of 1320, those of Joan of Arc when she declared her desire 'to kick the Englishman out of all France' or those of Albrecht Achilles when he declared at the end of the fifteenth century that 'the Emperor should not be a non-German'.[24] The nation, in the political sense, did indeed exist, but in the region which concerns us neither Olivier de la Marche nor George Chastelain nor Jean Molinet used this term to denote the politico-cultural unit constituted by the Burgundian territories.

A multitude of 'imagined communities'

To avoid the stark choice between a modern-focused constructivism of the state and an essentialist search for origins, or, to put it another way, between the idea of a late ideological construction and that of a form of grouping on ethnic lines characteristic of all humanity, we can instead immerse ourselves in medieval culture, armed with a well-defined set of questions to enable us to measure the will and the capacity of particular peoples to establish themselves as a nation. By this I mean not only an ethnic group living in the same territory and sharing a common culture but the unification of men and women behind a common political project. Yet if we follow the list of questions used by certain members of the Leiden group mentioned earlier, concentrating on language, historical writing, the identification of common enemies and so forth, what emerges is a list of the handicaps which the dukes of Burgundy encountered in their attempts at unification. Indeed, the Burgundian territorial complex was composed of multiple counties and duchies, with powerful ideas based on languages, customs and histories which did not include, at least until very late on, the story of the Valois dukes of Burgundy.

One language, one nation?

Let us begin with the question of language. This has been at the heart of modern nationalist preoccupations, since German Romantics including Herder and Fichter attached a philosophy of language to the question of the nation. It is thus no surprise to come across the famous phrase of the Flemish poet Prudens van Duyse (1804–59): 'de tael is gantsch het volk' ('the language is the whole people').[25] But is it not an anachronism to take the defence of a language as a marker of national consciousness? It is true that the Great Principality of Burgundy was faced with a multiplicity of languages, which led to occasional controversies about which language should be used. But we need to analyse the precise meaning of these debates. The subject of language was apparently particularly sensitive in Flanders, where a francophone administration was established in a region where the majority spoke Flemish Dutch. Just before his marriage to Margaret of Flanders, Philip the Bold promised his father-in-law, Louis de Male, not to grant the castellany of Lille to anyone who was not 'a Flemish speaking Fleming, born in Flanders'.[26] A little later, in 1405, amongst the petitions from the Four Members of Flanders in Ghent, we find the request for the count to reside in the county and, in the case of his absence, to leave his countess there, so that she could govern with full powers supported by a council who knew the nature of the said county.[27] In the same text, the young prince was asked to establish his council chamber in 'Flanders, behind the [river] Lys, in the Flemish tongue'.[28] Nevertheless, it had been the practice in Flanders to govern in three languages (Latin, French and Flemish) since the twelfth century, without this apparently posing any problem, and linguistic controversies were relatively rare.[29]

The attachment to a particular language seems to have been stronger, and more closely engaged with political reality, in Brabant. According to Philippe Godding, the text which accompanied the Joyous Entry of 1430 was slightly modified from the original of 1356 in order to take account of the fear that a prince as powerful as Philip the Good might neglect the duchy's distinctive characteristics. It was specified that the prince's councillors, who ought traditionally to be of legitimate birth, natives of Brabant and should hold possessions and live there, were also, in 1430, supposed to speak the local dialect of Dutch, Thiois, a specification probably intended to prevent any invasion of French-speaking councillors.[30] Yet the need to speak the local language was normally the result of simple common sense. This was why Philip the Good recognised the need to appoint bilingual officers in Holland 'because there were few people in his council who knew how to speak the local language [*sachans le langaige du pays*]'. In practice the *stadhouders* who represented him, even if they were from outside the county, were all Dutch speakers.[31]

We thus need to be careful and to make two further sets of remarks. The first of these relates to the practical problems which could be produced by linguistic clashes, without necessarily originating in a 'national' movement. This is clearly seen in the complaints addressed to Philip the Bold after 1384, when his councillors were accused of holding trials in French before subjects who hardly understood this language and who did not understand the decisions taken at all, impeding the application of the judgements reached.[32] Moreover, the attachment to a local language for reasons of efficiency did not necessarily correspond to the frontiers of a particular duchy or county. The case of the Vale of the Voer or Foron, a triangle of territory between Maastricht, Liège and Aachen around a tributary of the Meuse of that name, shows how even within the duchy of

Brabant, to which this land pertained at the end of the Middle Ages, the population could be particularly sensitive to the question of local language. In reply to the chancery of Brussels, local representatives demanded that each village keep its own language (either 'Romance', a French dialect, or 'Diets', a Dutch one) for the purpose of transcribing its customs and that no other language should be tolerated in official correspondence with the village in question.[33] Should we see this as a nationalist demand or simply as the defence of local privileges by local interests threatened by a centralising government? As Joep Leerssen explains, the defence of a particular language should not be seen as the manifestation of a desire for autonomy but rather as evidence of diversity, namely the recognition and acceptance of different cultures and different laws within the same state.[34]

The second set of remarks concerns the fact that the desire to be ruled by officers who spoke the same language as those they governed was not the result of a passionate attachment to a particular language but rather of a desire to deal with intermediaries who knew the concerns of that region – who, in a word, were natives. As Claude de Seyssel wrote, 'All nations and reasonable men prefer to be governed by men of their own land or nation who know their own habits, laws, customs, sharing the same language and the same way of life, rather than by foreigners.' This demand, connected with the use of a language understood by everyone, was not limited to Dutch-speaking areas. In Hainault, the people of Valenciennes were also sensitive to the need to defend their privileges. In the course of a number of petitions delivered in 1434, they complained that the castellan was not native or a son of a burgess of the town and that he knew nothing of their customs and established practices.[35] This was why they asked Philip the Good to appoint only local men, a request rejected by the duke. In 1423, in the treaty by which Duke Frederick IV agreed to restore her widow's portion of Upper Alsace to Duchess Catherine, wh owas Philip the Good's aunt and the widow of Frederick's brother Leopold IV, it was also specified that the introduction of foreign vassals and foreign officers in Upper Alsace was forbidden.[36] As a general rule, historians from John Armstrong in 1965 to Marc Boone in 2009 have concluded that the language question never posed the kind of problem in this greater Burgundy that it did elsewhere.[37] We should no doubt accept this point of view in the main, whilst noting a number of more emphatic protests which presaged the coming of a new era.

For Malcolm Vale, who addressed this issue in 2005, the relative harmony shown by the use of different languages within the Burgundian administration need not imply the absence of political implications in the use of one language or another.[38] We can indeed point to a number of examples in which, at moments of crisis, tensions over language are apparent. During times of fundamental disagreement between the duke and his subjects, people sometimes used their language as a banner under which to group their objections. On the duke's side, the use of French was sometimes regarded as a punishment. On 31 July 1453, when Philip the Good received the excuses of the people of Ghent after the battle of Gavre, the peace treaty insisted that the petition for grace be made in the 'French language'.[39] A few years later, the town did not seem to have forgotten this affront when it greeted its prince first in French, outside the walls, and then, within the city, in Flemish.[40] Equally famous is the episode of the chapter meeting of the Golden Fleece at The Hague in 1456. Just before this meeting, Philip the Good had imposed his illegitimate son, David, as bishop of Utrecht. This move met with the opposition of the local population and of the Brederode family, one of whose members was the disappointed candidate to the bishopric and another of whom, his brother Reinhoud van Brederode, was a member of the Order of the Golden Fleece. The latter first refused to attend the chapter and then, when he finally did appear, would only talk in Thiois – to which the other members replied to him in French – and even demanded to consult the statutes of the order in Dutch.[41]

Reinhoud's attachment to his mother tongue was largely shared by a population hostile to the Burgundian dominance of the region. When George Chastelain narrates the punitive expedition of Philip the Good against Deventer, in rebellion against David, he summed up the opposition of different communities in terms of linguistic divisions:

> For the people and the nobles of all this land there around Guelders and Cleves are by their nature never willingly favourable to those of the French tongue or especially to the Picards, whom amongst everyone in this world they [most] fear and hate.[42]

Later, at the moment of the final crisis of 1477, Mary of Burgundy was forced to concede in the 'Great Privilege' that all public acts would henceforth by recorded in Dutch.[43] But the instructions given by Maximilian to his ambassadors to the Three Members of Flanders, who were resisting recognising him as regent on Mary's death in 1482, suggest that the crisis of transition had intensified tensions over identity. Article 26 specifies that it was not desirable to reject men on the pretext that they were Burgundian or spoke Walloon French, since 'in all nations there are good folk'.[44] Here, the rejection of one group by another appears, as it were, in negative, confirming the idea which we have already explored in the context of the war song 'Awake, Picards and Burgundians'.

Although different languages could easily co-exist in the fifteenth century without too much trouble, the emergence of a *koiné* or common language can probably be observed more clearly at the opening of the sixteenth century. Yet would this cultural community defined by a shared language be enough to ensure the transition to nationhood?

Multiple histories

Language is certainly not the only necessary ingredient for a nation: a sense of shared history is another. Indeed, the lands assembled by the dukes of Burgundy were all more or less well provided with a solid tradition of history writing. We have already alluded to the efforts of the Valois dukes to insert themselves into the history of Brabant, Flanders, Hainault, Burgundy and so on.[45] In this series of historical re-compositions, on the basis of more or less fantastical genealogies, Philip the Good in particular used a range of stratagems to present himself as the worthy heir of all kinds of lands won by marriage alliances or by the sword, one after the other.[46] For de Dynter, he was the duke of Brabant legitimated by Trojan and Carolingian ancestors; for Wauquelin, thanks to the same genealogy, he was the natural heir to the noble lineage of Hainault. Whereas the chronicles of Flanders logically placed him as the successor to the legendary founders of the county called 'Forestiers de Flandre', the history of Burgundy reminded him of the glorious foundation provided by his original lands. In a nutshell, the figure of the duke, in a typically feudal approach, was based in local histories, once again failing to bring them together into the same melting pot. For that matter, did the duke have any such intention?

Admittedly, at a time when the inheritance of Charles the Bold was in danger, Olivier de la Marche's prologue to his *Mémoires* does seem to bring all these elements together when he describes the origins of the cross of Saint Andrew, the adventures of the Forestiers of Flanders, the creation of the arms of various different territories and especially, in a fresh invention, the Herculean origins of Burgundy. Indeed, Olivier argues, on the basis of the *Universal History* of Diodorus of Sicily, that Hercules had married Alise, a Burgundian princess, thus founding a dynasty of the kings of Burgundy which was superior to that of the kings of France, since the conversion of Clovis ought to be attributed to the merits of his wife, Clotilde, a Burgundian princess. The primary purpose of this courtier was to use all his talents as a writer to integrate the Burgundian past with the history of the Habsburgs. For as Jean Devaux has commented, Burgundian historical writing, in the hands of exceptional writers, was a history of the here and now ('une histoire immédiate'), a history which related the great deeds of princes and a history of magnificence which was itself magnificent ('une histoire de la magnificence'). In other words, it was an aspect of the art of creating power through illusion which we considered at the beginning of this book.[47] In the wake of Michael Zingel's monograph, there is no need to insist upon proving that Burgundian history writing failed to assemble the elements necessary to provide solid ideological foundations for the constitution of a Burgundian state or of a Burgundian nation, at least before 1477.[48] Great deeds, lavish banquets, the prestige and superiority acted out in court ceremony or on the field of battle, all served to hide, as if by dazzling the audience, the lack of an original system of political thought. The multi-territorial reality of the great principality did not come through in the speeches of the dukes or their officers, and the chroniclers and annalists never worked to imagine a coherent and unified political community around their princes, whether they were 'loyal Frenchmen' (*léal françois*), like Chastelain, or convinced of the need to recognise the universal sovereignty of the emperor, like Olivier de la Marche or Jean Molinet.[49]

This observation is essential if we are to describe the cultural policy of the Burgundian dukes without over-interpreting it. From this point of view, we must once more 'free ourselves from all the judgements which have accumulated over time', not only to stop making Italy into the land of the Renaissance and the Burgundian Low Countries into the land of the autumn of the Middle Ages, but also in order to liberate our thinking from a teleological view which seeks out signs of the coming of the 'modern state' in every fifteenth-century governmental act. The dukes of Burgundy were indeed the heirs to the kings of France and to Charles V's bibliophilia. The nine hundred manuscripts in Philip the Good's library are ample proof of his appetite for collecting, which served, once again, as a means of demonstrating the power of the duke of Burgundy through luxury and riches. This interest in beautiful books was a fashion, one shared throughout Europe in the fifteenth century, which enabled court nobles to raise themselves up in order to impress the prince and to show in turn their own superiority through competition in the patronage of books. Yet, as Céline Van Hoorebeeck notes in her study of the books and reading of Burgundian officials, the unification of the Burgundian nobility around its prince, through a shared common taste, did not go further than the court, and this supposed 'literary Burgundianisation' did not spread into the world of the prince's administrators.[50]

The dukes of Burgundy imitated the kings of France in every way, equipping themselves with a common burial site, majestic rituals and a highly superior library, but they did not conceive of their history outside this relationship of feudal dependence with the king before 1473. If we want to take up this question from the fundamental point of view of the impact of this reading on the prince, we must also remember that the past, as brought to mind for example in Roman works, had been 'expropriated', to use the nice formula of Arjo Vanderjagt.[51] We thus cannot deduce from the fact that Cicero was being read in a French translation in which *militaris* became *chevalerie* and *patria* became *pays* that the *res publica* or the common good, in its Roman sense, had become familiar notions at the court which served to build an ideology of state. Burgundian history writing, even as it has recently been described by Maria Golubeva, was still, before 1477, writing for the glory of the prince, the defender of the public weal, guided by an ideal of virtue and honour.[52]

In this sense, I am arguing as much against Richard Vaughan and his successors, who see in Burgundian political construction the failure to construct a nation-state, as against certain current historians who, on the contrary, see in the policies of Philip the Good and his councillors a conscious plan designed to establish this same form of government. For me, the dukes did not fail in this regard, because they were not actually trying to impose an ideal of government which was absent from their culture. If the dukes had wanted to establish a unified, autonomous state, we might have expected that the court historians would have been in the front line of this project. But it is enough to read the prologues of George Chastelain, Jean Molinet and Olivier de la Marche to see that these men directed their rhetoric towards promoting the 'victorious reigning princes, guides of the public weal',[53] each of whom embodied in turn the virtues of the great, which were prudence, fortitude, temperance and justice. The writings of these men sought to record the glorious deeds of their masters, assessing their good government by the measure of their conquests and the expansion of their territory, by the destruction of their enemies and by the riches they accumulated. The history of the here and now that they recorded in no way served to establish the foundations of an independent state or of a nation.

Nevertheless, other forms of writing, used elsewhere, might have served the state-building aims of princes who had been so well educated and whose libraries were so well stocked. The genre of the 'monarchical autobiography', of which Charles IV of Bohemia and the kings of Aragon furnish us with examples, might have provided a way to forge the link between 'self government and the government of other people'.[54] The *Vita* of Charles IV, which served to promote the dynastic pretensions of the House of Luxembourg, the stabilisation of royal power in Bohemia and the conquest of the imperial crown, alongside the *Majestas carolina* of 1355 and the Golden Bull of 1356, demonstrates the existence of real political ambitions and a genuine system of political thought.[55] Similarly, in the autobiographical fiction of James I of Aragon, the king wrote a book, or at least had it written, with the avowed aims of reinforcing the monarchy as an institution and confirming the supremacy of public authority, as the memory of the king gradually became the memory of a people.[56] We might have thought that the composition of a history of the kingdom of Lotharingia would have allowed the dukes to make their subjects understand that they had much more in common than they imagined. But instead, in this Great Principality of Burgundy, the accumulation of regional histories demonstrates perfectly the limits of a form of political authority which had succeeded in conquering numerous new regions by respecting local identities, but which had not gathered sufficient means to go beyond this territorial accumulation, to leave behind plurality and finally to succeed in creating an imagined community.

Consolidation through opposition

Although not the most respected of intellectual tools, the history of events sometimes provides powerful arguments for unity. The appearance of common enemies rallied the troops in England, in France and in the Empire. However, we have already seen how war, as long, recurrent and hungry for men and money as it was, did not succeed in bringing about an awakening of Burgundian national consciousness up prior to the death of Charles the Bold. And yet, as if to drive home the point, the House of Burgundy did work as a unifying factor in the formation of a common identity amongst its enemies. If Burgundian unity did not come about within the duke's territories, the fear of the Burgundians did nevertheless contribute to the mobilisation or re-awakening of neighbouring peoples.

Around the edges of the Great Principality, resistance to the domination of the dukes, or simply to the threat they posed, could be expressed through the emergence of national sentiment. This was the case in Guelders, where as a result of the violent dispute between Duke Arnold and his son Adolf, Charles the Bold ultimately succeeded in seizing the duchy by force, after having been recognised as the new duke of Guelders by Frederick III at Trier in 1473. The local population nevertheless remained hostile to the House of Burgundy, and the word 'Burgundy' gradually acquired a negative connotation, becoming a synonym for tyranny and encouraging an alliance with the Empire.[57] Through an analysis of fifteenth-century chronicles, in particular that of Willem van Berchen, a native of Nijmegen, Aart Noordzij has successfully proved that the attachment to the Burgundian court in Guelders was very superficial and that nobles as much as townsmen disliked being absorbed into the Burgundian dominions.[58] At the moment of the creation of the Parlement of Malines, van Berchem denounced the duke's sin of pride in setting up this 'abominable idol' so that all his subjects would worship him. Similarly, according to him, this feeble imitation of justice was in the hands of those Picard infidels who would tolerate no appeal. As one friar from Doesburg wrote, the French and Picard officers put in place by Charles the Bold had conquered the land only in order to ravage it and they had all run away in the wake of the duke's death.[59]

This opposition from 'Burgundy' was not directed against a dynasty but against a policy. The word 'Burgundy' denoted a kind of government characterised by the loss of liberties and independence. The French way embodied by the dukes of Burgundy opened the door to the establishment of a kind of sovereignty which excluded any other power, whereas the imperial way proposed a sovereignty shared between the emperor, the duke, the nobles and the towns. The nation of Guelders was not only constructed around a language and the rejection of any foreigner who did not speak the local dialect; it was also based on a form of political thought which could lead to rather surprising results.[60] In the complex history of the duchy of Guelders, which oscillated between Burgundy, France and the Empire, the Emperor Charles V was regarded not as a member of the Germanic House of Habsburg but as a Burgundian and thus as a threat to the duchy's particular identity. What happened after 1477, however, genuinely changed the frame of reference, and Burgundy, as a political entity grafted on to an ideology, now began to exist.

What we could call the 'Charles the Bold moment', so important were the latter's ambitions, decisions and ultimately brutal death in changing the political situation, also had important consequences in the Empire. There, as elsewhere, Charles the Bold's advance provoked fear and could also lead to a similar defence of urban liberties. The last Valois duke inspired an ample literature which both fed his evil reputation and contributed to accelerating or re-launching the process of the formation of national consciousness. As we have seen, the man known as the Grand Turk of the West coveted the imperial crown, and Petra Ehm has asssembled examples which demonstrate how the strong feeling of rejection provoked by a man who did not speak the language and who ought not, as a result, to have pretentions to the imperial title reinforced feelings of solidarity within the German nation.[61] Aside from the citation of Albrecht Achilles earlier this chapter, the *Reim-Chronik* ('Rhymed chronicle') of Hans Erhard Tüsch explains the Burgundian's defeat in these terms:

> It was thus that those of the German nation
> Who were in alliance
> Gave such a good and great aid
> That the power of the Burgundian was broken.[62]

In the same way, Johannes Knebel appealed to divine omnipotence to help the righteous of the German nation (*Tutsche nacion*) of the Holy Roman Empire to protect the imperial crown. It is true that, for Claudius Sieber-Lehmann, the Burgundian wars were not a significant reference point in the development of nationalism in the Empire or in Switzerland.[63] Nonetheless, the texts cited from the towns of the upper Rhine and the Swiss Confederation did not fail to appeal to the 'German nation' in their opposition to the duke of Burgundy. It matters little whether the influence was religious or commercial; the expression made its way insidiously into a quite specific context. Although the German chroniclers lacked a generic term to denote the party of Charles the Bold and so preferred to speak of the Grand Turk of the West, all of them worked to rally the *Tutsche nacion* against the man who wanted to seize the Empire for himself and to destroy urban liberties.[64]

This animosity towards the dukes' policies, which was particularly notable during the rule of Charles the Bold, had already provoked a resurgence of nationalism in England during the time of Philip the Good. As we have seen, after the Treaty of Arras and the war of 1436, the duke's change of camp provoked a wave of national feeling across the Channel. For although the population was sick of the French war, the felony of Philip the Good led to the granting of a new tax for saving Calais, thereby avoiding a great dishonour to the kingdom of England.

It is clear that the Great Principality of Burgundy succeeded in stimulating the awakening of national consciousness amongst its enemies, following the relatively simple principle that a political entity often consolidates itself through opposition to an external threat. Yet this process did not work in the opposite direction, since the dukes of Burgundy did not succeed in provoking a common enemy who might threaten all at once the people of Flanders, Brabant, Burgundy, the Franche-Comté and so on. It is true that periods of tension could provoke a communitarian reaction, as in the case of Chastelain in 1463. The latter, disappointed by the attitude of the French, invoked on that occasion a Burgundian whole which went beyond the borders of the duchy and which corresponded with a party, that of the duke:

> ... and I do not only mean by 'Burgundians' from the country of Burgundy, but also I mean by 'Burgundians' all those of different countries who supported his cause.[65]

Yet Chastelain quickly made it clear that 'French and Burgundians' are 'all however of one kingdom', before pointing out in the next chapter that he was 'French by birth and one who honours the nation' ('exaltateur de la nation') and that his words were meant to attack not France but the ungrateful ones who hated the duke.[66] If we decode this passage, we can see that the Burgundians of the nation of France are simply those who had adopted the cause of the House of Burgundy against their fraternal enemy from the same country. Of course, given that the feudal framework was still the primary socio-political reference in this region, it is clear that one did not sacrifice oneself for an abstract *patria* or for a country held up as an ultimate value, but for one's lord, one's master. That was what the people of the Mâcon asserted, for example, in 1423, when they repeatedly promised as 'true and obedient subjects ... to live and die in the name of the king and of the duke, Philip'.[67] Yet this Burgundian party, limited in time and purpose, existed only under Chastelain's cynical pen. The prince's war against Henry VI was not fought for the Flemish, whose trade was always closely reliant on good relations with England. The Swiss Confederates, meanwhile, posed no threat to Zeeland. 'To live and to die' was an expression often pronounced by the prince, but it was not at all linked to the idea of the defence of a fatherland. It occurs, for example, in Philip the Good's manifesto of 1452, which urged all the people of his territories 'to live or to die' with him, 'as good and loyal subjects must do with their lord and prince', with the aim of reducing to submission not a foreign enemy but the community of Ghent which was in revolt.[68] The contrast is clear with, for example, Philip IV of France, who in 1302 asked for financial support from the clergy after the disaster of Courtrai 'for the defence of the fatherland of [their] birth' ('ad defensionem natalis patrie').[69]

Without any linguistic or historic common denominator, unable to unite against a threat which attacked the interests of both the prince and all his subjects, and despite an intense propaganda effort, the peoples of the dukes of Burgundy, in a territory with fluid boundaries, most certainly did not succeed in coming together to form a nation which might have made it possible to strengthen the basis of this political entity and perhaps even to construct a state. Benedict Anderson's famous idea of the nation as an 'imagined community', one which contributed to the success of his book but which was also widely criticised for its weak definition, does make clear the necessity of the imagined link between all the people who made it up, since 'even the members of the smallest nations will never know most of their fellow citizens, they will never meet them nor hear about them, even though in the spirit of each and all of them lives the image of their communion'.[70] Although it is true that the imagination feeds every social relationship, whether national or not, in this case this affective and transcendent element was restricted to particular parts of the Burgundian mosaic without embracing the whole. Even when we cross the frontiers of the different duchies and counties, it is difficult to discern any supra-regional community. Contrary to what is argued by certain historians who think they have detected the birth of a 'Burgundian nobility' in the lands of the Valois dukes, which is then supposed to have contributed to the creation of a national identity, Frederik Buylaert has recently shown, through a thorough study of the Flemish nobility, that interregional networks existed before the arrival of the Valois. It was only in the sixteenth century that the nobility adopted a perspective that took in not only Flanders, Hainault or Brabant on their own but the whole Low Countries.[71] From a feudal point of view, it was obviously the prince who should have encouraged this imaginative world, especially by stimulating the love of his people and a sense of a community.

The Great Principality of Burgundy: neither state nor nation

The coupling of 'nation' and 'state' is certainly not indivisible. There have been states without a nation, if we think for example of the former USSR, or nations without a state, such as the Kurds today, and there have been other forms of political organisation. Yet the state, insofar as it provides a model of government, can embody a political abstraction which is useful for the awakening of national consciousness.

Loyalty at the heart of the medieval nation

The Hungarian historian Jenö Szücs has pointed to a number of developments which make it possible to distinguish between the 'medieval nation' and the 'modern nation'. He notes in particular the importance of the principle of sovereignty, identifying the specific set of problems which were characteristic of Ancien Régime societies and allowing us, in the process, to qualify the definitions offered by Anthony Smith which we discussed earlier in this chapter. For Szücs, the conceptual model which we call the nation is 'the product of the association of three categories which had earlier been separated: political fidelity, the abstract entity of the state or the monarchy, and common membership of an identical cultural group'.[72] But in the medieval context, authority had to deal with two separate demands. On the one hand, there was the drive to create 'subjection', namely that power relation between individuals defined as different from each other. On the other, there was the desire to create 'association', that is to say a relationship of community between two individuals defined as identical. For these two apparently opposed requirements to be reconciled, the loyalty or *fidelitas* which underlay the principle of interpersonal subjection had to tend towards an abstraction which transcends physical persons. Close to the political theology described by Ernst Kantorowicz or the sentimental, even intuitive idea of the nation which we find in chapter 26 of Machiavelli's *The Prince*, this idea of the recognition of a superior authority accompanied by loyalist feelings directed towards this authority is at the heart of the definition of the modern state proposed by Joseph Strayer or Albert Rigaudière.[73] The love of the prince, of the king and of the community which the king embodies makes possible the fusion of peoples into a national spirit.

This model works for England, and for Scotland, where the 'regnal solidarity' discussed by Susan Reynolds brought together crown, lands and peoples, but not for Wales or Ireland, where no such symbiosis took place.[74] In France, the love of the king was part of this national movement which made him the keystone of the whole political edifice but also the spouse and protector of 'Lady France', whose presence in literature as in iconography bears witness to the transformation of the kingdom into a political abstraction.[75] The prince's love for his subjects and his subjects' love for their prince is one key theme of the *De regimine principum* of Giles of Rome. This love is learnt partly thanks to the efforts of the wise, who know the king's good actions and publicise them until they 'much moved the people to love the king', and partly thanks to the parents who should teach their children to love the king: 'all those of the kingdom must teach their children in their youth to love the king and their lord'.[76] Here, the social construction of a sentimental unit can stimulate the construction of a nation which becomes the imaginary incarnation of a people united around their sovereign. This line of thought leads on to the argument of Karl Ferdinand Werner, Bernard Guenée or more recently Jean-Marie Moeglin, for whom, in the medieval and modern period, 'it is the dynasty that would establish itself (or perhaps rather would be established) as the central reference for the affirmation of a feeling of regional or national identity'. Yet this personal reference-point to a ruling family was not enough on its own, since it must also be accompanied by the idea of a community of rights and privileges which are the proud possession of its inhabitants and on which the feeling of pertaining to the same regional or national unit is founded.[77] Although it goes without saying that these ideological constructions needed time to take root, it was particularly difficult to force the development of a feeling of belonging to a nation when country, dynasty and community of laws did not correspond with each other.

A contractual prince

It can hardly be denied that attachment to the prince was weak in the Great Principality of Burgundy. The year 1477 once more provides a useful point of reference, for example when Mary of Burgundy tried to resist Louis XI's threats to her inheritance by calling on her southern peoples to show their loyalty to the 'faith of Burgundy' which she embodied. In the southern territories, even though there were a number of revolts in these years of transition, the ultimate loyalty of the people was to the king of France. In the Franche-Comté, imperial overlordship made it possible to resist the incursions of the same king of France. On the other hand, these years of real danger did indeed stimulate the awakening of the consciousness of some kind of unified identity, and a noble like Adolph of Cleves could declare in 1491 that Marie 'was the creature in the world whom he loved the most'.[78] Before this date, although the preferred strategy was to blame the prince's counsellors for bad governance rather than the prince himself, this was more out of respect for his office than out of any real attachment to the dynasty. In Flanders, the county had seen numerous dynasties go by, as it placed its destiny one after another in the hands of the House of Baldwin, of Alsace, of Dampierre and of the Valois, with the result that this succession of different lineages became a familiar part of the structures of government in region and one of the elements of its political organisation. The same could be said of Brabant, where the constitution granted at the Joyous Entry of 1356 served as a kind of handbook for the prince who took on the government of this country.

From this point of view, we should not be surprised that, in 1477, the Flemish took up arms not to defend their mistress but rather out of fear of losing their privileges. Mary and Maximilian were quite aware of this. In the manifesto which they published in their northern lands, they invited the populations of Flanders and Brabant to resist the French armies, partly out of love of God and the prince but especially to preserve their liberties, which had been imperilled by the men of the kingdom. Under the king of France, prosperity would give way to the worst poverty, the state of insecurity would be permanent and brigandage would spring up everywhere.[79] Yet in this same document, the Burgundian myth began to take form. Whilst Jean Molinet worked hard to present Mary as a poor damsel in distress, the manifesto co-signed by Mary and her young husband insisted on a past in which the dukes' subjects were supposed to have been men and women of unshakeable loyalty.[80] All the desertions in the heat of battle, all the revolts, were forgotten in favour of an almost patriotic mythology in which the details were skipped over, officially for want of time.

Propaganda texts were issued at regular intervals during the short and disturbed rule of Mary of Burgundy, but the detailed analysis of the reactions of the court, of the nobility and of the towns in the county of Flanders leads Jelle Haemers to conclude that each of these different social groups acted in its own interest, without being conscious of acting to preserve the state, if such a thing existed.[81] The nation, too, beyond the level of the regions, did not develop into a community which could have laid the foundations of a finished state ideology on the basis of a cultural identity proper to a particular social category. In reality, under cover of the common good, the court promoted a dynasty in order to guarantee the public interest; the nobles defended their privileges by invoking services rendered during periods of crisis; the towns asserted that their privileges were essential to the prosperity of a land whose good health they ensured; whilst within the city walls the textile artisans considered themselves more important than the merchants in this enterprise and vice versa. By focusing on periods of crisis, the historian can observe under a magnifying glass, as it were, the lines of fracture between different groups and so understand better the expectations of the peoples in question. In these years in which Habsburg power was put into question, as earlier in the revolt of 1447–53 or in that of 1379–85, it was not Maximilian who was rejected, any more than Philip the Good or Philip the Bold had been in their day, but rather the kind of power which he represented. In the same way, it was not the idea of a centralised state which was fought against; rather it was the distribution of power within this state which was debated, more or less violently. The prince was still 'the most redoubted lord' who must respect the rights and duties of his people if he were to rule them, being as it were on a temporary but renewable contract.

It is this absence of love for the monarch, compensated by a powerful attachment to economic and juridical liberties, which explains amongst other things the ultimate move made by the Estates General assembled at The Hague on 26 July 1581 when they declared the deposition of King Philip II in the principalities of the Low Countries. Article 26 of the list of conditions agreed by these same Estates one year before, fixing the conditions for the reception of a new prince in these territories, stated that if the prince contravened any part of this treaty, the Estates would be freed from their oath and could even take 'another prince' or 'provide for their affairs otherwise as they see fit'.[82] The political contract thus established was inspired, by the end of the sixteenth century, by Protestant resistance theorists but also by reciprocal feudal relationships in which either party could consider himself freed from his obligations if the other failed to meet his.[83] Already detectable in the Joyous Entry of Brabant from 1356 onwards, or in the Great Privilege of 1477 extracted from Mary of Burgundy, in which it was specified that the subjects would not be liable to provide military service if the clauses of the charter were not respected by the monarch, the revocability of the office of prince also appears as a central argument when Guillaume Zoete tried to set in motion the deposition of Maximilian in 1488.[84] In all these texts, which draw on the urban rhetoric of common profit, of liberties, of peace, of justice, of the free circulation of goods and people, of monetary stability and so on, we might, following Jan Dumolyn and Jelle Haemers, insist on the precocity of the political contract in these territories, but we might also note the impossibility of going further than an agreement fixed in particular limited circumstances, to work towards a pact of alliance.[85]

Could economic concerns have provided the foundations of a national union on which a trans-regional state might have been founded? The state of European construction in the present day tends to make me think that this route is a dead-end, but beyond this obviously anachronistic judgement, the fragility of the markets and the rivalry between different towns and different crafts in the same town immediately disqualify this model. The desire to live together in a union going beyond the defence of local interests would have been the only possible basis on which to build such a vast, diverse and complex political edifice. But the cultural gulf between the territories of the north and south, or between the prince and those he ruled, was too deep to allow a nation to bridge them.

We should remember the warning of Pierre Nora: 'The nation itself is entirely a representation. Not a regime, nor a policy, nor a doctrine, nor a culture, but the framework in which all of these are expressed.'[86] If the nation is the result of a construction, an elaboration, a long-term building project, it cannot be denied that the Burgundian enterprise lacked the materials and the time needed to finish the job. Always thinking of themselves first and foremost as princes of the *fleur-de-lys*, at least until the accession of Charles the Bold, the dukes had no desire to promote a unifying national spirit on the edge of the kingdom of France. Part of a feudal pyramid which made their lords either subjects of the kings of France or else imperial vassals, the men of ducal Burgundy or the Franche-Comté did not want to unite in a single entity. As for the peoples of the north, their political destiny, conditioned since the twelfth century by the fierce defence of their liberties, took form only in the sixteenth century, when first the French threat and then the appearance of a common Spanish enemy incited them to take up arms for the love of this conglomerate of territories, this fatherland of liberties: the *Gandsche Nederlanden*, the whole Low Countries.[87]

Neither the state nor the nation can therefore be considered the right framework in which to understand the Burgundian political adventure. Indeed, it would be hard to identify a logical process or mechanism by which the state stimulated the elaboration of a nation so that in turn this nation might support the state when the latter was weakened. Burgundian governance was built on the power of its networks, of interest groups, those of princes, of the court, of nobles, of artisans or of merchants, and not on the basis of an ideological framework which might have led to the construction of a modern state. Was it just that there had not been enough time for this mutually supportive relationship to become established? Perhaps, but the loyalty of the men which led them simply to serve the prince who provided for them, or the patron of the crafts who gave them their means of subsistence, was not enough to construct a nation.[88]

Notes

1 Duke, 'The Elusive Netherlands', and B. Schnerb, 'La croix de saint André'. Both of these note the use of Burgundian symbols in the propaganda of the Belgian fascist party of Léon Degrelle.
2 On the Franche-Comté, see N. Vernot, 'La croix de saint André, facteur d'unité entre les Pays-Bas et le comté de Bourgogne, de Maximilien aux archiducs (1493–1633)', in L. Delobette and P. Delsalle (eds), *La Franche-Comté et les anciens Pays-Bas, XIIIe–XVIIIe siècles*, vol. I: *Aspects politiques, diplomatiques, religieux et artistiques* (Besançon: Cêtre, 2009), pp. 95–128.
3 W. Paravicini, 'La fin du mythe bourguignon?', in Paravicini (ed.), *La cour de Bourgogne et l'Europe*, pp. 9–17.
4 See T. Van Hemelryck, 'Qu'est ce que la littérature … française à la cour de Bourgogne', and H. Wijsman, '"Bourgogne", "bourguignon"

... un style de manuscrits enluminés?', in Paravicini (ed.), *La cour de Bourgogne et l'Europe*, respectively pp. 351–359 and pp. 361–376.
5   See E. Renan, *Qu'est-ce qu'une nation?* (Paris: Calmann Lévy, 1882; new edn, 1997). For a clarification of the background of the development of this thought, see J.-J. Guinchard, 'Le national et le rationnel', *Communications* 45 (1987), 17–49.
6   H. Pirenne, *La nation belge* (Brussels: Lamertin, 1899), p. 8.
7   M. Boone, 'Langue, pouvoirs et dialogue. Aspects linguistiques de la communication entre les ducs de Bourgogne et leurs sujets flamands (1385–1505)', *Revue du Nord* 379 (2009), 9–33. See also E. Bousmar, 'Siècle de Bourgogne, siècle des Grands ducs: variations de mémoire en Belgique et en France du XIXe siècle à nos jours', *PCEEB* 52 (2012), 235–250.
8   P. Monnet, 'La *patria* médiévale vue d'Allemagne, entre construction impériale et identités régionales', *Le Moyen Âge* 107:1 (2001), 71–99; D. Menjot, 'L'historiographie du Moyen Âge espagnol: de l'histoire de la différence à l'histoire des différences', *e-spania*, December 2009, https://doi.org/10.4000/e-spania.19028.
9   Boulton and Veenstra (eds), *The Ideology of Burgundy*.
10 I follow here the reflections of Bourdieu, *Sur l'État. Cours au Collège de France*, pp. 345–346.
11 Van Hemelryck, 'Qu'est ce que la littérature ... française à la cour de Bourgogne', and Wijsman, '"Bourgogne", "bourguignon" ... Un style de manuscrits enluminés?'.
12 See R. Stein, 'Nationale identiteiten in de late Middeleeuwen. Een verkenning', *Tijdschrift voor sociale geschiedenis* 28 (2002), 222–246. The first results of this project are published in R. Stein and J. Pollmann (eds), *Networks, Regions and Nations: Shaping Identities in the Low Countries, 1300–1650* (Leiden: Brill, 2009).
13 P. Hoppenbrouwers, 'The Dynamics of National Identity in the Later Middle Ages', in Stein and Pollmann (eds), *Networks, Regions and Nations*, pp. 19–42.
14 S. Lenherr, 'La vision de la Bourgogne et des Bourguignons dans les sources anglaises (1420–1468)', unpublished master's thesis, University of Lille, 2011.
15 See, for example, 'Mockery of the Flemings' (1436), in F. W. D. Brie (ed.), *The Brut, or the Chronicles of England* (London: Oxford University Press and Kegan Paul, 1960), pp. 582–584.
16 'On the Duke of Burgundy', in Wright (ed.), *A Collection of Political Poems*, pp. 148–149.
17 'Philippus dux Burgundiae ad Jacobum regem Scottorum', in *ibid.*, pp. 150–151.

18 *Ibid.*, pp. 151–156.
19 *Journal de Jean de Roye, connu sous le nom de Chronique scandaleuse*, ed. B. de Mandrot (Paris: H. Laurens, 1894–96), vol. II, p. 42: 'aucuns paillars tenans le parti de Bourgogne'.
20 Chastelain, *Chronique de G. Chastelain*, ed. J.-C. Delclos (Geneva: Droz, 1991), second fragment (October 1458–July 1461), XVI, pp. 76, 154.
21 E. Gellner, *Nations and Nationalism* (Oxford: Basil Blackwell, 1983); B. Anderson, *Imagined Communities: Reflections on the Origins and Spread of Nationalism* (London: Verso, 1983); E. Kedourie, *Nationalism* (London: Hutchinson, 1960); E. J. Hobsbawm, *Nations and Nationalism since 1870* (Cambridge: Cambridge University Press, 1990).
22 R. R. Davies, 'Nations and National Identities in the Medieval World: An Apologia', *Belgisch tijdschrift voor nieuwste geschiedenis* 34:4 (2004), 567–579.
23 A. Smith, *The Antiquity of Nations* (Cambridge: Polity, 2004), p. 245.
24 G. Barrow (ed.), *The Declaration of Abroath: History, Significance, Setting* (Edinburgh: Society of Antiquaries of Scotland, 2003).
25 Some medieval documents mentioning the issue of languages were included in the Policy Address of the Leiden Draft in 1787–88 with the aim of strengthening nationalistic arguments. See M. Boone and M. Prak, 'Rulers, Patricians and Burghers: The Great and the Little Traditions of Urban Revolt in the Low Countries', in K. Davids and J. Lucassen (eds), *A Miracle Mirrored: The Dutch Republic in European Perspective* (Cambridge: Cambridge University Press, 1995), pp. 99–134.
26 This quotation and other examples from Flanders in Boone, 'Langue, pouvoirs et dialogue'.
27 Cauchies (ed.), *Ordonnances de Jean sans Peur (1405–1419)*, pp. 5–9, at p. 5.
28 *Ibid.*, p. 6.
29 On this topic, see W. Prevenier and T. De Hemptinne, 'La Flandre au Moyen Âge. Un pays de trilinguisme administratif', in O. Guyotjeannin (ed.), *La langue des actes,* 2005, elec.enc.sorbonne.fr/CID2003/de-hemptinne_prevenier (accessed 19 July 2021).
30 Godding, *La législation ducale en Brabant*, p. 17.
31 See M. Damen, 'Linking Court and Counties: The Governors and Stadholders of Holland and Zeeland in the Fifteenth Century', *Francia* 29:1 (2002), 257–268. Bilingual nobles were also involved in the administration of Alsace and Luxembourg.
32 Boone, 'Langue, pouvoirs et dialogue', p. 21.
33 See J. Leersen, 'Macht, afstand en culturele diversiteit: bijvoorbeeld Overmaas', *Theoretische geschiedenis* 18:4 (1991), 423–433.

34 J. Leersen, 'Medieval Heteronomy, Modern Nationalism: Language Assertion between Liège and Maastricht, 14th–20th Century', *Belgisch tijdschrift voor nieuwste geschiedenis* 34:4 (2004), 581–593.
35 L. Devillers, *Cartulaire des comtes de Hainaut* (Brussels: Commission Royale d'Histoire, 1881), vol. VI, p. 225.
36 See G. Bischoff, 'La "langue de Bourgogne". Esquisse d'une histoire politique du français et de l'allemand dans les pays de l'entre-deux', *PCEEB* 42 (2002), 101–118.
37 C. A. J. Armstrong, 'The Language Question in the Low Countries: The Use of French and Dutch by the Dukes of Burgundy and their Administration', in J. R. Hale *et al.* (eds), *Europe in the Late Middle Ages* (London: Faber & Faber, 1965), pp. 386–409; Boone, 'Langue, pouvoirs et dialogue'.
38 M. Vale, 'Language, Politics and Society: The Uses of the Vernacular in the Later Middle Ages', *English Historical Review* 120:485 (2005), 15–34.
39 Gachard (ed.), *Collection de documents inédits*, vol. II, pp. 151–152.
40 E. Varenbergh, 'Fêtes données à Philippe le Bon et Isabelle de Portugal à Gand en 1457', *Annales de la Société royale des Beaux-Arts et de littérature de Gand* 12 (1869–72), 1–36.
41 See the report of the twenty-seventh feast of the Order of the Golden Fleece in 1456 at The Hague in Dünnebeil (ed.), *Die Protokollbücher*, vol. I, pp. 112–125.
42 Chastelain, *Chronique*, vol. III, book IV, ch. XXXV, pp. 170–171.
43 See W. P. Blockmans, 'La signification "constitutionnelle" des privilèges de Marie de Bourgogne, 1477', in W. P. Blockmans (ed.), *1477. Het algemeen en de gewestelijke privilegien van Maria van Bourgondie*, Standen en Landen 80 (Courtrai: Heule, 1985), pp. 496–516.
44 See the document in W. P. Blockmans, 'Autocratie ou polyarchie? La lutte pour le pouvoir politique en Flandre de 1482 à 1492, d'après des documents inédits', *Bulletin de la Commission Royale d'Histoire* 140 (1974), 257–368, at p. 328.
45 Lecuppre-Desjardin, 'Maîtriser le temps pour maîtriser les lieux'.
46 Lecuppre-Desjardin, 'Un prince, des fiefs, des ancêtres'.
47 J. Devaux, 'L'historiographie bourguignonne, une historiographie aveuglante?', in Paravicini (ed.), *La cour de Bourgogne et l'Europe*, pp. 83–96.
48 Zingel, *Frankreich, das Reich und Burgund*.
49 On this point, I disagree with Hanno Wijsman, who is convinced that the political ambition of Philip the Good was to found a state independent of the French kingdom. See H. Wijsman, 'Bibliothèques princières entre Moyen Âge et humanisme: à propos des livres de Philippe le Bon et de

Mathias Corvin et de l'interprétation du XVe siècle', in J.-F. Maillard et al. (eds), *Matthias Corvin, les bibliothèques princières et la genèse de l'État moderne* (Budapest: Országos Széchényi Könyvtar, 2009), pp. 121–134, at p. 134: 'Il voulait s'émanciper du royaume de France, se représenter comme un prince indépendant, unifier ses territoires morcelés, créer une histoire et une culture communes, tenter de fonder un État propre'.
50 C. Van Hoorebeeck, *Livres et lectures des fonctionnaires des ducs de Bourgogne (ca 1420–1520)* (Turnhout: Brepols, 2014).
51 A. Vanderjagt, 'Expropriating the Past: Tradition and Innovation in the Use of Texts in Fifteenth Century Burgundy', in R. Suntrup and J. Veenstra (eds), *Tradition and Innovation in an Era of Change/Tradition und Innovation im Übergang zur Frühen Neuzeit* (Frankfurt-am-Main: Peter Lang, 2001), pp. 177–201.
52 See the introduction in M. Golubeva, *Models of Political Competence: The Evolution of Political Norms in the Works of Burgundian and Habsbourg Court Historians, c. 1470–1700* (Leiden and Boston: Brill, 2013).
53 Molinet, *Chroniques*, vol. I, prologue, p. 3.
54 Quotations from Pierre Monnet and Jean-Claude Schmitt, 'Introduction', in P. Monnet and J.-C. Schmitt, *Autobiographies souveraines* (Paris: Les Belles Lettres, 2012), pp. 7–32.
55 See the introduction in P. Monnet and J.-C. Schmitt (ed. and trans.), *Vie de Charles IV de Luxembourg* (Paris: Les Belles Lettres, 2010).
56 J. Aurell, 'La chronique de Jacques Ier, une fiction autobiographique. Auteur, auctorialité et autorité au Moyen Âge', *Annales histoire, sciences sociales* 63:2 (2008), 301–318.
57 On this topic, see A. Noordzij, 'Against Burgundy: The Appeal of Germany in the Duchy of Guelders', in Stein and Pollmann (eds), *Networks, Regions and Nations*, pp. 111–130.
58 *Ibid.* This argument can qualify those of G. Nijsten, *In the Shadow of Burgundy. The Court of Guelders in the Late Middle Ages* (Cambridge: Cambridge University Press, 2004).
59 Quotation from Noordzij, 'Against Burgundy', pp. 116–117.
60 P. Van Peteghem, 'La "souveraineté" du pays de Gueldre. De l'avènement des Bourguignons au Cercle de Bourgogne (1548)', *PCEEB* 24 (1984), 17–31.
61 Ehm-Schnocks, 'L'empereur ne doit pas être un non-Allemand'. For discussion of these developments, see Rapp, *Le Saint Empire Romain Germanique*, pp. 292–304.
62 *Die Burgundisch Hystorie, eine Reim-Chronik von Hans Erhard Tüsch* (1477), lines 317–320, in E. Picot and H. Stein (eds), *Recueil de pièces*

historiques imprimées sous le règne de Louis XI (Paris: Francisque Lefrançois Librairie, 1923), p. 89.
63 Sieber-Lehmann, Spätmiterlalterlicher Nationalismus.
64 J.-M. Moeglin, '"Welsches" et "Allemands" dans l'espace bourguignon, germanique et suisse du XIIIe au XVe siècle', PCEEB 46 (2006), 45–75.
65 Chastelain, Chronique, vol. IV, book VI:2, ch. XXXVII, p. 392.
66 Ibid.; ibid., vol. IV, book VI:2, ch. XXXVIII, pp. 393–394.
67 I would like to thank Bruno Lethenet for allowing me to use some documents from his PhD thesis (Archives Municipales de Mâcon, BB13, fols 84r–v, 85).
68 Manifesto of Philip the Good against the people of Ghent, 31 March 1452, in Gachard (ed.), Collection de documents inédits, vol. II, pp. 109–111.
69 Quotations from Kantorowicz, 'Mystères de l'État', pp. 93–125.
70 Anderson, Imagined Communities, p. 19.
71 F. Buylaert, 'Les anciens Pays-Bas: nouvelles approches. La noblesse et l'unification des Pays-Bas: naissance d'une noblesse bourguignonne à la fin du Moyen Âge?', Revue historique 312:1 (653) (2010), 3–25.
72 See J. Szücs, Les trois Europes (Paris: L'Harmattan, 1985), and a reflection on that book in L. Pinto, 'Une fiction politique: la nation. À propos des travaux de Jenö Szücs', Actes de la recherche en sciences sociales 64 (September 1986), 45–50.
73 See the Introduction of this book.
74 For Susan Reynolds, it is 'regnal solidarity' which is at the origin of the English nation. See S. Reynolds, Kingdoms and Communities in Western Europe 900–1300 (Oxford: Oxford University Press, 1984; 2nd edn, 1997). The example of Wales under the Tudor kings shows that the English Crown was able to integrate ethnic communities which were not English, thanks to the principle of allegiance. See P. Jenkins, 'The Plight of Pygmy Nations: Wales in Early Modern Europe', North American Journal of Welsh Studies 2:1 (2002), 1–11.
75 C. J. Brown, 'Allegorical Design and Image-Making in Fifteenth-Century France: Alain Chartier's Joan of Arc', French Studies 53:4 (1999), 385–404.
76 For these quotations and other examples, see L. Scordia, 'Concepts et registres de l'amour du roi dans le De regimine prinicipum de Gilles de Rome', in J. Barbier et al. (eds), Amour et désamour du prince. Du haut Moyen Âge à la Révolution française (Paris: Kimé, 2011), pp. 45–57, at p. 57.
77 Quotation from J.-M. Moeglin, 'Nation et nationalisme du Moyen Âge à l'époque moderne (France-Allemagne)', Revue historique 301:3 (611) (1999), 537–553.

78 Adolph of Cleves, Defence of the Order of the Golden Fleece (BnF, ms. fr. 28, fols 72–101), ed. in Sterchi, *Über den Umgang*, p. 642.
79 'La défense de Monseigneur le duc et madame la duchesse d'Austriche et de Bourgongne', Bruges 1477, in Picot and Stein (eds), *Recueil de pièces historiques imprimées sous le règne de Louis XI*, pp. 213 ff.
80 On the political communication promoted by Molinet, see E. Bousmar, 'Duchesse de Bourgogne ou "Povre désoléee pucelle"? Marie face à Louis XI dans les chapitres 45 et 46 des *Chroniques* de Jean Molinet', in J. Devaux *et al.* (eds), *Jean Molinet et son temps*, Burgundica 22 (Turnhout: Brepols, 2013), pp. 97–113.
81 Haemers, *For the Common Good*, *passim* and p. 263.
82 See W. P. Blockmans, 'Du contrat féodal à la souveraineté du peuple. Les précédents de la déchéance de Philippe II dans les Pays-Bas (1581)', in *Assemblee di stati e istituzioni rappresentative nelle storia del pensiero politico moderno (secoli XV–XX)* (Rimini: Maggioli, 1983), pp. 135–150.
83 Lecuppre-Desjardin, *La ville des cérémonies*, pp. 141–148.
84 We should note that in 1339, urban elites from Flanders, Brabant, Hainault, Holland and Zeeland decided to form a sort of joint committee with the aim of judging the actions of princes and removing them in case of non-compliance with their duties. M. Boone, 'The Dutch Revolt and the Medieval Tradition of Urban Dissent', *Journal of Early Modern History* 11 (2007), 351–375.
85 J. Dumolyn and J. Haemers, 'Les bonnes causes du peuple pour se révolter. Le contrat politique en Flandre médiévale d'après Guillaume Zoete (1488)', in F. Foronda (ed.), *Avant le contrat social. Le contrat politique dans l'Occident médiéval (XIIIe–XVe siècle)* (Paris: Éditions de la Sorbonne, 2011), pp. 327–346.
86 Pierre Nora, 'Présentation de Pierre Nora', in Pierre Nora (ed.), *Les lieux de mémoire*, vol. II:1: *La nation* (Paris: Gallimard, 1986), p. x.
87 See A. Duke, 'In defence of the Common Fatherland: Patriotism and Liberty in the Low Countries, 1555–1576', in Stein and Pollmann (eds), *Networks, Regions and Nations*, pp. 217–239.
88 See the reflections of Johan Huizinga about this point in 'Uit de voorgeschiednis van ons nationaal besef'.

Conclusion

> History is not just a game for princes. But history is a game, nonetheless, in the sense that it has no hidden purpose. Matters could always have turned out differently. To want at any price to propose mechanistic explanations for historical processes is to underestimate the weight of the human will.[1]

On 26 June 1477, the head of the ducal council and president of the Parlements of the two Burgundies, Jean Jouard, was killed in the street in Dijon by rioters who ripped off the signs of his authority to the cry of 'Long live Burgundy! Down with the fat men!' This was a sad end for the lord of Échevannes and Gatey, this magistrate who, as his biographer writes with some embarrassment, had been raised to the peak of the hierarchy by the generosity of the duke and who ended up abandoning his former masters and entering the service of Louis XI as soon as the latter seized the lands of his goddaughter.[2] Jean Jouard, that skilled jurist, that righteous man who had always attempted to reconcile the interests of his lords with those of their subjects, who had found the money needed for ducal business, reformed local customs and reorganised the University of Dole, as well as acting as a diplomat in the matter of Besançon's rebellion and the interminable litigation over Chalon, that trusted adviser of Philip the Good, nonetheless did not hesitate to supress Mary's letters of 23 January 1477 calling for resistance, in order to ensure the agreement of the Estates and their allegiance to the king of France.

How can we explain Jean's actions? Did he act out of respect for the feudal law which made the king of France the lord of the duke of Burgundy? For the money which Louis XI distributed largely to the authorities of Dijon? From a personal desire to keep himself in office, whoever his master might be? For fear of a king like Louis XI, who had not hesitated to have Oudart de Bussy beheaded when the latter denied him a position in the Parlement and attempted to raise a rebellion in Artois?[3] Or, as Blondeau argued, did he act in the name of a *raison d'État* imposed on him by the march of events'? After all, Burgundy was once more going to change master and pass under foreign domination. Did these diplomatic concerns necessitate a change of allegiance? In assessing the strength of the powers involved and the risks to be run, was Jean Jouard not simply hoping to save his country, his *pays*, as he had previously done on 26 September 1467, when he petitioned the duke to leave men-at-arms in Burgundy for defence, or in 1475, when he insisted to Guillaume Rolin that the ducal troops based at Neuss come back at once to defend the people of Dijon in their battle against royal troops? To talk in terms of *raison d'État* is certainly an anachronism, but to talk of the love of the land of one's birth and the desire to protect one's fellow countrymen from the disasters of a new war does seem, to me, to be appropriate. The idea of loyalty to a particular government probably never left the mind of Jean Jouard, whose service record pleads in his favour. But for this senior civil servant to the dukes, who was still *bailli* of Fouvent and Graylois by birth, even as one served different masters, out of obedience, one remained loyal to one's natal *patria* out of an almost filial piety. It was a sad fate indeed, then, to die like a traitor, for this man who seems to have been committed to defending his people, whereas his killer, Chrétiennot Vyon, an impoverished local notable, had probably adopted the 'faith of Burgundy' merely to settle his own scores.

Jean Jouard was one of those men who, in action, had a care for the preservation of the lands, for the respect for the law of the places where he held office and for the good order of the finances he managed. Just like the members of the Chamber of Accounts who, in their correspondence, revealed their concern to defend the interests of the prince's domains against all predators, the prince himself included, Jouard knew how to play on his contacts and to use his social skills in order to reconcile contradictory interests until the time came to choose a party, in a period of trials and danger where every decision brought its own risks. Jean Jouard had nothing in common with the favourite always on the lookout for reward, whose origins were not important, or with the 'bourgeois calculators' who were always on the take, or with those courtiers who used their positions to lay their hands on honours and wealth. The president of the Parlement of Burgundy was one of those men who served the prince out of habit, for the honour of a job well done, but whose loyalty was above all to a land and its people. His choice is perhaps proof that state-consciousness, by which I mean the desire to protect institutions, forms of government and the integrity of a territory, independent of the authority of a prince, can appear in the exercise of power even without any explicit statement of political philosophy. The love of money did not determine the decisions of Jean Jouard, any more than the rules of feudal precedence, which might have led naturally to the acknowledgement of the French king's power but which would certainly not have carried much weight with a man used to dealing with Charles VII and Louis XI on the subject of the enclaves that we have observed before, and in which the kings did not hesitate to go back on their word.[4] The decisions of the lord of Échevannes were not taken in the name of a Burgundian nation, of a princely state which needed preserving or of a political entity which went beyond the limits of his *pays*. The limits of his state-consciousness were defined by his office as a magistrate: it was based in Dijon, went as far as Dole and Besançon, walked the banks of the Saône, and fortified itself in Beaune, but took the road to Brussels only to have itself confirmed.

This observation could equally well be made in the case of Jean Bonost, clerk, auditor and then master of accounts at Dijon between 1400 and 1443, who, inspecting the Chamber of Accounts at Lille in the wake of the exactions of Roland du Bois and Guérin Sucquet, recommended that the central accounts be sent to the Chamber of Accounts at Dijon.[5] One might also cite Henri van Goethals, diplomat and councillor of John the Fearless and Philip the Good, who nonetheless always worked in the interests of Ghent, the city of his birth, or Pierre Bladelin, diplomatic and financial adviser of Philip the Good, who used the prince's networks to compete with him, even going so far as to build his own town, but never forgot Bruges, his fatherland.[6] Their lives provide examples of servants of the prince whose political imagination had difficulty in going beyond the centre of gravity of their own power.

Things were rather different, however, at the end of the period under study, for Guillaume Hugonet, whose homilies to the sessions of the Estates General were charged with supporting Charles the Bold's quest for sovereignty. Different points of view are to be understood as a function of different cultures, responsibilities, events or desires. These men of Burgundian institutions, like Hugonet, indubitably mastered what Guido Castelnuovo calls an 'administrative lingua franca' ('*koiné* administrative'), sharing among themselves the same savoir-faire, sometimes even the same training and often identical personal ambitions. Yet, contrary to Castelnuovo's analysis, it is difficult to 'think that we are dealing with a homogeneous group of technicians, committed at any cost to an almost ideological defence of a state which is just as modern as it is immanent', for the simple reason that these men, as servants of the prince, always acted as both ducal officers on the one hand and as urban notables or noble lords on the other.[7] Their identities were multiple and they piled up one upon the other, but they did not yet lead to unity behind one man, one idea, one destiny.

Were the dukes of Burgundy responsible for this lack of unifying bonds? Did they fail to construct a composite state? The answer, which has already been put forward in the course of this book, is clearly 'no', insofar as they had no desire to proceed in this direction in the first place. The dukes of Burgundy were above all princes of their time, and in that they were neither 'modern' nor archaic. Of course, they were the heirs of a culture which made the Emperor Charles V present himself as a knight of Christ in the sixteenth century, in contrast, say, to François I, who leaves the impression of a king who was constantly looking for novelty and who did not hesitate to renege on his promises, for example when, as a prisoner of the emperor in 1525, he swore to cede the duchy of Burgundy in exchange for his freedom. But who would argue that Charles V was less powerful than the king of France? Their idea of power was certainly different, no doubt as a result of their different education and upbringing as well as of a different set of historical circumstances. Although an arbitrary set of dynastic circumstances had allowed Charles V to bring together an immense area under his sovereignty, it was his culture and his education which made him into a man who took on both his ancestors' painful dispute with the French monarchy and the struggle to defend the Catholic faith, either in the ideal of crusade in the distant Orient or on his doorstep in the confrontation with Protestantism. The early sixteenth-century afterlife of Burgundian history shows that the sense of a dynastic inheritance which was to be protected, recovered or extended was the primary motor of action in the heart of these princes, above and beyond any other intention. From this point of view, we would be wrong to ignore the analysis of Joachim Stieber, who sees all European policy between 1330 and 1650 as being marked by a logic of ownership, led by princes who thought of their authority and their possessions as their personal goods.[8] In western Europe, at the end of the Middle Ages, the political systems developed by France and England were the exceptions, not the models which ought to guide historians as they fix their definition of the 'modern state'.

How indeed can we call this multi-territorial complex a 'state'? After all, since certain historians do not hesitate to talk about, say, the modest 'state' of Bar, it is perhaps not surprising that they are even less burdened by scruples when referring to the far more elaborate Burgundian entity. But the concept of the 'state' is not neutral and conjures up in the historical imagination such notions as rationality, unity, monopoly and stability, which lead us insidiously towards over-interpretation. One of the ways to avoid this danger and to legitimate our historiographical position is to swiftly qualify the state we are studying as a 'feudal state', as Jean-Philippe Genet does for England until the sixteenth century, or as a 'princely state', as Bertrand Schnerb does for the Great Principality of Burgundy. We might even use 'territorial state', borrowing from the work of a good number of historians working on the Italian peninsular.[9] Let us briefly reconsider these expressions.

The terms 'feudal state' and 'state feudalism' certainly have the advantage of acknowledging the importance of human relations in the construction of power, but they arguably also involve a contradiction. If we accept that the 'state' is a sovereign authority distinguished from partial forms of authority, such as those of the Church and the nobility, and if we agree with what is perhaps now a rather dated historiography that feudalism implies a pyramid of powers where public authority is mediated by the levels which compose it, then it seems impossible that such a state could be reconciled with feudalism. We could define feudalism differently, but where would that get us? Why wrestle with such false problems, dictated in the final analysis by how we define our terms, not by the historical phenomena they are supposed to explain?[10]

The alternative of the 'princely state' makes the dynast into the keystone of the political edifice. In a society where power was conceived of as being embodied, there is nothing surprising about this expression, which could have made it possible to unify a varied group of territories in the beloved person of the prince.[11] Yet, on the one hand, we have shown how fragile this love for the prince could be. On the other, this dynastic state developed according to the familial logic of the 'House', where this House transcended the individuals of which it was composed, including the first amongst them. But before the House of Burgundy took the road to an independent identity under Charles the Bold, the dukes presented themselves as the children of France.[12] Moreover, power relations were not independent of kinship and client networks – which the language of diplomacy also reveals, using and abusing such terms as 'cousin', 'fair uncle of Burgundy', 'goddaughter' and so on. The characteristics of the 'princely' or 'dynastic' state, that is to say transmission by inheritance, the strength of ties of blood and birth, fatally compromise the notion of the 'state'. For the establishment of the state requires a rupture, even if a progressive one, of kinship ties in favour of another kind of loyalty.

If we turn to Italy and its history, spatial factors here might prompt a new lexical suggestion, namely the idea of a 'territorial state'. Italian historiography, with the aim of understanding the specificities of the peninsula in debates concerning the development of the modern state in Europe, has reconsidered the formation of Ancien Régime political entities separately from the model of a bureaucratic, centralised and rational state. The reflections of historians of late-medieval Italy have been close to those of Otto Brunner and Otto Hinze for Germany, another region characterised by political fragmentation and the multiplication of decision-making centres. These historians insist upon the composite character of political agglomerations, on legal pluralism and the contractual nature of government, from the point of view of what is called a 'territorial' state, since what is at issue is a system of government capable of handing down justice, imposing tributes and raising an army in a given territory.[13] This coinage might perhaps fit the Burgundian mosaic, and the concept of a 'Burgundian territorial state' on the Italian model might potentially be satisfactory, if we are prepared to put aside the system of political thought which, in Italy, took shape around a balanced ideal of the common good formed between centralising tendencies and the respect of personal and collective privileges. For it is there that the problem lies: Italian political ideology has only a few points in common with that of the dukes of Burgundy. If high levels of urbanisation were common to the Low Countries and to northern and central Italy, the town did not play the same role in both.[14] As Giorgio Chittolini has repeatedly demonstrated, the structures of lordship in northern Italy 'are in clear continuity with city institutions', which makes them 'very different from the superposition exercised by the Burgundian ducal court on the city and mercantile society of Flanders and the Low Countries'. In Italy, city communes had repelled imperial and papal assaults, creating city-states by dominating their *contado* and establishing strong governmental jurisdictions there.[15] The establishment of princely authority in these contexts absorbed communal jurisdictions, thanks notably to the retention of city chanceries. In the Low Countries, by contrast, the towns had no intention of developing a juridical and political culture of full autonomy and could not thus provide the kernels for the territorial construction of the state.

We might then turn to the Germanic region and the process of territorialisation. When we observe the geopolitical structure of the German territories, which led to the establishment of principalities (*Fürstenstaaten*) in the hands of dynastic groups which were almost independent of the emperor's authority and whose authority was limited but recognised, we might imagine that the dukes of Burgundy had before their very eyes a model of multi-territorial organisation which could have been adapted to the contours of their own sphere of power.[16] If we allow ourselves a little counter-factual indulgence, we might imagine that a prince of Burgundy might have placed a member of his family in each of his *pays* with the title of count of Flanders, duke of Brabant, count of Hainault and so on. He would then have allowed each of his peoples to recognise themselves in a prince and would have received a title which would have made him the uncontested leader of this federation. But this would be to ignore the many realities which meant that, on the one hand, the attachment of the duke to each of his territories was strictly personal and that, on the other, the subtleties of the German model seem to have been unknown or held in contempt at the court of Burgundy, if we recall the episode at Trier.[17] Once again, the political culture of these

Valois princes did not encourage them to take on board the geopolitics of their sphere of power, but instead meant that they continued to draw inspiration from their ancestors, the kings of France.

Thus, to return to the words of Jean-Frédéric Schaub, the question of how power might be exercised is ultimately summed up by determining 'what relationships to time, to experience and to accumulation are evident in different societies'.[18] This means assessing the different relationships with the past and their impact on future constructions in a dispersed territory where distances model this relationship to time. The dukes of Burgundy were noble lords whose dynastic memory attached them to the kingdom of France, at least until the accession of the last amongst them. The horizon of their thought was fully conditioned by this inheritance. The history that they ordered to be written, which was meant to serve as the dynastic and institutional story of their political regime, records this filiation and, as a result, proves until very late their visceral attachment to the kingdom of France. When Charles the Bold founded the Parlement of Malines in 1473, the desire to affirm his full sovereignty over his territories certainly shows a rupture with the family of France. The ordering of these institutions in the name of the implacable justice which he sought to embody demonstrates his will to turn the page and to align his economic power with his status as a prince who was now a sovereign. It was no longer a time for negotiation and the delegation of power, for sympathetic and complicit friendships. But we must not see in this duke's furious determination to win a crown simply the last piece of a jigsaw puzzle which, once assembled, would serve as a collective history dedicated to the gathering-together of his peoples. Charles pursued a very personal ambition which allowed him to compete with his perpetual enemy, Louis XI, but which also gave him, aside from the petty rivalry between these two men, a superior position in the European diplomatic game. The conquest of a supreme title, either royal or imperial, would perhaps not have changed anything in the political construction of this territorial complex, but it would have transformed the life of this prince who, as a man of his time, could envisage the justification of his power only through the acquisition of a title.[19] Words, because they refer to a state, a *status*, are certainly important, and it is wise to borrow those of the day. The sources are there to save us from the risk of constructing a vision of reality which is inappropriate for the Burgundian fifteenth century. Without speaking of a 'state', the sources use a rich vocabulary where domains, countries or *pays*, lordships, principalities, kingdoms, the Empire, governments and so on naturally take their place. To be sure, there is no more evidence here of the idea of a single principality than there is of a Burgundian state. The prince 'lords over his countries' (*seigneurie des pays*). But, since 'the Burgundian state' was a creation intended to assist historical writing, so 'the Great Principality of Burgundy', which suggests a political construction, whilst avoiding any confusion with the territorial principalities of Flanders, Brabant, the duchy of Burgundy and so on, seems to me a more neutral modern creation, one less subject to the distortions associated with the lexical field of the 'state'. Although modern historians can certainly use a practical term of art to bring everything together on the basis of a political entity which would have been recognisable in the fifteenth century, namely a principality, their investigations of the political imagination of the men of this period should never forget their realities, which were *pays* or lordships, counties or duchies, nor that their dreams of grandeur took the form of a crown. This book has given pride of place to 'understanding in context', being careful to distinguish, on the one hand, the tools being used by historians and, on the other, the thought and action of the men of the past.[20]

The year 1477 is certainly a key date in this Burgundian adventure. It built on a moment of rupture the chaotic destiny of the countries of the north, whose 'circle of Burgundy' (*Burgundischer Reichskreis*), in the absence of a crown, served temporarily in 1512 to assemble the northern lands of the dukes' inheritance. But it also brought an end to the princely revolt led by Charles the Bold against a king of France determined to respect his consecration oath and to expand his kingdom as far as he could, in Catalonia as in Burgundy. This date does not, however, mark the end of a world. The Emperor Charles V still issued challenges in the name of his honour and that of his subjects, and King Henry II of France died in a joust. The kings of Spain continued to negotiate their taxes separately with the different parts of society, and the king of France relied on collegiality in his provinces to maintain his authority. The year 1477 does, however, mark, in a moment, a brutal end to almost a century of shared power during which the prince's necessity was not that of his peoples. Through men's love of taking refuge in mourning for a lost golden age when the anxiety of the times grows too painful, it became the era of a mythical Burgundy which was paradoxically too fragile to help in constructing a political reality in the fifteenth century, whilst being sufficiently strong to give fuel for endless historiographical debates.

A nation only in fantasy, a grouping of lordships, a princely state on the cusp of sovereignty, on 5 January 1477 the Great Principality of Burgundy remained simply an immensely rich territory, definitively composite, with the look of an unfinished kingdom ... an illusion of a Burgundian state.

Notes

1. M.-A. Arnould, 'Les lendemains de Nancy dans les "pays de par-deça" (janvier–avril 1477)', in Blockmans (ed.), *1477. Het algemeen en de gewestelijke privilegien van Maria van Bourgondie*, p. 57.
2. G. Blondeau, *Jean Jouard, seigneur d'Échevannes et de Gatey, président des parlements des duché et comté de Bourgogne* (Besançon: De Dodivers, 1909).
3. Oudart de Bussy was the leader of the embassy sent to Mary of Burgundy asking for her support. They were arrested in Lens, brought to Hesdin and beheaded. Murray-Kendall, *Louis XI*, p. 375.
4. See above, pp. 252–256.
5. Regarding Jean Bonost, see J.-B. Santamaria, *La Chambre des comptes de Lille de 1386 à 1419. Essor, organisation et fonctionnement d'une institution princière* (Turnhout: Brepols, 2012), *passim*.
6. M. Boone and J. Dumolyn, 'Henri Goethals, doyen de Liège († 1433): un homme d'Église gantois au service des ducs de Bourgogne Jean sans Peur et Philippe le Bon', *PCEEB* 38 (1998), 89–105. On Pierre Bladelin, see J. Braekevelt, *Pieter Bladelin, de Rijselse Rekenkamer en de stichting van Middelburg-in-Vlaanderen (ca. 1444–1472): de ambities van eenopgeklommenhofambtenaar versus de bescherming van hetvorstelijkedomein* (Brussels: Commission Royale d'Histoire, 2012).
7. See the important reflections of G. Castelnuovo in 'Service de l'État et identité sociale. Les chambres des comptes princières à la fin du Moyen Âge', *Revue historique* 303:2 (618) (2001), 489–510.
8. J. W. Stieber, *Pope Eugenius IV, the Council of Basel, and the Secular and Ecclesiastical Authorities in the Empire: The Conflict over Supreme Authority and Power in the Church*, Studies in the History of Christian Thought 13 (Leiden: Brill, 1978), pp. 410–412.

9. This abundance of adjectives used to qualify the medieval state is also underlined by J.-F. Schaub in 'La notion d'État moderne est-elle utile? Remarques sur les blocages de la démarche comparatiste en histoire', *Cahiers du Monde russe* 46/1–2 (2005), 51–64.
10. See E. A. R. Brown, 'The Tyranny of a Construct: Feudalism and Historians of Medieval Europe', *American Historical Review* 79:4 (1974), 1063–1088.
11. See R. J. Bonney, *The European Dynastic States (1494–1660)* (Oxford: Oxford University Press, 1991).
12. Note moreover that this independence lasted only a very short time, since after the death of Charles the Bold, chroniclers sought to incorporate the House of Burgundy into that of the Habsburgs.
13. See the introduction in J. Boutier, S. Landi and O. Rouchon (eds), *Florence et la Toscane (XIVe–XIXe siècles). Les dynamiques d'un État italien* (Rennes: PUR, 2004), pp. 7–11.
14. See the comparison between Flanders and Italy in Crouzet-Pavan and Lecuppre-Desjardin (eds), *Villes de Flandre et d'Italie*.
15. See G. Chittolini, 'Paysages urbains du comté de Flandre et du duché de Milan au XVe siècle', in Paravicini (ed.), *La cour de Bourgogne et l'Europe*, pp. 503–514.
16. These power games are clarified in P. Johaneck, 'Imperial and Free Towns of the Holy Roman Empire: City-States in Pre-Modern Germany?', in M. H. Hansen (ed.), *A Comparative Study of Thirty City-States* (Copenhagen: Royal Danish Academy of Sciences and Letters, 2000), pp. 295–320.
17. See above, pp. 158–162.
18. Schaub, 'La notion d'État moderne est-elle utile?', pp. 51–64.
19. The situation can be compared with that of Cosimo de Medici who wanted to become Grand Duke of Tuscany. See O. Rouchon, 'L'invention du principat médicéen, 1512–1609', in Boutier, Landi and Rouchon (eds), *Florence et la Toscane (XIVe–XIXe siècles)*, pp. 65–90.
20. On this idea, see F. Cosandey and R. Descimon, *L'absolutisme en France. Histoire et historiographie* (Paris: Points Seuil, 2002).

Bibliography

Bibliographic material is hosted independently in the section 'Le royaume inachevé des ducs de Bourgogne (XIVe-XVe siècle), Paris, Belin, 2016 -BIBLIOGRAPHIE INTÉGRALE SOURCES' at: https://univ-lille.academia.edu/ElodieLecuppreDesjardin/Books.

Index

Note: pages in italics are maps or illustrations.

Aa, river 256–257, *257*
Abbeville 201, 204, 208
Achilles, Albrecht (margrave de Brandebourg) 161, 306, 316
Alençon, Jean II, duke of 47, 107
Alexander the Great 200, 239n.69
Alfonso V (king of Aragon) 34
Alost, city and county of 182, 255
Alsace *x*, 1–2, 159, 197, 201, 215, 217–218, 309, 322
    Alsace, bailiff of *see* Hagenbach
Amiens *x*, 109, 189, 214, 257
Anjou 46, 270, 279
    Anjou, René (king of Naples/Sicily) 147, 157, 166
    Anjou, Robert of (king of Naples) 151
Antwerp 166, 257, 283
Aragon 34, 151, 154, 215, 290, 314
    see also Alfonso V (king of Aragon); Ferdinand (king of Aragon); James I (king of Aragon); John II (king of Aragon)
Arbrestein, count of 3
Arc, Joan of 101, 206, 306, 330n.75

Armagnac 41n.34, 46, 71, 116n.2, 181, 304
Armagnac, Jacques (duke of Nemours) 57, 107
Arras 35, 96–102, 105, 153, 155, 183, 227–228, 279
Arras, bishop of 51, 97
Arras, Treaty of 76, 122, 124, 128, 131, 147, 178, 183, 192, 194, 221, 228, 252, 275, 304–305, 317
Arras, *Grande Vauderie* of 96–102, 155
Arson, Jean d' 43
Artevelde, Jacob van 74, 98
artillery 203–206, 211
Artois, county of *x*, 25, 32, 50, 71–72, 91, 94, 99, 122, 128, 153, 166, 182, 185, 189, 223, 236n.12, 248, 255, 261, 279, 287, 333
Athis-sur-Orge, Treaty of 92
Auffay, Jean d' (Burgundian lawyer) 122, 275
Austria, house of 161–162, 178
    Austria, Maximilian, duke of 12, 26, 72–76, 122, 161, 179, 182, 249, 260, 288, 311, 322–324
    Austria, Sigismund, count of Tyrol and duke of 197, 215

see also Burgundy (Catherine, duchess of Austria)
Auxerre *x*, 187, 229, 275

Bailliage 124, 250–253
banners and emblems 124, 152, 196, 213, 227, 230, 271–273, 290, 300
Basel 3, 76, 150, 183, 217
  Basel, council of 163, 263
Basin, Thomas (bishop of Lisieux and chronicler) 43, 63–64, 151, 158
Baudricourt, Jean de (marshal of France) 46
Bavaria, Isabeau of (queen of France) 85, 127, 168n.18
Bavaria, Jacqueline of (countess of Hainault, Holland and Zeeland) 128, 184, 191, 227, 249
Bavaria, William of (count of Hainault, Holland and Zeeland) 126, 214
  see also Burgundy, Margaret of Bavaria, duchess of
Beaujeu, Anne de (Anne de France) 76, 110
Beaufort, Henry (cardinal) 221
Beaune 1, 178, 186, 334
Berry, duke of *see* France, Charles of
Besançon 166, 178, 332, 334
Bische, Guillaume (lord of Clary) 48
Bladelin, Pierre (financial advisor and civil servant) 229, 334
Bodin, Jean (political thinker) 141
Boendale, Jan van (writer) 269, 283, 289
Bois, Roland du (master of accounts) 153, 334
Borssele family, the 73
Bonost, Jean (master of accounts) 153, 334

Bourbon, Jean II, duke of 107, 185, 187
Brabant *x*, 12, 28, 32, 39n.9, 48, 73, 113, 123–124, 162–165, 186, 189, 194, 251, 258, 259, 263, 267, 269, 273, 282–285, 308–309, 322
Brabant, Antoine, duke of 126
Brabant, John III, duke of 283
Brabant, John IV, duke of 128, 191
Brederode, Reinhoud van (lord of Vianen) 310
Brimeu, Athis de (lord of Ligny) 127
Brittany, duchy of 76, 134–135, 150, 157, 181, 188, 260
Brittany, Anne, duchess of 76
Brittany, Francis II, duke of 107–113, 214, 264
Brouwershaven 191
Bruges *x*, 2, 18, 21, 23, 25–26, 31, 33, 62–63, 91–95, 112, 150, 155–156, 182, 203, 211–212, 223–225, 230, 265, 279, 287–289
Bruges, franc of 142, 229, 232
Brussels *x*, 25, 36, 100, 108, 150, 156, 269, 282–283
Burgundy, county of *x*, 33, 42n.48, 47, 50, 52, 75, 95, 129, 179, 185, 187, 205, 216, 218, 232, 240n.81, 253–254, 275
Burgundy, duchy of *x*, 33, 50, 52, 74, 75, 102–103, 115, 117n.26, 128–129, 133–134, 160, 165, 178–179, 183–190, 205, 232, 240n.81, 252–253, 255, 260, 271, 273, 274, 275, 278, 285, 318, 325, 335, 340
Burgundy, Estates and General Estates of 15–16, 64, 69, 76, 98, 105–6, 108, 113–114, 130, 138, 140–141, 156,

163, 187, 197–198, 201, 211, 223, 233, 239n.62, 264, 266, 286
Burgundy, Agnes (countess of Clermont) 40n.32, 129
Burgundy, Anne (duchess of Bedford) 128, 168n.6
Burgundy, Antoine, Great Bastard of (count of La Roche, lord of Beveren and of Beuvry) 46, 50, 52, 55
Burgundy, Baudouin de Lille, Bastard of 43–44, 55, 71
Burgundy, Catherine (duchess of Austria) 126, 309
Burgundy, Charles the Bold, duke of x, 3, 6, 11n.10, 12, 16, 18, 22–23, 25, 29–32, 43–46, 48–52, 54–55, 57, 60–66, 68–75, 106–109, 111–116, 122, 124–125, 133–134, 136–137, 139–151, 154–167, 176n.129, 177n.141, 179, 183, 187, 196–221, 226–228, 230–234, 239n.62, 241n.94, 242n.115, 247, 252–253, 256–257, 265–266, 268–269, 275–279, 276, 281, 285, 291n.1, 315–317, 339–340
Burgundy, David, bishop of Utrecht, Bastard of 310
Burgundy (Isabelle of Bourbon, second wife of Charles the Bold, duke of) 26, 94–95
Burgundy (Isabella of Portugal, third wife of Philip the Good, duke of) 21, 23, 83n.86, 142, 147, 196, 223
Burgundy, John the Fearless, duke of 7, 12, 35, 41n.34, 46–47, 59, 63, 65, 71, 85–96, 106, 108, 113–114, 123–124, 126–128, 130–131, 150,

154–156, 173n.90, 189–192, 194, 206, 214, 228–232, 279, 282, 285
Burgundy, John (count of Etampes) 60, 97, 109, 186
Burgundy, Margaret (duchess of Guyenne) 126
Burgundy, Margaret (countess of Richmond) 128
Burgundy, Margaret of Bavaria, duchess of 126, 154–155, 190
Burgundy, Marguerite de Male, duchess of 55, 250
Burgundy, Margaret of York, duchess of (third wife of Charles the Bold) 18, 62, 265
Burgundy, Mary, duchess of (daughter of Charles the bold) 133–134, 161, 170n.41, 233, 261, 269, 273, 275, 311, 321–322, 324, 333
Burgundy, Mary (duchess of Clèves) 128
Burgundy, Mary (duchess of Savoy) 126
Burgundy, Philip the Bold, duke of 16, 35, 46–47, 55, 71, 85, 88–90, 95, 123, 125–130, 136–137, 155–156, 169n.21, 174n.90, 189, 203, 249, 271, 279, 281–282, 308
Burgundy, Philip the Good, duke of x, 5, 15–16, 18–19, 21–23, 25, 27–29, 31–33, 35–37, 39n.9, 45–51, 55–56, 59–61, 65–66, 68, 71, 96–103, 105–109, 112–113, 123–124, 126–129, 131–133, 135, 139–140, 143, 146, 148, 150–156, 162–164, 168n.6, 182, 185,

Index

190–195, 198, 203, 211, 213, 218, 221–230, 232–233, 236n.21, 250, 252–256, 269, 271–273, 272, 279, 282, 286–287, 302, 304–305, 308–311, 313–314, 317–318, 332, 334
Burgundy, Philip (count of Nevers) 85, 126
Burgundy, Philip the Fair, duke of 136, 148, 226, 260

Cabochienne ordinance 89, 106
Caesar, Julius 201, 213
Calais x, 27, 95, 189, 192–193, 218, 221–225, 229, 305
Calfvel (tax in Bruges) 89–96
Cassel 157, 263
Catalonia 180
Cateau–Cambrésis, Treaty of 253
ceremonies 13–17, 21–25, 35
Chalon family, the 47, 50, 74–76, 154
Chamber of Accounts 1–3, 16, 153, 165, 185, 251, 267, 279
Chambers of Rhetoric *see* rederijkers
Champagne, county of 184–185
Champmol (Chartreuse) 138, 278
Charles IV (Emperor and king of Bohemia) 314
Charles V (emperor) 34, 130, 166, 249, 316, 335
Charles VI (king of France) 20, 84–88, 124, 127, 190
Charles VII (king of France) 102, 124, 131, 139, 147, 196, 253, 281
Charles VIII (king of France) 76, 168n.18
Charolais, count of 31, 93, 106–113, 126–127, 137, 155–156

Chassa, Jean de 43, 50
Chastelain, George (chronicler) 23–29, 45–49, 61–66, 131–139, 305–306, 318
Cicero 151, 313
Circle of Burgundy 167, 340
Cleves, Adolph (count of La Mark and lord of Ravenstein) 72–73, 322
Cleves (Philippe, son of Adolf) 70, 73
cloth/clothing 18, 20–21, 55, 86, 149
Clugny, Guillaume de (archdeacon of Avallon) 48–49
coinage 80n.43, 104–105, 153, 288
Cologne 197, 215–216
Common good/weal (idea of) 13, 69–70, 110, 139, 196, 199, 213, 230, 286–289
Commynes, Philip de (chronicler) 31, 44–52, 63, 108–109, 115, 247
Conflans, Treaty of 111–112
Contault, Mongin (master of accounts at Dijon) 1–2
Coquillards 102–105, 114
Cornille, Martin (receiver general) 100, 153
Coustain, Jean (Burgundian officer) 43, 49, 101–102, 156
Crévecoeur, Philippe of (lord of Esquerdes) 46, 50–52
Croÿ family, the 45, 51–53, 56, 66–67, 73, 100–101
Crusade 35–37, 124, 151–152, 226, 282

Delft, Treaty of 191
Deschamps, Eustache (poet) 160, 270
Deventer, Jacob van (mapmaker) 259

Dijon x, 1–3, 15–16, 33, 52, 102–105, 133–134, 165, 207, 278–279, 332–334
Dinant 182, 197, 211
Dit de Péronne 254
Dixmude, Olivier van (chronicler) 92
Dole x, 74–76, 155–157, 208
Dominicans 97
Douai 12, 36, 140, 183, 249, 254, 262
Driessche, Jean de la/Jan van der (magistrate of the council of Flanders) 153–154
Du Clercq, Jacques (chronicler) 36, 97
Dutch (language) 307–311
Dynter, Edmond de (chronicler) 25

Ecorcheurs (mercenary troops) 104, 181–186
Edward I (king of England) 210, 227
Edward IV (king of England) 201, 214–216
Ee, Adrien van der (charters keeper) 162–163
Empire, the 160–163, 197, 201, 214–215, 254–255, 315–317
England 32, 94–96, 127–128, 180, 190–192, 210, 214–216, 221–223, 234, 304–305, 317–320, 336
Estates General 15, 88, 108, 113–114, 211, 232–233, 285, 323, 335

Faith of Burgundy 75, 321, 333
Feudalism 58, 70–75, 140, 158, 203–205, 225–226, 254, 273, 287–290, 313, 323–324, 336
Fillastre, Guillaume (bishop of Tournay) 19, 36, 67

Flanders x, 12–18, 25–26, 91–95, 146–147, 153–156, 166, 182, 189–194, 204, 224, 230–232, 249–257, 258, 282–285, 307–308, 311–312, 322–323
Flanders, Louis de Male, count of 189, 283, 288
Formelis, Simon van (lawyer) 3, 7
France, Charles of (Dauphin) see Charles VIII (king of France)
France, Charles of (duke of Berry and Guienne) 107–109
Franche-Comté 47, 74–76, 197, 322, 325
François I (king of France) 335
Frederick III (emperor) 158–163
French (language) 36, 91, 149, 182, 203, 205, 251, 301, 308–313
Frisia, Kingdom of 159, 162–165
Frontiers 248–252, 258–260

Garter, Order of the 32
Germain, Jean (bishop of Chalon) 163, 263–264
Germans 200, 217, 302–307, 317
Gerson, Jean (theologian) 87–88
Ghent x, 16, 93, 98–99, 124, 150, 154–157, 182, 192–196, 224–225, 230–232, 256, 281–282, 287–289, 310
Gloucester, Humphrey, duke of 191, 221–228
Golden Bull 264, 314
Golden Fleece, Order of the 21, 32–37, 47–49, 66–78, 72–74, 124, 131, 265, 310
Golden Tree, Order of the 33, 56
Görlitz, Elisabeth von (duchess of Luxembourg) 193, 214
Goethals, Henry (councillor) 127, 334
Grandson, Battle of 150, 197, 210–212, 217–219, 227, 281
Great Privilege Charter (1477) 261

Gros, Jean (audiencier) 48–49, 165
Gruuthuse manuscript 92, 288
Guelders (duchy) x, 197, 215, 310, 315–316
Guelders (family) 159–161, 189, 315
Guyenne, Charles, duke of 30, 196
Guyenne, Louis of (dauphin of France) 85

Habsburg (house) 73, 161, 283, 316, 323
Hagenbach, Peter von 2–3, 161, 215–216
Hague, The 152, 191, 310, 323
Haidroits 191, 228
Hainault (county) 56, 62, 73, 128, 164, 184–186, 191, 199, 254, 301, 309–311
Hameyde, Hernoul, Bastard of la 62
Haynin, Jean de (lord of Louvignies) 107, 218
Henry V (king of England) 127, 130, 138, 190
Henry VI (king of England) 48, 214, 221–222, 304
heraldry 265–266, 270–275
heralds of arms 23, 262
Hesdin 126
Holland (county) x, 48, 59, 101, 165, 191–192, 214, 286, 308
honour 43–45, 104, 129–135, 188–195, 219–232, 334
Hornes, Jean de (sénéchal de Brabant) 223
Hugonet, Guillaume (lord of Saillant, chancellor) 112–113, 137–138, 198–201, 334–335
Hulst, Jan van (poet) 92
Hundred Years War, The 181, 216

James I (king of Aragon) 314
James I (king of Scotland) 305
jewels 56, 150, 227

John II (king of France) 94, 128–129, 138–139, 278
Jouard, Jean (president of the parlements of Burgundy) 2–3, 134, 165, 332–334
Jouffroy, Jean (bishop of Arras and Cardinal) 50–51
Joyous Entry (ceremony) 12, 17, 25, 140, 308
Joyous Entry (Text) 322–324
Jülich, William of (duke of Guelders) 189
justice 12–13, 62, 109–110, 143–144, 275, 339
Juvénal des Ursins, Jean 86–88

Knebel, Johannes 305, 317

La Clite, Colard II de (*souverain bailli* of Flanders) 154, 192
La Hire 185
Lalaing (family) 33, 66, 70, 226
La Marche, Olivier de (chronicler) 31, 65, 136, 144, 158, 190–193, 226, 260
Lancaster, House of 214
Lannoy (family) 54, 58–59, 222–223, 256
Lausanne 218
Le Baud, Pierre (chronicler) 260
Le Franc, Martin (writer) 271–273, 272
Lèse-majesté 47, 66, 71, 99, 104–106, 143, 152–156
Liège (city and bishopric) x, 156, 191, 197, 251
Lille x, 16, 35–36, 93, 182–183, 249, 271, 279, 307
Lineage 26, 73–75, 125, 131, 136–138, 160, 271–273
London 304
Lorraine (duchy) x, 150, 197, 232
Lorraine, René II, count of Vaudémont and duke of 197, 247
Lotharingia 162–163, 314

Louis XI (king of France) 19, 28, 30–32, 46–52, 71–76, 109–112, 128, 132–134, 143, 146, 157, 184, 187, 208–209, 214, 255, 273, 274, 321, 332–333
Louvignies, Lord of *see* Haynin
Loyet, Gérard (goldsmith) 159
Luxembourg (duchy) *x*, 193–194, 214–215, 227
Luxembourg (family) 50, 52, 162, 185, 314

Machiavelli 53, 115, 320
Mâcon *x*, 275, 318
majesty 18–23, 101–105, 141–142, 148–152
magnificence 19–22, 312
Male, Louis de (count of Flanders) 25, 182
Malines, Parlement of 16, 73, 141–144, 148, 315, 339
Manifestos 41n.34, 43–45, 84–86, 89, 94, 109, 126, 155–156, 189, 195, 318, 322
marches 248–249
Members of Flanders (Three and Four) 91–93, 146–147, 200, 222, 230, 285, 307, 311
Meuse (river) *x*, 218
Milanese ambassadors 37, 200, 212, 305
Molinet, Jean (chronicler) 28, 65, 136, 322
Mons *x*, 22, 29, 139–140, 186, 199
Mons–en–Vimeu 190, 213
Montbéliard 104, 215
Montdidier 231, 250
Montereau 127, 190
Montil–lès–Tours, Ordinance of 106
morality plays 107, 110
Morat *x*, 197, 212, 217–219, 231–232
Mortagne 27
mottoes 161, 270, 275
Murten *see* Morat
music 24, 26, 36, 132, 178–179, 218, 223, 268
Mutemaque (Dijon Rebellion) 52, 165
mystery plays 103

Namur (county) *x*, 72, 251
Nancy *x*, 65, 72, 158, 163, 217, 219, 231, 247, 277–279
nation 300–325
Neuss *x*, 197–200, 211, 216–219, 233–234, 256, 333
Nevers, Jean de Bourgogne, count of Etampes and 16, 45, 48, 54, 66
Nicopolis 35
Nijmegen 197, 206
Normandy 185, 215–216

'On the Duke of Burgundy' 305
'On the Siege of Calais' 305
'ordinance companies' 6
Ordinances 11n.10, 47, 56, 59–63, 72–73, 91–93, 104–106, 202–212, 218–219, 220
Orléans, Charles of 124
Orléans, Louis of 85–88, 95
Ostrevant 254
Othée 65, 191, 214, 228

Panigarola, Johanne Petro (Milanese ambassador) 200
Paris *x*, 89–91, 94–95, 123–124, 132, 189, 279–281
Paris, Parlement of 50, 97, 142–148, 255, 275
Pensions 52–60, 76, 90, 109
Péronne, Treaty of 124, 144–146, 252
Philip II (king of Spain) 323
Picards 36, 178, 304, 310–311, 316
Picquigny, Treaty of 216

Pippe, Roland (master of accounts) 154
Pizan, Christine de 53, 69, 87, 127
Pope/papacy 35–36, 338, 79n.28
Pot (family) 46, 50, 52–55
privileges 47, 73, 99, 140, 156–157, 165–166, 222, 250, 309, 323
processions 17, 21–22, 25, 35–37, 69, 131
propaganda 8, 13–14, 17–18, 23, 85, 91–92, 98, 107, 126–127, 149–150, 188, 197–199, 201–202, 217, 222, 224, 322–323
Properheden van den steden van Vlaenderen 263
public weal 9, 33, 106–112, 198–199, 207–210, 313–314
    War of the Public Weal 27, 56, 65, 112, 133, 196, 204, 214

Quesnoy 184

Rabustel, Jean (town prosecutor of Dijon) 102–104
Rederijkers 28, 288
reform 56–60, 106–110, 114–115, 180, 202–204
regalia 150, 275
reliquaries 22, 159
residences 279–283
Rheims 128, 131
Rhine (towns) 216
Richard II (king of England) 20
Roovere, Anthonis de (rederijker) 29, 230–231
Rolin (family) 45, 50, 55, 60–61
Rome, Giles of 321
Roosebeke 213
Rossano, Troylo da (condottiere) 205
Rouvres 186
Roye 52, 196, 250
Roye, Jean de (chronicler) 305

Rubempré, Antoine, Bastard of 30–31, 101, 108
rumours 29–31, 51, 186

Sablon, Our Lady of the 283
Saligny, Lourdin de 47, 63
Salins *x*, 200, 264
Salmon, Pierre ('Le Fruitier') 86
Saint Andrew 36, 230, 273–275, 300, 312
Saint–Bertin Abbey 256, 257
Saint–Maximin, abbey of 159, 204, 208
Saint–Maur, Treaty of 111
Saint–Omer 55, 71, 133, 140, 229, 249, 256
Saint–Pol, Philippe, count of 126, 251
Saint–Quentin 214
Saveuse, Philippe de (captain of Amiens) 99–100
Savoy (duchy) 190, 201, 249–251
Savoy (house) 65, 126
Saxony, Wilhelm of 193, 228
Schilling, Diebold (chronicler) 218
Scutelare (family) 93, 96
Seventeen (number) 266–269
Seyssel, Claude de (lawyer and political thinker) 54, 309
Sigismond (duke of Austria, count of Tyrol) 159
Sluys 95, 224–225
Soillot, Charles (Burgundian clerk) 64–65
Soleuvre, Treaty of 217
Somme (towns) *x*, 51, 109
sovereignty 71–72, 106, 111, 140–157, 253–255, 312, 316, 320, 335
sumptuary laws 21
Swiss, the 197, 200–201, 216–218

Talmont 52
tapestries 150, 159

taxation 19, 52, 85–96, 189, 194, 197, 217–219, 250–254, 285–287, 317, 340
'The Maid of Ghent' 288
'The Seven Gates of Bruges' 92, 288
Thiois (language) 308–310
Thionville, Ordinances of 73, 144, 279
Thymo, Petrus a (chronicler) 283
Tournai 27, 101, 253–254
tournaments and jousts 55, 132, 227, 264, 340
tours 266
traitors 44–49, 333
Transport de Flandre 92
Tremoille (family) 47, 56, 76
Trier 158–162, 204, 215, 315
Troyes, Treaty of 127, 228
Turks 100, 151
tyranny 19, 107–112, 134, 195–196, 302, 315

Utrecht, Peace of 303
Uutkerke, Roland van (lord of Heemstede) 225

Valenciennes 29, 68, 139, 186, 281, 309
Van de Lore, Boudin (poet) 288–289
Van der Goes, Hugo (painter) 265
Van Eyck, Jan (painter) 2, 25

Van menych sympel 25, 269, 283
Vaudémont, Antoine de (lord of Joinvelle) 214
Vienne 255, 271
Villandrando, Rodrigue de (mercenary) 184
Vrijdagmarkt (Ghent market) 150, 166
Vyon, Chrétiennot (Burgundian rioter) 333

Waas 255
Warbeck, Perkin 20
Warwick, Richard Neville, earl of 48, 214
Wauquelin, Jean (writer) 311
Wavrin, Jean de (lord du Forestel, writer) 223–224
Wielant, Philippe (lawyer) 209–210, 260
William V (count of Hainaut, Holland, Zeeland) 165
wine 1, 95, 134, 178–179, 265
Witches 96–97, 101, 105
Wittelsbach, Frederick of 160

York, house of *see* Burgundy (Margaret of York, third wife of Charles the Bold, duchess of)
Ypres 12, 146, 204, 229, 285

Zeeland *x*, 192, 222, 286, 318
Zoete, Guillaume (lawyer) 324
Zutphen *x*, 215

EU authorised representative for GPSR:
Easy Access System Europe, Mustamäe tee 50,
10621 Tallinn, Estonia
gpsr.requests@easproject.com

www.ingramcontent.com/pod-product-compliance
Lightning Source LLC
Chambersburg PA
CBHW051556230426
43668CB00013B/1872